Financial and Managerial Accounting for School Administrators

Tools for School

Ronald E. Everett
Donald R. Johnson
Bernard W. Madden

Published in partnership with the
Association of School Business Officials International

Rowman & Littlefield Education
Lanham, Maryland • Toronto • Plymouth, UK
2007

Published in partnership with the
Association of School Business Officials International

Published in the United States of America
by Rowman & Littlefield Education
A Division of Rowman & Littlefield Publishers, Inc.
A wholly owned subsidiary of The Rowman & Littlefield Publishing Group, Inc.
4501 Forbes Boulevard, Suite 200, Lanham, Maryland 20706
www.rowmaneducation.com

Estover Road
Plymouth PL6 7PY
United Kingdom

British Library Cataloguing in Publication Information Available

Library of Congress Cataloging-in-Publication Data

Everett, Ronald Edmond, 1942–
Financial and managerial accounting for school administrators : tools for school / Ronald E. Everett, Donald R. Johnson, Bernard W. Madden.
p. cm.
Includes bibliographical references.
ISBN-13: 978-1-57886-581-9 (hardcover : alk. paper)
ISBN-13: 978-1-57886-295-5 (pbk. : alk. paper)
ISBN-10: 1-57886-581-6 (hardcover : alk. paper)
ISBN-10: 1-57886-295-7 (pbk. : alk. paper)
1. Schools—Accounting. 2. Managerial accounting. 3. School administrators—In-service training. I. Johnson, Donald R., 1941– II. Madden, Bernard W., 1940– III. Title.
LB2830.E94 2007
371.2'06—dc22 2006035614

™The paper used in this publication meets the minimum requirements of American National Standard for Information Sciences—Permanence of Paper for Printed Library Materials, ANSI/NISO Z39.48-1992.
Manufactured in the United States of America.

We dedicate this book to our wives and families. It is also dedicated to our colleagues and students.

Contents

Preface

In 1960, the book *Public School Fund Accounting Principles and Procedures* by Sam B. Tidwell was published by Harper and Brothers Publishers, New York, NY. This was followed by a second and a third edition the latter published by the Research Corporation of the Association of School Business Officials International in 1985. Over the past 50 years, a continuous stream of publications and circulars on accounting has become available. These publications have come from agencies of the federal government, professional associations that serve accountants and school administrators, nonprofit organizations and university faculty. These publications have satisfied a variety of professional needs such as:

- Better definitions of terms crucial to the accounting process.
- Improved standards of financial and managerial accounting.
- The development and improvement of revenue and expenditure classifications.
- The development and improvement of generally accepted accounting principles and reporting procedures.
- The creation and expansion of auditing standards.

During this 50-year period, significant accounting changes have occurred. The school business administration profession has also changed dramatically. Those who administered the public schools began to realize that knowledge of liabilities, assets, cash and the like was important information if organizational goals were to be met. In today's school financial environment school business administrators are concerned with the total fiscal structure of the district. This includes the financial position and the current status of the various funds and accounting groups used.

Between 1960 and today, publication of *Handbook II—Principles of Public School Accounting* by the United States Office of Education (USOE) was a major step in managerial and financial accounting for governmental and nonprofit accounting. *Handbook II* illustrated and encouraged the use of double-entry bookkeeping as the basis for financial accounting for educational agencies. With this action, the emphasis shifted from the cash basis of recording only selected financial transactions to a basis of financial accounting that is referred to in the literature as generally accepted accounting principles. This new basis of accounting complied with the reporting requirements of federal and state laws.

The Association of School Business Officials in the United States and Canada (now called ASBO International) was very active in accounting developments during this time. During the 1970s, guidelines were established for what is now called the Certificate of Excellence (COE) in Financial Reporting by School Systems Program. This association service encouraged school districts to use generally accepted accounting principles and budgetary and reporting procedures that met high standards.

Other agencies, associations and organizations were also very active in the accounting changes and refinements that were evolving and that would influence governmental accounting and financial accounting for school districts. Some of these not already referenced were:

- American Association of School Administrators.
- National School Boards Association.
- Council of Chief State School Officers.

- American Institute of Certified Public Accountants.
- Municipal Finance Officers Association of United States and Canada.
- National Committee on Governmental Accounting.
- National Center for Education Statistics of the United States.
- Office of Education Financial Accounting Standards Board (FASB).
- Financial Accounting Foundation.

Out of all of these, FASB was established as the organization in the private sector that created the rules and standards governing the preparation of financial statements. In the public sector, the Governmental Accounting Standards Board (GASB) performs a similar function and provides much of the leadership in the continuing study and efforts to improve governmental accounting at all levels, including the public schools.

This book builds on the monumental foundation of Tidwell's three editions. His works have become classics, and their contribution to the elevation of accounting knowledge and skills in the school business administration profession are well documented. This work adds to Tidwell, but, with his permission, also draws on his earlier work. The three authors of this text have used Tidwell's earlier editions in graduate level courses over the past three decades. As we began our work, a deeper appreciation of Tidwell's earlier works developed. In some instances minor updating of his work was all that was needed. In other instances major revisions to his work have been made. Several new chapters and original new material have been inserted.

This work is designed to be much more than an introduction. It is designed for all school administrators. It deals with creating and expanding the user's knowledge base concerning school fund accounting. It is designed to expand and enhance understanding of financial and managerial accounting and reporting principles as well as the procedures as applied to fund and account groups.

This book assumes that the user has no, or at best, an introductory understanding of accounting. It is intended to serve those totally unfamiliar with accounting as well as those who bring some formal accounting training and experience to this stage of their professional development. While it is normal for those who have no formal training or background in accounting to be very anxious as they begin their serious study of the subject, *no* accounting background is necessary to benefit from the use of this book. This book is designed to be used primarily as a textbook at the graduate level with students training to be school administrators, school business administrators or principals. The appropriate audience for this book is anyone who is responsible for creating and/or using accounting-produced information about school districts.

The book consists of 28 chapters, each of which can be covered in one class period. Professors or instructors who select this work for the basic text for their courses are encouraged to enrich the material in each chapter with additional examples and supplemental material specific to a school district in their particular state so the students are exposed to their state's documents, forms and procedures. This book should lend itself to the teaching style of a wide variety of instructors.

We now go to the organization of this book. The book has two parts: The first part spans chapters 1 through 12 and part two covers chapters 13 through 28. The first twelve chapters and chapters 26 and 28 comprise the content normally covered in a one-semester course. For those who cover this material more rapidly, one or two chapters from the second part could be added. In those programs that offer or require two semesters of accounting work, chapters 13 through 28 can serve as the content for the second semester. The authors recognize that some chapters address topics that may not be appropriate or even required in some states or provinces.

The chapter organization consists of:

- Brief introduction.
- Short list of learner outcomes.
- Chapter content.
- Summary.
- Activities.

References/Selected Readings can be found before the appendix. The appendix is a very important part of this book and should be carefully studied when suggested by the text or chapter activities.

To the students or readers who use this book for whatever reason, the authors wish to point out that:

- This book will not make you accountants or CPAs.
- Going through the chapters in sequence is important.
- The illustrations and examples should be carefully studied and reviewed.
- Chapter activities have been carefully designed to teach basic ideas, skills and concepts.
- The activities which refer to the glossary are intentionally redundant.
- The glossary and appendix are very important components of this book.

While there are many different and correct ways to demonstrate accounting principles and concepts, only one method generally is given in this book. The instructors and students are encouraged to develop the additional problems as needed.

The authors acknowledge that many people have contributed to the completion of this work. The first one we wish to acknowledge is Sam Tidwell, who not only pioneered school fund accounting but provided the classic editions that will remain as monumental contributions for years to come. Students in Northern Illinois University's School Business Management program contributed to chapters 7, 8 and 20. Specific thanks go to Anthony Cozzi, Andrea Gorla, Sherry Koerner, Risa Hanson, Steve Miller and Hillarie Siena.

To avoid the real possibility of leaving someone out, we wish to thank ALL those who provided great insight and assistance in the initial organization of this and earlier editions of this book and contributed material to some of the chapters.

The authors appreciate the contributions made by the International staff. Last but certainly not least, the authors appreciate the secretarial and clerical support provided by the Illinois ASBO staff, specifically Julie Warner. There are many whose patience, encouragement and cooperation really made this book happen.

Ronald E. Everett
Donald R. Johnson
Bernard W. Madden

1

Accounting and School Business Administration

INTRODUCTION

School business administrators in the United States will receive, expend and account for the use of over $300 billion during 2004–05 to provide the staff, materials, facilities, supplies and services to deliver educational programs for public school children pre-K–12 according to statistics provided by the National Center for Educational Statistics (NCES). This massive consumption of public money will only increase in the years ahead. Few, if any, can really comprehend the size of this commitment and investment in human capital, but the fact that what is spent in the United States each year for education exceeds the total economic output of many countries does provide a crude perspective. While the tasks and functions performed by school business administrators are extensive and complex, the knowledge and skills of accounting are basic to all of them and contribute to the understanding of how these resources are deployed and the impact of their use.

One should not overlook that dollars for education are also expended in private schools and that higher education (both public and private) spends huge sums of money as well. Combined, it is safe to state that well over a half trillion dollars will be expended during 2004–05, and this amount will only increase in terms of inflated dollars or constant dollars. Private business and industry also invest dollars in educating their employees.

This chapter will explore the importance of accounting in the school environment and demonstrate the overall binding effect it has on all of the tasks and functions performed by the school district business administrator. The point will be made that knowledge about accounting and accounting skills pervades *all* aspects of the day-to-day operation of a school and school district. The proper day-to-day operation of the schools and quality planning and decision-making cannot realistically take place unless administrators and Board members have an understanding of school fund accounting.

OUTCOMES

In this chapter, you will learn:

1. How school districts are organized to manage the resources made available to them.
2. What the tasks, functions, duties and responsibilities are of those individuals a school district retains to manage its resources.
3. How important financial and managerial accounting is to a school district and how it is evolving.
4. How accounting spans and impacts every aspect of the school business administration profession.
5. How the use and importance of accounting information is relating resource inputs to instructional outputs.

Note: Throughout this book the reader will find the expressions school district, school system, local educational agency, educational institution, district and the like. These terms are interchangeable.

A FRAMEWORK

One of the ways to establish a context or framework for this text is to examine some basic information about educational spending. The following statements are taken from NCES document 95–169.

- Current expenditures are expected to increase by 38.6 percent in real dollars and average annual teacher salaries in public elementary and secondary schools are projected to increase by 11.6 percent between school years 1991–92 and 2004–05 (also in real dollars). (page 75)
- Current expenditures per pupil in average daily attendance are projected to increase by 17.7 percent to $6,576 from 1991–92 to 2004–05. (page 76)
- Total current expenditures as a percentage of total disposable income are projected to increase from 4.9 percent in 1990–91 to 5.1 percent in 2004–05. One cause of this projected increase is the 17.8 percent increase in enrollment projected for this period. (page 76)

While these figures are interesting and important, the facts reported will change over time. In the context of the material the reader will find in this book, the data given demonstrate two important and related concepts.

First, some form of accounting was necessary to produce these facts and figures. Without some system of organizing, recording, describing, analyzing and reporting, this information could not have been presented. Without a system of accounting, appropriate and useful comparisons and classifications could not exist.

Second, the sheer volume of dollars needed to provide products and services to public school children and the pressures to relate the use of these dollars to some type(s) of outcome measures makes an accounting (accountability) system essential. Society should and does expect excellence in accounting just on the basis of the number of dollars used, if for no other reason.

For the purpose of this book, two accounting distinctions will be made and used. The two distinctions are between *financial accounting* and *managerial accounting.* In his book *Finance and Accounting for Nonfinancial Managers*, Finkler (1992, 3–4) gives the following definitions:

> *Financial Accounting*: a formalized system designed to record the financial history of an organization over time and report that history to interested individuals normally in an annual or some other regular report(s).
>
> *Managerial Accounting*: provides information that can be used for making improved decisions regarding the future. This assumes that virtually any decisions that could be improved by a forecast or an analysis is the responsibility of the managerial accountant.

The recognition of these two distinctions does not mean that the two practices are mutually exclusive. Financial and managerial accounting can be provided by a single individual or by different individuals and systems. This dichotomy is consistent with the living systems theory (LST) of Miller and Swanson (1989, 55–73), which separates accounting quantities into: Measurement of concrete process; and Interpretation of those measurements. The most fundamental information produced by accounting is the measurement of concrete processes and thereby is information prepared to be disclosed in public reports. The spinoff of this publicly reported information, however, is its use in general and specific decision-making settings. There was a time when resources for education were fairly plentiful and expectations were not as high, delivery of desired services was relatively simple and technology was practically nonexistent as we know it today. At that time, most if not all accounting was financial in nature, i.e., simple recording sources, timing and amounts of revenue received and reporting on what these revenues purchased in terms of products and services, when, and what each cost. It was during this time period that school business administrators earned the description of "bean counter." While some look down on this term, the fact is that "bean counting" is necessary and it must be done well. Managerial accounts were created in response to: calls for greater accountability, the growing complexity of society, increased competition for limited resources, expanding technological capabilities and the requirement that resources be more accurately related to outcomes. This also spurred a growth and maturation in accounting that promises sophistication in the future that is currently beyond our imagination.

The present and the future will see the need for both financial and managerial accounting. One will not overshadow the other. Both will continue to evolve and develop to satisfy the needs of society and the education community. Financial and managerial accounting together can be thought of as the process that gathers, produces, organizes and presents information that can be consumed by a wide variety of users for the purpose of keeping an organization operating, growing, improving and changing.

If financial and managerial accounting is not done well, then the survival of the organization is at risk and difficult times will be created for not only the organization, but for the clientele it serves. This is true for public sector and private sector organizations and especially for public education.

HISTORY OF SCHOOL BUSINESS MANAGEMENT AND SCHOOL BUSINESS ADMINISTRATION IN THE UNITED STATES

Before anyone begins the study of school financial accounting and school managerial accounting, some understanding of the school organization is helpful. Public schools exist in the United States to provide *mass* public education at public expense (and some use of private resources) to all those who present themselves to receive instruction. Many people refer to public education as the most important service government is expected to provide and teaching as the profession that makes all other professions possible. While some may argue the relative importance of education, few will argue that education is not important.

In order to provide educational opportunities to the masses, society must commit a tremendous amount of its resources to this purpose. Society rightfully expects that the resources that are made available be effectively and efficiently managed so that the purposes for which these resources have been committed are maximized (or nearly so). The basic resource that we are referring to here is money. Dollars are received directly from the taxpayers, students, parents and others and indirectly from taxpayers through state, federal, municipal or intermediate governmental units that collect and distribute dollars to school districts. These dollars are used to purchase other resources like teachers, administrators, support staff, textbooks, supplies, materials, buildings, busses, electrical power, heat, food, water and on and on. Those who provide the dollars directly and/or indirectly expect and require that the receipt and use of these resources be described and explained on a regular, complete, accurate, comprehensive, detailed, understandable and useful basis. The public requires accountability. Accountability is the obligation to report, explain and justify. Financial and managerial accounting strives to at least partially satisfy these obligations.

One of the many great experiments that the settling of the western hemisphere by Europeans allowed to take place was the creation and development of public school systems that were locally controlled by school committees, school trustees, school boards and the like. In early colonial times, when schools were small and education was fairly simple, the day-to-day operation of the school or schools within a geographic area was provided by one of these groups. These school boards were the educational policy arm of their area *and* its administration. These committees were also the "chief cooks and bottle washers" of the schools. They had to see to every detail of the local school operation. For nearly 200 years this approach to operating and managing the public schools in the United States worked reasonably well. Colonial life, however, changed and so did education.

School systems grew in size; education became more complex; the expectations for the schools expanded to include more than reading, writing and arithmetic; and the time demands and expertise needed to provide a livelihood for a family increased. Communities began to recognize that the day-to-day operation of the school(s) had become too complex and time-consuming to adequately be performed by lay volunteers regardless of their intelligence, willingness, desire, enthusiasm and energy. Even attempts at compensating one or more board members to perform specific tasks proved only to be an intermediate solution. Whether the manager/clerk was paid or unpaid, it became evident that in terms of both time and expertise, these individuals were overextended. In response to this condition, Hill (1982, 3) reported that in the 1840s the Cleveland, Ohio, city school district became the first to hire a full-time "acting manager" to "keep the books, prepare the payroll and care for the school buildings."

Early school business managers were not considered educators expected (or allowed) to participate in educational decision-making. History makes it clear that educators were not to make school business decisions and the business managers were to keep their noses out of the educational domain. The position of school business manager was not viewed as very important at its inception. In fact, it was not until the last quarter of the 19th century and early 20th century that educators started to recognize and stress the importance of the school business administrator role. During this time period some specific defining of the role began and people started to take an interest in how individuals prepared themselves to perform this role. As the country moved into the 21st century, the relationship between quality educational opportunities being available and sound business practice/accounting was still not universally understood or accepted.

It was also in the early 1900s that leading school business administrators realized the importance of their duties, the effects of their services on education and the need for defining specific aspects of their duties and responsibilities. Specific course work at the university level started to pop up and books and journal articles devoted exclusively to school business management started to appear. The multidimensional aspects of school business management became apparent from reading the literature and from the certification and licensing requirements that were developing.

It is clear today that decisions relating to the teaching, learning and curriculum dimension of a school district are interdependent upon decisions that are accepted as being in the school business domain. Understanding and accepting this relationship between curriculum and resource allocation are crucial to understanding a school district and what it can and cannot provide. National initiatives like No Child Left Behind (NCLB) and state school finance systems of funding schools that relate general state aid to student test results or penalize schools for poor performance reflect the growing dependence on solid accounting information as well as the need for improved student assessments.

School business administrators must be trained and experienced in the field of education with emphasis on school business administration or trained and experienced in various phases of business with knowledge of educational practices. The school business manager must be viewed as a crucial element in school reform and school improvement if educational opportunities are to be available to all students, now and in the future.

WHAT IS SCHOOL BUSINESS ADMINISTRATION?

A majority of those who use this book will either be preparing themselves to function in one or more of the roles within the profession of school business administration or will be enhancing their knowledge base and accounting skills to more effectively and efficiently perform current duties and responsibilities. Therefore, an understanding of what school business administration is all about as a profession and role, with its accompanying tasks, functions, duties and responsibilities is useful. To facilitate this understanding, ASBO International created a professional registration program to enhance the credentials of those seeking to demonstrate that they possess superior skills and knowledge relevant to school business administration. This program is particularly important in states and provinces where certification is not required.

Within this registration program three distinctions are defined: registered school business administrators (RSBA), registered school business officials (RSBO), and registered school business specialists (RSBS). Those with RSBAs deal with the total area of school business, and with subordinates.

Those with RSBOs deal with specific phases of school business administration, but not to the breadth and scope of the RSBA. The RSBS is even more focused, having highly specialized skills in a single area of school business administration. These nomenclatures serve only as a guide and are helpful only to the degree that they expand the understanding of these roles.

Like every other key role involved in the central office administration of the public schools, no two school business administrator positions are exactly alike even though there is a commonality in terms of duties, tasks, functions, knowledge base, skills and attitudes. Often characterized as the "invisible, add-on" profession, the role has been supportive and subordinated to the board and superintendent.

The school business administrator's job description, when viewed from a historical perspective, reveals that over the years the list of responsibilities of a school business administrator has become longer as new programs and mandates trickle down to the school business administrator's desk. Over the past 50 years very little has been removed from the school business administrator's duties, but much has been added.

The role of school business administrators has been the subject of specific research for over 70 years. The nature of much of these research efforts has focused on attempts to summarize, define, delimit and bring understanding to what the school business administrator does. Carnahan (1965, 16) categorized major responsibilities of the school business administrator as follows:

- School funds excluding student activity funds.
- School audits and school accounting, except attendance accounting.
- Records and supervision of non-instruction personnel.
- School insurance.
- Establishment of standards and specifications for supplies.
- Managing rentals.

Many other researchers have arrived at very similar conclusions. Hill, in his book *The School Business Administrator* (1982), took the earlier works of Linn (1965), Knezevich and Fowlkes (1960), Jordan (1969), Kaiser and Webb (1957), McGuffey (1980) and others to delineate the work areas usually associated with school business administration and generated the following specific task clusters:

- Capital Fund Management
- Cash Management
- Classified Personnel Management
- Community Relations
- Construction Management
- Data Processing
- Educational Facilities Planning
- Educational Resource Management
- Financial Planning and Budgeting
- Fiscal Accounting and Financial Reporting
- Fiscal Audits and Reports
- Food Service
- Grantsmanship
- Insurance and Risk Management
- Legal Control
- Office Management
- Payroll Management
- Plant Management
- Plant Operations
- Plant Security and Property Protection
- Professional Negotiations
- Property Management
- Purchasing
- Staff Development
- Student Activity Funds
- Transportation Services
- Warehousing and Supplies Management

This list was never intended to be all-inclusive of what school business administrators do. Over the past few years many new tasks have been created and assigned to this role, for example, energy management, environmental issues, legal concerns, legislative management and the like. Hill's categories have been used to organize and assign responsibilities as well as to help give definition to the profession of school business administration.

While these tasks and work areas do help to identify what the school business administrator does, this list and related lists do not set forth the particular functions that are so necessary to insure that efficient and effective business services are delivered at all times. The basic management functions, like the aforementioned tasks, have also undergone the scrutiny of researchers over time.

The following eight processes (Hill, 1982) are most commonly suggested:

- Planning
- Organizing
- Staffing
- Influencing or Directing
- Controlling

- Controlling
- Coordinating
- Decision-making
- Evaluating

Figure 1.1

FUNCTIONS: HOW WE DO THINGS—PROCESSES											
Planning	Organizing	Staffing	Influencing/ Directing	Controlling	Coordinating	Decision-making	Evaluating	Reporting	Budgeting	Professional Develop-ment*	**THE TOPICS OF WHAT WE DO**
											Capital Fund Management
											Cash Management
											Classified Personnel Management
											Community Relations
											Construction Management
											Data Processing
											Educational Facilities Planning
											Educational Resource Management
											Financial Planning and Budgeting
											Fiscal Accounting and Financial Reporting
											Fiscal Audits and Reports
											Food Service
											Grantsmanship
											Insurance and Risk Management
											Legal Control
											Office Management
											Payroll Management
											Plan Management
											Plant Operations
											Plant Security and Property Protection
											Professional Negotiations
											Property Management
											Purchasing
											Staff Development
											Student Activity Funds
											Transportation Services
											Warehousing and Supplies Management

* (Perhaps another discussion of what school business administrators do is to "prepare themselves professionally" to do their job, i.e., update changes in old program and learn the new rules, regulations and guidelines of new mandates and should be added to the list of functions.)

To begin to grasp what school business management and administration is really all about, it must be recognized that each of the above functions can and usually is applied to each of the earlier mentioned tasks. Figure 1.1 suggests a means of visualizing exactly how these tasks and functions work together to define school business management and administration in the 1970s. This grid has dramatically expanded on the task dimension over the past 30 years as will become obvious over the next few pages of this chapter. This grid also adds three functions/processes to the Hill list above.

While the actual skills and knowledge base necessary to adequately perform in each of the cells created by the above grid vary from school district to school district, the magnitude of what might be expected is clear. It becomes evident that there is a common core of cells that will be done every day, week, month and/or year regardless of the district type, size or location. It should also be evident that some cells are repeated, but in a random chaotic cycle over time. Over time, it may be completely unnecessary to perform certain tasks or function cells at all.

The task and function approach is useful as a means of ordering our thinking about school business administration, but using the "typical duties" approach expands the understanding of the role. Once again, drawing from Hill's work, a broader understanding can be obtained. Such a listing of typical duties can be useful to board members, superintendents, lay citizens and others who have an interest in the role.

The following list taken from Hill (1982, 28–32), while fairly comprehensive, is not all-inclusive:

I. Financial Planning and Budgeting
   A. Budget compilation, in coordination with educational planning
   B. Long-term fiscal planning—operating budget
   C. Estimating
      1. Receipts
      2. Disbursements
   D. Budget control
   E. Fiscal relationships with other government units
   F. Use of systems analysis and Program Planning Budgeting Evaluation System (PPBES)
   G. Cash flow management

II. Accounting
   A. General fund
   B. Capital reserve funds, trust funds and special purpose grants
   C. Construction funds
   D. Internal accounts
   E. Student activity funds
   F. Voucher and payroll preparation
   G. Inventory
   H. Attendance, census, tax roll accounting
   I. Government tax and pension accounting—categorical aids
   J Special trust funds
   K. Cost accounting—cost analysis—unit and comparative costs—cost distribution
   L. Student stores, bookstores
   M. Source documentation
   N. PPBES—Evaluation Resource Management (ERM) concepts and procedures
   O. Employer benefits accounting—vacations, sick leave, seniority status
   P. Petty cash funds

III. Debt Service and Capital Fund Management
   A. Long-term and short-term financing
   B. Maturities and debt payments
   C. Long-range capital programs
   D. Investments and cash flow
   E. Reporting

- F. Bond and note register
- G. Debt service payment procedures
- H. Short-term debt management
- I. Revenue anticipation loans; emergency loans
- J. Bond prospectus
- K. Credit data—credit ratings

IV. Auditing
- A. Pre-audit, or internal procedures
- B. Determination that prepared statements present fairly the financial position
- C. Propriety, legality and accuracy of financial transactions
- D. Proper recording of all financial transactions
- E. Post-audit procedures
- F. External audits
- G. Reconciliation of internal and external audits
- H. Legal advertising and reporting

V. Purchasing and Supply Management
- A. Ethics in purchasing
- B. Official purchasing agent designation
- C. Legal aspects of purchasing and contracting
- D. Purchase methods—seasonal and off-season buying
- E. Stock requisition and buying cycles
- F. Standards and specifications
- G. Requisition and purchase orders
- H. Purchase bids
- I. Cooperative purchasing—state contracts, local contracts
- J. Testing and value analysis
- K. Purchases of supplies and equipment
- L. Warehousing and distribution procedures
- M. Storage, delivery, trucking services
- N. Inventory controls
- O. Management of supplies, furniture, equipment
- P. Computerized purchasing and supply management

VI. School Plant Planning and Construction
- A. Establishment of educational standards for sites, buildings and equipment
- B. Plant utilization studies
- C. Projections of facility needs
- D. Design, construction and equipment of plant
- E. Safety standards
- F. Contracts management
- G. Architect selection

VII. Operation of Plant—Custodial, Gardening, Engineering Services
- A. Standards and frequency of work
- B. Manpower allocations
- C. Scheduling
- D. Inspection and evaluation of services
- E. Relationship with educational staff

- F. Operating of related school-community facilities, such as recreation, park, museum, library programs, etc.
- G. Community use of facilities
- H. Protection of plant and property
- I. Security and police forces
- J. Salvage, surplus and waste disposal

VIII. Maintenance of Plant
- A. Repair of buildings and equipment
- B. Upkeep of grounds
- C. Maintenance policies, standards and frequency of maintenance
- D. Scheduling and allocation of funds and manpower
- E. Modernization and rehabilitation versus replacement

IX. Real Estate Management
- A. Site acquisition and sales
- B. Rental, leases
- C. Rights-of-way and easements
- D. Assessments and taxes
- E. After school use of buildings
- F. Dormitories, student unions, concessions

X. Personnel Management
- A. Records
  1. Probationary and tenure status of employees
  2. Sick leave and leave of absence
  3. Official notices of appointments and salaries
  4. Retirement data and deductions
  5. Salary schedules and payments
  6. Individual earnings records
  7. Withholding, tax and group insurance or fringe benefits
  8. Civil Service and Social Security
  9. Substitute and part-time employees
  10. Dues check-offs
- B. Supervision of noninstructional staff
  1. Recruitment
  2. Selection
  3. Placement
  4. Training
  5. Advancement
  6. Working conditions
  7. Disciplinary action
  8. Termination of services
- C. Relationship to instructional staff
  1. Goodwill and service concept
  2. Cooperation in procurement
  3. Cooperation in budget preparation
  4. Information on pay and retirement
  5. Personnel records and reports

XI. Permanent Property Records and Custody of Legal Papers
  A. Security and preservation of records
  B. Maintenance of storage files
  C. Purging of records no longer legally required
XII. Transportation of Pupils
  A. Policies, rules, regulations and procedures
  B. Contract versus district-owned equipment
  C. Routing and scheduling
  D. Inspection and maintenance
  E. Staff supervision and training
  F. Utilization and evaluation of services
  G. Standards and specifications
XIII. Food Service Operations
  A. Policies, rules, regulations and procedures
  B. Staffing and supervision
  C. Menus, prices and portion controls
  D. Purchasing, storage and distribution
  B. Accounting, reporting and cost analysis
  F. In-service training
  G. Coordination with educational program
  H. Procurement and operation of contract services
XIV. Insurance
  A. Insurance policies
  B. Insurable values—buildings and contents
  C. Coverage to be provided
  D. Claims and reporting
  E. Insurance and procurement procedures
  F. Insurance and claims record
  G. Distribution of insurance to companies, agents and brokers
XV. Cost Analysis
  A. Unit costs
  B. Comparative costs
  C. Cost distribution studies
XVI. Reporting
  A. Local financial and statistical reports
  B. State financial and statistical reports
  C. Federal financial and statistical reports
  D. Miscellaneous reports
  E. Required legal advertising
  F. Relationships with public information media
XVII. Collective Negotiations
  A. Service on management team when required
  B. Preparation of pertinent fiscal data for management team
  C. Development of techniques and strategies of collective negotiations
  D. Sharing of proper information with employee units
  E. Use of outside negotiations, agencies

F. Mediation, arbitration, grievances

XVIII. Data Processing
- A. Selection of system
- B. Programming
- C. Utilization of systems analysis
- D. Forms preparation
- E. Broad use of equipment for all pertinent applications

XIX. School Board Policies and Administrative Procedures as Related to Fiscal and Non-instructional Matters

XX. Responsibilities for Elections and Bond Referenda

XXI. Responsibilities for School Assessment, Levy and Tax Collection Procedures as May Be Set by Law

The Association of School Business Officials International (ASBO International) has developed an updated definition of what encompasses the role of school business administrator. This new view can be reviewed by visiting the website at www.asbointl.org. Shown below is the table of contents of a brochure titled *Association of School Business Officials International's Professional Standards* (July 2001) which appears on the website. While this overlaps with the work of Hill, it is a current validation of what the present-day school business administrator does.

Reviewing the definitions of financial accounting and managerial accounting and applying them to the list of duties and/or each of the cells in Figure 1.1, even with a minimal amount of understanding, one thing should become very clear: Accounting spans all tasks, functions and duties of the school business administrator. The more one learns about school business administration and accounting, the more evident this becomes. Accounting is the glue that binds all aspects of school business administration together.

I. The Educational Enterprise
- A. Organization and Administration
- B. Public Policy and Intergovernmental Relations
- C. Legal Issues

II. Financial Resource Management
- A. Principles of School Finance
- B. Budgeting and Financial Planning
- C. Accounting, Auditing and Financial Reporting
- D. Cash Management, Investments and Debt Management

III. Human Resource Management
- A. Personnel and Benefits Administration
- B. Professional Development
- C. Labor Relations and Employment Agreements
- D. Human Relations

IV. Facility Management
- A. Planning and Construction
- B. Maintenance and Operations

V. Property Acquisition and Management
- A. Purchasing
- B. Supply and Fixed Asset Management

C. Real Estate Management

VI. Information Management
   A. Strategic Planning
   B. Instructional Support Program Evaluation
   C. Instructional Program Evaluation
   D. Communications
   E. Management Information Systems

VII. Ancillary Services
   A. Risk Management
   B. Transportation
   C. Food Service

HOW SHOULD SCHOOL BUSINESS ADMINISTRATORS BE TRAINED?

A strong case can be made that if a person really wants to find out how important a particular skill and/or knowledge base is to a particular role, it can be obtained by asking those (or at least a sample) who are incumbents in the role of interest. If one wants to know how important knowledge about accounting skills is to the school business administrator, ask practicing school business administrators.

Studies done in the 1960s and 1970s pointed to accounting as being one of the top responsibilities (if not the top) of the school business administrator. Whether the researchers were examining perceptions, competency statements, harvesting ideas on pre-service training or just organizing and categorizing statements from job descriptions, the results ranked accounting at or near the top of all lists. McGuffey (1980), using survey techniques, rank ordered 28 task duties and established the following "importance scores" (nine being the highest possible). The range of scores for all 28 items was 7.94 to 3.44. The top five items were:

- Financial Planning and Budgeting 7.94
- Fiscal Accounting and Financial Reporting 7.47
- Cash Management 7.34
- Fiscal Audits and Reports 7.28
- General Management 7.18

Clearly, accounting knowledge, understanding and skills are an important area of study for those already in the school business administration profession and for those preparing to enter it.

In 1986, a survey of school business administrators in the United States and Canada was conducted by Everett and Glass (1986, May) to investigate what tasks business administrators performed on a daily basis, the perceived importance of these tasks and the types of training school business administrators had received prior to employment. The survey also asked school business administrators what types of professional preparation and training they wanted and how they wanted it delivered. In 1992, Everett and Glass (1992, 28–36) replicated the 1986 survey. It examined whether a shift in function and opinions of school business administrators had taken place. The survey produced the following general findings:

- Even though most school districts carry on without professionally prepared school business administrators, the importance of the role is increasing. For example, the annual budgets of school districts climbed during the 1980s and despite the economic recession of the early 1990s, promise to continue rising in future years but at a reduced rate.

- The complexity of school operations has increased in the past due to expanding government regulations, court decisions and statutory requirements.
- In addition to being stewards of public monies, school business administrators are now expected to be responsible for problem solving and planning in important management functions such as collective bargaining, risk management, investments and contracting. These functions require knowledge and skills that must be current and relevant.
- The contemporary school business administrator is no longer the chief bookkeeper or "bean counter" for the school district, but instead, an important member of the district management team responsible for leading significant numbers of employees in the business office and making competent decisions (Candoli et al., 1973). While this statement reflects that the role has and is changing, it would be inappropriate to conclude that accounting (chief bookkeeper/bean counter) is becoming less important compared to other functions now expected of the school business administrator.

The overall goal of the Everett-Glass study was to form a composite picture of the professional characteristics of today's school business administrator. The findings of this survey along with the 1986 survey can be used by those individuals responsible for the development of pre-service and in-service training of school business administrators.

Unpublished research completed by Everett at the beginning of the 21st century replicated the Everett and Glass surveys of the 1980s and 1990s. The recent survey results provided no significant shifts in the results reported in 1991.

So what do school business administrators do as they enter the new century? School business administrators are responsible for a variety of management tasks in school districts. Many of these tasks and functions are not necessarily within the framework of the management of funds. Many have to do with employees (collective bargaining) or with educational programs (special education and compensatory programs).

The respondents were asked to prioritize the relative importance of each function to job success using a Likert type scale (1–5) with the designators being: Absolutely essential = 1; Very important = 2; Medium importance = 3; Not very important = 4; Not appropriate = 5. The respondents rated the top three absolutely essential and the remaining 13 as very important.

1. Budget Planning
2. Accounting
3. Finance
4. Cash Management
5. Purchasing
6. Data Processing
7. Risk Management
8. Auditing
9. Salary Administration
10. Strategic Planning
11. Collective Bargaining
12. Federal Programs
13. Auxiliary Services

14. Property Management
15. Facilities
16. Special Education

The first three, budget planning, accounting and finance, are commonly thought to be the heart of the position. However, there was not much common agreement among the respondents in how the three should be ranked. Probably, respondents felt the top three should be of equal importance.

The types of preparation/formal training that school business administrators generally receive follows what they think to be their most important job functions and responsibilities (Figure 1.2).

Accounting and auditing are two of the top five priority functions in which school business administrators generally have received their pre-service training. In budget planning and finance, about half received formal training before employment and half afterwards. Data processing, risk management, purchasing, strategic planning, collective bargaining and facilities are areas that have not been generally addressed in academic preparation programs until recently. Overall, the data seemed to indicate that a majority of school business administrators receive the major part of their job preparation training on the job during in-service sessions. There are advantages and disadvantages to this. In-service sessions can be more current but can also be superficial with little, if any, follow-up and supervision by trainers.

Figure 1.2
Training and Preparation Received

	Pre-Service	In-Service
Budget Planning	191	189
Accounting	236	135
Finance	185	181
Cash Management	166	166
Purchasing	137	203
Data Processing	151	191
Risk Management	92	228
Auditing	194	141
Salary Administration	97	218
Strategic Planning	106	205
Collective Bargaining	98	217
Federal Programs	73	244
Auxiliary Services	70	236
Property Management	151	170
Facilities	93	201
Special Education	47	257

OTHER INDICATORS OF THE IMPORTANCE OF ACCOUNTING TO SCHOOL BUSINESS ADMINISTRATION

If the reader is still not convinced of the importance of studying school accounting as part of preparing to become a school business administrator, perhaps an examination of the state certification requirements to be a chief school business official (CSBO) will provide some added insight. The specific requirements vary dramatically from state to state and province to province but most include an accounting component.

In 1990, ASBO International finalized its *Model Preparation Program for School Business Administrators* (ASBO International, 1991) and had them approved in 1991 by the National Council for the Accreditation of Teacher Education (NCATE). From 1992 to 1999, any NCATE college or university unit that offered a graduate degree in school business administration had to comply with these standards.

What did these guidelines say about accounting? The major division of the guideline, "Financial Resource Management," was composed of four subsections, one of which was "Accounting, Auditing and Financial Reporting." Ten competency statements relating to this subsection were specified. They were:

1. Present fairly and with full disclosure the financial position and results of financial operations of the funds and account groups of the school district in compliance with generally accepted accounting principles.
2. Establish and verify compliance with finance-related legal and contractual provisions.
3. Develop and maintain all fixed assets in a general fixed asset account group.
4. Utilize the appropriate basis of accounting in measuring financial position and operating results: modified accrual basis of accounting; accrual basis of accounting; or cash basis of accounting.
5. Prepare appropriate interim and annual financial statements and reports of financial position, and operating results to facilitate management control of all financial operations and funds using appropriate technology.
6. Prepare revenue and expenditures by fund (use appropriate state chart of accounts, electronic data processing, etc.)
7. Communicate the relationships between the institution program and process to the budget and available resources of the school district.
8. Analyze both monthly and annual financial statements and reports.
9. Develop specifications for the employment of an independent auditor.
10. Understand the use and role of an internal auditor.

State certification requirements and NCATE standards were further indications that the study of school fund accounting is necessary and proper for anyone interested in becoming a school business administrator.

DIFFERENCE BETWEEN GOVERNMENTAL/PUBLIC SCHOOL ACCOUNTING AND PRIVATE SECTOR ACCOUNTING

Profit-oriented businesses must operate in a free enterprise/market environment. These entities must report to owners who have a vested interest in earning a return on their investments. Accounting reports for these organizations focus on the profitability and resources of the business entity often referred to as "the bottom line." Part of this reporting is to determine whether resources are being managed efficiently and effectively. This can, in part, be assessed by examining the earnings performance of the business.

In a school district, resource allocation is often set by policy rather than by the forces of supply and demand. The revenues resulting from the sale of goods and services by a public school district do not necessarily reveal the demand of consumers for these goods or services, and costs cannot be compared to earned revenues to determine whether the operating costs of the public school district are at an acceptable level.

Without the components of a free market economy, public school districts are at a disadvantage relative to businesses in assessing the quantity and quality of goods and services to provide. Many of the unique features of public school district accounting and reporting result from the special needs these organizations have for controlling resources and costs and for providing accountability in the absence of market forces.

Ingram and others (1991, 1–16) were quick to point out that in addition to the lack of market forces, governmental organizations such as public school districts differ from businesses in that operating procedures and policies are heavily influenced by legal and political constraints and issues. Authority to spend may be conveyed by a legally adopted budget enacted by elected or appointed members of a board of education. Additionally, external sources of funding may come with legal constraints as to their use. Authority for action is based on laws or rules derived from a political process.

Accountability is often a response to political demands rather than a response to the need for financial information that helps determine profitability. Thus, unlike corporate accounting and reporting, demonstration of compliance with laws and regulations and/or political agendas is a major objective of public school district accounting and reporting.

It is important to understand that public school districts can be thought of as a single entity, but also as an entity made up of a variety of different types of entities sometimes called auxiliary enterprises. Some of these entities operate similarly to business enterprises in that they sell goods and services to customers. For example, bookstores and cafeterias often operate as business enterprises within a public school district. The general operation of public school districts is an example of a non-business type organization. By focusing on examples of business organizations at one end of the spectrum and public school districts as non-business organizations at the other end of the spectrum, the extreme types of differences that may be observed between business and nonprofit educational organizations may be presented.

BASIC PUBLIC SCHOOL DISTRICT ACCOUNTING CONCEPTS

The basic concepts of public school district accounting are examined in this section and are contrasted with profit-oriented accounting concepts. These concepts apply to those activities of public school districts that result in products and services that are not sold to customers as part of a business enterprise.

In accounting for business organizations, revenues are inflows or other enhancements of assets of an entity or settlements of its liabilities from delivering or producing goods, rendering services or other activities that constitute the entity's ongoing major or primary operations.

Therefore, business revenue arises from the sale of products or services. The right to receive cash (accounts receivable) from sales is as legitimate a revenue as a cash receipt. In contrast, public school district revenues arise from taxes, fees or donations. Public school districts currently record the right to receive cash as revenue only when it is reasonably certain that the cash will be available to finance the operations of the current fiscal period.

SUMMARY

This chapter sets the stage for the remainder of this book. It establishes a comprehensive definition of what the role of the school business administrator is. This was done by listing most of the tasks and functions currently assigned to the individuals who perform these important roles. The relative importance of the accounting function and its overlapping nature with the various duties and responsibilities of the school business administrator were presented. Accounting was described as the product/service that ties everything together in a school district.

The accounting process not only satisfies the reporting needs of multiple users of such information but also produces information for decision-making. Those who currently provide school business administration services validate the absolutely essential nature of having accounting knowledge and skills. The chapter closed by suggesting that the accounting performed by governmental/school district/nonprofit agencies is significantly different from that used in the business/private sector.

ACTIVITIES

1. Read the preface of this book.

2. Carefully review the definition of the following terms as given in the glossary:

   a. Financial accounting
   b. Managerial accounting
   c. School Business Administration
   d. School Business Official
   e. School Business Specialist
   f. School Business Manager

3. Log on to the Association of School Business Officials International website, www.asbointl.org, and review the professional standards (2001) for the preparation of chief school business officials. Compare and contrast these standards with the work of Hill, Everett and Glass, and others cited in this chapter.

4. Obtain a copy of your state/provincial chart of accounts for public schools. These may be available by going to their website(s).

2

What Is Accounting?

INTRODUCTION

If a person wants to keep track of the financial transactions that occur in a school district during any given period of time, it would soon become apparent that one needs a method to summarize the different types of transactions and the number of transactions within categories. For the school business official it is essential to be able to plan for financial aspects of school operations, to implement and maintain the financial plan and to summarize the results of financial transactions associated with school operations.

OUTCOMES

In this chapter, you will learn how to:

1. Define accounting.
2. Define a school budget—a plan for financial aspects of school operations for a given period.
3. Recognize the layout of a typical budget document.
4. Define an audit—an examination of the financial aspects of school operations for a given period.
5. Recognize the layout for a typical independent audit.
6. Recognize the layout for the Annual Financial Report (AFR).
7. Recognize the layout for the Comprehensive Annual Financial Report (CAFR).

ACCOUNTING

The accounting profession has defined accounting as the art of analyzing, recording, summarizing, interpreting and communicating the results of financial transactions. State and local school administrators realize the need to have a well-organized system for managing and reporting comparable financial transactions. The National Center for Education Statistics (NCES) has a responsibility to provide and interpret comprehensive statistics about the condition of education. In order to facilitate the task of obtaining comparable statistics, NCES regularly revises documents designed to promote the collection of comparable information. *Financial Accounting for Local and State School Systems, 2003 edition* (Johnson, 2003) is the latest document prepared by NCES to facilitate the collection of comparable financial data from school districts across the United States.

Although there is no federal law mandating the use of the handbook, many state school systems use terms and definitions presented in the handbook. The state school systems may use *Financial Accounting for Local and State School Systems, 2003 edition* to develop state-specific accounting manuals (e.g., *Illinois Program Accounting Manual for Local Education Agencies: Chart of Accounts and North Carolina Public Schools: Chart of Accounts*).

BUDGETING

In *Financial Accounting for Local and State School Systems, 2003 edition*, Johnson (2003, 13–15) describes the budgeting process as follows:

> A major element of financial data activity rests in the act of budgeting. Budgeting is the process of allocating finite resources to the prioritized needs of an organization. In most cases, for a governmental entity, the budget represents the legal authority to spend money. Adoption of a budget in the public sector implies that a set of decisions has been made by the governing board and administrators that culminates in matching a government's resources with the entity's needs. As such, the budget is a product of the planning process.
>
> The budget also provides an important tool for the control and evaluation of sources and the uses of resources. Using the accounting system to enact the will of the governing body, administrators are able to execute and control activities that have been authorized by the budget and to evaluate financial performance on the basis of comparisons between budgeted and actual operations. Thus, the budget is implicitly linked to financial accountability and relates directly to the financial reporting objectives established by the GASB.
>
> The planning and control functions inherent to any organization, including schools, underscore the importance of sound budgeting practices for the following reasons:
>
> - The type, quantity and quality of goods and services provided by governments often are not subject to the market forces of supply and demand. Thus, enacting and adhering to the budget establishes restrictions in the absence of a competitive market.
> - These goods and services provided by governments are generally considered critical to the public interest and welfare.
> - The scope and diversity of operations in an organization make comprehensive financial planning essential for good decision-making.
> - The financial planning process is critical to the expression of citizen preferences and is the avenue for reaching consensus among citizens, members of the governing board and staff on the future direction of the governmental unit's operations.
>
> The link between financial planning and budget preparation gives the budget document a unique role in governmental organizations. Budgets in the public arena are often considered the definitive policy document because an adopted budget represents the financial plan used by a government to achieve its goals and objectives.
>
> When a unit of government legally adopts a financial plan, the budget has secured the approval of the majority of the governing board and reflects:
>
> - Public choices about which goods and services the unit of government will or will not provide
> - The prioritization of activities in which the unit of government will be involved

- The relative influence of various participants and interest groups in the budget development process
- The governmental unit's plan for acquiring and using its resources

> In an educational environment, budgeting is an invaluable tool for both planning and evaluation. Budgeting provides a vehicle for translating educational goals and programs into financial resource plans—that is, developing an instructional plan to meet student performance goals should be directly linked to determining budgetary allocations. The link between instructional goals and financial planning is critical to effective budgeting and enhances the evaluation of budgetary and educational accountability.

Although the above description seems to reflect the *cash basis* of accounting, the budget may reflect operations which are recorded on the *accrual basis* of accounting. The *cash basis* of accounting implies that transactions are recorded when cash changes hands. (Tax monies are actually distributed to school districts; equipment is paid from district monies.) On the other hand, the *accrual basis* of accounting implies that transactions are recorded when they are reduced to legal obligations. (Taxes are levied; supplies are received but not yet paid for.) Although state legislatures may permit school districts to record transactions on a cash basis, the accounting profession recognizes that the accrual basis of accounting provides a more complete picture of the financial condition of the district.

The simple statement that a school district must provide a statement of cash on hand at the beginning of the fiscal year causes one to ask questions about the comparability of data across school districts. What is cash (assets)? How much is in "cash in the bank"? How much is in investments? How much is on loan?

The NCES has attempted to compile a comprehensive list and description of all items which reflect "cash" or current assets. *Financial Accounting for Local and State School Systems, 2003 edition* (Johnson, 2003) identifies and defines the following current assets: cash, cash with fiscal agents, investments, taxes receivable, interfund receivables, other receivables, bond proceeds receivable, inventories, prepaid expenses and other current assets. The manual also provides sub-classifications and descriptions to facilitate consistent reporting across districts of assets in each of the categories.

NCES has also attempted to develop a comprehensive list and description of expenditure items. NCES has established several *dimensions* that may be used to describe expenditure transactions. Three basic dimensions are fund, function and object.

- *Funds* are established to carry on specific activities in accordance with legislation, rules or regulations
- *Function* describes the activity for which a service or material object is acquired.
- *Object* is the service or commodity bought.

The use of fund, function and object enables NCES, state and local education agencies to gain a better understanding of the operations of a school district.

AUDITING

At the most general level, an audit is a methodical examination of use of resources and a written report of the findings. The audit may be conducted by independent public accountants, governmental accountants or by internal auditors. The audit may focus on selected areas—financial and compliance audits, program compliance audits, or performance audits. *Financial and compliance audits* are concerned with fairness of presentation of basic financial statements in conformity with Generally Accepted Accounting Principles (GAAP). *Program Compliance Audits* are concerned with the extent to which the school district conformed to requirements of the funding agency. *Performance Audits* are concerned with the economy and efficiency of the school district and the extent to which the program objectives are being attained. Everett, Lows and Johnson (1996, 13) cite Sam Tidwell's comments on the audit: "… for purposes of school fund accounting, the word audit involves examination of the documents, records, reports, system of internal control, accounting procedures, and other evidence for the purpose of determining the legality and propriety of proposed or consummated transactions, or for the purpose of ascertaining whether all transactions have been recorded and properly reported."

Generally speaking, the external financial audit is a way for the school district to show stewardship in the use of resources granted by the taxpayers in the school district. Although few persons may actually examine the external audit, it nevertheless compels the school district to greater accountability than might occur without an external audit.

ANNUAL FINANCIAL REPORTS

Annual financial reports are detailed financial statements that conform to state guidelines for reporting revenues and expenditures and are parallel to information contained in the budget. NCES has developed guidelines for reporting financial information that will facilitate collecting and reporting annual general education statistics at the federal level. Each state is expected to develop a manual that will outline comparable account classifications across school districts within the respective states. In addition, each state is expected to develop a set of models of the reporting formats used with the account classifications. The account classifications of the annual financial report include revenues, expenditures (fund, function and object), assets, liabilities and fund equities. To facilitate analysis, the structure of the budget and annual financial report are similar. The budget sets forth the planned financial transactions for a given period of time and the annual financial report sets forth the actual financial transactions for that period of time.

COMPREHENSIVE ANNUAL FINANCIAL REPORT (CAFR)

NCES does not mandate that each state adopt identical accounting manuals as suggested by *Financial Accounting for Local and State School Systems, 2003*. Each state is encouraged to use the manual as a guide in developing accounting systems that are uniquely suited to that state. A major difference that arises in reporting summary information is that there is considerable variance in the "funds" used by each state. Therefore, NCES has established general guidelines to group the various funds used by the states into "broad funds":

- General fund
- Special revenue funds
- Capital projects funds
- Debt service funds
- Enterprise funds
- Internal service funds

- Trust funds
- Agency funds

A "permanent fund" (code 5) was added in the draft 2003 handbook to account for resources that are legally restricted to the extent that only earnings, and not principal, may be used by the school district. Codes for enterprise funds and internal service funds were moved up to make room for the new permanent fund code. The trust and agency fund in the 1990 handbook was broken out into two funds in the 2003 handbook; trust funds (code 8) and agency funds (code 9). The general fixed assets (in the 1990 handbook) was deleted. The new fund classifications are presented below.

Governmental Fund Types

1. *General Fund.* This fund is the chief operating fund of the school district. It is used to account for all financial resources of the school district except for those required to be accounted for in another fund. A district may have only one general fund.

2. *Special Revenue Funds.* This fund is used to account for the proceeds of specific revenue sources (other than trusts or major capital projects) that are legally restricted to expenditure for specified purposes. Some examples of special revenue funds are:

   - Restricted state or federal grants-in-aid
   - Restricted tax levies

   A separate fund may be used for each identified restricted source, or one fund may be used, supplemented by the classification Project/Reporting code.

3. *Capital Projects Funds.* This fund is used to account for financial resources to be used to acquire or construct major capital facilities (other than those of proprietary funds and trust funds). The most common source of capital projects funding is the sale of bonds or other capital financing instruments. A separate fund may be used for each capital project or one fund may be used, supplemented by the classification Project/Reporting code.

4. *Debt Service Funds.* This fund is used to account for the accumulation of resources for, and the payment of, general long-term debt principal and interest.

5. *Permanent Funds.* This fund is used to account for resources that are legally restricted to the extent that only earnings, and not principal, may be used for purposes that support the school district's programs.

Proprietary Fund Types

6. *Enterprise Funds.* This fund may be used to account for any activity for which a fee is charged to external users for goods or services. Enterprise funds are required to be used to account for any activity whose principal revenue sources meet any of the following criteria:

- Debt backed solely by revenues from fees and charges (thus, not debt that is backed by the full faith and credit of the school district)
- Legal requirement to recover costs through fees and charges
- Policy decision of the governing board of management to recover the costs of providing services through fees or charges

Some examples of enterprise funds are activities such as the food service program, the bookstore operation, the athletic stadium or the community swimming pool.

7. *Internal Service Funds*. This fund may be used to account for any activity within the school district that provides goods or services to other funds, departments, component units or other governments on a cost-reimbursement basis. The use of an internal service fund is appropriate only for activities in which the school district is the predominant participant in the activity. Otherwise, the activity should be reported as an enterprise fund. Examples of internal service funds are such activities as central warehousing and purchasing, central data processing and central printing and duplicating.

Fiduciary Fund Types

8. *Trust Funds*. These funds are used to account for assets held by a school district in a trustee capacity for others (e.g., members and beneficiaries of pension plans, external investment pools or private purpose trust arrangements) and therefore cannot be used to support the school district's own programs. Trust funds are generally accounted for on the economic resources measurement focus and the accrual basis of accounting (except for the recognition of certain liabilities of defined benefit pension plans and certain post-employment healthcare plans; refer to GASB 26 and 27 for guidance on the recognition of these liabilities). Trust funds include pension trust funds, investment trust funds and private-purpose trust funds (as described below).

   - *Pension Trust Fund*. This fund is used to account for resources that are required to be held in trust for members and beneficiaries of defined benefit pension plans, defined contribution plans, other post-employment benefit plans or other benefit plans. Typically, these funds are used to account for local pension and other employee benefit funds that are provided by a school district in lieu of or in addition to any state retirement system.
   - *Investment Trust Fund*. This fund is used to account for the external portion (i.e., the portion that does not belong to the school district) of investment pools operated by the school district.
   - *Private-Purpose Trust Fund*. This fund is used to account for other trust arrangements under which the principal and income benefit individuals, private organizations or other governments.

9. *Agency Funds*. This account is used for funds that are held in a custodial capacity by a school district for individuals, private organizations or other governments. Agency funds may include those used to account for student activities or taxes collected for another government.

The only difference between the annual financial report and the CAFR is that state-specific information is presented in the annual financial report and information presented in the CAFR is aggregated by funds defined by NCES.

In order to carry out its mission, a school district may operate a number of funds. For the school business administrator, the term *fund* has come to hold a specific meaning, and the school business official will be quick to point out that a school district may use several funds.

The term *fund,* as it is used in governmental accounting, is defined as a fiscal and accounting entity with a self-balancing set of accounts recording cash and other financial resources, together with all related liabilities and residual equities or balances, and changes therein, which are segregated for the purpose of carrying on specific activities or attaining certain objectives in accordance with special regulations, restrictions or limitations (MFOA, 1980).

ACCOUNTS WITHIN A FUND

A fund, as an independent accounting entity, uses a self-balancing set of accounts to provide full information about financial transactions pertinent to meeting the objective for which the fund was established. Accounts that record financial transactions of an LEA fund may be classified a follows:

- Asset accounts
- Liability accounts
- Fund equity accounts
- Estimated revenue accounts
- Revenue accounts
- Appropriation accounts/estimated expenditure accounts
- Expenditure accounts
- Encumbrance accounts
- Summarizing and closing accounts

The estimated revenue accounts and appropriations/estimated expenditures accounts are not separate accounts; they are the budgetary elements of the respective revenue and expenditure accounts. Encumbrance accounts likewise are not separate accounts; they are an element of the expenditure accounts except for the reserve for encumbrance account which is part of the fund equity. These will be explained more fully in chapter 7 "Revenue Accounting" and chapter 8 "Expenditure Accounting."

SUMMARY

In this chapter, accounting, budgeting and auditing were defined. Descriptions of layouts for the budget document, audit, annual financial report, and comprehensive annual financial report were presented. The term *fund* was defined and several types of funds were described. The accounts necessary for the self-balancing set of accounts for a fund were listed.

ACTIVITIES

1. Access two different school district websites and carefully examine the budget, annual financial report and comprehensive annual financial report provided.

2. Study the definitions of the following terms as provided in the glossary:

    a. Budget
    b. Annual Financial Report (AFR)
    c. Comprehensive Annual Financial Report (CAFR)
    d. Cash
    e. Asset
    f. Cash basis
    g. Accrual basis
    h. Current asset
    i. Fund
    j. Function
    k. Object
    l. Audit
    m. Financial and compliance audit
    n. Program compliance audit
    o. Performance audits
    p. General fund
    q. Special revenue fund
    r. Capital projects fund
    s. Debt service fund
    t. Enterprise fund
    u. Internal service funds
    v. Trust and agency funds

3

Basic Principles of Accounting

INTRODUCTION

The information presented in this chapter is designed to acquaint the superintendent, school business administrator or principal with a rudimentary understanding of accounting processes in order that they may communicate accounting information and reports to school personnel, board of education members and the public, as well as to enable them to communicate with certified public accountants, state auditors and others with respect to accounting matters. This text is not designed to prepare public accountants nor to eliminate the need for persons with advanced accounting training or certified public accountants.

Everett, Lows and Johnson (1996) cite Tidwell's statement that the objectives of financial accounting for school systems may be summarized as follows:

1. To provide a complete record of all financial transactions of the school system.
2. To summarize, with reasonable promptness, financial transactions of the school system in financial reports required for proper, effective and efficient administration.
3. To provide financial information that would be helpful for budget preparation, adoption and execution.
4. To provide financial controls or safeguards for the school system's money and property.
5. To provide a basis whereby the governing board can place administrative responsibility and minimize the possibility of waste, carelessness, inefficiency and possible fraud.
6. To provide clear and concise financial reports to the public as a basis for judging past, present and future financial operation of the school system.
7. To provide a historical record which, over a period of years, can be studied and analyzed critically and constructively for the purpose of aiding citizens, the governing board and the school system's administrative officers in keeping pace with changing concepts of education.

OUTCOMES

In this chapter, you will learn how to:

1. Perform selected accounting procedures (discover, record, classify and summarize financial transactions).
2. Distinguish between the cash and accrual basis of accounting.
3. Recognize the accounting equation.
4. Operate within the constraints of the accounting equation.
5. Use the accounting equation in the preparation of financial reports.

ACCOUNTS WITHIN A FUND

As noted in the previous chapter, a fund, as an accounting entity, uses a self-balancing set of accounts to provide full information about financial transactions pertinent to meeting the objectives for which the fund was established. Accounts that record financial transactions of a school district fund which will be used in the next few chapters may be classified as follows:

1. Asset accounts
2. Liability accounts
3. Fund equity accounts
4. Revenue accounts
5. Expenditure accounts
6. Summarizing and closing accounts

ACCOUNTING RECORDS

To record accounting transactions a local education agency uses a variety of books. *Book* of course is a term derived when records were maintained manually, but the term is still used today even though most records are maintained electronically and the books are merely printouts of the electronic records. The two most common terms associated with these books are *ledgers* and *journals* (sometimes referred to as *registers*). The primary permanent accounting record for an entity is the general ledger. Transactions are not normally posted directly to the general ledger. Transactions are usually recorded in one of the journals, which is why they are referred to as books of original entry. There are a number of special journals; in education most common are the payroll journal, the cash receipts journal, the cash disbursements journal and the purchases journal. If a transaction does not fit in one of the special journals then it is recorded in the general journal. In this electronic age these journals are usually identified as elements of an accounting software package. The ledgers and journals will be described in more detail in later chapters in this book.

ACCOUNTING PROCEDURES

Accounting procedures discover, record, classify and summarize financial information to produce financial reports and to provide internal control. Procedures used in analyzing and recording transactions are as follows:

1. Determine the specific fund to which the transaction is related. (What fund?)
2. Determine the specific accounts that are affected by the transaction. (What accounts?)
3. Record each transaction in the book of original entry. (Keep a journal.)
4. Post each part of the transaction to the specific account affected. (Post to ledger or journal.)
5. Prepare financial statements from the accounts. (Summarize and report.)

BASIC FINANCIAL STATEMENTS

Basic financial statements present information concerning a school district's financial position on a specific date, *or* changes in that position and results of operation during a period ending on that date. Financial statements presenting the financial positions as of a certain date are called *balance sheets* and statements reflecting changes in that position and results of operation during a period ending on that date are called *operating statements.*

BALANCE SHEETS

The financial position information presented on the balance sheet indicates what a school district owns (assets), what it owes (liabilities) and the excess of assets over liabilities (fund equity). Therefore, the basic accounting equation for a fund is expressed as:

Assets - Liabilities = Fund Balance

or

Assets = Liabilities + Fund Balance

Assets—defined as resources owned or held by a school district that have monetary value. Current assets are those assets that are available or can be made readily available to finance current operations or to pay current liabilities. General fixed assets are those that the school district intends to hold or continue to use over a long period of time. A partial list of current assets common to school districts follows.

Cash in bank—All funds on deposit with a bank or savings and loan institution, normally in non-interest-bearing accounts. Interest-bearing accounts are recorded in investments. (Also referred to as *cash*.)

Investments—Securities and real estate held for producing income in the form of interest, dividends, rentals or lease payments.

Taxes receivable—Uncollected portion of taxes levied by a school district or governmental unit which has become due including any interest or penalties that may be accrued.

Loans receivable—Amounts that have been loaned to people or organizations, including notes taken as security for such loans, where permitted by statutory authority.

Prepaid expenses—Expenses paid for benefits not yet received or expired.

A listing of current asset account titles with account code numbers, as recommended by the National Center for Education Statistics (NCES), can be found on pages 103–106 of *Financial Accounting for Local and State School Systems, 2003* (Johnson, 2003).

Liabilities—Liabilities may be defined as debt or other legal obligations arising out of transactions in the past that must be liquidated, renewed or refunded at some future date. Current liabilities are those debts the school district expects to pay within a short period of time, usually a year or less. Long-term liabilities are debts with a maturity of more than one year after date of issuance. A partial list of current liabilities common to a school district follows:

Interfund loans payable—A liability account used to record a debt owed by one fund to another fund in the same governmental unit.

Accounts payable—Liabilities on open account owing to private people, firms or corporations for goods and services received by a school district (but not including amounts due to other funds of the same school district or to other governmental units).

Warrants payable—Amounts due to designated payees in the form of a written order drawn by the school district directing the treasurer to pay a specific amount (i.e., unpaid teacher/employee salaries, unpaid payroll withholdings).

Contracts payable—Amounts due on contracts for assets, goods or services received by a school district.

Deferred revenues—A liability account that represents revenues collected before they become due or recorded as an asset.

A listing of current liability account titles, with account code numbers, as recommended by NCES, can be found on pages 107–109 of *Financial Accounting for Local and State School Systems, 2003* (Johnson, 2003).

Fund balance—These are accounts showing the excess in assets of fund over its liabilities. Portions of that balance may be reserved for future use. A partial list of fund balance accounts commonly used by school district's follows:

Reserve for encumbrances—A reserve representing that portion of a fund balance segregated to provide for unliquidated encumbrances. Separate accounts may be maintained for current encumbrances and prior-year encumbrances (see chapter 8).

Reserved fund balance—A reserve representing that portion of a fund balance segregated to indicate that assets equal to the amount of reserve are restricted and are, therefore, not available for appropriation. A separate reserve should be established for each special purpose. One example of a special purpose would be restricted federal programs.

Unreserved fund balance—The excess of the assets of a fund over its liabilities and reserves.

A listing of current fund balance account titles with account code numbers, as recommended by NCES, can be found on pages 109–110 of *Financial Accounting for Local and State School Systems, 2003* (Johnson, 2003).

Balance Sheet—The balance sheet is a basic financial statement that discloses the assets, liabilities and fund equities of an entity at a specific date in conformity with generally accepted accounting principles (GAAP) (MFOA, 1980).

The balance sheet should contain the following information:

- The name of the school district
- The name of the fund

- The name of the financial statement (balance sheet)
- The date
- All asset, liability and fund balance accounts which have non-zero balances

A balance sheet for the general fund of Kimberly Hills School District as of the end of 2009 is shown in Illustration 3.1.

Illustration 3.1
Kimberly Hills School District
General Fund
Balance Sheet
June 30, 2009

Assets		
Cash in Bank		$ 20,000
Investments		80,000
Taxes receivable	$300,000	
less: Est. Uncollectible Taxes	15,000	285,000
Loan receivable		30,000
Total Assets		$415,000
Liabilities and Fund Balance		
Liabilities:		
Accounts Payable	$ 27,000	
Warrants Payable	82,000	
Loan Payable	161,000	$270,000
Fund Balance:		
Reserved for Encumbrances	$115,000	
Unreserved Fund Balance	30,000	
Total Fund Balance		145,000
Total Liability & Fund Balance		$415,000

Financial Accounting for Local and State School Systems, 2003, Johnson (2003, 62) changed the terminology from fund equity to fund balance. Within governmental funds, equity is reported as fund balance. Proprietary and fiduciary fund equity is reported as net assets.

OPERATING STATEMENTS

Results of operation can be measured and reported in several different ways. A statement of revenues, expenditures and fund balance, or statement of changes in financial position, summarize the effect revenues and expenditures have had on the fund balance during a specific period of time.

Revenues increase the net assets of a fund and expenditures decrease the net assets of a fund. Revenues of a fund recognized in a certain period have a direct positive impact upon the fund balance account.

Expenditures refer to the charges incurred, whether paid or unpaid, which are presumed to benefit the current fiscal year. A fund's revenues increase the fund balance and expenses decrease the fund balance. Given these relationships, the basic accounting equation can be expanded to the following:

Assets = Liabilities + (Fund Balance + Revenues – Expenditures)

or,

Assets = Liabilities + Fund Balance + Revenues – Expenditures

Illustration 3.2 shows a Statement of Revenues, Expenditures and Fund Balance for the Kimberly Hills School District.

Illustration 3.2
Kimberly Hills School District
General Fund
Statement of Revenues, Expenditures and Fund Balance
For the period ended June 30, 2009

Fund Balance, July 1, 2008 (beginning of period)		$ 25,000
Add excess of revenues over expenditures:		
Revenues	$300,000	
less Expenditures	180,000	120,000
Fund Balance, June 30, 2009 (end of period)		$145,000

The balance sheet provides information regarding the financial condition of a fund as of a specific date and the statement of revenues, expenditures and fund balance provide information regarding the results of operation for a specified period of time.

Examples 1A, 1B and 2 illustrate the use of the balance sheet and the statement of revenues, expenditures and fund balance in summarizing transactions in a school district.

Example 1A

On July 1, 2008, the unreserved fund balance of Cape Jennifer School District was $323,000. During the year, revenues amounting to $420,000 were realized and expenses amounting to $300,000 were paid. Asset and liability account balances in the general fund on June 30, 2009 were as follows:

Cash in Bank	$ 20,000
Investments	370,000
Taxes Receivable	640,000
Prepaid Expense	3,000
Accounts Payable	590,000

Given the above information:

- Prepare a statement of revenues, expenditures and fund balance for the general fund for the period ending June 30, 2009
- Prepare a balance sheet for the general fund as of June 30, 2009

Illustration of Example 1A
Cape Jennifer School District
General Fund
Statement of Revenues, Expenditures and Fund Balance
For the period ended June 30, 2009

Fund Balance, July 1, 2008		$323,000
Add excess of revenues over expenditures:		
Revenues	$420,000	
less: Expenditures	300,000	120,000
Fund Balance, June 30, 2009		
		$443,000

Cape Jennifer School District
General Fund
Balance Sheet
June 30, 2009

Assets	
Cash in Bank	$ 20,000
Investments	370,000
Taxes Receivable	640,000
Prepaid Expense	3,000
Total Assets	$1,033,000
Liabilities and Fund Balance	
Liabilities:	
Accounts Payable	$590,000
Fund Balance:	
Unreserved Fund Balance	443,000
Total Liabilities and Fund Balance	$1,033,000

Example 1B

On July 2, 2009, Cape Jennifer School District (refer to Example 1A) sold its investments for cash and received cash for the total amount due in taxes receivable. The balance sheet for the general fund for Cape Jennifer School District on July 2, 2009, would be as follows:

Illustration of Example 1B

Cape Jennifer School District
General Fund
Balance Sheet
July 2, 2009

Assets		
Cash in Bank		$1,030,000
Prepaid Expense		3,000
Total Assets		$1,033,000
Liabilities and Fund Balance		
Liabilities:		
Accounts Payable	$ 590,000	
Fund Balance:		
Unreserved Fund Balance	443,000	
Total Liabilities and Fund Balance		$1,033,000

Example 2

Timton School District has the following account balances in the general fund on June 30, 2008:

Unreserved Fund Balance	$353,000
Accounts Payable	35,000
Investments	420,000
Loans Receivable	180,000
Contracts Payable	300,000
Cash in Bank	6,000
Taxes Receivable	560,000
Prepaid Expense	12,000
Warrants Payable	40,000
Accrued Salaries and Benefits	450,000

(Hint: Identify and group assets, liabilities and fund equities accounts and list in order of liquidity or by account number.)

The balance sheet for the general fund for Timton School District on June 30, 2008, would appear as shown in the illustration for Example 2.

SUMMARY

Definitions were given of accounting and descriptions were given of selected account subcategories. Illustrations were provided for selected accounting procedures and examples of balance sheets and statements of revenues, expenditures and fund balance were shown. The accounting equation was introduced and reports were derived through the use of that equation.

Illustration of Example 2

Timton School District
General Fund
Balance Sheet
June 30, 2008

Assets	
Cash in Bank	$ 6,000
Investments	420,000
Taxes Receivable	560,000
Loans Receivable	180,000
Prepaid Expense	12,000
Total Assets	$1,178,000
Liabilities and Fund Balance	
Liabilities:	
Accounts Payable	$ 35,000
Warrants Payable	40,000
Contracts Payable	300,000
Accrued Salaries and Benefits Fund Balance	450,000
Unreserved Fund Balance	353,000
Total Liabilities and Fund Balance	$1,178,000

ACTIVITIES

(Note: The suggested solutions to numeric problems can be found on the CD inside the cover of this book.)

1. Define each of the following terms:

   a. Accounting
   b. Fund
   c. Accounting entity
   d. Asset
   e. Liability
   f. Fund balance
   g. Balance sheet accounts

2. Review the definitions of the following terms found in the glossary:

a. Transaction
b. Journalize
c. Post
d. Post to ledger
e. Operating statement
f. Current assets
g. General fixed assets
h. Cash in bank
i. Interfund loans payable
j. Accounts payable
k. Warrants payable
l. Contracts payable
m. Deferred revenue
n. Reserve for encumbrances
o. Reserved fund balance account
p. Unreserved fund balance
q. Investments
r. Taxes receivable
s. Prepaid expenses
t. Liabilities
u. Current liabilities
v. Long-term liabilities
w. Loans receivable

3. What types of accounts are included in the school fund accounting equation?

4. What is the purpose of the Statement of Revenues, Expenditures and Fund Equity Report?

5. On June 30, 2008, the account balances of the general fund of Christopher Point School District were:

Cash in bank	$ 20,000
Accounts payable	30,000
Investments	25,000
Taxes receivable	200,000
Unreserved fund balance	120,000
Contracts payable	95,000

Instructions:

- Prepare a balance sheet as of June 30, 2008, for Christopher Point School District.

6. On July 1, 2008, the fund balance of the general fund of Randyville School System was $75,000. During the year, revenues amounting to $96,000 were realized and expenditures amounting to $474,000 were paid. Prepare a statement of revenues, expenditures and fund balance for the period ending June 30, 2009.

7. On July 1, 2008, the fund balance of the general fund of New Douglas School System was $97,455. During the year, revenues amounting to $346,000 were realized and expenditures amounting to $213,613 were incurred. Asset and liability account balances as of June 30, 2009 were as follows:

Taxes receivable	$600,050
Accounts payable	54,965
Cash in bank	29,415
Warrants payable	422,381
Contracts payable	242,227
Investments	317,950
Loans receivable	2,000

Instructions:

- Prepare a statement of revenues, expenditures and fund balance for the year ended June 30, 2009.
- Prepare a balance sheet as of June 30, 2009.

4

Basic Accounting Techniques

INTRODUCTION

Although most accounting in school systems has been automated, the best way to learn accounting is to study and apply paper and pencil techniques. This chapter harkens back to the day before modern technology when "real people did real work." Electronic data processing is fast and efficient. However, if one does not understand what is being done, then one is in the position of placing blind trust in a silicon monster.

What is the accounting mystery? What are debits and credits? How do you know you haven't made mistakes? What do the numbers tell you? Grab a paper and pencil and probe the mysteries of accounting.

OUTCOMES

In this chapter, you will learn how to:

1. Define *debits* and *credits*.
2. Debit and credit accounts.
3. Define a *trial balance*.
4. Compute a trial balance.

DEBITS AND CREDITS DEFINED

Financial transactions may result in increases or decreases to an account. A convenient method of displaying the increases or decreases is through the use of debits and credits to T-accounts. A T-account, shown in Figure 4.1, looks like a "T," and the left side of the T-account is called the debit side and the right side is called the credit side.

Figure 4.1
T-Account

Name of the Account
(Debit side) | (Credit side)

The terms *debit* and *credit* are of Latin origin and do not carry any increase/decrease meaning in and of themselves. As an adjective, *debit* means "left" and *credit* means "right"; as a noun, *debit* means "an entry in the debit or left-hand side of an account" and *credit* means "an entry in the credit or right-hand side of an account"; and as a verb, *debit* means "to enter a sum on the debit or left-hand side of an account" and *credit* means "to enter a sum on the credit or right-hand side of an account."

The terms *debit* and *credit* do carry increase/decrease meaning when used in conjunction with a specific group of accounts. The relationship between accounts, debits and credits, and increases and decreases is shown in the basic accounting equation as follows (dr = debit; cr = credit):

Assets	=	Liabilities	+	Fund Balance	+	Revenues	-	Expenditures
dr cr	=	dr cr	+	dr cr	+	dr cr	-	dr cr
+ -	=	- +	+	- +	+	- +	-	+ -

RELATIONSHIP BETWEEN ACCOUNTS, DEBITS AND CREDITS

The relationship between accounts, debits and credits, and increases and decreases may be stated as follows:

To increase an asset account, debit.
To decrease an asset account, credit.
To increase a liability account, credit.
To decrease a liability account, debit.
To increase a fund balance account, credit.
To decrease a fund balance account, debit.
To increase a revenue account, credit.
To decrease a revenue account, debit.
To increase an expenditure account, debit.
To decrease an expenditure account, credit.

The above relationships may be summarized as follows:

1. To increase asset and expenditure accounts, debit.
2. To decrease asset and expenditure accounts, credit.
3. To increase liability, fund balance and revenue accounts, credit.
4. To decrease liability, fund balance and revenue accounts, debit.

EQUALITY OF DEBITS AND CREDITS

In a self-balancing set of accounts, the debit amounts must equal the credit amounts. Therefore, each transaction has at least one debit and at least one credit, and the total amount of debits must equal the total amount of credits. A transaction may have more than one debit and/or more than one credit. Such a transaction is called a compound entry. For example, the use of cash (credit: reduction of an asset) to pay principal (debit: reduction of a liability) and interest (debit: increase in expenditures) results in a compound entry.

Illustrations of the use of debits and credits in recording transactions are presented in the following examples.

TRIAL BALANCE

If all transactions have been recorded correctly, then the total of all debits should be equal to the total of all credits (Examples 1–4). After all transactions have been recorded, a trial balance

(Illustration 4.1) is prepared to prove the equality of debits and credits.

Example 1

Assume that the Kimberly Hills School District began the year with assets of $30,000, liabilities of $10,000 and fund equity of $20,000 in the general fund.

	Assets	=	Liabilities	+	Fund Balance	+	Revenues	-	Expenditures
	dr cr	=	dr cr	+	dr cr	+	dr cr	-	dr cr
(1)	30000	=	10000	+	20000	+		-	
(T)	30000	=	10000	+	20000	+		-	

Note: Transaction (1) has equal debits and credits ($30,000) and the totals (T) of debits and credits are equal ($30,000).

Example 2

Assume that property taxes are assessed and levied in the amount of $40,000. What accounts are affected? (Assets are increased/debited and revenues are increased/credited.)

	Assets	=	Liabilities	+	Fund Balance	+	Revenues	-	Expenditures
	dr cr	=	dr cr	+	dr cr	+	dr cr	-	dr cr
(1)	30000	=	10000	+	20000	+		-	
(2)	40000	=		+		+	40000	-	
(T)	70000	=	10000	+	20000	+	40000	-	

Note: Transaction (2) has equal debits and credits ($40,000) and the totals (T) of debits and credits are equal ($70,000).

Example 3

Assume supplies in the amount of $8,000 were purchased on account. What accounts are affected? (Expenditures are increased/debited and liabilities are increased/credited.)

	Assets	=	Liabilities	+	Fund Balance	+	Revenues	-	Expenditures
	dr cr	=	dr cr	+	dr cr	+	dr cr	-	dr cr
(1)	30000	=	10000	+	20000	+		-	
(2)	40000	=		+		+	40000	-	
(3)		=	8000	+		+		-	8000
(T)	70000	=	18000	+	20000	+	40000	-	8000

Note: Transaction (3) has equal debits and credits ($8,000) and the totals (T) of debits and credits are equal ($78,000).

Example 4

Assume the school district borrows $15,000 from the bank. What accounts are affected? (Assets are increased/debited and liabilities are increased/credited.)

	Assets	=	Liabilities	+	Fund Balance	+	Revenues	-	Expenditures
	dr cr	=	dr cr	+	dr cr	+	dr cr	-	dr cr
(1)	30000	=	10000	+	20000	+		-	
(2)	40000	=		+		+	40000	-	
(3)		=	8000	+		+		-	8000
(4)	15000	=	15000	+		+		-	
(T)	85000	=	33000	+	20000	+	40000	-	8000

Note: Transaction (4) has equal debits and credits ($15,000) and the totals (T) of debits and credits are equal ($93,000).

The Municipal Finance Officers Association (1980, 76) defines a trial balance as: a list of the balances of the accounts in a ledger kept in double entry, with the debit and credit balances shown in separate columns. If the totals of the debit and credit columns are equal or their net balance agrees with a control account, the ledger from which the figures are taken is said to be "in balance."

To prepare a trial balance, the following steps should be followed:

1. Find the total debits and total credits of each account. Make sure to include any beginning balance in the appropriate total.
2. Determine the account balance by calculating the difference between the debit and credit totals in each account.
3. List each account and its balance on paper that has two amount columns. Debit balances will be placed in the left column and credit balances in the right column.
4. Compare the sum of the two columns. (The sum of the column of debits should be equal to the sum of the column of credits.)

Illustration 4.1
Kimberly Hills School District
General Fund
Trial Balance
June 30, 2008

Accounts	Debits	Credits
Assets	$85,000	
Liabilities		33,000
Fund Equity		20,000
Revenues		40,000
Expenditures	8,000	
Total	$93,000	$93,000

SUMMARY

Debits and credits were defined and their use was illustrated in the accounting equation. Trial balance was defined and an example was given.

ACTIVITIES

1. Define each of the following terms:

    a. Debit (adjective, noun and verb)
    b. Credit (adjective, noun and verb)
    c. Trial balance
    d. T-account
    e. Compound entry
    f. Debit account
    g. Credit account
    h. Transaction

2. Give an example of a compound entry.

3. What is the purpose of preparing a trial balance?

4. Describe which accounts are to be debited and which are to be credited for each of the following transactions:

    a. General state aid is received.
    b. Teacher salaries are paid.
    c. Money is borrowed from the bank.
    d. A utility bill is paid.
    e. Investments are purchased.
    f. Custodial salaries are paid.
    g. Investments are sold.
    h. A loan from a bank is repaid.
    i. Supplies are purchased for cash.
    j. Equipment is purchased on account.

5. Fort Steven School District began the year with assets of $95,000, no liabilities and fund balance of $95,000 in the general fund. During the year which ended June 30, 2008, the following transactions were completed:

    a. Property taxes were assessed and levied in the amount of $85,000.
    b. An amount of $65,000 was borrowed from the Fort Steven National Bank by means of tax anticipation warrants.
    c. Cash was received for the entire amount of the property tax levy as specified in transaction (a).
    d. Teacher salaries of $40,000 were paid.

e. Supplies and materials in the amount of $35,000 were purchased on account.
f. Paid tax anticipation warrants of $50,000 (See transaction (b)).
g. Received $90,000 in general state aid.

Instructions:

- Record the beginning balances and enter the transactions in T-accounts.
- Prepare a trial balance.

6. The Markham City School System began the year with assets of $125,000, liabilities of $30,000 and a fund balance of $95,000 in the general fund. During the year which ended June 30, 2009, the following transactions were completed:

    a. Property taxes were assessed and levied in the amount of $75,000.
    b. A general state aid payment of $70,000 was received.
    c. A loan was obtained from the Markham City State Bank in the amount of $35,000.
    d. Tuition in the amount of $3,300 was collected.
    e. School property was sold for $5,500.
    f. Teacher salaries of $45,000 were paid.
    g. Equipment in the amount of $123,000 was purchased on account.
    h. Investments of $40,000 were sold for $30,000. (Loss on investments is an expenditure.)
    i. Heating costs of $12,000 were paid.
    j. Auditor's fee of $8,000 was paid.

Instructions:

- Record the beginning balances and enter the transactions in T-accounts.
- Prepare a trial balance.

7. Briancon School District began the year with assets of $220,000, some liabilities and a fund balance of $85,000 in the general fund. During the year which ended June 30, 2009, the following transactions were completed:

    a. Property taxes were assessed and levied in the amount of the liabilities.
    b. Cash was received for the entire amount of the property tax levy.
    c. Cash was used to pay all liabilities.
    d. A loan was obtained from the Briancon National Bank in the amount of $135,000.
    e. Equipment in the amount of $85,000 was purchased for cash from the Randyville Lawn and Garden Center.

Instructions:

- Record the beginning balances and enter the transactions in T-accounts.
- Prepare a trial balance.
- Prepare a statement of revenues, expenditures and fund balance.
- Prepare a balance sheet.

5

General Ledger

INTRODUCTION

An organization, such as a school district, may have numerous accounting transactions during a month, week or day. In order to facilitate record keeping, it is necessary to identify all accounts the organization expects to use during the accounting period. The accounts should then be grouped by type of accounts and arranged in such a manner as to be similarly located across accounting periods. The general ledger is the "book" that accommodates all accounts, grouped by type of account, which is necessary to reflect the financial operations of a school district.

OUTCOMES

In this chapter, you will learn how to:

1. Define *general ledger*.
2. Recognize accounts, grouped by type of account, within the general ledger.
3. Analyze financial transactions.
4. Debit and credit entries in the general ledger.
5. Obtain an account balance for accounts in the general ledger.

GENERAL LEDGER DEFINED

The National Center for Educational Statistics (Roberts and Lichtenberger, 1973) defines the general ledger as: a book, file, or other device in which accounts are kept to the degree of detail necessary, that summarized the financial transactions of the LEA (local education agency). General ledger accounts may be kept for any group of items of receipts or expenditures on which an administrative officer wishes to maintain a close check.

Financial Accounting for Local and State School Systems, 2003 recommends the following accounts and account code numbers for asset, liability, fund equity, revenue and expenditure accounts.

ASSET CLASSIFICATION

Assets and other debits include what is owned and what is not owned but is expected to become fully owned at some future date.

101 Cash in Bank
102 Cash on Hand
103 Petty Cash
104 Change Cash
105 Cash with Fiscal Agents
111 Investments

112 Unamortized Premiums on Investments
113 Unamortized Discounts on Investments (Credit)
114 Interest Receivable on Investments
115 Accrued Interest on Investments Purchased
121 Taxes Receivable
122 Allowance for Uncollectible Taxes (Credit)
131 Interfund Loans Receivable
132 Interfund Accounts Receivable
141 Intergovernmental Accounts Receivable
151 Loans Receivable
152 Allowance for Uncollectible Loans (Credit)
153 Other Accounts Receivable
154 Allowance for Uncollectible Accounts Receivable (Credit)
171 Inventories for Consumption
172 Inventories for Resale
181 Prepaid Items
191 Deposits
192 Deferred Expenditures/Expenses
193 Capitalized Bond and Other Debt Issuance Costs
194 Premium and Discount on Issuance of Bonds
199 Other Current Assets
200 Capital Assets
211 Land and Land Improvements
221 Site Improvements
222 Accumulated Depreciation on Site Improvements
231 Buildings and Building Improvements
232 Accumulated Depreciation on Buildings and Building Improvements
241 Machinery and Equipment
242 Accumulated Depreciation on Machinery and Equipment
251 Works of Art and Historical Treasures
252 Accumulated Depreciation on Works of Art and Historical Collections
261 Infrastructure
262 Accumulated Depreciation on Infrastructure
271 Construction in Progress

LIABILITIES, RESERVES AND FUND BALANCE CLASSIFICATION

Liabilities, reserves and fund balance are LEA debts plus items that are not debts but which may become debts at some future time. Also included are other budgeting accounts that normally appear only on the interim financial statements.

Interfund Accounts Payable

411 Intergovernmental Accounts Payable
421 Accounts Payable
422 Judgments Payable

423 Warrants Payable
431 Contracts Payable
432 Construction Contracts Payable—Retainage
433 Construction Contracts Payable
441 Matured Bonds Payable
442 Bonds Payable—Current
443 Unamortized Premiums on Issuance of Bonds
451 Loans Payable
452 Lease Obligations—Current
455 Interest Payable
461 Accrued Salaries and Benefits
471 Payroll Deductions and Withholdings
472 Compensated Absences—Current
473 Accrued Annual Requirement Contribution Liability
481 Deferred Revenues
491 Deposits Payable
499 Other Current Liabilities
511 Bonds Payable
512 Accreted Interest
513 Unamortized Gains/Losses on Debt Refundings
521 Loans Payable
531 Capital Lease Obligations
551 Compensated Absences
561 Arbitrage Rebate Liability
590 Other Long-Term Liabilities
711 Reserve for Inventories
712 Reserve for Prepaid Items
713 Reserve for Encumbrances
714 Other Reserved Fund Balance
720 Designated Fund Balance
730 Unreserved Fund Balance
740 Invested in Capital Assets, Net of Related Debt (This account is to be used in Proprietary funds only.)
750 Restricted Net Assets (This account is to be used in Proprietary funds only.)
760 Unrestricted Net Assets (This account is to be used in Proprietary funds only.)

REVENUE AND OTHER FUND SOURCES CLASSIFICATION

Revenues are classified by type and source for the various funds of an LEA. Revenues are defined as additions to assets that do not increase any liability, do not represent the recovery of an expenditure and do not represent the cancellation of certain liabilities with a corresponding increase in other liabilities or a decrease in assets.

1000 Revenue from Local Sources
1100 Taxes Levied/Assessed by the School District
1110* Ad Valorem Taxes

1120* Sales and Use Taxes
1130* Income Taxes
1140* Penalties and Interest on Taxes
1190* Other Taxes
1200* Revenue from Local Governmental Units Other Than School Districts
1210* Ad Valorem Taxes
1220 Sales and Use Tax
1230 Income Taxes
1240 Penalties and Interest on Taxes
1280 Revenue in Lieu of Taxes
1290 Other Taxes
1300 Tuition
1310* Tuition from Individuals
1320* Tuition from Other Government Sources within the State
1321* Tuition from Other School Districts within the State
1330* Tuition from Other Government Sources Outside the State
1331* Tuition from School Districts Outside the State
1340* Tuition from Other Private Sources (other than individuals)
1350* Tuition from the State/Other School Districts for Voucher Program Students
1400 Transportation Fees
1410* Transportation Fees from Individuals
1420* Transportation Fees from Other Government Sources within the State
1421* Transportation Fees from Other School Districts within the State
1430* Transportation Fees from Other Government Sources Outside the State
1431* Transportation Fees from Other School Districts Outside the State
1440* Transportation Fees from Other Private Sources (other than individuals)
1500* Investment Income
1510 Interest on Investments
1520 Dividends on Investments
1530 Net Increase in the Fair Value of Investments
1531 Realized Gains (Losses) on Investments
1532 Unrealized Gains (Losses) on Investments
1540 Investment Income from Real Property
1600* Food Services
1610 Daily Sales—Reimbursable Programs
1611 Daily Sales—School Lunch Program
1612 Daily Sales—School Breakfast Program
1613 Daily Sales—Special Milk Program
1614 Daily Sales—After-School Program
1620 Daily Sales—Non-Reimbursable Programs
1630 Special Functions
1650 Daily Sales—Summer Food Program
1700* District Activities
1710 Admissions
1720 Bookstore Sales
1730 Student Organization Membership Dues and Fees

1740 Fees
1750* Revenue from Enterprise Activities
1790 Other Activity Income
1800* Revenue from Community Services Activities
1900 Other Revenue from Local Sources
1910* Rentals
1920* Contributions and Donations from Private Sources
1930* Gains or Losses on the Sale of Capital Assets
1940* Textbook Sales and Rentals
1941 Textbook Sales
1942 Textbook Rentals
1950* Miscellaneous Revenues from Other School Districts
1951 Miscellaneous Revenue from Other School Districts within the State
1952 Miscellaneous Revenue from Other School Districts Outside the State
1960* Miscellaneous Revenues from Other Local Governmental Units
1970* Operating Revenues
1980* Refund of Prior Year's Expenditures
1990* Miscellaneous
2000* Revenue from Intermediate Sources
2100* Unrestricted Grants-in-Aid
2200* Restricted Grants-in-Aid
2800* Revenue in Lieu of Taxes
2900* Revenue for/on Behalf of the School District
3000* Revenue from State Sources
3100 Unrestricted Grants-in-Aid
3200 Restricted Grants-in-Aid
3800 Revenue in Lieu of Taxes
3900* Revenue for/on Behalf of the School District
4000 Revenue from Federal Sources
4100* Unrestricted Grants-in-Aid Direct from the Federal Government
4200* Unrestricted Grants-in-Aid from the Federal Government through the State
4300* Restricted Grants-in-Aid Direct from the Federal Government
4500* Restricted Grants-in-Aid from the Federal Government through the State
4700* Grants-in-Aid from the Federal Government through Other Intermediate Agencies
4800* Revenue in Lieu of Taxes
4900* Revenue for/on Behalf of the School District
5000* Other Financing Sources
5100 Issuance of Bonds
5110* Bond Principal
5120 Premium or Discount on the Issuance of Bonds
5200 Fund Transfers In
5300 Proceeds From the Disposal of Real or Personal Property
5400 Loan Proceeds
5500 Capital Lease Proceeds
5600 Other Long-Term Debt Proceeds
6000 Other Items

6100 Capital Contributions
6200 Amortization of Premium on Issuance of Bonds
6300 Special Items
6400 Extraordinary Items

*Account codes that are necessary for the NCES reporting are noted with an asterisk (*).

EXPENDITURE CLASSIFICATION

Expenditures can be classified along several dimensions. *Financial Accounting for Local and State School Systems, 2003* specifies the classifications that are essential to meet many of the important federal (and most state) reporting requirements that are found within the following dimensions:

- Program
- Function
- Object
- Project/Reporting (formerly called Source of Funds)

EXPENDITURE CLASSIFICATION BY PROGRAM

A program is a plan of activities and procedures designed to accomplish a predetermined objective or set of objectives. This dimension provides school districts the framework to classify expenditures to determine costs by program.

100 Regular Elementary/Secondary Education Programs
200 Special Programs
300 Vocational and Technical Programs
400 Other Instructional Programs—Elementary/Secondary
500 Non-Public School Programs
600 Adult/Continuing Education Programs
700 Community/Junior College Education Programs
800 Community Services Programs
900 Co-curricular and Extra-curricular Activities

EXPENDITURE CLASSIFICATION BY FUNCTION

Financial Accounting for Local and State School Systems, 2003 describes the function dimension as follows: The function describes the activity being performed for which a service or material object is acquired. The functions of an LEA are classified into five broad areas: Instruction, Support Services, Operation of Non-Instructional Services, Facilities Acquisition and Construction Services, and Other Outlays. Functions are further classified into sub-functions. Functions and sub-functions consist of activities which have somewhat the same operational objectives. Furthermore, categories of activities comprising each of these divisions and subdivisions are grouped according to the principle that the activities should be combinable, comparable, relatable and mutually exclusive.

1000* Instruction

2000 Support Services
2100* Support Services—Students
2110 Attendance and Social Work Services
2120 Guidance Services
2130 Health Services
2140 Psychological Services
2150 Speech Pathology and Audiology Services
2160 Occupational Therapy—Related Services
2190 Other Support Services—Student
2200* Support Services—Instruction
2210 Improvement of Instruction
2212 Instruction and Curriculum Development
2213 Instructional Staff Training
2219 Other Improvement of Instruction Services
2220 Library/Media Services
2230 Instruction-Related Technology
2240 Academic Student Assessment
2290 Other Support Services—Instructional Staff
2300* Support Services—General Administration
2310 Board of Education
2320 Executive Administration
2400* Support Services—School Administration
2410 Office of the Principal
2490 Other Support Services—School Administration
2500* Central Services
2510 Fiscal Services
2520 Purchasing, Warehousing and Distributing Services
2530 Printing, Publishing and Duplicating Services
2540 Planning, Research, Development and Evaluation Services
2560 Public Information Services
2570 Personnel Services
2580 Administrative Technology Services
2590 Other Support Services—Central Services
2600* Operation and Maintenance of Plant
2610 Operation of Buildings
2620 Maintenance of Buildings
2630 Care and Upkeep of Grounds
2640 Care and Upkeep of Equipment
2650 Vehicle Operation and Maintenance (Other Than Student Transportation Vehicles)
2660 Security
2670 Safety
2680 Other Operation and Maintenance of Plant
2700* Student Transportation
2710 Vehicle Operation
2720 Monitoring Services
2730 Vehicle Servicing and Maintenance

2790 Other Student Transportation Services
2900* Other Support Services
3000 Operation of Noninstructional Services
3100* Food Services Operations
3200* Enterprise Operations
3300* Community Services Operations
4000* Facilities Acquisition and Construction
4100 Land Acquisition
4200 Land Improvement
4300 Architecture and Engineering
4400 Educational Specifications Development
4500 Building Acquisition and Construction
4600 Site Improvement
4700 Building Improvements
4900 Other Facilities Acquisition and Construction
5000* Debt Service

*Account codes that are necessary for the NCES reporting are noted with an asterisk (*).

EXPENDITURE CLASSIFICATION BY OBJECT

Financial Accounting for Local and State School Systems, 2003 describes *object* as the service or commodity obtained as a result of a specific expenditure. Major object categories are:

- Personnel Services—Salaries
- Personnel Services—Employee Benefits
- Purchased Professional and Technical Services
- Purchased Property Services
- Other Purchased Services, Supplies
- Property, and Other Objects

Representative Object categories and corresponding code numbers are listed below.

100* Personal Services—Salaries
    101 Salaries Paid to Teachers
    102 Salaries Paid to Instructional Aides or Assistants
    103 Salaries Paid to Substitute Teachers
110 Salaries of Regular Employees
    111 Salaries of Regular Employees Paid to Teachers
    112 Salaries of Regular Employees Paid to Instructional Aides and Assistants
    113 Salaries of Regular Employees Paid to Substitute Teachers
120 Salaries of Temporary Employees
    121 Salaries of Temporary Employees Paid to Teachers
    122 Salaries of Temporary Employees Paid to Instructional Aides and Assistants
    123 Salaries of Temporary Employees Paid to Substitute Teachers
130 Salaries for Overtime

- 131 Salaries for Overtime Employees Paid to Teachers
- 132 Salaries for Overtime Employees Paid to Instructional Aides and Assistants
- 133 Salaries for Overtime Employees Paid to Substitute Teachers

140 Salaries for Sabbatical Leave
- 141 Salaries for Sabbatical Leave Paid to Teachers
- 142 Salaries for Sabbatical Leave Paid to Instructional Aides and Assistants
- 143 Salaries for Sabbatical Leave Paid to Substitute Teachers

150 Additional Compensation Such as Bonuses, or Incentives
- 151 Additional Compensation Paid to Teachers
- 152 Additional Compensation Paid to Instructional Aides and Assistants
- 153 Additional Compensation Paid to Substitute Teachers

200* Personnel Services—Employee Benefits
- 201 Employee Benefits for Teachers
- 202 Employee Benefits for Instructional Aides or Assistants
- 203 Employee Benefits for Substitute Teachers

210 Group Insurance—Employer's Share of Any Insurance Plan
- 211 Group Insurance for Teachers
- 212 Group Insurance for Instructional Aides or Assistants
- 213 Group Insurance for Substitute Teachers

220 Social Security Contributions
- 221 Social Security Payments for Teachers
- 222 Social Security Payments for Instructional Aides or Assistants
- 223 Social Security Payments for Substitute Teachers

230 Retirement Contributions
- 231 Retirement Contributions for Teachers
- 232 Retirement Contributions for Instructional Aides or Assistants
- 233 Retirement Contributions for Substitute Teachers

240* On-Behalf Payments
- 241 On-Behalf Payments for Teachers
- 242 On-Behalf Payments for Instructional Aides or Assistants
- 243 On-Behalf Payments for Substitute Teachers

250 Tuition Reimbursement
- 251 Tuition Reimbursement for Teachers
- 252 Tuition Reimbursement for Instructional Aides or Assistants
- 253 Tuition Reimbursement for Substitute Teachers

260 Unemployment Compensation
- 261 Unemployment Compensation Paid for Teachers
- 262 Unemployment Compensation Paid for Instructional Aides or Assistants
- 263 Unemployment Compensation Paid for Substitute Teachers

270 Workers' Compensation
- 271 Workers' Compensation Paid for Teachers
- 272 Workers' Compensation Paid for Instructional Aides or Assistants
- 273 Workers' Compensation for Substitute Teachers

280 Health Benefits
- 281 Health Benefits Paid for Teachers
- 282 Health Benefits Paid for Instructional Aides or Assistants

283 Health Benefits Paid for Substitute Teachers
290 Other Employee Benefits
291 Other Employee Benefits Paid for Teachers
292 Other Employee Benefits Paid for Instructional Aides or Assistants
293 Other Employee Benefits for Substitute Teachers
300* Purchased Professional and Technical Services
310 Official/Administrative Services
320 Professional Educational Services
330 Professional Employee Training and Development Services
340 Other Professional Services
350 Technical Services
351 Data Processing and Coding Services
352 Other Technical Services
400* Purchased Property Services
410 Utility Services
420 Cleaning Services
430 Repairs and Maintenance Services
431 Non-Technology-Related Repairs and Maintenance
432 Technology-Related Repairs and Maintenance
440 Rentals
441 Renting Land and Buildings
442 Rental of Equipment and Vehicles
443 Rentals of Computers and Related Equipment
450* Construction Services
490 Other Purchased Property Services
500* Other Purchased Services
510 Student Transportation Services
511* Student Transportation Purchased from Another School District within the State
512* Student Transportation Purchased from Another School District Outside the State
519 Student Transportation Purchased from Other Sources
520 Insurance (Other Than Employee Benefits)
530 Communications
540 Advertising
550 Printing and Binding
560 Tuition
561* Tuition to Other School Districts within the State
562* Tuition to Other School Districts Outside the State
563* Tuition to Private Sources
564* Tuition to Educational Service Agencies within the State
565* Tuition to Educational Service Agencies Outside the State
566* Tuition to Charter Schools
567* Tuition to School Districts for Voucher Payments
569* Tuition—Other
570 Food Service Management
580 Travel
590 Intereducational, Interagency Purchased Services

591* Services Purchased from Another School District or Educational Services Agency within the State
592* Services Purchased from Another School District or Educational Service Agency
600* Supplies
610 General Supplies
620 Energy
621 Natural Gas
622 Electricity
623 Bottled Gas
624 Oil—Expenditures for Bulk Oil Normally Used for Heating
625 Coal
626 Gasoline
629 Other
630 Food
640 Books and Periodicals
650 Supplies—Technology-Related
700* Property
710* Land and Land Improvements
720* Buildings
730* Equipment
731 Machinery
732 Vehicles
733 Furniture and Fixtures
734 Technology-Related Hardware
735 Technology Software
739 Other Equipment
740* Infrastructure
790 Depreciation
800 Debt Service and Miscellaneous
810* Dues and Fees
820 Judgments Against the School District
830 Debt-Related Expenditures/Expenses
831* Redemption of Principal
832* Interest
833 Amortization of Bond Issuance and Other Debt-Related Costs
834 Amortization of Premium and Discount on Issuance of Bonds
890 Miscellaneous Expenditures
900 Other Items
910 Fund Transfers Out
920 Payments to Escrow Agents for Defeasance of Debt
930 Net Decreases in the Fair Value of Investments
931 Realized Losses on Investments
932 Unrealized Losses on Investments
940 Losses on the Sale of Capital Assets
950 Special Items
960 Extraordinary Items

*Account codes that are necessary for the NCES reporting are noted with an asterisk (*).

EXPENDITURE CLASSIFICATION BY PROJECT

Financial Accounting for Local and State School Systems, 2003 permits school districts to account for and report separately expenditures to meet a variety of specialized reporting requirements at local, state and federal levels. Refer to that document for information regarding this classification.

USE OF CODE NUMBERS

In this text the code numbers provided in this chapter will be used as account numbers for consistency. Actual practice varies with respect to account numbers. In some electronic systems the account numbers are a combination of the classification/dimension codes for fund, function, object, program, location, etc. from *Financial Accounting for Local and State School Systems, 2003.* In other electronic systems the account numbers are separate numbers unrelated to the codes. However, they do have a feature that attaches the *Financial Accounting for Local and State School Systems, 2003* codes to the accounts so they can be used for sorting and accumulation of data for state and other financial reports.

ANALYSIS OF FINANCIAL TRANSACTIONS

According to Lynn and Thompson (1974):

> A transaction is an economic event that affects the asset or equities of a fund. The effects of the event must be recorded as changes in the accounting equation; that is, they must be recorded in the proper accounts. The recording of every transaction will be composed of an equal dollar amount of debits and credits.

The analysis of transactions involves the following questions:

1. What type of account(s) is (are) affected (asset, liability, fund balance, revenue, expenditure)?
2. What specific accounts are affected (cash in bank, accounts payable, unreserved fund balance)?
3. What is the change (increase or decrease) in the account balance?
4. Does the increase or decrease in an account balance require a debit or credit entry?

The general ledger consists of all accounts, grouped by type of accounts, which are necessary to reflect the financial operations of each fund of a school district. Accounts in the general ledger follow the order in which the accounts appear on the financial statements—assets, liabilities, fund equities, revenues and expenditures. The account form should provide for the following information:

1. The complete title of the account.
2. The code number of the account.
3. A column for the date of the transaction (year/month/day).
4. A posting reference column (P.R.).

5. A column for the debit amount.
6. A column for the credit amount.

The format for the general ledger accounts that will be used in illustrations and activities is demonstrated in Examples 1 to 5.

Name of account in full					Account No. XX
Date	P.R.	Amount	Date	P.R.	Amount
01/01/XX	T1	$ ###,###	02/02/XX	T2	$ ###,###

Example 1

Assume that Kimberly Hills School District began the fiscal year 20XX with account balances as follows: cash in bank, $10,000; investments, $20,000; contracts payable, $10,000; and unreserved-fund balance, $20,000. Record the balances in the appropriate accounts. (Note: throughout the textbook, "T1" refers to the first transaction, "T2" refers to the second transaction, and continuing.)

Cash in Bank					Account No. 101
Date	P.R.	Amount	Date	P.R.	Amount
07/01/XX	T1	$ 10,000			

Investments					Account No. 111
Date	P.R.	Amount	Date	P.R.	Amount
07/01/XX	T1	$ 20,000			

Contracts Payable					Account No. 431
Date	P.R.	Amount	Date	P.R.	Amount
			07/01/XX	T1	$10,000

Unreserved Fund Balance					Account No. 730
Date	P.R.	Amount	Date	P.R.	Amount
			07/01/XX	T1	$20,000

Example 2

Assume that local property taxes are assessed and levied in the amount of $40,000.

Cash in Bank					Account No. 101
Date	P.R.	Amount	Date	P.R.	Amount
07/01/XX	T1	$ 10,000			

Investments					Account No. 111
Date	P.R.	Amount	Date	P.R.	Amount
07/01/XX	T1	$ 20,000			

Taxes Receivable					Account No. 121

Date	P.R.	Amount	Date	P.R.	Amount
07/01/XX	T2	$ 40,000			

Contracts Payable — Account No. 431

Date	P.R.	Amount	Date	P.R.	Amount
			07/01/XX	T1	$10,000

Unreserved Fund Balance — Account No. 730

Date	P.R.	Amount	Date	P.R.	Amount
			07/01/XX	T1	$20,000

Revenue—Local Ad Valorem — Account No. 1110

Date	P.R.	Amount	Date	P.R.	Amount
			07/01/XX	T2	$40,000

Example 3

Assume general supplies in the amount of $8,000 were purchased on account:

Cash in Bank — Account No. 101

Date	P.R.	Amount	Date	P.R.	Amount
07/01/XX	T1	$ 10,000			

Investments — Account No. 111

Date	P.R.	Amount	Date	P.R.	Amount
07/01/XX	T1	$ 20,000			

Taxes Receivable — Account No. 121

Date	P.R.	Amount	Date	P.R.	Amount
07/01/XX	T2	$ 40,000			

Accounts Payable — Account No. 421

Date	P.R.	Amount	Date	P.R.	Amount
			07/01/XX	T3	$8,000

Contracts Payable — Account No. 431

Date	P.R.	Amount	Date	P.R.	Amount
			07/01/XX	T1	$10,000

Unreserved Fund Balance — Account No. 730

Date	P.R.	Amount	Date	P.R.	Amount
			07/01/XX	T1	$20,000

Revenue—Local Ad Valorem — Account No. 1110

Date	P.R.	Amount	Date	P.R.	Amount
			07/01/XX	T2	$40,000

Expenditures—General Supplies					Account No. 630
Date	P.R.	Amount	Date	P.R.	Amount
07/01/XX	T3	$8,000			

Example 4

Received $120,000 in unrestricted grants-in-aid from the state:

Cash in Bank					Account No. 101
Date	P.R.	Amount	Date	P.R.	Amount
07/01/XX	T1	$ 10,000			
07/01/XX	T4	$120,000			

Investments					Account No. 111
Date	P.R.	Amount	Date	P.R.	Amount
07/01/XX	T1	$ 20,000			

Taxes Receivable					Account No. 121
Date	P.R.	Amount	Date	P.R.	Amount
07/01/XX	T2	$ 40,000			

Accounts Payable					Account No. 421
Date	P.R.	Amount	Date	P.R.	Amount
			07/01/XX	T1	$8,000

Contracts Payable					Account No. 431
Date	P.R.	Amount	Date	P.R.	Amount
			07/01/XX	T1	$10,000

Unreserved Fund Balance					Account No. 730
Date	P.R.	Amount	Date	P.R.	Amount
			07/01/XX	T1	$20,000

Revenue—Local Ad Valorem					Account No. 1110
Date	P.R.	Amount	Date	P.R.	Amount
			07/01/XX	T2	$40,000

Revenue-State-Grants					Account No. 3110
Date	P.R.	Amount	Date	P.R.	Amount
			07/01/XX	T4	$120,000

Expenditures—General Supplies					Account No. 610
Date	P.R.	Amount	Date	P.R.	Amount
07/01/XX	T3	$8,000			

Example 5

Paid salaries of regular employees in the amount of $30,000.

Cash in Bank — Account No. 101

Date	P.R.	Amount	Date	P.R.	Amount
07/01/XX	T1	$ 10,000	07/01/XX	T5	$30,000
07/01/XX	T4	$120,000			

Investments — Account No. 111

Date	P.R.	Amount	Date	P.R.	Amount
07/01/XX	T1	$ 20,000			

Taxes Receivable — Account No. 121

Date	P.R.	Amount	Date	P.R.	Amount
07/01/XX	T2	$ 40,000			

Accounts Payable — Account No. 421

Date	P.R.	Amount	Date	P.R.	Amount
			07/01/XX	T1	$8,000

Contracts Payable — Account No. 431

Date	P.R.	Amount	Date	P.R.	Amount
			07/01/XX	T1	$10,000

Unreserved Fund Balance — Account No. 730

Date	P.R.	Amount	Date	P.R.	Amount
			07/01/XX	T1	$20,000

Revenue—Local Ad Valorem — Account No. 1110

Date	P.R.	Amount	Date	P.R.	Amount
			07/01/XX	T2	$40,000

Revenue—State Grants — Account No. 3110

Date	P.R.	Amount	Date	P.R.	Amount
			07/01/XX	T2	$120,000

Expenditures—Salaries—Reg. Emp. — Account No. 110

Date	P.R.	Amount	Date	P.R.	Amount
07/01/XX	T5	$30,000			

Expenditure—General Supplies — Account No. 610

Date	P.R.	Amount	Date	P.R.	Amount
07/01/XX	T3	$8,000			

TRIAL BALANCE

The trial balance is prepared by computing the balance of each account or by summing the debits in each account and the credits in each account. If the sum of the debits exceeds the sum of the credits, then the difference is a debit balance. If the sum of the credits exceeds the sum of the debits, then the difference is a credit balance. The debit and credit balances of each account are used to prepare a trial balance. The trial balance for Kimberly Hills School District is shown in Illustration 5.1.

Illustration 5.1
Kimberly Hills School District
General Fund
Trial Balance
(Date)

Cash in Bank	$100,000	
Investments	20,000	
Taxes Receivable	40,000	
Accounts Payable		$ 8,000
Contracts Payable		10,000
Unreserved Fund Balance		20,000
Revenue—Local Ad Valorem Taxes		40,000
Revenue—State Unrestricted Grants		120,000
Expenses—Salaries—Employees	30,000	
Expenses—General Supplies	8,000	
Total	$198,000	$198,000

SUMMARY

General ledger was defined and accounts in the general ledger recommended by the National Center for Educational Statistics were presented. A methodology for analyzing financial transactions was presented. Debiting and crediting accounts in the general ledger were illustrated. Computational procedures for preparing a trail balance were presented.

ACTIVITIES

1. Study the definitions of the following terms as provided in the glossary:

    a. General ledger
    b. Asset
    c. Current asset
    d. Fixed asset
    e. Liability
    f. Reserve
    g. Fund balance
    h. Debit balance
    i. Credit balance
    j. Current liability
    k. Long-term liability

l. Budgeting accounts
m. Fund equity account
n. Revenue type
o. Revenue source
p. Expenditures
q. Program dimension
r. Function dimension
s. Object dimension
t. Project/Reporting dimension

2. The Susanville School System had general ledger account balances in its general fund on July 1, 2008, as follows:

101 Cash in Bank	$ 30,000
111 Investments	180,000
121 Taxes Receivable	210,000
730 Unreserved Fund Balance	420,000

The following transactions occurred during the year:

a. Local property taxes of $250,000 were assessed and levied.
b. General supplies were purchased on account for $20,000.
c. General state aid in the amount of $145,000 was received.
d. Collected $200,000 from taxes receivable.
e. Paid salaries of regular employees, $215,000.
f. Paid the full amount of accounts payable.
g. Sold investments of $180,000 for $180,000.
h. Paid for electricity in the amount of $8,500.
i. Paid for natural gas in the amount of $4,800.
j. Paid salaries of regular employees in the amount of $215,000.

Assume the chart of accounts for the school district consists of the following:

Assets (code nos. 101, 111, 121)
Liabilities (421)
Fund balance (730)
Revenue (1110, 3100)
Expenditure (object codes 110, 610, 620)

Instructions:

- Record the beginning balances to the general ledger accounts.
- Record the transactions to the general ledger accounts.
- Prepare a trial balance for June 30, 2009.

3. Janet Ridge School System began the fiscal year July 1, 2008 with the following account balances in the general fund:

101 Cash	$ 5,000
111 Investments	90,000
730 Unreserved Fund Balance	95,000

During the year which ended June 30, 2009, the following transactions were completed:

a. Local property taxes were assessed and levied in the amount of $85,000.
b. Cash was received for the entire amount of the local property tax levy of transaction a.
c. Local property taxes were assessed and levied in the amount of $70,000.
d. An amount of $65,000 was borrowed from the Cape Jennifer National Bank against anticipated tax revenues.
e. Cash was received for the amount of the property tax levy in transaction c.
f. Paid the amount due on the tax anticipation warrants issued in transaction d.
g. Paid regular teacher salaries of $40,000.
h. Purchased general supplies in the amount of $35,000.
i. Paid regular custodial salaries of $20,000.
j. Paid salaries of regular bus drivers in the amount of $15,000.

Assume the chart of accounts for the school district consists of the following:

Assets (codes 101, 111, 121)
Liabilities (423)
Fund balance (730)
Revenue (1110)
Expenditure (object codes 110, 610)

Instructions:

- Record the beginning balances to the general ledger accounts.
- Record the transactions to the general ledger accounts.
- Prepare a trial balance for June 30, 2009.

4. Kimberly Hills School System began the fiscal year July 1, 2008, with the following account balances in the general fund:

101	Cash	$47,000
111	Investments	45,000
121	Taxes Receivable	33,000
730	Unreserved Fund Balance	?????*

* To be computed by reader

During the year which ended June 30, 2009, the following transactions were completed:

a. Local property taxes were assessed and levied in the amount of $150,000.
b. Received $200,000 in general state aid.
c. Paid salary of instructional staff of the special education program in the amount of $58,000.
d. Purchased equipment for the vocational home economics program in the amount of $35,000.
e. Paid salary of the instructional staff of the bilingual program in the amount of $15,000.
f. Collected $120,000 of the taxes that were previously assessed and levied.
g. Purchased general supplies in the amount of $35,000 for the special education program.
h. Paid salary of $15,000 for custodian for the bilingual program area.
i. General supplies for the bilingual program were purchased on account in the amount of $6,000.
j. An amount of $65,000 was borrowed from the New Douglas State Bank against anticipated tax revenues.

Assume the chart of accounts for the school district consists of the following:

Assets (101, 111, 121)
Liabilities (421, 423)
Fund balance (730)
Revenue (1110, 3100)
Expenditures (program codes 210, 260, 340)

Instructions:

- Record the beginning balances to the general ledger accounts.
- Record the transactions to the general ledger accounts.
- Prepare a trial balance for June 30, 2009.
- Prepare a statement of revenues, expenditures and fund balance.
- Prepare a balance sheet.

6

Journals

INTRODUCTION

The recording of debits and credits to separate accounts within the general ledger, as was done in the previous chapter, makes it difficult to directly reconstruct a given financial transaction after only a limited number of transactions. Obviously, a method is needed to facilitate tracing transactions over time. The journal is designed to fill this need.

OUTCOMES

In this chapter, you will learn how to:

1. Define the *general journal.*
2. Journalize financial transactions.
3. Post from the general journal to the general ledger.
4. Define *special journals.*
5. Record transactions in special journals.

GENERAL JOURNAL

The journal is the accounting record in which details of financial transactions are first recorded. Information is transferred from the general journal to the affected accounts in the general ledger.

Journal—A book of original entry (MFOA, 1980). The journal entry carries a summary of the transaction—date, the account(s) debited, the amount of the debit(s), the account(s) credited, the amount of the credit(s) and a brief description of the nature of the transaction. The journal satisfies the need to have a chronological record of transactions. It also is the record from which postings are made to ledgers. The ledger contains all accounts of a particular fund (general ledger) or all detail accounts that support a particular general ledger account.

For purposes of illustration, the following conventions relating to the use of the general journal should be noted:

Date—a column for the date is provided where the year, month and day are to be entered.

Theory of debits and credits—the theory of debits and credits is applied to each transaction.

Debit entry—the debited part (all of the debits if a compound entry) of the entry is always recorded first and indented.

Credit entry—the credited part (all of the credits if a compound entry) of the entry is always recorded next and indented.

Explanation—each entry is supported with a brief explanation of the transaction.

Posting reference—a column for the posting reference where the account number of the general ledger account is recorded after the transaction has been posted to that account.

An example of a general journal is shown in Illustration 6.1.

Illustration 6.1
Kimberly Hills School District
General Fund
General Journal

Date	Account Titles	Post	Debit	Credit
BB	Cash		$ 10,000	
	Investments		20,000	
	Contracts Payable			$ 10,000
	Unreserved Fund Balance			20,000
	To record beginning balances			
T1	Taxes Receivable		40,000	
	Revenue—Local Ad Valorem Tax			40,000
	To record levy of property tax			
T2	Expenditures—General Supplies		8,000	
	Accounts Payable			8,000
	To record purchase of supplies on account			
T3	Cash		120,000	
	Revenue—State Unrestricted Grant-in-Aid			120,000
	To record receipt of general state aid			
T4	Expenditures—Salaries—Regular Employees		40,000	
	Cash			40,000
	To record payment of salaries			
T5	Accounts payable		6,000	
	Cash			6,000
	To record payment on accounts payable			

	Debit	Credit
T6 Cash	35,000	
Taxes receivable		35,000
To record collection of taxes previously assessed and levied		
T7 Contracts payable	9,000	
Cash		9,000
To record payment on contracts payable		

POSTING TO THE GENERAL LEDGER

Posting is the process of transferring information from the general journal to the ledger accounts. A systematic process of posting can facilitate the reduction of errors that otherwise might occur. The following steps are recommended in posting from the general journal to the accounts in the general ledger:

1. Record in the proper ledger account
   a. amount for the account cited in the journal
   b. date of the transaction cited in the journal
   c. page number of the general journal on which the transaction is listed; enter the page number in the posting reference column of the general ledger account.
2. Record the account number of the ledger account in the posting reference column of the general journal

Illustration 6.2 shows transactions which have been recorded in the general journal and posted to the general ledger accounts.

Illustration 6.2
Kimberly Hills School District
General Fund
General Journal

Date	Account Titles	Post	Debit	Credit
BB	Cash	101	$ 10,000	
	Investments	111	20,000	
	Contracts Payable	431		$ 10,000
	Unreserved Fund Balance	730		20,000
	To record beginning balances			
T1	Taxes Receivable	121	40,000	
	Revenue—Local Ad Valorem	1110		40,000
	To record levy of property tax			
T2	Expenditures—General Supplies	610	8,000	
	Accounts Payable	421		8,000
	To record purchase of supplies on account			

T3 Cash	101	120,000	
Revenue—State Unrestricted Grant-in-Aid	3100		120,000
To record receipt of general state aid			
T4 Expenditures—Salaries—Regular Employees	110	40,000	
Cash	101		40,000
To record payment of salaries			
T5 Accounts payable	421	6,000	
Cash	101		6,000
To record payment on accounts payable			
T6 Cash	101	35,000	
Taxes receivable	121		35,000
To record collection of taxes previously assessed and levied			
T7 Contracts payable	431	9,000	
Cash in bank	101		9,000
To record payment on contracts payable			

After posting to the general ledger accounts, account balances are determined as shown in Illustration 6.3.

Illustration 6.3
Kimberly Hills School District
General Fund
General Ledger

Cash 101

Date	P.R.	Amount	Date	P.R.	Amount
BB		$10,000	T4		$40,000
T3		120,000	T5		6,000
T6		35,000	T7		9,000

Investments 111

Date	P.R.	Amount	Date	P.R.	Amount
BB		$20,000	T6		$35,000
T1		40,000			

Accounts Payable 421

Date	P.R.	Amount	Date	P.R.	Amount
T5		6,000	T2		8,000

Contracts Payable 431

Date	P.R.	Amount	Date	P.R.	Amount
T7		$9,000	BB		$10,000

Unreserved Fund Balance 730

Date	P.R.	Amount	Date	P.R.	Amount
BB		$20,000			

Revenue—Local Ad Valorem Taxes 1110

Date	P.R.	Amount	Date	P.R.	Amount
T1		$40,000			

Revenue—State Unrestricted Grants 3100

Date	P.R.	Amount	Date	P.R.	Amount
T3		$120,00			

Expenditures—Salaries—Regular Emp. 110

Date	P.R.	Amount	Date	P.R.	Amount
T4		$40,000			

Expenditures—General Supplies 610

Date	P.R.	Amount	Date	P.R.	Amount
T2		$8,000			

Illustration 6.4 presents a trial balance.

Illustration 6.4
Kimberly Hills School District
General Fund
Trial Balance
(Date)

Cash in Bank	$110,000	
Investments	20,000	
Taxes Receivable	5,000	
Accounts Payable		$ 2,000
Contracts Payable		1,000
Unreserved Fund Balance		20,000
Revenue—Local Ad Valorem Taxes		40,000
Revenue—State Unrestricted Grants		120,000
Expenditures—Salaries—Regular Employees	40,000	
Expenditures—General Supplies	8,000	
	$183,000	$183,000

CASH RECEIPTS JOURNAL

In order to improve internal control in the accounting for numerous cash receipts, a cash receipts journal may be used to record these transactions. The cash receipts journal is not used to record all transactions, but is used to record the debit and credit entries associated with the numerous cash receipts transactions that a district frequently encounters during the accounting period. There are a wide variety of practices and procedures for handling cash receipts.

CASH DISBURSEMENTS JOURNAL

Similar in nature to the cash receipts journal is the cash disbursements journal. As with the cash receipts journal, there are a variety of practices and procedures for handling cash disbursements.

SUMMARY

The purpose of the general journal was presented, and data fields commonly occurring in the general journal were listed. Procedures were presented for posting to the general ledger. Examples of special journals, the cash receipts journal and the cash disbursements journal, were illustrated.

ACTIVITIES

1. Carefully review the definition of the following terms given in the glossary:
   a. General journal
   b. Journal
   c. Post
   d. General ledger
   e. Special journal
   f. Journal entry
   g. Debit entry
   h. Credit Entry
   i. Cash Receipts Journal

2. Use the transaction information from Activity 2 of chapter 5.

Instructions:

- Journalize the transactions in the general journal.
- Post the general journal transactions to the accounts in the general ledger.
- Determine the account balances and prepare a trial balance.

3. Use the transaction information from Activity 3 of chapter 5.

Instructions:

- Journalize the transactions in the general journal.
- Post the general journal transactions to the accounts in the general ledger.
- Determine the account balances and prepare a trial balance.

4. Use the transaction information from Activity 4 of chapter 5.

Instructions:

- Journalize the transactions in the general journal.
- Post the general journal transactions to the accounts in the general ledger.
- Determine the account balances and prepare a trial balance.

5. Fort Steven School District began the fiscal year July 1, 2008, with the following account balances in the general fund:

101	Cash	$ 14,750
111	Investments	175,000
121	Taxes Receivable	23,000
730	Unreserved Fund Balance	212,750

The following transactions occurred during July:

a. Local property taxes of $350,000 were assessed and levied.
b. The district borrowed $120,000 from the First National Bank of Fort Steven by means of tax anticipation warrants.
c. The district received equipment for which it was billed $40,000.
d. The district paid regular instructional employees $114,500.
e. The district received $370,000 for payment of property taxes which were previously assessed and levied. (Note: Tax anticipation warrants must be paid as soon as tax monies are received.)
f. The district paid for equipment received in transaction c.
g. The district paid regular custodial employees $23,750.
h. The district purchased equipment on account in the amount of $80,000.
i. Defective equipment in the amount of $15,000 was returned for credit.
j. The district paid $45,000 on outstanding accounts.

Assume the chart of accounts for the school district consists of the following:

Assets (code nos. 101, 111, and 121)
Liabilities (code nos. 421 and 423)
Fund Equity (code no. 730)
Revenue (code no. 1110)
Expenditures (object code nos. 110 and 630)

Instructions:

- Journalize the beginning balances and the transactions for the month of July in the general journal.
- Post the general journal transactions to the account in the general ledger.
- Determine the account balances and prepare a trial balance as of July 31, 2008.

7

Revenue Accounting

INTRODUCTION

Revenue is an increase in assets or a decrease in liabilities that increases the fund equity. Some revenue results in increases in cash; however the accrual basis of accounting does recognize revenue without the receipt of cash. The budget is a plan of financial operation for a school district. As part of the plan, it is necessary to know the amount of estimated revenue and the amount of actual revenue.

OUTCOMES

In this chapter, you will learn how to:

1. Define *revenue*.
2. Distinguish between actual revenue and estimated revenue.
3. Identify the different revenue classifications.
4. Make allowances for estimated uncollectible taxes.

REVENUE DEFINED

Revenue is defined as an addition to assets that does not increase any liability, does not represent the recovery of an expenditure and does not represent the cancellation of certain liabilities without a corresponding increase in other liabilities or a decrease in assets (Fowler, 1990).

Financial Accounting for Local and State School Systems, 2003 provides the account code structure associated with revenues, and it is relatively straightforward because each revenue transaction is identified by source, ranging from general to specific.

There are two general types of accounts, budgetary and proprietary, used to track and manage revenue. Budgetary accounts are those accounts necessary to reflect budget operations and conditions, such as estimated revenues, appropriations and encumbrances, as distinguished from proprietary accounts. Proprietary accounts are those accounts that show actual financial conditions and operations such as actual assets, liabilities, reserves, revenues and expenditures. As shown in the expanded accounting equation revenue is an element of equity. It is one of the two most common elements, expenditures being the other, which causes fund equity to change.

Beyond the textbook definition, revenue is the inflow of financial resources into a school district. In most instances this involves the receipt of cash or promises of cash (accrual basis) from various sources. Public schools receive revenue from three primary sources—local, state and federal. Local and state sources are the primary sources of funds for most public schools; however the relative importance of each varies significantly from district to district. The largest local revenue source is usually a property tax on real property. Other local sources can include textbook/instructional materials fees, registration fees, interscholastic athletic fees and intramural fees, bookstore and cafeteria sales, gate admissions and earnings on investments. State sources can come in the form of restricted (restricted to a specific purpose such as transportation, special education, etc.) or unrestricted grants-in-aid. Many different allocation formulas are used to allocate state funds, with average daily attendance, local property values and the level of state education funding being the most significant variables in most plans. Use of some type of formula is the common allocation method for unrestricted aid, while restricted aid often involves an application and approval process. The federal government allocates funds to education. In most cases this funding is to supplement (not supplant) local and state plans to help disadvantaged (low-income and disabled) students.

This chapter will focus first on the estimation or budget process and second on the recording of actual revenue.

ESTIMATED REVENUE

Estimated revenue represents the amount of revenue expected to be received or to become receivable during the fiscal year. At the end of a fiscal year, estimated revenue is closed out and does not appear in the balance sheet. Actual revenue represents the amount of revenue actually realized during a period and represents an increase in fund equity during the period. During the fiscal period when interim balance sheets are prepared the system shows an account in the fund equity section that reflects the period to date net amount of revenue and expenditures. This is a system-generated account that does not actually exist. The software simply adds up all of the revenue and expenditures account balances and prints it with a year to date activity label.

The revenue budget is a detailed plan that outlines the many sources of revenue that flow into a school district annually. It represents a plan for the future expressed in formal quantitative terms. The budget allows managers to plan for the estimated amount of revenue and to predict the actual results of the fiscal year. The revenue budget also allows managers to estimate the financial condition of a school district in future periods. Estimating revenue is the critical first step in the budgetary process. Without an estimate of revenue, school districts would have no realistic basis for developing expenditure (discussed in chapter 8) and program plans.

At the time the budget is adopted, estimated revenue is recorded for each revenue source. There are many sources of revenue and it is necessary to maintain an account for each revenue source. In the old manual systems, in order to reduce the "size" of the general ledger, subsidiary control accounts and subsidiary ledgers were used for revenue. With the electronic systems and the related report extraction capabilities available today subsidiary control accounts are rarely used, and will not be used in this text.

Revenue Accounts

For each revenue item, i.e., Local Ad Valorem Taxes, there is a single ledger account that has elements to record both estimated/budgetary and actual activity. Illustration 7.1 is a visual depiction of the record for one such account. In an electronic system the unrealized balance column is calculated at the time the information is printed.

RECORDING ESTIMATED REVENUE

Estimated revenues are recorded at the beginning of the fiscal year for which a budget is adopted. Because the estimated (budget) amounts do not reflect actual financial activity many accounting software packages allow direct entries to be made to the budget component of individual revenue

Illustration 7.1
Ledger Format for Revenue Accounts

Revenue Account: Local Ad Valorem Taxes Account No: 1110

			Estimated Revenue		Actual Revenue		Unrealized
Date	Explanation	P.R.	Dr.	Cr.	Dr.	Cr.	Balance
AB	To adopt budget		$100,000				$100,000
T1	To record levy					$90,000	10,000

accounts and do not require a balancing or offsetting entry to another ledger account (effectively these are one-sided entries). Some systems may require a balancing entry, which is why the Illustration 7.2 has an account titled Unreserved Fund Balance (noted as memo only) with an Estimated Revenue component; this is a memo account only. Illustration 7.2 shows how the adopted revenue budget would be posted including the offset to the Unreserved Fund Balance for systems that require a balancing entry. You will note the convention used here is to post the estimated revenue items as debits to the revenue accounts.

RECORDING ACTUAL REVENUE

In accounting for profit-oriented enterprises, revenue is ordinarily not recognized until (1) a transaction has taken place (that is, the amount of revenue can be objectively measured), and (2) the earnings process is complete or substantially complete. Criterion (2) is not applicable to governmental entities (Haried, 1988). The revenue-recognition criteria for governmental entities can be stated as follows. Revenue is not ordinarily recognized until (1) it can be objectively measured, and (2) it is available to finance expenditures of the current period. Many sources of revenue do not meet the criteria of measurability and availability until they are received in cash. However, significant amounts of revenue, such as some types of grants and earnings on investments meet both criteria and are recognized as revenue prior to the receipt of cash.

Property Taxes

Property taxes also meet the measurability criteria prior to receipt—when levied. The amount of property tax is precisely determinable when levied. However, property taxes are only considered to be available in the period levied if they are collected in the current period or soon enough thereafter to pay current operating expenditures. Industry standards deem "soon enough thereafter" to be sixty days. The amounts levied that will be collected after sixty days are recorded as deferred revenue.

At the time taxes are assessed and levied, an entry is made in the general journal to debiting taxes receivable and crediting revenue from taxes. However, only the "eternal optimist" would expect that the entire amount of taxes assessed and levied would be collected.

Therefore, experience dictates that one should make an allowance for uncollectible taxes. The allowance for uncollectible taxes should be based upon past experience and knowledge of expected departures from previous collection and distribution practices.

Illustration 7.2
Recording Estimated Revenue

The Kimberly Hills School District adopted the following budget:

Revenue Local: Ad Valorem Taxes	$ 100,000
Revenue State: Unrestricted State Aid	$ 50,000
Revenue Federal: Revenue in Lieu of Taxes	$ 30,000

Revenue—Local Ad Valorem Taxes — Account No. 1100

			Estimated Revenue		Actual Revenue		Unrealized
Date	Explanation	P.R.	Dr.	Cr.	Dr.	Cr.	Balance
AB	To adopt budget		$ 100,000				$100,000

Revenue—State Unrestricted State Aid — Account No. 3100

			Estimated Revenue		Actual Revenue		Unrealized
Date	Explanation	P.R.	Dr.	Cr.	Dr.	Cr.	Balance
AB	To adopt budget		$ 50,000				$50,000

Revenue Federal—Revenue in Lieu of Taxes — Account No. 4800

			Estimated Revenue		Actual Revenue		Unrealized
Date	Explanation	P.R.	Dr.	Cr.	Dr.	Cr.	Balance
AB	To adopt budget		$ 30,000				$30,000

Unreserved Fund Balance — (memo acct only)

			Estimated Revenue		Actual Revenue		Unrealized
Date	Explanation	P.R.	Dr.	Cr.	Dr.	Cr.	Balance
AB	To adopt budget			$180,000			$180,000

A typical entry to show that taxes were assessed and levied and an allowance for estimated (estimate as used here is not the same as the term *estimate* that refers to budget amounts) uncollectible taxes was made, is as follows:

	Dr.	Cr.
Taxes receivable	$100,000	
Estimated uncollectible taxes		$ 3,000
Revenue form taxes		97,000
To record taxes assessed and levied		

When taxes receivable are collected, the following entry is made in the general journal to record the collection of taxes receivable:

	Dr.	Cr.
Cash	$60,000	
Taxes receivable		$60,000
To record collection of taxes receivable		

If an additional $38,000 were collected in taxes receivable, then the following entry would be made in the general journal:

Cash	$38,000	
Estimate uncollectible taxes	1,000	
Taxes receivable		$38,000
Revenue form taxes		1,000
To record collection of taxes receivable and to adjust the amount of the estimated uncollectible taxes and the amount of revenue from taxes.		

If $35,000 in taxes receivable had been collected instead of $38,000, then the entry to the general journal would be as follows:

Cash	$35,000	
Taxes receivable		$35,000
To record collection of taxes receivable		

The balance sheet should reflect the effect of estimated uncollectible taxes on the assets of the LEA. For example, after the collection of $60,000 and $35,000 in taxes receivable of the $100,000 of taxes that were assessed and levied, the balance sheet would show the following:

Taxes receivable	$5,000	
Less estimated uncollectible taxes	3,000	$2,000

If it was determined that no more taxes would be collected, then an adjustment would be required to write off the balance of taxes receivable and close the balance sheet accounts. The following entry should be made in the general journal:

Estimated uncollectible taxes	$3,000	
Revenue from taxes	2,000	
Taxes receivable		$5,000
To write off the remainder of taxes receivable		

As soon as revenue is actually realized, the unrealized balance would be reduced by the amount of the actual revenue. Illustration 7.3 and 7.4 reflect the posting of actual revenue to the accounts for which estimated amounts were set up in Illustration 7.2.

After posting transactions from the general journal to the appropriate accounts in the general ledger, the general ledger should appear as shown in Illustration 7.4. The Unreserved Fund balance memo account shows the totals for the estimated and actual revenue activity. You will note there was no entry shown to this account in the general journal.

INTERIM STATEMENT OF REVENUE

Interim financial statements should be prepared during the year to provide information to administrators and board members. The interim statement of revenue is shown in Illustration 7.5 for the period indicated, of July 1 through July 31, 2008, but could be for any interim period. The amounts used are from Illustration 7.4.

Illustration 7.3
Recording Estimated Revenue and Actual Revenue

Estimated revenue in this illustration is provided from Illustration 7.2.
Assume the Kimberly Hills School District received revenue from the following sources:

Revenue Local: Ad Valorem Taxes	$ 75,000
Revenue State: Unrestricted State Aid	$ 35,000
Revenue Federal: Revenue in Lieu of Taxes	$ 20,000

Kimberly Hills School District
General Fund
General Journal

Date	Account Title	P.R.	Debit	Credit
T1	Cash in Bank	101	$ 75,000	
	Revenue Local: Ad Valorem Taxes	1100		$ 75,000
	To record local tax collections			
T2	Cash in Bank	101	$ 35,000	
	Revenue State: Unrestricted State Aid	3100		$ 35,000
	To record local tax collections			
T3	Cash in Bank	101	$ 20,000	
	Revenue Federal: in Lieu of Taxes	4800		$ 20,000
	To record local tax collections			

GOVERNMENT-WIDE REPORTING

According to *Financial Accounting for Local and State School Systems, 2003* (Johnson 2003, 65), "GASB Statement 34 introduces a number of new reporting concepts for revenues in the governmentwide statements. Essentially, revenues must be classified as either program or general revenues on the Statement of Activities." The following subsection outlines the basic reporting criteria established for revenues.

Program Revenues

Program revenues are revenues that are directly attributable to a specific functional activity. GAAP requires these revenues to be presented separately in the appropriate functional areas, providing a calculation of net expense for each activity. This net expense often represents the level of support required from the government's own resources. Program revenues include fees collected from those who benefit from the program, grants and other contributions required by the resource provider to support a specific activity.

Illustration 7.4
Kimberly Hills School District
General Fund
General Ledger

Cash in Bank — Account No. 101

Date	Explanation	P.R.	Amount	Date	Explanation	P.R.	Amount
T1		GJ	$ 75,000				
T2		GJ	35,000				
T3		GJ	20,000				

Revenue Local: Ad Valorem Taxes — Account No. 1100

			Estimated Revenue		Actual Revenue		Unrealized
Date	Explanation	P.R.	Dr.	Cr.	Dr.	Cr.	Balance
AB			$100,000				$100,000
T1						$ 75,000	25,000

Revenue State: Unrestricted State Aid — Account No. 3100

			Estimated Revenue		Actual Revenue		Unrealized
Date	Explanation	P.R.	Dr.	Cr.	Dr.	Cr.	Balance
AB			$ 50,000				$ 50,000
T1						$ 35,000	15,000

Revenue Federal: Revenue in Lieu of Taxes — Account No. 4800

			Estimated Revenue		Actual Revenue		Unrealized
Date	Explanation	P.R.	Dr.	Cr.	Dr.	Cr.	Balance
AB			$ 30,000				$ 30,000
T1						$ 20,000	10,000

Unreserved Fund Balance — (memo account only)

			Estimated Revenue		Actual Revenue		Unrealized
Date	Explanation	P.R.	Dr.	Cr.	Dr.	Cr.	Balance
AB				$180,000			$180,000
T1					$130,000		50,000

Program revenues are reported on the Statement of Activities in the following three categories, if applicable:

- Charges for services are revenues that arise from charges to customers or applicants who purchase, use, or directly benefit from the goods, services or privileges provided. Examples are rental fees for school buses or facilities, athletic participant or spectator fees, summer school tuition or library fines.
- Program-specific operating grants and contributions are revenues that occur from mandatory and voluntary non-exchange transactions with other governments, organizations, or individuals that are restricted for use in a particular program. An example is a business grant to provide a scholarship for staff training.
- Program-specific capital grants and contributions are grants and contributions that consist of capital assets or resources that are restricted for capital purposes, such as purchasing, constructing, or renovating capital assets associated with a specific program. These revenues should be reported separately from grants and contributions that may be used either for operating or capital expenses at the judgment of the reporting government. An example is a grant to purchase a school bus.

Program revenues are reported at gross amounts. The Statement of Activities also reports program expenses net of applicable program revenues. GASB Statement 37 clarified that difference captions and additional categories for program revenues may be used.

Illustration 7.5
Kimberly Hills School District
General Fund
Interim Statement of Revenue
For the period July 1, 2008, through July 31, 2008

Revenue from:	Estimated Revenue	Revenue	Unrealized Revenue
1110 Local—Ad Valorem Tax	$100,000	$75,000	$25,000
3100 State—Unrestricted Grant	50,000	35,000	15,000
4800 Federal—Revenue in Lieu of Taxes	30,000	20,000	10,000
Total	$180,000	$130,000	$50,000

General Revenues

All revenues are general revenues unless they are required to be reported as program revenues. General revenues are reported in the governmentwide statement of activities after program revenues have been subtracted from functional expenses.

Classification of Revenues

Programs are financed from essentially four sources:

- Type A. Those who purchase, use or directly benefit from the goods or services of the program
- Type B. Parties outside the reporting government's citizenry
- Type C. Taxpayers (regardless of whether they benefit from a particular program)

- Type D. The governmental institution itself (primarily investment income)

Table 7.1 lists the different revenue classifications.

Table 7.1
Classification of Revenues

Source Type	Program Revenue	General Revenue
Type A	Yes	No
Type B	Yes, if restricted	Yes, if unrestricted
Type C	No	Yes
Type D	No	Yes (usually)

SUMMARY

Revenue was defined. The difference between actual and estimated revenue was described. Procedures were illustrated for actual revenue and estimated revenue. Procedures for accounting for uncollectible taxes were shown. The interim statement of revenue was illustrated.

ACTIVITIES

1. Carefully review the definition of the following terms given in the glossary:
   a. Revenue
   b. Estimated revenue
   c. Actual revenue
   d. Proprietary accounts
   e. Subsidiary control account for revenue
   f. Revenue subsidiary ledger

2. Review procedures for handling estimated revenue and actual revenue. Obtain copies of relevant subsidiary ledgers from your school district.

3. The following transactions occurred during the fiscal year in Timton School District:
   T1 Property taxes were levied in the amount of $100,000. It is estimated that 3 percent of these taxes will be uncollectible.
   T2 The district received $44,000 in payment of property taxes previously levied (T1).
   T3 Unrestricted grant-in-aid from the state was received in the amount of $30,000.
   T4 Tuition in the amount of $4,000 was collected.
   T5 Earning on investments in the amount of $3,000 was received.
   T6 Revenue in lieu of taxes from the federal government was received in the amount of $9,000.
   T7 The district received $47,000 in payment of property taxes previously levied (T1).
   T8 Tuition in the amount of $6,000 was collected.
   T9 Unrestricted grant-in-aid from the state was received in the amount of $45,000.

T10 Revenue in lieu of taxes from the federal government was received in the amount of $15,000.

Instructions:

- Record all transactions in the general journal.
- Post all general journal entries to the general ledger and to the revenue ledger.
- Prepare an interim statement of revenues.

4. During the fiscal year, the following transactions were completed in the general fund in Randyville School District:
   - T1 Property taxes were assessed and levied in the amount of $270,000 and past history indicates 10% of local property taxes will be uncollectible.
   - T2 The district received $125,000 in payment of property taxes previously assessed and levied (T1).
   - T3 Unrestricted grant-in-aid from the state was received in the amount of $45,000.
   - T4 Received $100,000 in collections from property taxes assessed and levied (T1).
   - T5 A general state aid payment of $70,000 was received.
   - T6 Revenue in lieu of taxes from the federal government was received in the amount of $75,000.
   - T7 The district received $22,000 in payment of property taxes previously levied (T1).
   - T8 Tuition in the amount of $6,000 was collected.
   - T9 Unrestricted grant-in-aid from the state was received in the amount of $65,000.
   - T10 Revenue in lieu of taxes from the federal government was received in the amount of $65,000.

Instructions:

- Record all transactions in the general journal.
- Post all general journal entries to the general ledger and to the revenue ledger.
- Prepare an interim statement of revenues.

5. From July 1, 2008, to September 30, 2008, the following transactions were completed in the general fund of New Douglas School District:
   - T1 Property taxes were assessed and levied in the amount of $147,000. It is estimated that 5% of local property taxes will be uncollectible.
   - T2 The district received $145,000 in payment of property taxes previously assessed and levied (T1).
   - T3 Unrestricted grant-in-aid from the state was received in the amount of $44,000.
   - T4 State revenue in lieu of taxes in the amount of $15,000 was received.
   - T5 A general state aid payment of $120,000 was received.
   - T6 Revenue in lieu of taxes from the federal government was received in the amount of $45,000.
   - T7 Tuition from students in the amount of $24,000 was received.
   - T8 State revenue in lieu of taxes in the amount of $12,000 was received.
   - T9 Unrestricted grant-in-aid from the state was received in the amount of $110,000.

T10 Revenue in lieu of taxes from the federal government was received in the amount of $22,000.

Instructions:

- Record all transactions in the general journal.
- Post all general journal entries to the general ledger and to the revenue ledger.
- Prepare an interim statement of revenues.

8

Expenditure Accounting

INTRODUCTION

Expenditures are charges incurred, whether paid or unpaid, which are presumed to benefit the current fiscal year. Some expenditures are paid with decreases in cash, however, the accrual basis of accounting does recognize expenditures without a decrease in cash. Just as revenue is part of the plan of financial operations for a school district, so are expenditures. As part of the budget, or financial plan, it is necessary to know about appropriations, encumbrances, reserve for encumbrances and expenditures/expenses.

OUTCOMES

In this chapter, you will learn how to:

1. Define *expenditures*.
2. Distinguish between appropriations, expenditures, encumbrances and reserve for encumbrances.
3. Identify the different expenditure dimensions.
4. Make debit and credit entries to the appropriate accounts.

EXPENDITURES DEFINED

Expenditures are decreases of net financial resources (MFOA, 1980). Expenditures include current operating expenses that require current or future use of net assets.

Financial Accounting for Local and State School Systems, 2003 provides the account code structure associated with expenditures that uses a series of levels in a hierarchy to identify the following:

- The fund from which funds are being expended
- The program that is spending the funds
- The function for which the funds are being spent
- The object on which the funds are spent
- The project for which funds are being spent (used mainly for reporting, e.g., grants)
- The level of instruction associated with the expenditure
- The operational unit on which the funds are being spent
- The subject matter on which the funds are being spent
- The job class associated with the expenditure

As stated in the previous chapter, budgetary accounts are those accounts necessary to reflect the budget operations and conditions, such as revenue, appropriations, encumbrances, as distinguished from proprietary accounts. Proprietary accounts are those that show actual financial conditions and operations such as actual assets, liabilities, reserves, revenues and expenditures.

In the previous chapter, revenue and estimated revenue were discussed. In this chapter, the discussion continues with appropriations (budget accounts), expenditures, encumbrances and reserve for encumbrances. As was mentioned in chapter 7, in the old manual systems, in order to reduce the "size" of the general ledger, subsidiary control accounts and subsidiary ledgers were used for expenditures. With the electronic systems and the related report extraction capabilities available today, separate subsidiary ledgers and control accounts are rarely used and will not be used in this text. The electronic ledger systems include the individual revenue and expenditure accounts as well as assets, liabilities and equity accounts. It should be remembered, however, that the revenue and expenditures accounts are considered temporary, that is, they are closed out each year. At the beginning of each new fiscal year the revenue and expenditure accounts start at zero. This is in contrast to the balance sheet accounts which are considered permanent and balances carry forward from year to year. The concept of closing entries will be discussed in chapter 9.

APPROPRIATIONS, ENCUMBRANCES AND EXPENDITURES

Illustration 8.1 shows the information each expenditure account contains related to appropriations, expenditures and encumbrances. The unencumbered balance is calculated by the system and is the appropriation/budget amount less the actual expenditures and encumbrances.

Illustration 8.1
Example of an Expenditure Account Format

Account Title | Account No.

			Appropriations/Budget		Expenditures		Encumbrances		Unencumbered
Date	Explanation	P.R.	Debit	Credit	Debit	Credit	Debit	Credit	Balance
	Totals		$0	$0	$0	$0	$0	$0	

Appropriations (Budget)—The term *appropriation* is synonymous with budget. Most governmental (federal, state and local) organizations use the term *appropriation* when they establish the amounts authorized to be expended in a fiscal year. While school districts in a number of states also use the term *appropriation*, many school districts never refer to appropriations, instead they use the term *budgets*. There are some instances where organizations will combine the terms and refer to an appropriations budget. As was true of recording the budget estimates for revenue, recording appropriations is an activity where entries are unusually one-sided. In practice amounts are posted directly to the appropriation/budget area of the expense accounts. For demonstration and practice the appropriation/budget amounts will be posted to the ledger by way of a general journal (see Illustration 8.2). It should be noted that there is no offsetting or balancing debit.

Encumbrances—Encumbrances are commitments to pay another individual or entity upon their delivery of a product or completion of a service. These commitments are usually evidenced by a formal document. The most common item resulting in an encumbrance is the issuance of a purchase order; however, they can be based on other contractual commitments. The issuance of a contract to a teacher could be considered an encumbrance, but it is rarely recorded as such.

Illustration 8.2
General Journal Format for Recording Appropriations Budget

Date	Account Title/Description	PR	Debit	Credit
	Appropriations:			
	Regular salaries	110		$85,000
	Group insurance	210		$11,000
	General supplies	610		$32,000
	Energy	620		$44,000
	Books & periodicals	640		$45,000
	To record the adoption of the budget			

Unlike appropriations, encumbrances in many systems are recorded with a regular journal entry with both a debit and credit element. The offset entry is to the reserve for encumbrances, which is described next. In this text encumbrance entries will have both the debit and credit element and will be recorded through the general journal (see Illustration 8.3). In an interim balance sheet encumbrances are deducted, along with expenditures from the appropriations, to arrive at the unexpended or encumbered amount of appropriations.

Illustration 8.3
Recording Encumbrance

A purchase order was issued for supplies in the amount of $2,500

Date	Account Title/Description	PR	Debit	Credit
T1	Encumbrances—General Supplies	610	$25,000	
	Reserve for Encumbrances	753		$25,000
	To record issuance of a purchase order			

Reserve for Encumbrances—Some systems set up Account No. 753 as an element of the equity section of the balance sheet. This reserve represents that portion of the fund balance that is segregated to provide for unliquidated encumbrances. Separate accounts may be maintained for current encumbrances and prior year encumbrances.

Expenditures/Expenses—As shown in the expanded accounting equation expenditures are an element of equity. It is one of the two most common elements, revenue being the other, which causes fund equity to change. Expenditures are outflows of district financial resources. Individual expense accounts provide the detail as to the type of item resources were expended for, such as salaries, benefits, services, supplies, etc. Individual accounts are provided to track items at a minimum in sufficient detail to comply with state annual financial reporting requirements. In addition to state required data, many districts breakdown the expense information by program, school, etc. For purposes of this text expenses will be entered through the general journal. Illustration 8.4 shows the recording of a transaction where no encumbrance was involved.

Illustration 8.4
Record the payment of regular salaries of $25,000

Date	Account Title/Description	PR	Debit	Credit
T1	Expenditure: Regular Salaries	110	$22,000	
	Cash in Bank	101		$22,000
	To record payment of regular salaries			

THE ENCUMBRANCE SYSTEM

In order to keep track of purchase orders and contracts outstanding, it is recommended that the appropriate expenditure account be charged and the reserve for encumbrances credited as each purchase order or contract is issued. However, multiple purchase orders issued at the same time may be combined for a single entry to the reserve for encumbrances. When goods or services are received, two entries are necessary: (1) the expenditure account is debited and the appropriate balance sheet account (for example cash or accounts payable) is credited for the actual amount; and (2) the reserve for encumbrance account is debited and the encumbrance category of the expenditure account is credited (in most electronic systems this is done as part of recording the invoice).

Illustration 8.5
Recording Expenditure and Encumbrance Impact

Supplies were received and paid for that were part of the encumbrance recorded in 8.3

Date	Account Title/Description	PR	Debit	Credit
T3a	Expenditure—General Supplies	610	$10,000	
	Cash in Bank	101		$10,000
	To record payment of regular salaries			
T3b	Reserve for Encumbrances	753	$10,000	
	Encumbrance—General Supplies	610		$10,000

Illustration 8.6
Recording Expenditure and Reversing the Encumbrance

All of the supplies were received and paid for that were encumbered in 8.3

Date	Account Title/Description	PR	Debit	Credit
T3a	Expenditure—General Supplies	610	$24,500	
	Cash in Bank	101		$24,500
	To record payment of regular salaries			

T3b	Reserve for Encumbrances	753	$25,000	
	Encumbrance—General Supplies	610		$25,000

Illustration 8.5 shows the record for the receipt of a partial order. It is not unusual for the amount of an invoice to be different from the amount of the purchase order. This does not present a problem. Simply reverse the encumbrance section of the expenditure account and the reserve for encumbrances for the original amount of the purchase order (see Illustration 8.6). After receipt of supplies and the related invoice, a disbursement is made or liability created, the expenditure account is charged and the encumbrance ceases to be necessary to reserve the appropriation.

INTERIM FINANCIAL REPORTS

Interim financial reports may be prepared during the year to provide information to administrators and board members. The interim statement comparing expenditures and encumbrances provides that information. The illustrations which follow (8.7, 8.8 and 8.9) will show the recording of appropriations, encumbrances and expenditures using the general journal, general ledger and then show an interim statement.

Illustration 8.7
Sample Activity for Kimberly Hills School District

The Kimberly Hills School District Board of Education approved a budget that had appropriations totaling $217,000, consisting of:

Regular salaries	$85,000
Group insurance	$11,000
General supplies	$32,000
Energy	$44,000
Books & periodicals	$45,000

During the period the district issues purchase orders for:

General supplies	$25,000
Books	$32,000
Fuel oil (open purchase order)	$12,000

The following transactions occurred:
1. Paid salaries of $25,000
2. Paid a group insurance bill of $11,000
3. Received and paid for $10,000, partial order of supplies, from the $25,000 ordered
4. Received and paid $2,000 for fuel oil
5. Received and paid for all of the books ordered; the actual cost was $43,000

Illustration 8.8
General Journal Recording Transactions

Kimberly Hills School District
General Fund
General Journal

Date	Account Title/Description	PR	Debit	Credit

	Appropriations:			
AB	Regular salaries	110		$85,000
	Group insurance	210		$11,000
	General supplies	610		$32,000
	Energy	620		$44,000
	Books & periodicals	640		$45,000
	To record the adoption of budget			
T1	Encumbrances—General Supplies	610	$25,000	
	Reserve for Encumbrances	753		$25,000
	To record issuance of a purchase order			
T2	Encumbrances—Books & Periodicals	640	$32,000	
	Reserve for Encumbrances	753		$32,000
	To record issuance of a purchase order			
T3	Encumbrances—Energy	620	$12,000	
	Reserve for Encumbrances	753		$12,000
	To record issuance of a purchase order			
T4	Expenditure—Regular Salaries	110	$25,000	
	Cash in Bank	101		$25,000
	To record payment of regular salaries			
T5	Expenditure—Group Insurance	210	$11,000	
	Cash in Bank	101		$11,000
	To record payment of regular salaries			
T6a	Expenditure—General Supplies	610	$10,000	
	Cash in Bank	101		$10,000
	To record payment of regular salaries			
T6b	Reserve for Encumbrances	713	$10,000	
	Encumbrance—General Supplies	610		$10,000
	To record payment of partial supply order			
	Expenditure—Energy	620	$9,000	
	Accounts Payable	421		$9,000
	To record receipt of fuel oil on account			
T7b	Reserve for Encumbrances	753	$9,000	
	Encumbrance—Energy	620		$9,000
	To record payment of partial fuel order			
T8a	Expenditure—Book & Periodicals	640	$31,000	
	Cash in Bank	101		$31,000
	To record payment of books full order received			
T8b	Reserve for Encumbrances	713	$32,000	
	Encumbrance—Books and periodicals	640		$32,000
	To record receipt of full book order			

Illustration 8.9
General Ledger Activity

Kimberly Hills School District
General Fund
General Ledger

Cash in bank — Acct. No. 101

Date	Amount	Date	P.R.	Amount
		T4	GJ	$25,000
		T5	GJ	$11,000
		T6	GJ	$10,000
		T8a	GJ	$31,000

Accounts Payable — Acct. No. 421

Date	Amount	Date	P.R.	Amount
		T7a	GJ	$9,000

Reserve for Encumbrances — Acct. No. 753

Date	P.R.	Amount	Date	P.R.	Amount
T6b	GJ	$10,000	T1	GJ	$25,000
T7b	GJ	$ 9,000	T2	GJ	$32,000
T8b	GJ	$32,000	T3	GJ	$12,000

Regular Salaries — Account No. 110

			Appropriations		Expenditures		Encumbrances		Unencum.
Date	Explanation	P.R.	Debit	Credit	Debit	Credit	Debit	Credit	Balance
AB	Budget adoption			$85,000					$85,000
T 4	Paid salaries				$25,000				$60,000
	Totals			$85,000	$25,000	$0	$0	$0	$60,000

Group Insurance — Account No. 210

			Appropriations		Expenditure		Encumbrances		Unencum.
Date	Explanation	P.R.	Debit	Credit	Debit	Credit	Debit	Credit	Balance
AB	Budget adoption			$11,000					$11,000
T 4	Paid insurance				$11,000				$0
	Totals		$0	$11,000	$11,000	$0	$0	$0	$0

General supplies							Account No.		610
			Appropriations		Expenditures		Encumbrances		Unencum.
Date	Explanation	P.R.	Debit	Credit	Debit	Credit	Debit	Credit	Balance
AB	Budget Adoption			$32,000					$32,000
T1	Purchase order						$25,000		$7,000
T6a	Received supplies				$10,000				($3,000)
T6b	Adjust encum.							$10,000	$7,000
	Totals		$0	$32,000	$10,000	$0	$25,000	$10,000	$7,000

Energy							Account No.		620
			Appropriations		Expenditures		Encumbrances		Unencum.
Date	Explanation	PR..	Debit	Credit	Debit	Credit	Debit	Credit	Balance
AB	Budget adoption			$44,000					$44,000
T3	Purchase order						$12,000		$32,000
T7a	Received fuel oil				$9,000				$23,000
T7b	Adjust encum.							$9,000	$32,000
	Totals		$0	$44,000	$9,000	$0	$12,000	$9,000	$32,000

Books & periodicals							Account No.		640
			Appropriations		Expenditures		Encumbrances		Unencum.
Date	Explanation	P.R.	Debit	Credit	Debit	Credit	Debit	Credit	Balance
AB	Budget adoption			$45,000					$45,000
T2	Purchase order						$32,000		$13,000
T8a	Received books				$31,000				($18,000)
T8b	Adjust encum.							$32,000	$14,000
	Totals		$0	$45,000	$31,000	$0	$32,000	$32,000	$14,000

Illustration 8.10
Kimberly Hills School District
General Fund
Interim Statement Comparing
Expenditures and Encumbrances with Appropriations
For the period July1, 2008, through July 31, 2008

Account Code	Account Name	Appropriations	Expenditures	Encumbrances	Unencumbered Balance
110	Exp—Regular salaries	$85,000	$25,000	$0	$60,000
210	Exp—Group insurance	11,000	11,000	-	-
610	Exp—General supplies	32,000	10,000	15,000	7,000
620	Exp—Energy	44,000	9,000	3,000	32,000
640	Exp—Books periodicals	45,000	31,000	-	14,000
	Totals	$217,000	$86,000	$18,000	$113,000

INTERIM FINANCIAL REPORTS

Interim financial reports may be prepared during the year to provide information to administrators and board members. The interim statement comparing expenditures and encumbrances with appropriations provides that information and is shown in Illustration 8.10.

SUMMARY

Appropriations, expenditures, encumbrances and reserve for encumbrances were defined. Procedures were illustrated for recording appropriations, expenditures, encumbrances and reserve for encumbrances. The interim statement comparing expenditures and encumbrances with appropriations was illustrated.

ACTIVITIES

1. Carefully review the definition of the following terms given in the glossary:
   a. Appropriation
   b. Encumbrances
   c. Expenditures/expenses
   d. Accrual basis
   e. Reserve for encumbrances
   f. Budgetary account

2. The following appropriations were approved in Timton School District at the beginning of the fiscal year:

110	Regular Salaries	$350,000
210	Group Insurance	5,000
610	General Supplies	20,000
620	Energy	10,000
640	Books and Periodicals	20,000

The following transactions occurred during the year:

- T1 An order was placed for general supplies estimated to cost $10,000.
- T2 The material ordered in T1 was received and the actual cost was $12,000.
- T3 Salaries were paid in the amount of $20,000.
- T4 Salaries in the amount of $10,000 were paid.
- T5 Group insurance in the amount of $3,000 was paid.
- T6 Purchased general supplies on account in the amount of $3,000.
- T7 Paid regular teacher salaries of $115,000.
- T8 Regular teacher salaries were paid in the amount of $90,000.
- T9 General supplies in the amount of $1,000 were purchased on account.
- T10 Paid regular teacher salaries in the amount of $45,000.

Instructions:

- Record the budget as adopted in the general journal.
- Record all transactions in the general journal.
- Post all general journal entries to the general ledger and to the expenditure ledger.
- Prepare an interim statement comparing expenditures and encumbrances to appropriations.

3. The general ledger account balances in the general fund of the New Douglas School District at the beginning of the fiscal year were:

Cash in Bank	$200,000
Investments	150,000
Accounts Payable	85,000
Contracts Payable	45,000
Unreserved Fund Balance	220,000

The New Douglas School District approved the following appropriations on the first day of the fiscal year:

110	Regular Salaries	$85,000
210	Group Insurance	11,000
610	General Supplies	32,000
620	Energy	44,000
640	Books & Periodicals	45,000

The following transactions occurred during the fiscal year:

T1	A purchase order, in the amount of $31,000, was issued for general supplies.
T2	The general supplies ordered in T1 were received and the actual cost was $35,500.
T3	Salaries were paid in the amount of $3,750.
T4	Salaries were paid in the amount of $54,000.
T5	Group insurance in the amount of $12,000 was paid.
T6	Periodical subscriptions in the amount of $14,000 were issued.
T7	A purchase order, in the amount of $9,000, was issued for books.
T8	The books ordered in T7 were received and the actual cost was $8,500.
T9	Charges for electricity in the amount of $11,000 were paid.
T10	A purchase order for paper supplies was issued in the amount of $6,000.

Instructions:

- Enter the account balances in the ledger accounts.
- Record the appropriations in the general journal.
- Record all transactions in the general journal.
- Post all general journal entries to the general ledger and to the expenditure ledger.
- Prepare an interim statement of expenditures and encumbrances compared with appropriations.

4. The general ledger beginning account balances in the general fund of the ABC School District at the beginning of the fiscal year were:

Cash in Bank	$ 45,000
Investments	130,000
Accounts Payable	75,000

Unreserved Fund Balance	395,000

The ABC School District approved the annual budget for expenditures (appropriations) on September 1, 2008, for the following amounts:

110	Salaries	$325,000
220	Benefits	60,000
310	Purchased Services	45,000
410	Supplies	38,000
440	Utilities	40,000
540	Equipment	85,000

The following transactions occurred during the first quarter of the fiscal year:

T1 Merchandise was received and payment was authorized for outstanding purchase order (accounts payable) in the amount of $24,000.

T2 Employee salaries and benefits were paid in the amount of $81,250 and $15,000, respectively.

T3 A purchase order, in the amount of $10,000, was issued for contractual services for site repairs.

T4 A purchase order, in the amount of $3,000, was issued for office supplies.

T5 Charges for electricity in the amount of $8,000 were paid.

T6 The repairs ordered in T2 were partially completed and payment of $5,000 was made.

T7 The office supplies from T3 were received and the actual cost was $3,100.

T8 A purchase order was issued for classroom computers in the amount of $55,000.

T9 The repairs ordered in T2 were completed and final payment of the balance due was made.

T10 The classroom computers ordered in T8 were delivered and payment was authorized for $58,000 that includes shipping charges of $3,000.

Instructions:

- Enter the beginning general ledger account balances in the ledger accounts.
- Record the annual expenditure budget in the general journal.
- Record all transactions in the general journal.
- Post all general journal entries to the general ledger and to the expenditure ledger.
- Prepare an interim statement of expenditures and encumbrances compared with appropriations (budget).

9

Special Entries

INTRODUCTION

In chapters 7 and 8 the recording of budgetary and actual financial data was described. It was also mentioned that the revenue and expenditure accounts were actually temporary accounts. The revenue and expenditure accounts provide the detail that supports the changes in the equity account that were a result of operations for the fiscal year. Because they are temporary accounts they must be closed out each year.

Likewise, closing the books to provide for separation of transactions into fiscal periods requires certain entries to the general journal. In order that results of operation can be determined at the end of the fiscal year, all revenue and expenditure accounts must be summarized. The use of "closing accounts" facilitates this procedure.

OUTCOMES

In this chapter, you will learn how to:

1. Record the budget.
2. Record closing entries.
3. Prepare a post-closing trial balance.

CLOSING THE BOOKS

The process of closing the books prior to the introduction of electronic systems was a time-consuming manual process. Most software systems have a built-in year-end closing process, which permits the user to simply select the process and the software closes the revenue and expenditure accounts to the equity (fund balance) account. For purposes of instruction and understanding, this chapter and the activities will go through the manual process.

CLOSING ENTRIES

During the fiscal year, transactions in the general fund are analyzed, recorded in the general journal, posted to accounts in the general ledger, account balances are determined and worksheets and financial statements are prepared. What happens at the end of the fiscal year? How does one "end" or "close the books" of one fiscal year and "start" or "open the books" to another fiscal year?

The objective of the closing process is to transfer balances from "temporary accounts" (i.e., revenues and expenditures) into the fund balance account at the end of the fiscal year (or accounting period). Although there are several different ways of making the closing entries, the method to be used in this text is simple and direct. The procedure is a straightforward two-step process:

1. Close each revenue account into the unreserved fund balance account.

2. Close each expenditure account into the unreserved fund balance account.

A necessary procedure at the end of the fiscal year is to "close the books." This implies recording the necessary entries in the general journal to close out revenue and expenditure accounts that have been active during the year. These temporary accounts are closed into the fund balance account to obtain the actual end-of-the-year fund balance. After the temporary accounts have been closed, the only accounts in the general ledger which will have a non-zero balance are assets, liabilities and fund balance accounts.

At the end of the fiscal year, a pre-closing trail balance should be prepared to check the equality of debits and credits prior to recording the closing entries. The pre-closing trial balance will probably contain non-zero balances for assets, liabilities, fund balances, revenues and expenditures. If the trial balance indicates equality of debits and credits, then the process of "closing the books" may begin.

Revenue accounts will normally have a credit balance. Therefore, in order to close out a revenue account the account should be debited in the amount of the credit balance and the unreserved fund balance account should be credited for this amount. Since the revenue account has been debited in the amount of the credit balance, the new balance in the revenue account is zero. If the balance at the end-of-the-year is zero, the account is said to be closed.

Expenditure accounts will normally have a debit balance. Therefore, in order to close out an expenditure account (produce a zero balance) the account should be credited in the amount of the debit balance and the unreserved fund balance should be debited in that amount.

ILLUSTRATION OF CLOSING ENTRIES

Assume the general ledger for Kimberly Hills School District contains the account balances shown in Illustration 9.1.

Illustration 9.1
Kimberly Hills School District
General Fund
General Ledger

	Cash in Bank		*Account No. 101*		
Date	P.R.	Amount	Date	P.R.	Amount
BB		$75,000			

	Investments		*Account No. 111*		
Date	P.R.	Amount	Date	P.R.	Amount
BB		$125,000			

Unreserved Fund Balance			*Account No. 730*		
Date	P.R.	Amount	Date	P.R.	Amount
			BB		$180,000

Revenue—Local Ad Valorem Tax			*Account No. 1110*		
Date	P.R.	Amount	Date	P.R.	Amount
			BB		$230,000

Expenditures—Salaries—Regular Emp.			*Account No. 1110*		
Date	P.R.	Amount	Date	P.R.	Amount
BB		$210,000			

The pre-closing trial balance for Kimberly Hills School District with the above account balances is shown in Illustration 9.2.

Illustration 9.2
Kimberly Hills School District
General Fund
Pre-Closing Trial Balance
June 30, 2008

Accounts		
Cash	$ 75,000	
Investments	125,000	
Unreserved Fund Balance		$180,000
Revenue—Local Ad Valorem Tax		230,000
Expenditures—Salaries—Regular Employees	210,000	
	$410,000	$410,000

Entries in the general journal which are necessary to close the revenue and expenditure accounts (i.e., leave them with a zero balance) are shown in Illustration 9.3.

Illustration 9.3
Kimberly Hills School District
General Fund
General Journal

Date	Account Titles	Post	Debit	Credit
C1	Revenue—Local Ad Valorem Tax		$230,000	
	Unreserved Fund Balance			$230,000
	To close revenue from local ad valorem tax			
C2	Unreserved Fund Balance		210,000	
	Expenditures—Salaries—Regular Employees			210,000
	To close expenditure for salaries of regular employees			

After the closing entries have been posted to the ledger accounts, then the "temporary accounts" (revenues and expenditures) can be ruled to indicate they are closed at the end of the fiscal year (or accounting period). Double-ruling after the closing entry in a revenue or expenditure account indicates that the account has been closed for that fiscal year.

After posting the closing entries to the general ledger accounts, the general ledger accounts would appear as shown in Illustration 9.4.

Illustration 9.4
Kimberly Hills School District
General Fund
General Ledger

Cash in Bank			*Account No. 101*		
Date	P.R.	Amount	Date	P.R.	Amount
BB		$75,000			

Investments			*Account No. 111*		
Date	P.R.	Amount	Date	P.R.	Amount
BB		$125,000			

Unreserved Fund Balance			*Account No. 770*		
Date	P.R.	Amount	Date	P.R.	Amount
C2	2	$210,000	BB		$180,000
			C 1		230,000

Revenue—Local Ad Valorem Tax			*Account No. 1110*		
Date	P.R.	Amount	Date	P.R.	Amount
C 1	2	$230,000	BB		$230,000

Expenditures—Salaries—Regular			*Account No. 1110*		
Date	P.R.	Amount	Date	P.R.	Amount
BB		$210,000	C2	2	$210,000

Balance sheet accounts (i.e., assets, liabilities and fund equities) are not "temporary accounts" and are not closed at the end of the fiscal year. However, balance sheet account balances are brought forward to the next fiscal year without general journal entry. Systematic procedures should be followed to ensure that appropriate balance sheet account balances have been brought forward to the next fiscal year.

POST-CLOSING TRIAL BALANCE

A post-closing trial balance is prepared after the "temporary" accounts have been closed and after each balance sheet account balance has been brought forward to the new fiscal year. The post-closing trial balance is taken directly from the general ledger to prove that the general ledger is in balance at the beginning of the new fiscal period. The post-closing trial balance is the last step in the accounting cycle.

The post-closing trial balance for the above example is shown in Illustration 9.5.

SUMMARY

Selected special entries were presented in this chapter. Special entries required for opening and closing temporary accounts were discussed. Illustrations were presented to show the closing of revenue accounts and expenditure accounts. Illustrations presented the unreserved fund equity account as an essential account in closing the temporary accounts.

Illustration 9.5
Kimberly Hills School District
General Fund
Post-Closing Trial Balance
June 30, 2008

Accounts		
Cash	$ 75,000	
Investments	125,000	
Unreserved Fund Balance		$200,000
	$200,000	$200,000

ACTIVITIES

1. Define the following terms:
   a. Closing Accounts
   b. Post-Closing Trial Balance

2. The trial balance for Kimberly Hills School District as of June 30, 2008, was as follows:

Kimberly Hills School District
General Fund
Pre-Closing Trial Balance
June 30, 2008

Accounts		
Cash in bank	$200,300	
Investments	70,050	
Interfund loan receivable	7,350	
Unreserved fund balance		$277,700
Revenue—local ad valorem tax		118,820
Revenue from tuition		44,558
Revenue from earnings on investments		29,705
Revenue from unrestricted state aid		89,115
Revenue from federal—revenue in lieu of taxes		14,852
Expenditures—salaries—regular	257,000	
Expenditures—employee benefits group insurance	38,550	
Expenditures—purchased service—rentals	1,500	
	$574,750	$574,750

Assume the chart of accounts for the school district consists of the following:

- Assets (101, 111, 131)

- Fund equity (730)
- Revenue (1110, 1300, 1500, 3100, 4800)
- Expenditures (object codes 110, 210, 440)

Instructions:

- Record the balances shown in the trial balance as of June 30, 2008, in T-accounts.
- Record the necessary closing entries in general journal form.
- Post closing entries to the T-accounts.
- Prepare a post-closing trial balance.

3. The trial balance of Randyville School District as of May 31, 2008, was as follows:

Randyville School District
General Fund
Trial Balance
May 31, 2008

Accounts	Debits	Credits
Cash in Bank	$150,000	
Interfund Loan Receivable	25,000	
Unreserved Fund Balance		$ 40,000
Revenue—Local Ad Valorem Tax		125,000
Revenue from Unrestricted State Aid		195,000
Expenditures—Salaries—Regular	150,000	
Expenditures—General Supplies	35,000	
	$360,000	$360,000

During the month of June, the following transactions were completed:

T1 Purchased general supplies in the amount of $25,000.
T2 Received a general state aid payment of $75,000.
T3 Paid employee health insurance of $42,000.
T4 Purchased equipment of $32,000.
T5 Payment of the entire amount due from other funds was received.
T6 Purchased investments for $100,000.

Instructions:

- Use accounts as needed.
- Record the balances shown on the Trial Balance as of May 31, 2008, in T-accounts.
- Record the transaction for June in a general journal.
- Post transactions from the general journal to the ledger accounts.
- Prepare a pre-closing trial balance.
- Record the necessary closing entries in the general journal.
- Post to the general ledger.
- Prepare a post-closing trial balance.

4. Account balances in the general fund of the New Douglas School System as of June 30, 2008, were as follows:

Cash in bank	$115,000
Taxes receivable	75,000
Expenditures—salaries—regular	200,000
Expenditures—supplies—general	55,000
Expenditures—purchase property services—utility services	23,000
Expenditures—supplies—food	20,000
Revenue from earnings on investments	15,000
Unreserved fund balance	?*
Revenue from tuition	35,000
Expenditures—employee benefits—retirement contributions	14,000
Revenue from local ad valorem tax	400,000

* To be computed by the reader.

Instructions:

- Use accounts as needed.
- Prepare a pre-closing trial balance as of June 30, 2008.
- Record the necessary closing entries in general journal form.
- Post closing entries to the T-accounts.
- Prepare a post-closing trial balance.

10

Basic Financial Statements

INTRODUCTION

Previously, *fund balance* was defined as the "balancing factor" reflecting the difference between assets and liabilities. In addition, fund balance was identified as one group of the three groups of balance sheet accounts. *Financial Accounting for Local and State School Systems, 2003* (2003) expands the concept of fund equity into fund balance. It is appropriate at this time to explore more fully the ramifications of fund balance.

One of the primary purposes of school fund accounting is to facilitate the communication of financial information to interested people. Of particular interest to people are the balance sheet and statement of revenue, expenditures and changes in fund balance. These reports may be combined reports that reflect financial conditions across all funds or they may be combined reports that compare budget and actual amounts.

OUTCOMES

In this chapter, you will learn how to:

1. Define *fund balance*.
2. Distinguish between reserved fund balance accounts and unreserved fund balance accounts.
3. Prepare a balance sheet.
4. Identify balance sheet accounts.
5. Prepare an interim balance sheet.
6. Prepare a statement of revenues, expenditures and fund balance.
7. Identify the purposes of combined financial reports.

FUND BALANCE

Financial Accounting for Local and State School Systems, 2003 (Johnson 2003, 65) defines *fund balance* as the "accounts showing the excess of a fund's assets over its liabilities." It further states that portions of the balance may be reserved for future use.

Throughout this text, the term *fund balance* has referred to balance sheet account number 730, unreserved fund balance. This convention has expedited discussion of accounting procedures, but does not accurately reflect the true meaning of balance sheet account number 730. Unreserved fund balance refers to the excess of the assets of the fund over its liabilities and reserves.

Fund balance consists of the following accounts:

711 Reserve for Inventories
712 Reserve for Prepaid Items
713 Reserve for Encumbrances
714 Other Reserved Fund Balance

720 Designated Fund Balance
730 Unreserved Fund Balance

Since the purpose of this text is to introduce individuals to basic concepts of school fund accounting, a discussion of fund equity accounts other than 730, unreserved fund balance, will not be presented. Such discussion is left to advanced topics in school fund accounting.

Financial Accounting for Local and State School Systems, 2003 (Johnson (2003, 62–66) reports that within governmental funds, equity is reported as *fund balance*; proprietary and fiduciary fund equity is reported as *net assets*. Fund balance and net assets are the difference between fund assets and liabilities reflected on the balance sheet or statement of net assets. Johnson (2003, 62–66) continues,

> Because of the current financial resources measurement focus of governmental funds, fund balance is often considered a measure of available expendable financial resources. This is a particularly important measure in the general fund because it reflects the primary functions of the government and includes both state aid and local tax revenues. The relative amount of unreserved fund balance reflected in the general fund is used by rating agencies as a measure of financial strength of the government. Declines in the amount of unreserved fund balance may signal deterioration in the financial condition of the entity.
>
> Governmental fund balances are categorized as follows:
>
> - Reserved
> - Unreserved
>   —Designated
>   —Undesignated
>
> **Reserved Fund Balances**
>
> Reservations of fund balance should be used in governmental financial reporting to identify the portion that is
>
> - not available for appropriation or expenditure (e.g., reserve for inventories, reserve for long-term receivables) and/or
> - legally earmarked by external parties or entities for a specific future use, that is, a legal restriction on the use of assets (e.g., reserve for encumbrances).
>
> The amount and nature of the reservation of fund balance should be disclosed on the face of the financial statements. The description may need to be supplemented by disclosure in the notes to the financial statements. Examples of reservations of fund balance follow:
>
> - Inventories
> - Debt service
> - Endowments
> - Prepaid items
> - Outstanding encumbrances

- Construction
- Federal and state programs

The aggregate fund balance in the debt service fund is legally reserved for the payment of bonded indebtedness and is not available for other purposes until all bonded indebtedness is liquidated.

The fund balance of the capital projects fund reflects an amount designated for construction and major renovation projects, and it usually represents unexpended proceeds from the sale of bonds that have restricted uses. However, in all instances in which the name of the fund communicates the legal segregation, the fund balance should be reported as unreserved.

Unreserved Fund Balances

Unreserved fund balance is the difference between the total and reserved fund balance. It has two components: designated and undesignated. The unreserved fund balance of the general fund represents the balance available for legal appropriation and expenditure for general operating expenditures.

Prudent financial management requires accumulating a sufficient undesignated, unreserved fund balance in the general fund representing available expendable financial resources to meet the net cash outflows during the fiscal year.

Designated, Unreserved Fund Balances

Portions of fund balance may be designated by management to reflect tentative plans or commitments of governmental resources. *Designations* generally reflect board action to earmark the balance for purposes that will be fulfilled at a later time, but specific board action is not required. Designations represent planned actions, rather than actual commitments. Because they typically arise from internal actions (management decisions) rather than actions external to the entity (encumbrances), designations are reported as part of unreserved fund balance.

The amount and nature of the designation should be explained in a

- separate line of the balance sheet,
- parenthetical comment, or
- note to the financial statements.

Designations may be related to

- construction or other capital expenditures,
- claims and judgments, or
- self-insurance contingencies.

Undesignated, Unreserved Fund Balances

Undesignated, unreserved fund balance is the difference between total fund balance and the portion that is reserved and designated. This is the balance available for legal appropriation and expenditure if a government budgets on a GAAP basis for its governmental funds.

FINANCIAL STATEMENTS

School personnel are frequently asked to relate the financial condition of the school district. One way to respond is to present a balance sheet and/or a statement of revenues, expenditures and fund equity. The balance sheet is able to provide information about the financial condition *as of* a particular point in time. On the other hand, the statement of revenues, expenditures and fund equity is used to provide information about the financial condition of a school district *during* a specific period of time. Drawing information from the two different reports, an individual may gain a better indication of the financial condition of the school district than could be obtained from an analysis of only one of the reports.

The balance sheet contains account balances in balance sheet accounts only. Therefore, prior to preparing an end of the year balance sheet, the revenue and expenditure accounts must be closed into the fund balance account. One must first prepare the statement of revenues, expenditures and fund equity and then prepare the balance sheet after the new fund balance is determined.

The following examples demonstrate the procedures for preparing the statement of revenues, expenditures and fund balance, and a balance sheet.

Example 1

On July 1, 2008, the unreserved fund balance of Cape Jennifer School District was $323,000. During the year, revenue amounting to $420,000 was realized and expenses amounting to $300,000 were incurred. Asset and liability account balance in the general fund on June 30, 2009, were as follows:

Cash in bank	$ 20,000
Investments	370,000
Taxes receivable	640,000
Prepaid expenses	3,000
Accounts payable	590,000

Prepare the statement of revenues, expenditures and fund balance for the period ending June 30, 2009.

Cape Jennifer School District
General Fund
Statement of Revenues, Expenditures and Fund Balance
For the period ended June 30, 2009

Fund Balance, July 1, 2008		$323,000
Add excess if revenues over expenditures		
Revenues	$420,000	
less: Expenditures	300,000	120,000
Fund Balance, June 30, 2009		$443,000

Example 2

Use the new ending fund balance to prepare a balance sheet as of June 30, 2009.

Cape Jennifer School District
General Fund
Balance Sheet
June 30, 2009

Assets	
Cash in bank	$ 20,000
Investments	370,000
Taxes Receivable	640,000
Prepaid expenses	3,000
Total assets	$1,033,000
Liabilities and Fund Balance	
Liabilities:	
Accounts payable	$ 590,000
Fund Balance:	
Unreserved fund balance	443,000
Total liabilities and fund balance	$1,033,000

INTERIM FINANCIAL STATEMENTS

Interim financial statements may be prepared during the year to provide information to administrators and board members. The financial statements should contain an interim statement of revenue (chapter 7), an interim statement comparing expenditures and encumbrances with appropriations (chapter 8), and an interim balance sheet. Preparation of an interim statement of revenues, expenditures and fund balance would permit preparation of a balance sheet (at an interim point in time) in the format shown in Example 2. In the activities for this chapter, however, an interim balance sheet refers to the format presented in Illustration 10.1. The interim balance sheet as shown provides information about the balance sheet accounts as well as the revenue and expenditure activity.

Illustration 10.1
New Douglas School District
General Fund
Interim Balance Sheet
April 30, 2009

Assets and Resources	
Current assets:	
Cash in bank	$ 20,000
Investments	370,000
Accounts receivable	640,000
Prepaid expenses	3,000
Total current assets	$ 1,033,000

Resources:			
Estimated revenue		$ 500,000	
less: revenue		420,000	
Balance to be realized			80,000
Total assets and resources			$ 1,113,000
Liabilities, Appropriations and Fund Balance			
Current liabilities:			
Accounts payable		$ 590,000	
Total current liabilities			$ 590,000
Appropriations		500,000	
Less: Expenditures	$ 300,000		
Encumbrances	40,000	340,000	
Balance to be expended			160,000
Fund balance:			
Reserve for encumbrance		$ 40,000	
Unreserved fund balance		323,000	
Total fund balance			363,000
Total liabilities, appropriations and fund balance			$ 1,113,000

SUMMARY

Fund balance includes reserved and unreserved balances. This introductory discussion has been limited to the analysis of unreserved fund balances. This chapter has illustrated procedures used in preparing basic financial statements. A balance sheet, a statement of revenues, expenditures and fund equity were illustrated. Elements of interim financial reports were reviewed and expanded to include the interim balance sheet.

ACTIVITIES

1. Carefully review the definition of the following terms found in the glossary:
   a. Fund balance
   b. Fund equity
   c. Reserved fund balance accounts
   d. Unreserved fund balance accounts
   e. Balance sheet
   f. Statement of changes in financial position
   g. Combined financial report

2. The general ledger account balances in the general fund of the Timton School District as of July 1, 2009, were as follows:

Cash	$100,000
Investments	30,000
Accounts payable	70,000

Contracts payable	10,000
Unreserved fund balance	50,000

The Timton School District board adopted the following budget for the general fund on July 15, 2009:

301	Estimated revenues			
1000	From local sources:			
1110	Ad valorem taxes	$45,000		
1300	Tuition	6,000		
1500	Earnings on investments	5,000	$56,000	
3000	From state sources:			
3100	Unrestricted grants-in-aid	35,000		
3800	Revenue in lieu of taxes	9,000	44,000	$100,000
601	Estimated Expenditures:			
110	Regular salaries	35,000		
210	Group insurance	4,000		
610	General supplies	15,000		
620	Energy	11,000		
640	Books and periodicals	20,000		$85,000
730	Unreserved fund balance			$15,000

The following transactions occurred during the year:

T1	Property taxes were levied in the amount of $45,000. It is estimated that 3 percent of these taxes will be uncollectible.
T2	An order was placed for general supplies estimated to cost $10,000.
T3	The materials ordered in T2 were received and the actual cost was $12,000.
T4	Salaries were paid in the amount of $20,000.
T5	The district received $44,000 in payment of property taxes previously levied.
T6	The entire amount of accounts payable was paid.
T7	Unrestricted grants-in-aid from the state was received in the amount of $30,000.
T8	Tuition in the amount of $4,000 was collected.
T9	Earnings on investments in the amount of $3,000 were received.
T10	Revenue in lieu of taxes from the state was received in the amount of $9,000.
T11	Salaries in the amount of $10,000 were paid.
T12	Group insurance in the amount of $3,000 was paid.

Instructions:

- Enter the account balances in the ledger accounts.
- Record the budget as adopted in the general journal.
- Record all transactions in the general journal.
- Post all general journal entries to the general ledger.
- Prepare a trial balance.
- Prepare an interim statement of revenues.
- Prepare an interim statement of appropriations, encumbrances and expenditures.
- Prepare an interim balance sheet.

- Prepare a statement of revenues, expenditures and fund balance for the period.
- Prepare a balance sheet as of the end of the period.

3. The general ledger account balances in the general fund of the Randyville School District as of July 1, 2009, were as follows:

Cash	$291,000
Accounts payable	273,000
Unreserved fund balance	18,000

The Randyville School District adopted the following budget for the general fund on July 1, 2009:

301	Estimated revenues			
1000	From local sources:			
1110	Ad valorem taxes	$400,000		
1300	Tuition	20,000		
1500	Earnings on investments	5,000	$425,000	
3000	From state sources:			
3100	Unrestricted grants-in-aid	150,000		
3800	Revenue in lieu of taxes	30,000	180,000	$605,000
601	Estimated expenditures:			
110	Regular salaries	350,000		
210	Group insurance	35,000		
610	General supplies	150,000		
620	Energy	20,000		555,000
730	Unreserved fund balance			$ 50,000

The following transactions occurred during the year:

T1	Local property taxes were assessed and levied in the amount of $270,000 and past history indicates 10 percent of these taxes will be uncollectible.
T2	Purchased general supplies of $40,000 on account.
T3	Paid $55,000 on accounts payable.
T4	Paid regular teacher salaries of $115,000.
T5	The district received $45,000 from the state in unrestricted grants.
T6	A general state aid payment of $70,000 was received.
T7	Tuition in the amount of $4,000 was collected.
T8	Regular teacher salaries were paid in the amount of $90,000.
T9	Received $295,000 in collections from property taxes assessed and levied in T1.
T10	A general state aid payment of $70,000 was received.
T11	Salaries in the amount of $90,000 were paid.
T12	General supplies in the amount of $123,000 were purchased on account.
T13	The entire amount due on general supplies purchased in T12 was paid.
T14	Of the general supplies purchased in T12, $45,000 was returned and a cash refund was received.

Instructions:

- Enter the account balances in the ledger accounts.

- Record the budget as adopted in the general journal.
- Record all transactions in the general journal.
- Post all general journal entries to the general ledger.
- Prepare a trial balance
- Prepare an interim statement of revenue.
- Prepare an interim statement of appropriations, encumbrances and expenditures.
- Prepare an interim balance sheet.
- Prepare a statement of revenues, expenditures and fund balance for the period.
- Prepare a balance sheet as of the end of the period.

4. The general ledger account balances in the general fund of the New Douglas School District as of July 1, 2009, were as follows:

Cash in bank	$200,000
Investments	150,000
Accounts payable	85,000
Contracts payable	45,000
Unreserved fund balance	220,000

The New Douglas School District adopted the following budget for the general fund on August 1, 2009:

301	Estimated revenues			
1000	From local sources:			
1110	Ad valorem taxes	$45,000		
1300	Tuition	23,000		
1500	Earnings on investments	42,000	$110,000	
3000	From state sources:			
3100	Unrestricted grants-in-aid	68,000		
3800	Revenue in lieu of taxes	27,000	$ 95,000	$205,000
601	Estimated expenditures:			
110	Regular salaries	85,000		
210	Group insurance	11,000		
610	General Supplies	32,000		
620	Energy	44,000		
640	Books and periodicals	45,000		$217,000
730	Unreserved fund balance			($ 12,000)

The following transactions occurred during the year:

T1 Property taxes were assessed and levied in the amount of $147,000. It is estimated that 5 percent of these taxes will be uncollectible.

T2 A purchase order, in the amount of $31,000, was issued for general supplies.

T3 Contracts for employment of regular faculty and staff in the amount of $75,000 were signed and issued.

T4 Due to an unanticipated enrollment increase, additional contracts for employment of regular faculty and staff in the amount of $15,000 were signed and issued.

T5 The general supplies ordered in T2 were received and the actual cost was $35,500.

T6 Salaries were paid in the amount of $3,750.

T7 The district received $145,000 in payment of property taxes levied in T1.
T8 The district paid $65,000 of the amount in the accounts payable account.
T9 Salaries were paid in the amount of $54,000.
T10 A general state aid payment of $44,000 was received.
T11 State revenue in lieu of taxes in the amount of $15,000 was received.
T12 Tuition from students in the amount of $26,000 was received.
T13 State revenue in lieu of taxes in the amount of $12,000 was received.
T14 Group insurance in the amount of $12,000 was paid.

Instructions:

- Enter the account balances in the ledger accounts.
- Record the budget as adopted in the general journal.
- Record all transactions in the general journal.
- Post all general journal entries to the general ledger.
- Prepare a trial balance.
- Prepare an interim statement of revenue.
- Prepare an interim statement of appropriations, encumbrances and expenditures.
- Prepare an interim balance sheet.
- Prepare a statement of revenues, expenditures and fund balance for the period.
- Prepare a balance sheet as of the end of the period.

11

Changes in Financial Position

INTRODUCTION

The statement of changes in financial position is useful as a communication device between school districts and taxpayers because the statement identifies the amount of financial resources provided from all sources and shows how the amount was used during the fiscal period. The statement shows what money it takes to run the school district.

OUTCOMES

In this chapter, you will learn how to:

0. Identify financial resources.
0. Determine working capital.
0. Prepare a fund's statement of changes in financial position.

FINANCIAL RESOURCES CONCEPT

The statement of changes in financial position for a fund is more than a balance sheet, a statement of revenues and expenditures, a statement of changes in fund equity, an analysis of cash receipts and disbursements, a schedule of working capital or a schedule of changes in working capital. It presents financial information in a way that no other financial statement does. When using the "all financial resources" concept, it shows what it takes to run a school district. For the individual fund, the statement of changes in financial position shows the total financial resources that were required to operate the fund for a specific fiscal period. When combined with the statement of changes in financial position for each fund, it gives a picture of the economic magnitude of the school district that is not possible otherwise.

When the combined statement is published along with the combined balance sheet, combined statement of revenues, expenditures and changes in fund balance, it is possible for the taxpayer to have full information about the financial operations of the school district. A fully informed public is more likely to be sympathetic to the problems of elementary and secondary education and to be more willing to support its goals, aims and objectives. This is particularly important at the time voters are called upon to make decisions on financial matters of a school system by voting on tax rates and bond issues.

Managerial accounting is concerned with identifying all of the financial resources that are available to the school district and developing ways for a maximum use of each. This is essential if these resources, property and property rights are to be adequately safeguarded and effectively used for desired educational programs and activities. Financial resources are provided from any or all of the following. (Note that all are account credits.)

These resources are:

- Converting assets
- Incurring debt
- Increasing a fund's fund balance as a result of correcting a prior year's error or by transfers from another fund
- Recording revenue
- Recording an expenditure reimbursement

Management is also concerned with allocating financial resources to both short-term and long-term educational programs, goals and objectives in order that the highest quality of education can be offered with the financial resources that are available. Therefore, identification and control of the ways by which financial resources may be applied to educational goals and objectives are important. Financial resources may be applied to any or all of the following. (Note that all are account debits.) These are:

- Increasing assets
- Decreasing debts
- Decreasing a fund's fund balance as a result of correction of a prior year's error or by a transfer to another fund
- Recording revenue rebates
- Recording expenditures

The balance sheet is frequently referred to as a statement of financial position. Therefore, the statement of changes in financial position is prepared from a fund's comparative balance sheets—the balance sheet at the beginning of the fiscal period and the balance sheet at the end of the fiscal period—computing the difference between the beginning and ending balances of each account. The balance sheet preparation using the "all financial resources" concept shows gross revenue and gross expenditures, which are computed from the fund's statement of revenue and expenditures. Other financial resources and uses of financial resources may be found on the fund's statement of changes in fund equity.

Thus, a broader interpretation of the statement of changes in financial position is possible for school districts than is possible by using either the "working capital" concept, which includes only those transactions that affect the current assets or current liabilities, or changes in cash concept.

Example 1

Assume that a school district wishes to purchase land for $100,000 and construct a new school building costing $1,400,000. The school district plans to accomplish this by issuing bonds of $1,000,000 at 103 (103 is a method used to express the price as 103 cents for each 100 cents contained in the principal amount stated on the face of the bond). The school district additionally would pay $470,000 from cash. When the transactions are completed, the statement shows the source of $1,000,000 as proceeds from the principal of bonds sold, $30,000 from a premium on bonds issued, and $470,000 from a reduction in the cash balance. It shows a total of $1,500,000 to be applied to the purchase of land and construction of the new school building. This series of transactions results in the following:

Financial resources provided by:	
Decreasing assets	
Cash	$ 470,000
Increasing liabilities:	
Principal of bonds issued	1,000,000
Premium on bonds issued	30,000
Total financial resources provided	$1,500,000

Financial resources applied to:	
Increasing assets:	
Land	$ 100,000
Building	1,400,000
Total financial resources applied	$1,500,000

Example 2

Assume that certain general fixed assets of the school district are sold for $1,000 and the proceeds are deposited in the general fund. No other general fixed assets are purchased. The statement shows total revenue of $1,000 from the sale of general fixed assets and a corresponding $1,000 applied to increase the cash balance. This transaction results in the following:

Financial resources provided by:	
Increasing revenue:	
Sale of general fixed assets	$1,000
Financial resources applied to:	
Increasing assets:	
Cash	$1,000

Illustration 11.1 shows how the statement of changes in financial position is prepared from the statement of revenues, expenditures and fund balance and from the balance sheets at the beginning and end of the fiscal period for each fund used in the operation of the school district.

Part 1—Assume the general fund's statement of revenues, expenditures and fund balance appears as shown in Illustration 11.1, Parts 1, 2 and 3.

The debits in the "Net Change in Accounts" column represent resources applied and the credits represent resources provided. From the statement of revenues, expenditures and fund balance, revenues represent resources provided and expenditures represent resources applied.

The $200,000 net change in fund balance is eliminated by a debit because it is a net figure, the nature of which can be found by referring to the statement of changes in fund balance. There, it is found to be the net excess of revenues over expenditures and the net change in fund balance is substituted by a credit identified for what it is: excess of revenues over expenditures. When making this elimination and substitution, note that debits equal credits.

Illustration 11.1, Part 1

New Douglas School District
General Fund
Statement of Revenues, Expenditures and Fund Balance
For the period ended June 30, 2008

Fund Balance, July 1, 2007				$ 10,000
Add excess of revenues over expenditures:				
	Revenues			
	From local sources		$1,400,000	
	From intermediate sources		200,000	
	From state sources		1,230,000	
	From federal sources		120,000	
	From other school districts:			
	In state	$ 30,000		
	Out of state	20,000	50,000	
	Total Revenues		$3,000,000	
less:	Expenditures			
	Instruction		$2,000,000	
	Administration		200,000	
	Attendance and health services		10,000	
	Pupil transportation services		400,000	
	Operations of plant		40,000	
	Maintenance of plant		60,000	
	Fixed charges		20,000	
	Community services		40,000	
	Debt service		30,000	
	Total Expenditures		$2,800,000	$ 200,000
Fund Balance, June 30, 2008				$ 210,000

The $200,000 representing net excess of revenue over expenditures is also a net figure, which is eliminated by a debit. In its place is substituted the things that caused this net result. From the statement of revenue and expenditures, it is found to be the excess of revenue of $3,000,000 over expenditures of $2,800,000. When making this elimination and substitution, note that the debits equal the credits. The column totals for eliminations and substitutions must also be equal. Prior to drafting the formal statement of changes in financial position, the following observations can be made:

- Resources were provided by reduction or conversion of assets identified as temporary investments, due from other funds, and inventory of supplies. The reduction in these assets provided financial resources that are not reported when a school district uses a cash basis of recording financial transactions. Conversion of assets should come under the control of the board of education so that property of the school district can be properly safeguarded.
- Financial resources were also provided by increasing the liabilities of the general fund during the year, i.e., vouchers payable and the deferred revenue account, taxes collected in advance. Full

disclosure of financial transactions of the school district to the public requires that liability accounts be an integral part of the public school district's accounting structure.

- Financial resources were applied to increase asset account balances during the year. Cash, taxes receivable and accounts receivable were increased. A financial statement that shows how much money was spent for things other than operating expenses of the school district is important to an inquiring public.
- Financial resources were applied to the reduction of the liability due to other funds. Only the statement of changes in financial position has the capacity to show the amount of financial resources used during the year to reduce liabilities of the school district.
- Reserve for encumbrances was reduced during the period by $16,000, and such a reduction represented an application of resources (see Illustration 11.1, Part 4).

Assume further that the comparative balance sheets of the general fund are as follows:

Illustration 11.1, Part 2
New Douglas School District
General Fund
Comparative Balance Sheet

Assets:	July 1, 2007	June 30, 2008
Cash	$ 4,000	$ 21,000
Temporary investments	25,000	18,000
Taxes receivable	40,000	242,200
Accounts receivable	10,000	22,300
Due from other funds	20,000	1,000
Inventory of supplies	1,000	500
Total Assets	$ 100,000	$ 305,000
Liabilities and Fund Equity		
Liabilities		
Vouchers payable	$ 40,000	$ 50,000
Due to other funds	10,000	5,000
Taxes collected in advance	20,000	36,000
Total Liabilities	$ 70,000	$ 91,000
Fund Balance		
Reserve for inventories	$ 1,000	$ 500
Reserve for encumbrances	19,000	3,500
Unreserved fund balance	10,000	210,000
Total Fund Balance	30,000	214,000
Total Liabilities and Fund Balance	$ 100,000	$ 305,000

Illustration 11.1, Part 4 shows that resources were provided from sources other than revenue and while not large in this illustration they can be significant. Total resources were $3,052,500 of which $3,000,000 was provided by revenue. Where did the remaining $52,500 come from? The voluntary or involuntary conversion of assets, a common transaction, provided $26,500. It is important for the board of education and administration to monitor the amount realized from the disposition of assets, to insure that disposals such as sale of equipment, which may require their approval, are not sold without their authorization.

The illustration also shows that resources were provided by increasing the school district's liabilities by $26,000. It is important to emphasize that goods and services generally come from increasing liabilities, such as vouchers payable. A major source of cash can come from increasing interest-bearing, short-term or long-term notes payable or bonds payable. Therefore, the amount available for the board of education to allocate to educational programs, goals and objectives is not restricted to either budgeted or realized revenue. Purchasing power comes from many other sources that must be controlled.

In addition, the illustration shows that while $2,800,000 was applied to educational programs, significant financial resources can be applied to many other things. In this case a number of assets accounts were increased by a total of $231,599 while resources of $5,000 were applied to the reduction of the school system's liabilities. The reserves for encumbrances and inventories were reduced by $16,000. Note that broad classifications were used to show how financial resources were applied to operations, rather than showing one total amount.

From the balance sheet at the beginning and end of the fiscal year, comparisons are made to determine the net changes that have occurred in the balance sheet.

Illustration 11.1, Part 3

	July 1 2007	June 30 2008	Net Change in Accounts Debit	Net Change in Accounts Credit
Cash	$4,000	$21,000	$17,000	
Temporary investments	25,000	18,000		$7,000
Taxes receivable	40,000	242,200	202,200	
Accounts receivable	10,000	22,300	12,300	
Due from other funds	20,000	1,000		19,000
Inventory of supplies	1,000	500		500
Total	$100,000	$305,000		
Vouchers payable	$10,000	$50,000		10,000
Due to other funds	10,000	5,000	5,000	
Taxes collected in advance	20,000	36,000		16,000
Reserve for inventories	1,000	500	500	
Reserve for encumbrances	19,000	3,500	15,500	
Unreserved fund balance	10,000	210,000		200,000
Total	$100,000	$305,000	$252,500	$252,500

Illustration 11.1, Part 4
The formal Statement of Changes in Financial Position is prepared

General Fund
Statement of Changes in Financial Position
For the year ended June 30, 2008

Resources provided:			
From revenues			
Local sources		$1,400,000	
Intermediate sources		200,000	
State sources		1,230,000	
Federal sources		120,000	
From other school districts:			
In the state	$30,000		
In another state	20,000	50,000	$3,000,000
From reduction in assets:			
Temporary investments		$7,000	
Due from other funds		19,000	
Inventory of supplies		500	26,500
From increasing liabilities:			
Vouchers payable		$10,000	
Taxes collected in advance		16,000	26,000
Total resources provided			$3,052,500
Resources Applied:			
To operations			
Instruction		$2,000,000	
Administration		200,000	
Attendance and health services		10,000	
Pupil transportation services		400,000	
Operations of plant		40,000	
Maintenance of plant		60,000	
Fixed charges		20,000	
Community services		40,000	
Debt service		30,000	$2,800,000
To increase assets:			
Cash		$17,000	
Taxes receivable		202,200	
Accounts receivable		12,300	231,500
To reduction in liabilities:			
Due to other funds			5,000
To reduction in reserves:			
Reserve for inventories			500
Reserve for encumbrances			15,500
Total resources applied			$3,052,500

FINANCIAL STATEMENTS

A balance sheet for each fund accompanies the fund's statement of changes in financial position. The balance sheet is a statement of financial position that shows each asset, liability and fund balance at the end of the fiscal period. The balance sheet is not in the statement of changes in financial position nor is that statement a substitute for a balance sheet. Each presents different financial information. For preparation of the comprehensive annual financial report, GASB's Statement 1 lists those considered to be general purpose financial statements as:

1. Combined balance sheet—all fund types and account groups.
2. Combined statement of revenues, expenditures and changes in fund balances—all governmental fund types.
3. Combined statement of revenues, expenditures and changes in fund balances—budget and actual—general and special revenue fund types for which annual budgets have been legally adopted.
4. Combined statement of revenues, expenses and changes in retained earnings (or equity)—all proprietary fund types.
5. Combined statements of changes in financial position—all proprietary fund types.
6. Notes to financial statements.

For purposes of the comprehensive annual financial report, GASB's Statement 1 states that the general outline and minimum content of the CAFR of a governmental unit include:

1. Combining statements—by fund type—where a governmental unit has more than one fund of a given fund type.
2. Individual fund and account group statements, where a governmental unit has only one fund of a given type and for account groups and/or where necessary to present prior year and budgetary comparisons.
3. Schedules.
   a. Schedules necessary to demonstrate compliance with finance-related legal and contractual provisions.
   b. Schedules to present information spread throughout the statements that can be brought together and shown in greater detail (i.e., taxes receivable, including delinquent taxes; long-term debt; investments; and cash receipts, disbursements and balances).
   c. Schedules to present greater detail for information reported in the statements (i.e., additional revenue sources detail and object of expenditure data by departments).

Narrative explanations useful in understanding combining and individual fund and account group statements and schedules that are not included in the notes to financial statements should be presented on divider pages, directly on the statements and schedules, or in a separate section.

These CAFRs will be presented throughout the text by presenting annual financial reports that have earned ASBO International's Certificate of Excellence in Financial Reporting. For management purposes, financial statements of individual funds will be emphasized.

The statement of changes in financial position is prepared primarily for presentation of financial information in a manner meaningful to the public. For that reason, it shows revenues and expenditures by broad classification; to provide detail about revenues and expenditures, the statement of revenues, expenditures and fund equity should accompany the statement of changes in financial position.

The statement of changes in fund balance contains all elements that caused a change from the beginning to the ending balance of fund balance. In addition to showing the excess of revenue over expenditures or the excess of expenditures over revenue, transfers in and/or out may have occurred, and errors of prior years may have been detected and corrected through fund balance. Appropriations of fund balance may have been made or the purposes for which fund balance may have been appropriated in prior periods may have been completed which may have resulted in a return from an appropriated fund balance account to the unappropriated fund balance account.

Each of these transactions, if they occur, has an effect upon changes in financial position. Therefore, the statement of changes in fund balance should accompany the statement of changes in financial position to provide more detailed information than would appear on the statement. Generally, revenue provides the largest amount of financial resources for a school district during a fiscal period. As revenue is shown in detail on the statement of revenue and expenditures, only the total amount of revenue is shown on the statement of changes in financial position when the "all financial resources" concept is used.

Resources are provided if any asset account is reduced at the end of the fiscal period to a figure below its balance at the beginning of the fiscal period. For example, if $100,000 was invested in an asset at the beginning of the year and only $70,000 is reported as the account balance at the end of the period, $30,000 has been provided. The question arises: Where did the $30,000 go? A number of transactions, each having a different effect on an account, may have occurred. To provide complete information about an account balance, it is necessary to analyze all transactions in the account during the accounting period, if that is desired. In some cases, an asset account is reduced because of converting it into cash, exchanging it for another asset or recognizing it as a loss. However, whatever the cause, the amount of the reduction is reported.

Some accountants have prepared statements of changes in financial position that report only the excess of revenue over expenditures for the period as a source of working capital or as a source of cash. But, it must be emphasized that the statement is prepared primarily for public information and that offsetting revenue with expenditures by reporting the difference only, conceals the amount of revenue actually used to operate the school district. Therefore, for the public to understand what amount of financial resources is required for the operation of the school district, revenue should be reported by total amount on the face of the statement of changes in financial position.

A fund's financial resources may come from transfers of fund balance from another fund. This amount would be found on the statement of changes in the recipient fund's balance rather than on its statement of revenue and expenditures, but it does provide financial resources to the recipient fund and, therefore, should be reported in the statement of changes in financial position for the recipient fund.

All expenditures and expenses are applications of financial resources. Generally, operating expenditures, capital outlay and debt service consume the greatest amount of a school district's financial resources. Although the statement of changes in financial position could be presented in a shorter form by offsetting expenditures against revenue, such an offset would conceal the total amount of expenditures of a school system. Therefore, the full amount of expenditures should be reported on the statement of changes in financial position. The statement can present amounts by broad expenditure classification or in total because the required accompanying statement of revenue and expenditures shows the nature and amount of the expenditures in detail. Such a disclosure shows in large part what happened to the school district's financial resources.

Within a fund, an increase in the balance of any asset account at the end of the fiscal period over the balance at the beginning of the fiscal period represents an application of financial resources. For full information, it is important that the nature and amount of each asset account that is increased be shown in the statement of changes in financial position. Such a disclosure does show in part how the financial resources were used.

Financial resources are applied when any liability account is reduced at the end of the fiscal period to an amount less than at the beginning of the fiscal period. A number of transactions, each having a different effect on a liability account, may have occurred. Full disclosure of how a school district's financial resources were used requires reporting the nature and amount of each liability account that was reduced in the statement of changes in financial position. Reduction in liabilities may be a major cause of change in financial position of a school district.

Reductions in the balances of all fund balance accounts to an amount at the end of the fiscal period less than at the beginning of the fiscal period represents an application of a school district's financial resources. A reduction in the reserve for encumbrances or any other appropriated fund equity account to an amount at the end of the fiscal period less than at the beginning is a change in financial position. A transfer of fund balance unappropriated to another fund is a change in financial position of the fund and its disclosure should be reported. The amounts by which all fund balance accounts have been reduced should be found on the statement of changes in fund balance rather than on the statement of revenue and expenditures.

Some accountants have prepared the statement of changes in financial position by reporting only the excess of expenditures over revenue as an application or use of financial resources, working capital or cash. But it must be emphasized that the statement of changes in financial position is prepared primarily for public information and that offsetting expenditures with revenue by reporting the difference only conceals the amount of expenditures of the school district. Thus, total expenditures should be shown. Detailed information about each expenditure is reported in the accompanying required statement of revenues and expenditures. Therefore, broad classifications of expenditures or the total amount of expenditures may be shown in the statement of changes in financial position.

An individual statement of changes in financial position is prepared for each fund used. When these statements are combined for all funds, full disclosure of the financial size of the school district is made. This is the statement that can be compared meaningfully with the statement of changes in financial position of any other business entity. It will allow a comparison of the economic impact of the school system with the economic impact or size of the business entity in terms of dollars for a fiscal year.

Comparisons of combined balance sheets of the school district with balance sheets of business entities also provide information about comparative sizes, but this comparison is as of one day only because the balance sheet presents financial position on one date only. Comparisons of the combined statement of revenue and expenditures of the school district with income statements of business entities provide comparisons of income or revenue and comparisons of expenses or expenditures for a fiscal period, but these are only parts of the financial structure of both entities. Only the combined statement of changes in financial position of all funds provides the overall financial dimensions of a school district.

Complete financial accounting and reporting serves as one of the strongest ways that school districts can keep the public informed about the financial needs of education. Public support is needed as the school board and its administrators strive to provide the highest quality education possible with the financial resources of the school district. The remaining chapters discuss the nature and financial operation of each of the funds and account groups used by elementary and secondary school districts.

WORKING CAPITAL CONCEPT

In commercial enterprises, working capital is extremely important because it measures the ability of a firm to pay its current debts by computing the excess of current assets over current liabilities. A ratio of better than one dollar of current assets to each dollar of current liabilities is a management objective to be achieved consistently. Theoretically, in governmental accounting and financial accounting for school districts, the general fund is working capital because it should have only current assets and current liabilities, as its long-term fixed assets are carried in the general fixed assets account group and its long-term debts are carried in the general long-term debt account group.

Illustration 11.2
New Douglas School District
General Fund
Schedule of Working Capital
June 30, 2008

Current assets:	
Cash	$ 21,000
Temporary investments	18,000
Taxes receivable	242,200
Accounts receivable	22,300
Due from other funds	1,000
Inventory of supplies	500
Total current assets	$305,000
Current liabilities:	
Vouchers payable	$ 50,000
Due to other funds	5,000
Taxes collected in advance	36,000
Total current liabilities	$ 91,000
Working capital	$214,000

A schedule of working capital for any fund can be prepared for management use at any time or at the end of each month and submitted as a supporting schedule to interim and annual financial statements. Illustration 11.2 shows a schedule of working capital. A statement showing changes in working capital is shown in Illustration 11.3.

CASH CONCEPT

Cash presents a serious problem not only to school districts but in commercial enterprises also and that problem is how to have enough cash to pay currently maturing obligations. A schedule of cash receipts and disbursements can be prepared daily or presented as a supporting schedule to interim financial statements. A study of when cash is received from each source during the year, and an analysis of the consistency with which cash is received during certain periods of time during the year from each source, is an excellent cash management procedure. The study can be made by use of schedules of cash receipts and disbursements.

Illustration 11.3
New Douglas School District
General Fund
Statement of Changes in Working Capital
For the year ending June 30, 2008

Working capital:	July 1	Changes Increase Debit	Decrease Credit	June 30
Current assets:				
Cash	$ 4,000	$ 17,000		$ 21,000
Temporary investments	25,000		$ 7,000	18,000
Taxes receivable	40,000	202,200		242,200
Accounts receivable	10,000	12,300		22,300
Due from other funds	20,000		19,000	1,000
Inventory of supplies	1,000		500	500
Total current assets	$100,000			$305,000
Current liabilities:				
Vouchers payable	$ 40,000		10,000	$ 50,000
Due to other funds	10,000	5,000		5,000
Taxes collected in advance	20,000		16,000	36,000
Total current liabilities	$ 70,000			$ 91,000
Working capital	$ 30,000	$ 236,500	$ 52,500	$214,000

Illustration 11.4 shows the format of a schedule of cash receipts and disbursements and bank reconciliation for a fund.

Illustration 11.4
New Douglas School District
General Fund
Schedule of Cash Receipts and Disbursements
For the year ending June 30, 2008

Cash balance, July 1, 2007		$4,000
Add:		
Cash receipts to date		2,811,500
Cash available for use		2,815,500
Less:		
Cash disbursements to date		2,794,500
Cash balance, June 30, 2008		$ 21,000
Reconciliation		
Balance per bank statement		$ 111,467
Add:		
Deposits in transit		52,531
Total		163,998
Less:		
Outstanding checks:		
1096	$100	
1097	112,500	
1099	3,125	
1101	1,812	
1104	25,461	142,998
Cash balance, June 30, 2008		$21,000

SUMMARY

This chapter described the construction of the Statement of Changes in Financial Position and its uses as a communication vehicle. The statement identifies the amount of financial resources available from all sources and indicates how the amount was used. The Statement of Changes in Financial Position basically shows what amount of money it took to operate the school district over the period reported.

ACTIVITIES

1. Identify the statements used by a school district to prepare a Statement of Changes in Financial Position.

2. Discuss the differences between the all financial resources concept, working capital concept and cash concept for preparing a Statement of Changes in Financial Position for a school district.

3. Determine if financial resources have been provided or applied when:

a. A liability account is reduced at the end of a fiscal period to an amount less than it was at the beginning of the period.
b. Expenditures exceed revenue for a fiscal period.
c. Assets are sold for more money than their original cost.
d. The fund balance is increased at the end of a fiscal period as a result of finding that an invoice for $1,400 was paid at $1,500.
e. The fund balance was decreased due to a transfer of accumulated interest to another fund.

4. Comparative balance sheets at the beginning and end of the calendar year for the Fort Steven School District general fund are:

	January 1	December 31	Application	Source
Cash	$22,000	$ 40,000		
Temporary investments	30,000	19,000		
Taxes receivable	35,000	20,000		
Accounts receivable	22,000	19,500		
Due from other funds	12,000	15,000		
Inventory of supplies	800	1,200		
Total	$121,800	$114,700		
Vouchers payable	$ 28,000	$ 31,000		
Due to other funds	15,000	20,000		
Taxes collected in advance	45,000	32,000		
Reserve for encumbrances	20,000	15,000		
Matured bonds payable	10,000	8,000		
Fund balance	3,800	8,700		
Total	$ 121,800	$ 114,700		

Instructions:

- Compute the change in account balances and indicate whether the change provided or applied financial resources by recording the change in the appropriate column.

5. Comparative balance sheets for Michago School District are shown below:

	July 1	June 30
Cash	$ 180,000	$ 2,450,000
Temporary investments	340,000	0
Taxes receivable	900,000	900,000
Accounts receivable	210,000	210,000
Due from other funds	100,000	20,000
Inventory of supplies	35,000	35,000
Total	$ 1,765,000	$ 3,615,000
Vouchers payable	$ 265,000	$ 265,000
Due to other funds	100,000	100,000
Taxes collected in advance	150,000	220,000

Reserve for encumbrance	600,000	600,000
General fund balance	650,000	2,430,000
Total	$ 1,765,000	$ 3,615,000

The following transactions took place during the year:

a.	Collected additional taxes in advance	$ 70,000
b.	Collected revenue from state	4,400,000
c.	Collected state grant-in-aid	3,200,000
d.	Collected taxes from local sources assessed and levied during the year	2,500,000
e.	Collected revenue from federal sources	500,000
b.	Sold temporary investments (at a loss of $90,000)	250,000
g.	Collected revenue from intermediate sources	900,000
h.	Collected on amount due from other funds	80,000
i.	Paid administrative expenses	900,000
j.	Paid for pupil transportation	80,000
k.	Paid instructional salaries	6,500,000
l.	Paid cost of plant operation	1,250,000
m.	Paid fixed charges	300,000
n.	Paid community services costs	350,000
o.	Paid debt service items	250,000

Instructions:

- Prepare a Statement of Changes in Financial Position for the general fund of the district for the year ending June 30.

6. The statement of revenues, expenditures and fund balance for the year ended December 3, 2009 and the comparative balance sheets for January 1, 2009, and December 31, 2009, for Petersburg School System 10 are shown below.

Petersburg School System 10
General Fund
Statement of Revenues, Expenditures and Fund Balance
For the year ended December 31, 2009

Revenues:		
From local sources	$ 800,000	
From state sources	750,000	
From federal sources	50,000	
From other school systems in the state	15,000	
Total Revenues		$1,615,000
Expenditures:		
Administration	$ 75,000	
Instruction	1,215,000	

Health services	4,500	
Transportation services	16,000	
Operation of plant	8,000	
Maintenance of plant	9,500	
Food services	18,500	
Fixed charges	7,500	
Community services	10,000	
Debt service	6,800	
Total Expenditures		$1,370,800
Excess revenues over expenditures		$244,200
Fund Balance, January 1, 2009		15,000
Fund Balance, December 31, 2009		$259,000

Petersburg School System 10
General Fund
Comparative Balance Sheets
2009

Assets	January 1	December 31
Cash	$ 3,500	$ 37,800
Temporary investments	22,500	17,000
Long-term investments	50,000	47,500
Taxes receivable	20,000	300,000
Accounts receivable	8,500	12,100
Due from other funds	1,500	6,000
Inventory of supplies	1,500	300
Total Assets	$107,500	$420,500
Liabilities, Reserves and Fund Equity		
Vouchers payable	$ 25,000	$ 70,000
Due to other funds	15,000	4,500
Taxes collected in advance	34,500	83,300
Total Liabilities	$ 74,500	$157,800
Reserve for encumbrances	$18,000	$ 3,500
Fund balance	$15,000	$259,200
Total Liabilities, Reserves and Fund Balance	$107,500	$420,500

Instructions:

- Prepare a Statement of Changes in Financial Position for the general fund of Petersburg School System 10 for the year ended December 31, 2009, using:

a. All financial resources concept
b. Working capital concept
c. Cash concept

12

Special Revenue Funds

INTRODUCTION

Special revenue funds are used to account for revenue received from a source designated to be used for a specific educational purpose to supplement the basic educational or foundation program.

OUTCOMES

In this chapter, you will learn how to:

1. Create a special revenue fund.
2. Determine uses of a special revenue fund.
3. Use budgetary accounts to record special revenue fund transactions.
4. Prepare financial statements for a special revenue fund.

SPECIAL REVENUE FUND DEFINED

A special revenue fund is used to account for the proceeds of specific revenue sources (other than trusts or major capital projects) that are legally restricted to expenditure for specified purposes. Some examples of special revenue funds are:

- Restricted state or federal grants-in-aid.
- Restricted tax levies.

A separate fund may be used for each identified restricted source, or one fund may be used, supplemented by the classification Project/Reporting code (Johnson 2003, 93).

Special revenue funds may be used at the discretion of the board of education to provide a basis for better managerial control and public understanding. These funds have been found to be particularly useful to school districts when new or different sources of revenue for educational programs are of a temporary nature. Use of a special revenue fund for temporary educational programs can prevent such revenue from being placed in the general fund where it could become commingled or could give a distorted impression of the amount of money that is available for the basic educational program.

Special revenue funds require adoption of a budget by the board of education each year. The funds require use of budgetary accounts that serve special revenue funds in the same way that they serve the general fund. Some accountants hold the concept that any fund can be a special revenue fund if it has special sources of revenue to be used for special or restricted purposes, regardless of whether it is an educational program or a supporting service. These advocates say that a fund, such as a school food services fund, can be either a special revenue fund or an enterprise fund. They maintain that the decision or choice should be based upon the sources and amounts of revenue from each source. For example, if the majority of revenue comes from tax sources at the local, state or federal level, it should be classified as a special revenue fund. If the majority of revenue comes from charges for services rendered, it should be classified as an enterprise fund. Use of either fund type among districts is widespread, but usually once a district decides to use one type, the district seldom changes.

Such a classification technique defeats good financial reporting. Since the ratio of revenue from service charges to revenue from tax sources can be determined only at the end of the fiscal period, interim financial reports may not be consistent with the annual report. Comparing year-to-year operations of the school district is impossible when decisions are made to report a fund as a special revenue fund one year and as an enterprise fund the next. Statistical comparisons among school districts are impossible when such fund shifts are made.

TYPES OF SPECIAL REVENUE FUNDS

There may be any number of special revenue funds, each having a separate, self-balancing general ledger with subsidiary ledgers. Some may be required by statute or ordinance, and others may be established through policies of governmental agencies at the federal, state or local level. Others may be established by resolutions of the board of education for better administration. No fund or account group should be created unless by minutes of a meeting of the board of education. The Governmental Accounting Standards Board (GASB) Statement 1 recommends that the number of funds should be kept to a minimum consistent with legal and operational requirements. Special revenue funds may account for revenue from sources similar to the general fund's sources but they may also receive revenue from other sources that are restricted by the purposes for which expenditures can be made.

Many advantages may accrue to a school district by creating separate special revenue funds under certain circumstances. Although revenue may be from sources similar to those of the general fund, certain kinds of revenue may not be assured in future years. For instance, through federal grants-in-aid, state aid or aid from sources such as foundations, individuals or corporations, money may be provided on a temporary basis to a school district for experimental educational programs. Whether or not the programs will continue to be financed from these sources in the future may not be known and, as a result, it may not be considered a permanent part of the school district's educational program. In such a case, this temporary kind of program is accounted for separately from the on-going basic foundation program. In the event a temporary program proves to be one that will continue to be financed from sources that are relatively certain in the future, such programs may be transferred from special revenue funds to the school district's general fund where they may be considered part of the on-going educational program. When this occurs, the special revenue fund may cease to be needed.

Governmental agencies, foundations, individuals, corporations and others who contribute to special educational programs generally require periodic audits of accounts of the school district to determine that the financial resources are being used for the purpose for which they were provided. Interim and annual financial statements, which divide the revenues and expenditures for the continuing basic educational program from those that are temporary or experimental in nature, are much easier to understand and to control.

GASB identified some of the serious disadvantages of special revenue funds. It warned that if revenues raised through compulsory tax rates for special revenue funds exceed the normal use requirements, the fund may build up a balance, leading to unnecessary expansion of an activity in an effort to spend all of the available income. On the other hand, a low rate of revenue set by law may lead to a deficit in a special revenue fund, and the general fund may have to use its resources for purposes that are designated to be accomplished by the special revenue fund.

Transactions are recorded in a separate general journal or in a separate set of books of original entry designed specifically for use by each special revenue fund. Recording transactions of each special revenue fund in separate books of original entry assists in dividing the work of employees of the school district and avoiding confusion as to the fund to which a certain revenue or a certain expenditure is applicable.

SOURCES OF SPECIAL REVENUE

Special revenue may be provided from local, intermediate, state or federal sources for special programs. Local or intermediate revenue could be provided from a voted in but temporary tax, from tuition charges or fees, from gifts or from other sources. Revenue from these sources may be segregated from the general fund in order to assist administrative officers and the board of education to determine the adequacy of revenue and the limits that must be placed upon expenditures for these programs.

Revenue from state sources may come from direct grants by the state for special programs such as for mentally disabled, orthopedic, speech correction, visiting teacher, driver education or other categorical aid. The state may also provide revenue to a local school district that represents redistribution of federal grants-in-aid for vocational education, homemaking, trades and industry, cooperative training and many others.

Revenue from federal sources may be provided for special programs, which are of a temporary or experimental nature. The grants may be made for programs such as vocational education in agriculture, distributive education, health occupations, home economics, trades and industrial education, manpower development training, welfare education, public health training, vocational rehabilitation and many others. For example, the Elementary and Secondary Education Act (ESEA) provides programs for the educationally disadvantaged, supplementary education and special education. The Improving America's Schools Act reauthorized ESEA for five years. In 2004, the No Child Left Behind Act was signed into law. Federal grants may be made either directly to local school districts or through state departments of education to develop educational programs. Unless the revenues become permanent programs and a part of the foundation program of the school district, it is appropriate to account for these restricted revenues and expenditures through special revenue funds. As emphasis moves to and from areas of special concern, legislation at all levels will be developed to permit focused educational programs. In these cases, particularly if the program is temporary, experimental or uncertain of future financial support, the concept of special revenue funds provides timely and meaningful information for management, boards of education, governmental entities and taxpayer purposes.

Once a special revenue fund is created, it remains in operation until the purpose for which it was created is served or until it is abolished by an act of the board of education.

ACCOUNTS AND TRANSACTIONS

Because revenue of a special revenue fund can arise from public sources, formal budgets are required. When adopted by the board, the budget is recorded in the minutes of the board meeting. Therefore, budgetary accounts for appropriations, estimated revenues, encumbrances, reserve for encumbrances and budgeted fund balance are as effective for management accounting and financial control in special revenue funds as they are in the general fund.

The budgetary accounts compare estimated revenue with actual revenue and, as a result, assist the school district to realize the maximum revenue during the fiscal period from each source that is available to it. They also assist the board in controlling expenditures and encumbrances by requiring administrative officers to keep them within the limits established. Budgetary accounts record estimated revenue both from public sources and from the special sources. Appropriation accounts also are established to control all expenditures of the fund and not merely that portion of revenue raised through the tax levy. Accounting principles and procedures applicable to special revenue funds are identical to those used in financial and managerial accounting for the general fund.

Transactions that occur in the operation of a special revenue fund are similar to those that occur in the operation of a general fund. Budgetary accounts for estimated revenues, appropriations, encumbrances, reserve for encumbrances and budgeted fund balance are used in connection with proprietary accounts for assets, liabilities, fund equity, revenue and expenditures accounts for each special revenue fund.

FINANCIAL STATEMENTS

Reporting the interim and annual financial position and results of operation of each special revenue fund is important to effective administration of a school district. It is the individual special revenue fund that is most important for financial control and financial management purposes.

Illustration 12.1
Kimberly Hills School District
Special Revenue Fund
Comparative Balance Sheets
Assets July 1, 2008–June 30, 2009

Assets	July 1, 2008	June 30, 2009
Imprest cash fund	$1,000	$999
Cash in banks:		
First National Bank	167,187	43,034
Superior National Bank	83,130	88,772
Accounts receivable		38,413
Taxes receivable	47,909	42,283
Inventories	17,958	13,440
Prepaid insurance	2,293	1,994
Total Assets	$319,477	$228,935
Liabilities and fund balance		
Current and short-term loans	$210,000	$114,000
Accounts payable	1,556	2,083
Salaries payable	85,761	95,653
Accrued expenses payable		4,650
Total liabilities	$297,317	$216,386
Fund balance	22,160	12,549
Total liabilities and fund balance	$319,477	$228,935

Interim and annual financial statements for each special revenue fund include the balance sheet, the statement comparing estimated with actual revenue, the statement comparing expenditures and encumbrances with appropriations, the statement of changes in fund equity and the statement of changes in financial position.

The format for each financial statement for a special revenue fund is identical to the format of the financial statements used by the general fund. Interim financial statements, which compare estimated with actual revenues by source and which compare expenditures and encumbrances with appropriations by organizational unit and object are the most effective, efficient and economical ways to classify financial statements. Financial responsibility can be best placed and internal accounting and financial controls can be most effective when expenditures are classified by organizational unit and by object. Expenditures can be classified in many more ways if financial resources are available to permit it. Among additional ways that expenditures can be classified are by location, grade level, subject matter or program. Illustration 12.1 shows comparative balance sheets for a special revenue fund.

Illustration 12.2
Kimberly Hills School District
Special Revenue Fund
Statement of Revenues, Expenditures and Fund Balance
For the year ended June 30, 2009

Fund Balance, July 1, 2008		$ 22,160
Revenues:		
From local sources	$ 493,494	
From state sources	776,110	
From federal sources	102,375	
From gifts and bequests	260	
From other school districts in the state	68,754	
Total Revenues		$ 1,440,993
Expenditures:		
Instruction	$ 1,077,928	
Administration	49,378	
Attendance and health services	23,443	
Operation of plant	187,094	
Maintenance of plant	82,249	
Fixed charges	20,897	
Capital outlay	8,346	
Student services	1,267	
Total Expenditures		$ 1,450,602
Excess revenues over expenditures		$ (9,609)
Fund Balance, June 30, 2009		$ 12,551

A different kind of problem in financial reporting occurs when combining financial statements for all special revenue funds are prepared to present a comprehensive annual financial report for all funds and account groups used in financial administration of the school district. Individual special revenue funds require a separate set of books of original entry, a general ledger, subsidiary ledgers, adequate competent business papers (which provide evidence of financial transactions), and interim and annu-

Illustration 12.3
Special Revenue Fund
Statement of Changes in Financial Position
For the year ended June 30, 2009

Resources provided:		
From revenues:		
Local sources	$ 493,494	
State sources	776,110	
Federal sources	102,375	
Gifts and bequests	260	
Other school districts in the state	68,754	$ 1,440,993
From reduction in assets:		
Cash:		
Imprest cash fund	$ 27	
General fund	122,153	
Taxes receivable	5,624	
Inventories	4,517	
Prepaid insurance	298	$ 132,619
From increasing liabilities:		
Accounts payable	$ 504	
Salaries payable	9,891	
Accrued expenses	4,650	$ 15,045
Total resources provided		$1,588,657
Resources applied:		
To expenditures of school district:		
Instruction	$ 1,077,928	
Administration	49,378	
Attendance and health services	23,443	
Operation of plant	187,094	
Maintenance of plant	82,249	
Fixed charges	20,897	
Capital outlay	8,346	
Student services	1,267	$1,450,602
To increase assets:		
Increase in cash	$ 5,641	
Accounts receivable	36,410	$ 42,051
To reduction in liabilities:		
Reduction in amount due on loan		$ 96,004
Total resources applied		$1,588,657

al financial statements for effective financial administration and control. The technique effectively combines financial statements for all of the special revenue funds into one set composed of a combining balance sheet, a combining statement of revenue, expenditures and fund equity, and a statement of changes in fund balances. Users of financial statements for individual special revenue funds focus attention on the fact that combined statements without supporting financial statements for each special revenue fund can be misleading and create problems in the mind of the board and the general public about the status and management of the special revenue funds.

Illustration 12.2 shows a statement of revenues, expenditures and fund balance for a special revenue fund.

Illustration 12.3 shows a statement of changes in financial position for a special revenue fund. Additional illustrations of combined financial statements for the consolidated annual financial report can be found on ASBO International's website.

SUMMARY

A special revenue fund is created when a school district receives revenue from a special source designated to be used for a specific educational purpose that supplements the basic educational or foundation program. Special revenue funds may be used at the discretion of the board of education to provide a basis for better managerial control and public understanding. The budgetary accounts compare estimated revenue with actual revenue. Budgetary accounts compare estimated revenue with actual revenue.

ACTIVITIES

1. Review the definition of the following terms found in the glossary:

    a. Special revenue fund
    b. Enterprise fund
    c. Proprietary account
    d. Budgetary account
    e. Agency fund

2. Carefully study and review special revenue fund statements obtained from an annual audit report on a school district's website.

3. Fort Steven School District created a special revenue fund in order to account for revenues and expenditures associated with a vocational education project. The following transactions occurred:

    a. The budget adopted for the 2008–09 school year was as follows:

Estimated revenue—income taxes	$ 600,000
Estimated revenue—tuition	150,000
Estimated revenue—federal sources	1,200,000
Appropriations:	
Salaries	$1,100,000
Employee benefits	200,000
Materials and supplies	500,000

b. The 2008–09 school year encumbrances were closed into the special revenue fund's equity, leaving a reserve for encumbrances in the amount of $10,000. Commitments had been issued for supplies and materials.
c. The Fort Steven School District used an agency fund for collection of all taxes and an agency fund for central payroll.
d. Employee contracts in the amount of $1,100,000 were signed with a corresponding estimate of employee benefits amounting to $200,000.
e. The Department of Education formally approved the project in the amount of $1,200,000.
f. Student registration and cash tuition for the project realized $140,000.
g. First quarter income tax distribution to the district produced $150,000.
h. Payroll vouchers received from the central payroll fund billed the special revenue fund for $180,000 salaries and $21,000 employee benefits. A check in the amount of $201,000 was issued to the central payroll fund.
i. The tax collection agency fund remitted $150,000 to the special revenue fund (representing collections from (g).
j. Issued purchase orders for materials and supplies in the amount of $480,000.
k. Received the materials and supplies in (j) invoiced at $490,000. Checks were issued in the amount of $225,000 representing partial payment of the invoices for (j).

Instructions:

- Record the transactions in general journal form.

4. Michago School Corporation 2 Special Revenue Fund had the following accounts and balances on July 1, 2009:

2–101 Cash	$24,000
2–111 Investments	18,500
2–402 Accounts payable	2,200
2–730 Special revenue fund balance	43,300

During the year, the following transactions occurred:

a. The board of education adopted the following budget:

2–1100	Revenue from local sources—taxes	$200,000
2–1910	Revenue from local sources—rentals	4,000
2–3000	Revenue from state sources—grants in aid	80,000
2–4000	Revenue from federal sources—grants in aid	60,000
Appropriations		
2–1200	Special programs	85,000
2–1300	Adult/continuing education programs	26,000
2–2100	Support services—pupils	15,000
2–2120	Support services—guidance	12,000
2–2200	Support services—instructional staff	2,000

2–2220	Support services—instructional media	30,000
2–2320	General administration	20,000
2–2350	Facilities acquisition	28,000
2–2370	Food services	7,500
2–2384	Central support services	13,800
2–2390	Information services	5,000
2–2410	Operation of plant	18,800

b. The board of education authorized the sale of investments, and the investments were sold for $18,500.
c. Teacher's contracts were approved for special programs, $83,000, and for adult/continuing education, $24,000.
d. The special revenue fund received an invoice from operations and maintenance fund for $18,000, representing its share of costs for the year.
e. Received the state grant-in-aid in the amount of $82,000.
f. Cash was collected from rentals in the amount of $4,200.
g. The federal grant-in-aid was received for $43,500.
h. Taxes had been assessed and levied for the school corporation resulting in the special revenue fund's share amounting to $122,000.
i. Prior to the start of the school year, a special programs teacher resigned who previously had signed a contract with the district for $31,500.
j. During the year, vouchers were paid as follows:

	Expenditure	Encumbered
Special programs	$ 70,300	$70,000
Adult/continuing education programs	24,000	22,000
Support programs:		
Pupils	13,200	
Guidance	12,000	
Instructional staff	500	
Instructional media	31,200	
General administration	17,400	
Facilities acquisition	20,000	
Food services	4,000	
Central support services	11,000	
Information services	2,400	
Operation of plant	2,200	
	$208,200	$92,000

k. Collected $121,000 from the central tax collection agency fund.
l. Paid $222,000 on accounts payable.

Instructions:

- Record the account balances as of July 1, 2008, in general ledger accounts.
- Record transactions during the year in general journal form using general ledger accounts.
- Post to the general ledger.
- Prepare a trial balance as of June 30, 2009.

- Prepare a pre-closing balance sheet.
- Prepare supporting schedules of the revenue and expenditures ledgers for the balance sheet above.
- Record closing entries in general journal form for both the general ledger accounts.
- Post closing entries to the general ledger accounts.
- Prepare a post-closing trial balance.

13

Capital Projects Funds

INTRODUCTION

Changing demographics mean school districts are faced with the problem of securing the money necessary to acquire sites, construct facilities, equip facilities, repair and/or remodel facilities. Expenditures for these purposes are classified as capital outlay expenditures or capital projects fund expenditures.

If revenue of the general fund is adequate each year to meet the constantly changing needs for fixed assets, accounting for their acquisition could be handled through the capital outlay expenditure accounts in the general fund or in special revenue funds. Frequently this is not possible and other methods of financing have to be found. Capital projects funds are created to account for acquisition, construction or for major remodeling of fixed assets when not provided for in the general fund, special revenue funds, internal services funds or enterprise funds.

Capital projects funds are used to account for revenue from a bond issue or from other sources designated for capital outlay purposes. Capital projects fund revenue is provided by issuing bonds. Bonds may also be issued for other capital project fund purposes such as eliminating a deficit resulting from operation of the general fund, a special revenue fund, an internal services fund, an enterprise fund or refinancing, retiring or refunding maturing bond issues. Grants received from gifts or from other units of government at the local, state, province or federal level also provide major sources of revenue designated for capital projects of school districts.

OUTCOMES

In this chapter, you will learn how to:

0. Determine why school districts may issue bonds.
0. Properly use bond proceeds.
0. Differentiate between bond premium and bond discount.
0. Use budgetary accounts to record capital projects fund transactions.

TYPES OF BONDS

A bond, frequently referred to as a debenture, is a written promise to pay a certain amount of money at a fixed or determinable future date. The bond may be issued by a school district or the governmental unit under which the school district operates as evidence of debt and usually indicates a specific rate of interest payable on certain dates. A note is a form of a bond that is issued for a short period of time, while a bond is issued for a longer period of time. Investors find bonds issued by public school districts to be an attractive investment because income earned from the bonds is usually exempt from federal income tax and may be exempt from local and state income taxes as well.

In the past, bonds may have been issued as coupon bonds, registered bonds or a combination of both. A coupon bond had coupons attached, each indicating the amount of interest and the date on which interest is payable. On or within a reasonable time subsequent to the interest payment date, the bondholder presented the coupons to the school district or to its fiscal agent, and the interest was paid. Federal legislation has now required all municipal bonds to be registered. Ownership of every long-term, tax-exempt security issued now must be a matter of record. Today, a bond may be registered as to principal or interest or both. Registered bonds have no coupons attached. Instead, the name of the owner is registered on the books of the school district or its fiscal agent. On interest payment dates, interest checks are issued to the owners of record, and when the bond's maturity date arrives, checks for the maturity value of the bonds are issued to owners of record in exchange for the matured bonds.

The activities related to recording the liability as a result of issuing general long-term debt instruments are handled through the general long-term debt account group, while activities related to payment of interest and principal are handled through the debt service fund and/or the general fund.

SOURCES OF CAPITAL

The power to issue bonds may be vested in the school board or in the governmental unit under which the school district operates. If bonds are issued by the governmental entity over the school district, the proceeds of the issue may be transferred to the board of education for proper administration. If the board has the power and authority to issue its own bonds, all procedures necessary for securing proper authorization under the laws as well as those related to selling the bonds are the responsibility of the board of education. Under either procedure, the board of education is charged with the responsibility of accounting for the expenditure of proceeds in accordance with the purpose for which the capital projects fund was created.

Bonding power of the board or the governmental unit through which bonds are issued is restricted by law, and a favorable referendum vote is usually required before bonds can be issued. The purposes for which proceeds of a bond issue are to be used is information voters should have before they vote for or against a bond issue. As a result, the board is under an obligation to use the proceeds of a bond issue only for those purposes specified. There have been instances where money raised through bond issues intended to acquire fixed assets was used to pay current operating expenses. Whether intentional or unintentional on the part of the administrative officers who permitted such expenditures, or whether done with or without the knowledge of the governing board, the fact remains that the money was used for a purpose other than that for which it was raised.

Business operations of a school district that permit such a thing to happen destroy the confidence of the voters and taxpayers in the board and its administrative officers. This can be avoided by full disclosure of financial facts and by use of financial accounting principles and reporting procedures applicable to capital projects funds, segregating them from the general fund.

The Governmental Accounting Standards Board, American Institute of Certified Public Accountants, the National Center for Education Statistics and the Association of School Business Officials International recommend that a separate group of self-balancing accounts be maintained for each capital project. Differences in each bond issue's proceeds, interest rate, interest payment dates, maturity dates and in the purposes for which revenue may be used make it desirable to use separate and independent funds for each major capital project.

ACCOUNTS AND TRANSACTIONS

When a bond issue is authorized to be sold, an account entitled Bonds Authorized and Unissued is debited and appropriation is credited. Both are budgetary accounts. The difference between these amounts is applied to the budgeted fund balance account or to the capital projects unappropriated fund equity account. The bonds authorized and unissued account serves the same purpose for a capital projects fund as the estimated revenue account serves for the general fund. It is debited for the face value of the bonds. Although this is not an asset of the fund, it is a financial resource through which money is obtained. For that reason, the bonds authorized and unissued account is reported on the assets and resources side of interim and annual balance sheets.

Proceeds from a bond issue provide revenue to the capital projects fund because the capital projects fund does not assume the liability for retirement of the bonds or for the payment of interest on bonds outstanding. Once bonds are issued, the long-term liability is recorded in and reported by the general long-term debt account group as long as the bonds are outstanding. The responsibility for bond interest payment and bond principal retirement at maturity is placed upon a debt service fund and/or the general fund.

Authority to expend the proceeds of a bond issue is granted by the board of education when all procedures required by law have been fulfilled. Procedures necessary for issuing bonds and for securing other sources of revenue needed for a capital projects fund are initiated by the school board. If approval of the voters is required, a proposal setting forth the terms of the bond issue and the purposes for which the bond proceeds are to be used is presented to the voters as required by law. If approval of a governmental unit under which the school district operates is required, all procedures prescribed by that governmental unit must be completed. Therefore, budgetary accounts for both revenue and expenditures are as helpful to the board and to management during the life of a capital projects fund as they are to the general fund because large sums of money are required for capital projects and the life of a capital projects fund often extends over a number of years. Controlling accounts in the general ledger accounts for capital projects funds use the same format as previously used.

The amount of revenue that can be raised by a bond issue and from all other sources for specified capital projects is limited. To assist management in realizing all revenue that is available to a capital projects fund, budgetary accounting for revenue is as important as in the general fund. Therefore, estimated revenue and actual revenue accounts are used in each capital projects fund.

Authority granted by the board of education to administrative officers to make expenditures in a capital projects fund is an appropriation, just as it is in the general fund. As a result, budgetary accounts are established in capital projects funds to control expenditures and they serve the same purposes for capital projects funds as they serve for the general fund. Expenditure controls are provided by general ledger accounts for appropriations, encumbrances and the reserve for encumbrances.

Because of the amount of money involved, the number of contracts issued, the number of revisions made in contracts during the life of a capital projects fund and the length of time required to complete a capital project, it is as important to a school district that it have as effective control over expenditures for each capital projects fund as it is to have control over expenditures of the general fund. Budgetary control over expenditures is effectively gained in capital projects funds by using the expenditure account format from previous chapters in the general ledger .

These expenditure accounts are used as a basis for interim financial reporting during the life of each capital project fund. The budgetary expenditure accounts in the general ledger serve effectively to prevent expenditures and encumbrances from being made in excess of the appropriation for each object. The accounts of a capital projects fund operate on a basis similar to accounts in the general fund; however, there are some major differences. In fact, all revenue needed for a capital project is usually authorized before a capital projects fund is created, not on an annual or fiscal year basis as it is in the case of the general fund. Furthermore, appropriations that authorize expenditures in a capital projects fund do not lapse at the end of a year or fiscal period as they do in the case of the general fund.

Although many accountants continue to close all capital projects funds' revenue and expenditure accounts at the end of each year or fiscal period, a need for year-end closing entries in capital projects funds does not exist. All capital projects fund accounts, budgetary and proprietary, are kept open until the purposes for which the capital projects fund was created have been accomplished. The revenue accounts continue accumulating total revenue that is provided for a capital project and expenditure accounts continue to accumulate total costs until the project is completed. After all bonds have been issued and revenue from all other sources has been expended for the purposes authorized, the capital projects fund accounts are closed. The capital projects fund serves no further purpose other than to provide a record of what happened to the money.

The liability created by the bond issue is recorded and reported, as long as the bonds are outstanding, as a part of another group of accounts known as the general long-term debt account group. Because a capital projects fund is not responsible for retirement of the principal of bonds issued for capital projects purposes and for interest on them, a debt service fund is created when the bonds are issued to serve these purposes for the school system. A debt service fund is created for each bond issue.

General fixed assets acquired as a result of expenditures in capital projects funds are recorded and reported as a part of another separate self-balancing group of accounts known as the general fixed assets account group. As construction expenditures and/or other costs are incurred in the long period of time required for completing the capital project, construction-in-progress accounts may be recorded in the general fixed asset account group. If, on the other hand, a capital projects fund is created to acquire fixed assets for an enterprise fund or an internal service fund, the fixed assets become a part of the enterprise fund or the internal service fund where they are recorded as assets of these funds and not as assets in the general fixed assets account group. However, these fixed assets are reported in footnotes to the financial statements of the general fixed assets account group. Because internal services funds and enterprise funds can record long-term liabilities along with fixed assets, it is infrequent that capital projects funds would be used to acquire fixed assets for these special purpose funds.

In the event all assets of a capital projects fund are not used or needed to complete the capital projects, the remaining assets, by direction of the board of education in accordance with the bond indenture, may be transferred either to the general fund or to the debt service fund created to accumulate resources in amounts sufficient to retire the bonds that were issued to finance the capital projects at the maturity date of the bond issue.

The following entries illustrate typical capital projects fund transactions. When all legal procedures have been completed and $50,000 of bonds have been authorized to be issued by the Kimberly Hills School District, the following entry is made in the general journal of the capital projects fund:

Bonds authorized and unissued	$50,000	
Appropriations, capital improvements		$50,000
To record authorization to issue capital projects fund bonds		

As bonds are issued by the school system or the governmental unit under which the school district operates, the following entry is made:

Cash or due from other governmental unit	$50,000	
Revenue from bonds issued		$50,000
To record sale of bonds		

When the other governmental unit, if used, deposits the cash in the capital projects fund, the following entry is made:

Cash	$50,000	
Due from other governmental unit		$50,000
To record collection of cash from other governmental unit		

The cash now on hand can be used for the purposes designated. At this point, assume that the money is to be used for certain improvements. When a portion of the improvements are completed and payment amounting to $20,000 is approved, the following entry is made:

Expenditures, capital improvements	$20,000	
Accounts payable		$20,000
To record expenditures for improvements		

When purchase orders or other forms of financial commitment are issued for certain authorized improvements costing $20,000, the following entry is made:

Encumbrances, capital improvements	$20,000	
Reserve for encumbrances		$20,000
To record estimated cost of authorized improvements		

When authorized improvements have been completed and a final $21,000 contract price determined, the following two entries are made:

Reserve for encumbrances	$20,000	
Encumbrances, capital improvements		$20,000
To reverse encumbrances entry		

Expenditures, capital improvements	$21,000	
Accounts payable		$21,000
To record expenditures for authorized improvements		

Assuming that additional purchase orders and commitments are issued for authorized improvements in the amount of $8,000, the following entry is recorded:

Encumbrances, capital improvements	$8,000	
Reserve for encumbrances		$8,000
To record the estimated cost of authorized improvements		

The entry to record payment on accounts payable is recorded as follows:

Accounts payable	$15,000	
Cash		$15,000
To record payment of account		

Illustration 13.1 shows a trial balance of the capital projects fund prepared at this point:

Illustration 13.1
Kimberly Hills School District
Capital Projects Fund
Trial Balance
(Date)

Cash	$35,000	
Accounts payable		$26,000
Reserve for encumbrances		8,000
Bonds authorized and unissued	50,000	
Appropriations, capital improvements		50,000
Revenue from bonds issued		50,000
Expenditures, capital improvements	41,000	
Encumbrances, capital improvements	8,000	
Total	$134,000	$134,000

Assume that the capital projects fund makes a $7,600 expenditure for improvements, which were originally estimated to cost $8,000. The two following entries are made:

Reserve for encumbrances	$8,000	
Encumbrances, capital improvements		$8,000
To reverse the encumbrances entry		
Expenditures, capital improvements	$7,600	
Accounts payable		$7,600
To record the expenditure for authorized improvements		

When all accounts payable are paid, the following entry is made:

Accounts payable	$33,600	
Cash		$33,600
To record payment of accounts payable		

At this point, assume that all authorized improvements have been completed. Illustration 13.2 shows a trial balance of the accounts.

When the purpose for which the capital projects fund was created has been served the accounts of the fund are closed. The following entries close the appropriation and expenditures accounts:

Appropriations, capital improvements	$50,000	
Expenditures, capital improvements		$48,600

Revenue and expenditure summary		1,400
To close the expenditures and appropriation accounts		

Revenue and expenditure summary	$1,400	
Capital projects fund equity		$1,400
To close the revenue and expenditure summary account		

Illustration 13.2
Kimberly Hills School District
Capital Projects Fund
Trial Balance
(Date)

Cash	$ 1,400	
Expenditures, capital improvements	48,600	
Appropriations, capital improvements		$50,000
Total	$50,000	$50,000

The capital projects fund has a remaining cash balance of $1,400. The amount of cash represents the excess amount of bonds issued over the actual cost of authorized improvements. Reference to the trust agreement may provide a number of ways by which the board may make disposition of the remaining cash balance. Some may advocate transfer of the balance to the general fund. However, the expenditure of the cash by the general fund for purposes other than those authorized when bonds were issued would not be in accordance with the purposes for which the bonds were issued. Therefore, in this case, the board would probably direct that the cash be transferred to the debt service fund created for the purpose of accumulating sufficient cash to retire the bond issue when it matures. The entry to record the transfer of the remaining cash balance to the debt service fund appears as follows:

Capital projects fund equity	$1,400	
Due to debt service fund		$1,400
To record authority to transfer the remaining cash to the debt service fund, leaving an audit trail to indicate what happened to the remaining cash balance in the fund		
Due to debt service fund	$1,400	
Cash		$1,400
To record transfer of cash to the debt service fund		

When the cash balance is transferred to the debt service fund, the capital projects fund accounts are closed; the fund having served completely the purpose for which it was created.

A separate capital projects fund should be created for each capital project to provide financial management control of each capital project. A capital project may be to achieve one purpose such as acquisition of land or for construction of a building. Or a capital project may include a combination of objectives such as the acquisition of land, the construction of one or more buildings, the purchase of machinery and equipment, the remodeling, expansion or renovation of certain other fixed assets, the absorption of a fund deficit and/or the retirement of bonds payable. Each capital projects fund should have its own separate, self-balancing set of accounts.

Revenue accounts for both budgeted revenue and actual revenue from each revenue source would be maintained in the general ledger. It is necessary that adequate standards of budgetary accounting control for each source of revenue be maintained in each capital projects fund. For authorized expenditures of a capital projects fund appropriation, expenditure and encumbrance accounts for each object may be maintained in the general ledger. The reserve for encumbrances account is maintained in the general ledger. It is essential for each capital projects fund to have adequate standards of budgetary accounting control for each expenditure object.

FINANCIAL STATEMENTS

From the trial balance, all financial statements of capital projects funds can be prepared. As budgetary and actual revenue and expenditure accounts of each capital projects fund are not closed until the capital project is completed, interim financial statements are prepared for each fund. These interim financial statements—prepared for management purposes—are the balance sheet, statement comparing estimated and actual revenue, statement of expenditures and encumbrances compared with appropriations, statement of changes in fund equity and statement of changes in financial position. Because significant financial resources are provided for school districts through revenue accounts in capital projects funds and because material financial resources are applied through expenditure accounts of capital projects funds, the financial magnitude of a school district is not disclosed fully unless the financial statements for capital projects funds include a statement of changes in financial position. The problem of combining financial statements of all capital projects funds is similar to the problem of combining financial statements for special revenue funds.

If bonds are issued in a capital projects fund to eliminate a deficit of a fund, when money is transferred from the capital projects fund to a fund having a deficit, the following entry is made:

Transfers to _____ fund	XXX	
Due to ____fund		XXX
To record the expenditure to transfer money to absorb a deficit in the _____ fund		

Due to the _____ fund	XXX	
Cash		XXX
To record transfer of cash to the _____ fund		

When money in a capital projects fund is to be used in a debt service fund for the purpose of retiring matured bonds payable, the following entry is made:

Transfers to debt service fund	XXX	
Due to debt service fund		XXX
To record expenditure to transfer amount to the debt service fund to retire bonds		

Due to debit service fund	XXX	
Cash		XXX
To record transfer of cash to the debt service fund		

Transfer of money generated by revenue of a capital projects fund created for these purposes is recorded through a fund balance account such as "transfer to the general fund" to distinguish it from an expenditure account. When fund equity is no longer needed, a transfer is recorded by a debit to a fund equity account of the transferring fund as no additional expenditures are required for the purpose for which the fund was created. The recipient fund records the transfer by crediting a fund equity account such as "transfer from capital projects fund" to distinguish it from a revenue account as no additional revenue is generated for the school district by the transaction.

A bond premium exists when a bond issue is sold at a price in excess of the principal amount of the bonds. If a bond issue does produce a premium, the question arises as to its proper disposition because the money cannot be used as an additional expenditure in excess of the appropriation for the capital project. In all probability, the board of education would direct that the premium be transferred to the debt service fund charged with the responsibility of paying the principal and/or interest on the bonds issued to finance the capital projects fund.

A bond discount exists when a bond issue is sold at a price less than that of the principal amount of the bonds. In many instances, the sale of bonds at a discount is prohibited. However, in the event a bond issue does produce a discount, the facts of the case should be fully disclosed as shown in the following illustration. Assume that bonds are authorized in the amount of $100,000,000, and that the entire amount is to be used for the purchase of land. The entries to create the capital projects fund and to record their issue are as follows:

	Debit	Credit
Bonds authorized and unissued	$100,000,000	
Appropriations, land		$100,000,000
To record authorization to issue capital projects fund bonds for purchase of land		

	Debit	Credit
Cash	$98,800,000	
Appropriations, land	1,200,000	
Revenue from bonds issued		$100,000,000
To record the sale of bonds at a discount		

Illustration 13.3 shows the general ledger after posting these transactions. Observe that the appropriation is reduced to the amount of cash that is available for use.

Illustration 13.3

Cash

Date	P.R.	Amount	Date	P.R.	Amount
8		$98,800,000			

Revenue from Bonds Issued

			Bonds Auth & Issued		Rev from Bonds		Unrealized
Date	Explanation	P.R.	Debit	Credit	Debit	Credit	Revenue
3			$100,000,000				$100,000,000
8						$100,000,000	0

Expenditures: Land

Date	Explanation	P.R.	Encumbrances	Expenditures	Appropriation	Balance
3					$100,000,000	$100,000,000
				$1,200,000	$98,800,000	0

Not identified as a discount on bonds payable in the capital projects fund, the only accounting disclosure that the discount caused a reduction in the appropriation is the general journal entry. Therefore, for management to be informed through accounting reports and statements what did happen, it would be a sound business practice for the board of education to provide a budgeted fund balance at the time of appropriating money for capital project expenditures. The examples following Illustration 13.3 show how the facts may be fully disclosed. Observe that $1,200,000 remains in the budgeted fund balance account and may be appropriated by action of the board to cover future but presently unknown and unanticipated costs. This procedure does not authorize expenditures in excess of appropriations for purposes contained in the budget.

Example 1

Assume a bond issue is authorized for $100,000,000 and that the board appropriates $98,800,000 for capital projects expenditures:

Bonds authorized and unissued	$100,000,000	
Appropriations, building		$98,800,000
Budgeted fund balance		1,200,000
To record capital project budget		

Example 2

Assume that the bonds could be sold at $99,000,000. Prior to issuing the bonds, the board would authorize an additional appropriation of $1,000,000 to acknowledge that the discount on bonds issued is a part of the cost of the capital project:

Budgeted fund balance	$1,000,000	
Appropriation, discount on bonds issued		$1,000,000
To record approval to issue bonds at a discount		

Example 3

Assume that the bonds did sell for $99,000,000:

Cash	$99,000,000	
Expenditures, discount on bonds issued	1,000,000	
Revenue from bonds issued		$100,000,000
To record the sale of bonds at a discount		

A most effective management accounting technique can be used which includes accounts to record a provision in all capital projects fund construction contracts to withhold a stated percentage or stated amount of the total contract price for a reasonable period of time at the conclusion of each project to permit the school district to conduct a thorough and complete inspection of the project and to satisfy itself that the provisions of the contract have been satisfactorily completed. Inspection is usually a service of the architect, who notifies the contractors of unacceptable conditions in the project, if any. Upon correction of these conditions, the architect issues a certificate of satisfactory completion to the school district, which it uses as the basis for releasing the retained percentage to the contractors. The amount to be retained should be sufficient to encourage the contractor to correct all items identified by the architect at the earliest possible date. In this way, school systems can expedite early, total completion of capital projects.

An illustration of entries to record use of the contracts payable retained percentage accounting procedure is contained in the entries that follow. Typical of the use of capital projects funds is that of a state that permits a capital projects fund (identified as a building fund), to receive cash from the sale of bonds. In addition, this fund may receive revenue from a county school tax levy, state income tax distributions and revenue from other sources. If there is a balance left in the building fund after the building project has been completed and all claims against the building fund have been paid, the balance may be, according to the state's law, transferred to a fund established for the purpose of paying indebtedness incurred in the building project. If no indebtedness has been incurred, the unused balance in the building fund may be transferred to the general fund. Although the fund may be referred to as a building fund, it is accounted for through the use of principles of accounting applicable to capital projects funds.

In this particular case, expenditures authorized from this fund are land, buildings, new furniture and equipment, other building expenditures and transfers to other funds. Under the heading of new furniture and equipment, provisions are made for library books, office furniture and equipment, instructional furniture and equipment, engineers' and janitors' equipment, cafeteria and lunchroom equipment and transportation equipment. Because money for capital outlay also may be raised from sources other than bonds, this case illustrates that expenditures for a capital outlay project are controlled through one fund. The name by which a capital projects fund may be identified may vary but underlying principles of accounting remain the same.

Example 4

Assume that authorization had been granted to issue $500,000 of 5 percent bonds maturing in five years; a project had been approved by the state government to assist in construction in the amount of $300,000; and the project had been approved for a grant of $1,200,000 from the federal government. The governing board authorized creation of a capital projects fund for this project, designated as project number 93:

Step 1: A capital project fund for the Kimberly Hills School District is created by the following entry:

Bonds authorized and unissued	$500,000	
Estimated revenue from state sources	300,000	
Estimated revenue from federal sources	1,200,000	
Appropriations		$2,000,000
To record creation of capital projects fund		

Budget made appropriations as follows:

Land	$ 50,000
Building	1,650,000
Equipment	300,000
	$2,000,000

Step 2: Subsidiary appropriation and expenditure ledger accounts would be created to avoid the possibility of over-expenditure of resources available for the project:

Cash	$500,000	
Revenue from bonds issued		$500,000
To record issuance of 5-year bonds at face value, 5 percent		

At the time the bonds are issued, the school system becomes liable for both the principal and interest on indebtedness. As a result, a debt service fund is created to accumulate resources sufficient to pay interest throughout the life of the bonds and the principal at the maturity date of the bonds. Corresponding entries are made in the general long-term debt account group to record the long-term bonds payable. These entries will be illustrated in the following chapter and in the chapter on the general long-term debt account group.

Step 3: When the project is approved and the board authorizes notification of other governmental agencies of its claims, the following entry is made:

Due from state government	$ 300,000	
Due from federal government	1,200,000	
Revenue from state sources		$ 300,000
Revenue from federal sources		1,200,000
To record notification of state and federal agencies that the project is underway and that a claim is filed for each unit's share of its cost		

Cash	$300,000	
Due from state government		$300,000
To record collection of claim against the state government		

Cash	$1,200,000	
Due from federal government		$1,200,000
To record collection of claim against the federal government		

Encumbrances	$1,800,000	
Reserve for encumbrances		$1,800,000
To record issuance of purchase orders, signing of contracts for construction and other documents of commitment for:		
Land	$ 50,000	
Buildings	1,450,000	
Equipment	300,000	
	$1,800,000	

Account / Explanation	Debit	Credit
Expenditures	$195,000	
Cash		$195,000
To record expenditures for building materials not previously encumbered		
Reserve for encumbrances	$50,000	
Encumbrances		$50,000
To reverse original encumbrance		
Expenditures	$50,000	
Cash		$50,000
To record expenditure for project		
Reserve for encumbrances	$300,000	
Encumbrances		$300,000
To record reversal of original encumbrances		
Expenditures	$300,000	
Cash		$300,000
To record expenditure for equipment		
Reserve for encumbrances	$1,450,000	
Encumbrances		$1,450,000
To reverse original encumbrance for building construction		
Expenditures	$1,448,000	
Contracts payable		$1,448,000
To record expenditure for completion of building contract		
Contracts payable	$1,448,000	
Cash		$1,348,000
Contracts payable, retained percentage		100,000
To record payment of contract less amount to be retained until formal acceptance of building		
Contracts payable	$100,000	
Cash		$100,000
To record payment of retained percentage upon completion and acceptance of building		

Step 4: The general ledger, balance sheet and revenue accounts would appear as follows:

Cash

Date	P.R.	Amount	Date	P.R.	Amount
2		$500,000	7		$195,000
4		400,000	8		50,000
5		1,200,000	9		300,000
			10		1,348,000
			12		100,000

Due from State Government

Date	P.R.	Amount	Date	P.R.	Amount
3		$300,000	4		$300,000

Due from Federal Government

Date	P.R.	Amount	Date	P.R.	Amount
3		$1,200,000	4		$1,200,000

Contracts Payable

Date	P.R.	Amount	Date	P.R.	Amount
11		$1,448,000	10		$1,448,000

Contracts Payable, Retained Percentage

Date	P.R.	Amount	Date	P.R.	Amount
12		$100,000	10		$100,000

Reserve for Encumbrances

Date	P.R.	Amount	Date	P.R.	Amount
8		$50,000	6		$1,800,000
9		300,000			
10		1,450,000			

Revenue from Bonds Issued

			Bonds Auth & Issued		Rev Bonds Issued		Unrealized
Date	Explanation	P.R.	Debit	Credit	Debit	Credit	Revenue
		1	$500,000				$500,000
		2				$500,000	0

Revenue from State Sources

			Bonds Auth & Issued		Rev Bonds Issued		Unrealized
Date	Explanation	P.R.	Debit	Credit	Debit	Credit	Revenue
		1	$300,000				$300,000
		3				$300,000	0

Revenue from Federal Sources

			Bonds Auth & Issued		Rev Bonds Issued		Unrealized
Date	Explanation	P.R.	Debit	Credit	Debit	Credit	Revenue
		1	$1,200,000				$1,200,000
		3				$1,200,000	

Step 5: The expenditures accounts in the general ledger would appear as follows:

Expenditure: Land

P.R.	Explanation	Appropriations	Expenditures	Encumbrances	Unencumbered Balance
1		$50,000			$ 50,000
6				$50,000	0
8			$50,000	50,000	0

Expenditure: Building

P.R.	Explanation	Appropriations	Expenditures	Encumbrances	Unencumbered Balance
1		$1,650,000			$1,650,000
6				$1,450,000	200,000
7			$195,000		5,000
10			1,448,000	1,450,000	7,000

Expenditure: Equipment

P.R.	Explanation	Appropriations	Expenditures	Encumbrances	Unencumbered Balance
1		$300,000			$ 300,000
6				$300,000	0
9			$300,000	300,000	0

Step 6: A trial balance of the capital project fund would appear as follows:

Kimberly Hills School District
Capital Project Fund
Trial Balance
(Date)

Cash	$ 7,000	
Bonds authorized and unissued	500,000	
Revenue from bonds issued		$500,000
Estimated revenue from state sources	300,000	
Estimated revenue from federal sources	1,200,000	
Revenue from state sources		300,000
Revenue from federal sources		1,200,000
Appropriations		2,000,000
Expenditures	1,993,000	
	$4,000,000	$4,000,000

Step 7: The closing entries for all revenue and expenditure accounts, both budgetary and actual, are as follows:

Appropriations	$2,000,000	
Expenditures		$1,993,000
Revenue and expenditure summary		7,000

To close appropriations and expenditure accounts in the general ledger as follows:

Appropriations for:		
Land	$ 50,000	
Buildings	1,650,000	
Equipment	300.000	
	$2,000,000	
Expenditures for:		
Land	$ 50,000	
Buildings	1,643,000	
Equipment	300.000	
	$1,993,000	
Revenue from bonds issued	$500,000	
Revenue from state sources	300,000	
Revenue from federal sources	1,200,000	
Bonds authorized and unissued		$500,000
Estimated revenue from state sources		300,000
Estimated revenue from federal sources		1,200,000
To close all revenue accounts, budgetary and actual		
Revenue and expenditure summary	$7,000	
Capital project fund balance		$7,000
To close revenue and expenditure summary		

Step 8: Assume that the governing board authorized transfer of the unencumbered balance of the unappropriated fund equity balance to the debt service fund:

Capital project fund balance	$7,000	
Due to debt service fund		$7,000
To record authorization by board to transfer unencumbered balance of the capital project fund to the debt service fund		

Step 9: The entry to record transfer of cash to the debt service fund would appear as follows:

Due to debt service fund	$7,000	
Cash		$7,000
To transfer cash to the debt service fund		

As an exercise, using the general ledger presented before the preceding trial balance, post all closing entries and entries to record the disposition of the remaining cash balance to these ledgers. When this posting is completed, observe that all accounts of the capital project fund are in balance.

Illustration 13.4 shows the reporting format to combine all capital projects funds balance sheets for the year ending June 30, 2009, of the Kimberly Hills School District.

To complete the exercise, balance and rule all accounts in the general ledger. The fund has served its purpose. All books of original entry, financial statements and documents giving evidence of the financial transactions of this fund may be bound together and filed for future use by auditors of the school district. Illustration 13.5 shows the format for combining statements of revenues, expenditures and fund balances for capital project funds in Kimberly Hills for the same time period.

Illustration 13.4
Kimberly Hills School District
Capital Project Funds
Combining Balance Sheet
June 30, 2009, with Comparative Totals for June 30, 2008

	Capital Outlay	Capital Bonding Program	Totals 2009	2008
Assets				
Investments, at cost plus accrued interest	$4,251,334	$2,785,407	$7,036,741	$14,538,824
Delinquent property taxes receivable	353,360	0	353,360	369,601
Prepaid expenditures	3,145	0	3,145	246,750
Contracts receivable plus accrued interest	2,334,922	0	2,334,922	2,452,434
Total Assets	$6,942,761	$2,785,407	$9,728,168	$17,607,609
Liabilities and Fund Balance				
Liabilities				
Accounts payable	$888,249	$74,638	$962,887	$2,414,549
Due to Maint & Oper	99,724	0	99,724	13,227
Deferred property tax rev	460,396	0	460,396	258,207
Deferred revenue on contracts receivable	2,170,039	0	2,170,039	2,295,412
Total Liabilities	$3,618,408	$74,638	$3,693,046	$4,981,395
Fund Balance				
Reserve for encumbrance	$703,665	$493,110	$1,196,775	$6,146,161
Unreserved	2,620,688	2,217,659	4,838,347	6,480,053
Total Fund Balance	$3,324,353	$2,710,769	$6,035,122	$12,626,214
Total Liabilities & Fund Balance	$6,942,761	$2,785,407	$9,728,168	$17,607,609

SUMMARY

Capital projects funds are used to account for revenue from a bond issue or from other sources designated for capital outlay purposes. Capital projects fund revenue is provided by issuing bonds. Bonds may also be issued for other capital projects fund purposes such as eliminating a deficit resulting from operation of the general fund, a special revenue fund, an internal services fund or an enterprise fund, or refinancing, retiring or refunding maturing bond issues. Bonding power of the board or the governmental unit through which bonds are issued is restricted by law and a favorable referendum vote is usually required before bonds can be issued.

When a bond issue is authorized to be sold, budgetary accounts entitled bonds authorized and unissued are debited and appropriations are credited. Any difference between debits and credits is credited to the budgeted fund balance account or to the capital projects unappropriated fund equity account. The bonds authorized and unissued account serves the same purpose for a capital projects fund as the estimated revenue account serves for the general fund. It is debited for the face value of the bonds.

Illustration 13.5
Kimberly Hills School District
Capital Project Funds
Combining Statement of Revenue, Expenditures and Fund Balance
June 30, 2009, with Comparative Totals for June 30, 2008

	Capital Outlay	Bonding Program	Totals 2009	2008
Revenues				
Local sources	$3,815,917	$0	$3,815,917	$6,908,665
Federal sources	4,681	0	4,681	0
Total Revenues	$3,820,598	$0	$3,820,598	$6,908,665
Other Financial Sources				
Sale of bonds	$0	$0	$0	$7,000,000
Sale of real property	134,823	0	134,823	125,112
Total Revenue Other Sources	134,823	0	134,823	7,125,112
Total Revenues	$3,955,421	$0	$3,955,421	$14,033,777
Expenditures				
General Supervision	$75,517	$27,081	$102,598	$108,696
Site Acquisition & Improve	495,289	730,016	1,225,305	1,175,289
Construction	6,168,988	1,561,303	7,730,291	14,511,932
Equipment	341,371	982,941	1,324,312	727,448
Other Expenditures	164,007	0	164,007	170,388
Total Expenditures	$7,245,172	$3,301,341	$10,546,513	$16,693,753
Excess Revenue over Expenditures	($3,289,751)	($3,301,341)	($6,591,092)	($2,659,976)
Fund Balance—July 1, 2008	2,250,910	4,229,143	6,480,053	2,632,592
Decrease in Reserve for Encumbrances	3,659,529	1,289,857	4,949,386	6,507,437
Fund Balance—June 30, 2009	$2,620,688	$2,217,659	$4,838,347	$6,480,053

ACTIVITIES

1. Review the definition of the following terms found in the glossary:

    a. Capital projects fund
    b. Capital outlays
    c. Bond
    d. Bond proceeds
    e. Bond premium
    f. Bond discount
    g. Debt service fund
    h. Bond issue
    i. Maturity date
    j. Unappropriated fund equity account
    k. Face value of bonds
    l. Debenture
    m. Interest payable
    n. Rate
    o. Note
    p. Coupon bonds
    q. Registered bonds
    r. Self-balancing
    s. General fixed assets account group
    t. Internal service fund
    u. Retired bonds
    v. Indebtedness

2. Why do school districts issue bonds? Can districts issue bonds for the same project at varying times? If so, why would they do that?

3. Differentiate between a bond and a note.

4. Select a local school district and examine the capital needs and funding of bonds for the district. How does the district account for bonds? Does the district account for bonds for new construction differently than for remodeling?

5. Prepare journal entries necessary to record authorization of a $12,000,000 bond issue for a school system and for the cash sale of the entire issue.

6. Prepare the journal entries necessary to close the capital projects fund accounts created in Activity 5 above. Assume total expenditures were $11,500,000, and that they were paid. Also prepare the general journal entry to transfer any cash remaining to the debt service fund for payment of interest.

7. Why are budgetary accounts used in capital projects funds?

8. On June 25, 2008, Fort Steven School System received authorization to issue bonds in the amount of $7,500,000 for improvements on certain buildings. The following transactions occurred after the authorization:

   a. Bonds in the amount of $6,500,000 were sold on July 1 of that year.
   b. On July 6, 2008, contracts were issued for the improvements estimated to cost $6,750,000.
   c. The remaining bonds were sold on July 8, 2008.
   d. A partial payment invoice for work completed in the amount of $2,000,000 was received on July 25, 2008.
   e. On August 1, 2008, materials were purchased on account for $750,000.
   f. The improvements were completed on August 15, 2008. An invoice for the total balance due in the amount of $4,400,000 was received that day. Assume there were change orders issued and approved to the original contract price.
   g. Accounts payable were paid in full on September 15, 2008.

Instructions:

- Using a capital projects fund general journal, prepare entries to record the authorization of the bonds and the transactions that occurred as indicated above.

9. On September 1, 2008, the New Douglas School System Board of Education appropriated $11,500,000 to erect a new school building, furnish it and to repair the Columbus Manor School driveways and walks. Of this amount, $9,500,000 was appropriated for the new building, $1,800,000 to furnish it and $200,000 for repairing and replacing the Columbus Manor School driveways and walks. To finance these projects, the board received authorization to issue $11,500,000 in bonds. As of the following January 1, among account balances of the capital projects fund, the following appeared:

Cash	$ 9,700,000
Bonds authorized and unissued	11,500,000
Appropriations	11,500,000
Revenue from bonds issued	9,700,000

The following transactions took place during the calendar year beginning that January:

January 31, 2009	Remaining bonds were sold.
February 1, 2009	Contract for replacing/repairing driveways and sidewalks was signed at an estimated cost of $175,000.
February 15, 2009	Contract for $9,500,000 was signed for the new building.
April 1, 2009	Purchase orders totaling $1,750,000 to furnish the new building were issued.
May 15, 2009	Replacing/repairing driveway project was completed, and an invoice for $175,000 was received.
June 1, 2009	Invoice for the driveway project was paid in full.

Instructions:

- Record account balances in the general ledger.
- Prepare general journal entries for transactions that occurred during the year and post to the general ledger.
- Prepare an interim statement of appropriations, encumbrances and expenditures of the capital project fund as of July 1, 2009.
- Prepare a trial balance as of July 1, 2009.

14

Debt Service Funds

INTRODUCTION

Once a school district borrows money by issuing bonds, it is faced not only with the problem of paying interest on bonds payable annually but it is also faced with the problem of retiring the bonds when they mature. Debt service funds are used to account for the accumulation of resources for, and the payment of, general long-term debt principal and interest. Debt service funds are used to pay principal and interest on bonds payable and to accumulate resources over the outstanding life of a bond issue in an amount equal to the maturity value.

OUTCOMES

In this chapter, you will learn how to:

1. Determine why debt service funds are used.
2. Use budgetary accounts to record debt service fund transactions.
3. Prepare financial statements for a debt service fund.

TYPES OF DEBT SERVICE FUNDS

Two methods are frequently used by school districts to retire outstanding bonds and to pay interest on them. The method selected is determined, in part at least, by the type of bonds issued. One type of bonds can be retired and interest on them paid each year from the general fund when revenue of the general fund is adequate. This type is referred to as serial bonds, a part of which is retired annually over the outstanding life of the issue. The second type is referred to as term bonds, the entire principal of which comes due or matures on one date, the type usually retired through use of a debt service fund.

When debt service funds are used, interest can be paid either by the debt service fund or by the general fund. While accumulating resources, cash of the debt service fund is invested in income-producing securities. At the maturity date, the securities are converted into cash, which is used to retire the bonds. A set of accounting principles has been developed for debt service funds, which has been found to be effective for accumulating resources over the outstanding life of a long-term bond issue to retire it at maturity.

If the amount of serial bonds maturing at periodic dates is not too great each year, it is possible to pay annual interest and to retire the bonds from the general fund. This method of bond retirement requires general fund revenue annually from a tax levy or from some other source in an amount sufficient to retire the year's maturing bonds. In the general fund, appropriations can be made for debt service expenditures for bond interest and for bond principal. As retirement of serial bonds is ordinarily out of revenue of the year in which the bonds mature, there is no need to accumulate resources over a long period of time. In the general fund an appropriation usually lapses at the end of the budget period. For that reason, it is unusual that an accumulation of revenues from one year to another would be possible in the general fund. Illustration 14.1 shows how revenue from taxes in the general fund can be authorized for payment of principal and interest.

Illustration 14.1

	Debit	Credit
Budgeted fund balance	$55,000	
Appropriation, bond principal		$50,000
Appropriation, bond interest		5,000
To record the general fund appropriation for expenditures for bond principal retirement and bond interest expense		
Expenditures, bond interest expense	5,000	
Cash		5,000
To record check issued for payment of bond interest expense		
Expenditures, bond principal	50,000	
Matured bonds payable		50,000
To record liability for currently maturing long-term bonds		
Cash for bond principal	50,000	
Cash		50,000
To record check issued for retirement of bond principal		
Matured bonds payable	50,000	
Cash for bond principal		50,000
To record receipt of cancelled bonds completing the retirement of bonds matured		

Serial bonds mature in series during the last few years of a long life. For example, if 20 percent of the issue matures each year during the twenty-first, twenty-second, twenty-third, twenty-fourth and twenty-fifth years, debt service funds can also be used to retire what, in effect, are term bonds.

Debt service funds are established to account for the annual accumulation of resources for the retirement of long-term bonds over the outstanding life of term bonds. Annual accumulation spreads the tax burden equally over the life of the bonds. A separate group of accounts effectively provides information from each year's revenue requirements from taxation and interest earnings and provides information clearly throughout the life of the bonds about the adequacy of the fund. Published financial reports prepared by some accountants should contain this vital information for management, the board of education, taxpayers or the bondholder.

Revenue of a debt service fund usually is raised through taxation and earnings on investments. Taxes can be levied for the specific purpose of debt retirement. Accounting for the tax assessment, levy and collection should be the function of the debt service fund. To relieve the debt service fund of the tax assessment, levy and collection function, frequently the levy and collection is made by either the general fund or a central tax collection agency fund, which turns cash collected for it over to the debt service fund.

Chapter 19 on agency funds illustrates further operation of a tax collection agency fund.

When cash is received by the debt service fund, it can be placed in revenue-producing investments. Income earned on investments reduces taxation that otherwise would be required to retire bonds at maturity. Special accounting principles apply to debt service funds. Each year taxes are assessed, levied and collected either by the debt service fund, the general fund or a tax collection agency fund in an amount sufficient that the aggregate amount accumulated over the life of the bonds will be equal to the bonds' maturity value. The tax levy can be a special voted tax or it can be a portion of the general property tax assessment and levy.

Example 1

In order to accumulate a reserve for debt retirement of $100,000 by a series of five equal tax levies that earn 10 percent compounded annually, a tax levy of $16,379 is required. From an annuity table, the amount of an annuity of $1 per period at 10 percent for five periods is found to be 6.1051. The required tax levy of $16,379, therefore, is computed by dividing $100,000 by 6.1051. The accumulated total illustrated below is $99,997 due to rounding.

Debt Service Fund
Accumulation Schedule

Required Annual Year	Required Annual Earnings	Taxation	Total Additions Each Year	Accumulated Fund Total
1		$16,379	$16,379	$16,379
2	$1,638	16,379	18,017	34,396
3	3,440	16,379	19,819	54,215
4	5,422	16,379	21,801	76,016
5	7,602	16,379	23,981	99,997
	$18,102	$81,895	$99,997	

ACCOUNTS AND TRANSACTIONS

The page format for budgetary revenue accounts and revenue accounts in the debt service fund is identical to the page format used in the general fund. However, observe that some account titles are different. Because of the limited number of sources of revenue of a debt service fund, frequently a subsidiary revenue ledger is not necessary. However, if needed, a subsidiary revenue ledger can be used. The page format for budgetary expenditure accounts (appropriations, and accounts for expenditures and encumbrances) in debt services funds is identical to the page format of these accounts in the general fund. Because of the limited number of expenditure accounts needed in a debt service fund, frequently a subsidiary expenditure ledger can be used but may not be necessary. The following paragraphs provide definitions and explanations of selected terms.

Required Taxation—If the general fund collects taxes for debt retirement or if the tax is collected by the debt service fund, budgetary accounts are used. Budgetary accounts in debt service funds take on different titles, however. The title of one account is "required taxation." This account records the amount that had to be raised from taxation or from other revenue sources each year to meet the bonds' accumulation schedule requirements plus the amount required to meet annual interest costs if interest is to be paid from the debt service fund. An accumulation schedule is included in the bond prospectus prepared prior to the issuance of bonds and shows how much taxes and earnings are required each year until the fund accumulates the maturity value of the bonds at the maturity date. In a debt service fund, this account may have another title such as "required contributions," a title frequently used in the debt service fund when taxes are collected by the general fund as revenue of the general fund and transferred to the debt service fund. This account serves debt service funds in the same way that the "estimated revenue" account serves other budgetary funds like the general fund, special revenue funds and capital projects funds.

Required earnings—A second budgetary account is "required earnings." This account records the amount required by the bonds' accumulation schedule to be earned each year from investments. It, too, serves the debt service fund in the same way that the "estimated revenue" account serves other budgetary funds.

Budgeted fund balance—If interest is to be paid from the debt service fund annually, revenue from taxes or other sources must be provided in the budget through the budgetary account "required taxation" which is debited with a corresponding credit to "budgeted fund balance." If interest is to be paid from this fund, an appropriation has to be made by debiting "budgeted fund balance" and crediting "appropriation, bond interest expense." The budgeted fund balance account serves the debt service fund in the same way that it serves the general fund.

Reserve for encumbrances—The reserve for encumbrances account in the debt service fund is identical to the reserve for encumbrances account used in the general fund and it serves an identical purpose in the debt service fund.

Reserve for debt retirement—The reserve for debt service account is not a budgetary account, but rather an appropriation of the debt service fund equity and is introduced as a most effective debt management account. The account title is "reserve for retirement of principal of debt." Instead of crediting either the debt service fund unappropriated balance account or a budgeted fund balance account for the total, the reserve for retirement of principal of debt account is credited each year for the combined amounts of required taxation and required earnings if interest is not to be paid by the debt service fund. If the current year's interest is to be paid by the debt service fund, budgeted fund balance is credited for the amount of revenue required to meet the current year's interest cost. As a result, the reserve for retirement of principal of debt shows the amount required at the end of each year by the accumulation schedule throughout the life of the bonds outstanding. Annual variances between required taxation and revenue from taxes and between required earnings and revenue from earnings are closed into the revenue and expenditure summary, and the balance is closed into the debt service fund balance account. The debt service fund balance account indicates each year the amount that the fund exceeds or the amount the fund falls short of the requirements of the bonds' accumulation schedule.

When information provided by use of both budgetary and actual revenue and expenditure accounts is shown in interim and annual financial statements of each debt service fund, the board of education can take whatever action is necessary to bring the fund more closely into agreement with the accumulation schedule requirements. This information, not disclosed without use of the reserve for retirement of debt account or other similar account, is important as a way to focus the attention of the board on the amount of the cumulative variances to date. If the variance is an unfavorable variance, appropriate board decision and management actions can be taken each year throughout the outstanding life of each bond issue to meet the requirements rather than to discover at the maturity of the bonds that financial resources are not available to retire the bond issue. If the variance is favorable, decisions of the board may reduce the amount needed from taxation each year.

Appropriation, bond interest expense—If the debt service fund pays interest, the budgetary account, "appropriation, bond interest expense" is credited for the amount for the year and the "budgeted fund balance" account is debited. Because the amount is already committed, a corresponding debit is made to "encumbrances, debt service-interest," and a credit is made to "reserve for encumbrances."

Appropriation, principal of bond debt—The annual budget for each debt service fund must specify the amount to be appropriated for bonds maturing during the year that are to be paid from the debt service fund. The entry to record the budget debits is "budgeted fund balance" and to record credits is "appropriation, principal of bond debt." Because the amount is already committed, a corresponding debit is made to "encumbrances, principal of bond debt" and a credit is made to the "reserve for encumbrances." The amount of cash required to retire a bond issue can be accumulated by a series of tax levies, which are equal in amount when computed on an actuarial basis. As cash is collected from taxes and interest on investments, it is invested in income-producing investments. This plan to retire the principal of debt is commonly called an annuity program, a series of equal additions at equal periods of time. Annuity ordinarily refers to one year but the periods may be any length of time. The interest rate is the rate per period.

The bond prospectus contains a debt service fund accumulation schedule that generally provides that annual deposits from taxation be at a fixed amount which, when added to earnings each year, will produce the maturity value of the bonds at the maturity date. The accumulation schedule is based on compound interest and compound interest or annuity tables are used to determine the equal annual required taxation. Annuity tables are published that specify the amount of an annuity of $1 per period with interest rates which range up from 2 percent for one or more periods.

Assume that the tax levy resulted in revenue of $16,379 each year, all of which is collected. At the end of the first year, the reserve for debt retirement is $16,379. At the end of the second year, the reserve is increased by revenue from tax of an additional $16,379 plus interest of 10 percent. The total of the reserve for debt retirement is $34,396. Earnings in the following year are based on the total being invested at the beginning of the year. Observe that the accumulated amount equals $99,997 at the end of the fifth year due to rounding.

Various factors such as fluctuations in the rate of interest earned, fluctuations in the amount of revenue from taxation caused by differences between estimated and actual uncollectible taxes receivable and gains or losses on sale of investments frequently cause a variance between required earnings and actual earnings. If the reserve for debt retirement is to be maintained at the amount required by the accumulation schedule, revenue must be adjusted for earnings or for taxes that differ from the required amounts. If actual annual earnings on the investments do not equal the required earnings or if revenue from taxes does not equal required taxation, the amount of the annual tax levy or the amount of revenue required from other sources must be adjusted upward. If the actual earnings on investments exceed the required earnings, or if revenue from taxes exceeds the required taxation, the amount of the annual tax levy can be adjusted downward. The objective of the debt service fund is to accumulate sufficient but not excessive resources to be used to retire the bonds outstanding.

Example 2

Assume that the general fund or the central tax collection agency fund records all taxes receivable, makes allowances for estimated uncollectible taxes receivable and collects taxes as an agent for the debt service fund. The general fund or the central tax collection agency fund transfers the amount of taxes collected to the debt service fund. The amount is not revenue of the general fund or the central tax collection agency fund but instead is revenue of the debt service fund.

In the Debt Service Fund (First Year)		
Required taxation	$16,379	
Reserve for debt retirement		$16,379
To record debt service fund budget for the first year		

In the General Fund		
Taxes receivable	$ XXX	
Estimated uncollectible taxes receivable		$ XXX
Revenue from taxes		XXX
Due to debt service fund		16,379
To record the tax assessment and levy, a part of which is revenue of the debt service fund		

In the Debt Service Fund		
Due from the general fund	$16,379	
Revenue from taxes		$16,379
To record claim from the general fund for debt service fund taxes collected by it		

In the Tax Collection Agency Fund (if used)		
Taxes receivable	$ XXX	
Estimated uncollectible taxes receivable		$ XXX
Due to the general fund		XXX
Due to the special revenue fund		XXX
Due to debt service fund		16,379
To record tax assessment and levy and to distribute liability to each fund		

In the Debt Service Fund (if Tax Collection Agency Fund is used)		
Due from tax collection agency fund	$16,379	
Revenue from taxes		$16,379
To record claim for tax levy from the tax collection agency fund		

Example 3

After taxes are collected by the general fund, cash is transferred from the general fund to the debt service fund. Assume that $16,379 is collected by the general fund and transferred to the debt service fund.

In the General Fund		
Due to debt service fund	$16,379	
Cash		$16,379
To record transfer of cash from tax collections to the debt service fund		

In the Debt Service Fund		
Cash	$16,379	
Due from the general fund		$16,379
To record transfer of cash from the general fund for debt service fund revenue collections		
Investments	$16,379	
Cash		$16,379
To record investment in certificates of deposit		

At the end of the fiscal period, the following closing entries would be made:

Revenue from taxes	$16,379	
Required taxation		$16,379
To close budgetary and actual revenue accounts		

Example 4

Consistency in accounting principles and procedures requires that the accounts be closed through the revenue and expenditure summary. However, as no variances existed, no balance would appear in the account.

Assets:		
Investments	$16,379	
Fund equity:		
Appropriated:		
Reserve for debt retirement		$16,379

Example 5

For the second year in the debt service fund, entries for several situations are in the following steps.

Step 1: Record the budget entry from the accumulation schedule for the debt service fund for the second year as follows:

Required taxation	$16,379	
Required earnings	1,638	
Reserve for debt retirement		$18,017

To record the budget for the debt service fund for the second year

Step 2: When the general fund makes the tax assessment and levy, the following entry is made in the debt service fund:

Due from the general fund	$16,379	
Revenue from taxation		$16,379
To record the claim against the general fund at the time of the tax assessment and levy by the general fund		

Step 3: Assuming that the exact amount of taxes was collected by the general fund and was transferred to the debt service fund, the following entry is made in the debt service fund:

Cash	$1,738	
Revenue from interest earned		$1,738
To record collection of interest earned		

Step 4: As soon as cash is received, it should be invested. Therefore, the following entry records investment of total cash:

Investments	$18,117	
Cash		$18,117
To record investment in certificates of deposit		

Step 5: At the end of the fiscal year, the following closing entries are made:

Revenue from taxation	$16,379	
Revenue from interest earned	1,738	
Revenue and expenditure summary		$18,117
To close revenue accounts		

Revenue and expenditure summary	$18,017	
Required taxation		$16,379
Required earnings		1,638
To close budgetary revenue accounts		

Revenue and expenditure summary	$100	
Debt service fund balance		$100
To close the revenue and expenditure summary		

Step 6: The debt service fund balance sheet at the end of the second year would contain the following accounts:

Assets:	
Investments	$ 34,496
Fund Balance:	
Unappropriated	$ 100
Reserve for debt retirement	34,396
	$34,496

Example 6

Assume that an investment in bonds of $10,000 made at a premium of $200 plus accrued interest is purchased in the amount of $100.

Step 1: The entry to record the purchase follows:

Investments	$10,000	
Unamortized premium on investments	200	
Accrued interest receivable	100	
Cash		$10,300
To record purchase of bonds at a premium plus accrued interest		

Step 2: On the interest payment date, the following entry is made to record collection of interest:

Cash	$900	
Revenue from earnings, interest		$800
Accrued interest receivable		100
To record collection of interest on investments		

Budgetary accounts for each bond issue facilitate periodic comparisons of actual earnings with required earnings and periodic comparisons of actual revenue from taxation or other sources with required taxation or revenue from other sources. These comparisons throughout the outstanding life of each bond issue serve as effective debt management techniques for adjusting the amount of taxes required to retire each bond issue.

Step 3: Assume that an investment of $12,000 is made on which a discount of $240 is applicable. The following entry records the investment:

Investments	$12,000	
Unamortized discount on investment		$ 240
Cash		11,760
To record investments purchased at a discount		

Example 7

Assume that the $12,000 investment at a discount of $240 is to be held for four years. Either at each interest collection date or at the end of the fiscal year, the discount should be amortized. Amortization always affects interest earned on investments and is, as a result, amortized through the revenue from interest account. The following entry records amortization of one-fourth of the discount:

Revenue from interest	$60	
Unamortized discount on investments		$60
To amortize one-fourth of the discount on investments		

Example 8

Assume that the investment of $10,000 at a $200 premium is to be held for four years. The entry to amortize the premium at the end of the first year is as follows:

Unamortized premium on investments	$50	
Revenue from interest		$50
To amortize one-fourth of the premium on investments		

Observe that the reserve for debt retirement balance is in agreement with the debt service fund accumulation schedule at the end of each year throughout the outstanding life of the bonds. In this illustration, a favorable variance of $100 exists at the end of the second year. In future years, revenue from taxation or revenue from earnings may fall short of the requirements of the debt service fund accumulation schedule or losses may occur when converting investments into cash. In the event that the unappropriated debt service fund balance develops a deficit (a debit balance) attention of the board would be focused on the unfavorable variance and corrective action could be taken by the board of education.

The bond prospectus usually restricts the debt service fund to certain kinds of investments—investments that are conservative, yet able to provide income for the debt service fund. If investments in bonds are authorized, they may be purchased at a price in excess of face value (called a premium) or they may be purchased at a price less than face value (called a discount). An additional characteristic of investment in bonds is that if purchased between interest payment dates, interest accrued since the authorized date of issue or since the last interest payment date is included in the purchase price. The following illustrations will record the purchase at a premium, the purchase at a discount and the purchase including accrued interest to date of purchase.

When long-term investments are made at a discount or a premium, the discount or premium affects the amount of interest that will be earned on the investment. A prorata share of the discount or premium should be amortized or written off each year over the remaining outstanding life of the investment. Amortization of the premium or discount changes the rate of interest from the nominal rate (i.e., the rate stated on the face of the investment) to an effective rate of interest. Amortization of a discount increases the nominal rate of interest to the effective rate of interest while amortization of a premium decreases the nominal rate of interest to the effective rate of interest. In either case, interest earned each interest period on each investment will be the same amount, leaving the investment recorded at its maturity value.

Over the outstanding life of the investment, the discount or the premium will be written off through the revenue from interest earned account.

Each year the general fund makes provision in its budget for the amount required to retire bonds maturing during the budget period, and it may also make provisions to pay interest on general obligation bonds. The general fund's appropriation accounts record authorization to make such expenditures during the fiscal year. Later during the year the general fund will actually disburse money in payment of bond principal, and interest on bonded indebtedness.

When this occurs, business papers that give evidence that the transactions have occurred are prepared and support the following entry in the general journal:

Serial bonds payable	$20,000	
Amount to be provided for bond retirement		$20,000
To record general fund's payment for retirement of matured serial bonds		

Each year the preceding entry is made. Ultimately, the bonds payable account is eliminated as a result of annual retirement of the bonds. Each year the balance of the account entitled amount to be provided for bond retirement is reduced by the corresponding amount, ultimately eliminating it.

In the case of long-term bonds being retired by use of a debt service fund, it is possible that the general fund or a tax collection agency fund may serve as the agent to collect taxes for the debt service fund. In other cases, the debt service fund may collect its own taxes. In either case, however, taxes must be levied in an amount that sufficient assets can be accumulated over the life of long-term bonds in debt service funds to retire them at maturity.

At the end of the fiscal period the debt service fund's accounts are closed and the amount actually accumulated during the year for retirement of the long-term bonds is reflected in the accounts. To record the amount accumulated each year in the debt service fund, the following entry is made in the accounts of the general long-term debt group of accounts:

Amount provided in debt service fund—bond retirement	$29,865	
Amount to be provided for bond retirement		$29,865
To record the amount provided by taxes and earnings in the debt service fund for retirement of long-term bonds		

Because interest is paid annually by the general fund or debt service fund on both serial and long-term bonds, entries that reflect the transactions involving interest on general long-term debt are not, necessarily, made a formal part of this group of accounts. However, accounts that reflect the interest status may be effective management instruments.

Illustration 14.2
Kimberly Hills School District
Statement of General Long-Term Debt
(Date)

Amount provided in debt service fund or bond retirement	$100,000	
Long-term bonds payable		$100,000
Total	$100,000	$100,000

Each year as payments are made by the general fund or the tax collection agency fund to the debt service fund or as the debt service fund assesses, levies and collects its own taxes and earns interest on its investments, the account entitled amount provided in debt service fund for bond retirement is increased. At the maturity date of the long-term bonds, the amount provided in the debt service fund for bond retirement should equal the maturity value of the long-term bonds. Illustration 14.2 shows how the accounts relative to the bond issue appear at the maturity date of the long-term bonds.

The entry in the debt service fund to retire bonds is to debit the account entitled matured long-term bonds payable and credit the account entitled cash for $100,000. A corresponding entry is required to be made as follows:

Long-term bonds payable	$100,000	
Amount provided in debt service fund for bond retirement		$100,000
To record use of debt service fund assets to retire long-term bonds		

FINANCIAL STATEMENTS

Illustration 14.3 shows a trial balance of the debt service fund accounts.

Procedures are available for closing temporary and budgetary accounts of the debt service fund at the end of each fiscal period and are shown in Illustration 14.4. In this case, the difference between the actual earnings and the required earnings must be transferred to the debt service fund equity account through the revenue and expenditure summary at the end of the fiscal period by the following entry:

Debt service fund balance	$90	
Revenue and expenditure summary		$90
To close the revenue and expenditure summary account		

Illustration 14.3
New Douglas School District
Debt Service Fund Trial Balance
(Date)

Cash	$3,740	
Investments	22,000	
Unamortized premium on investment	180	
Unamortized discount on investment		$270
Required taxation	24,600	
Required earnings	1,200	
Revenue from taxation		24,600
Revenue from interest		1,110
Reserve for debt retirement		25,650
Debt service fund balance		90
Totals	$51,720	$51,720

The use of budgetary revenue accounts with actual revenue accounts on the same page puts important information together and easily indicates the variance between each source of budgeted revenue and actual revenue for the debt service fund.

Illustration 14.4

Revenue from taxation	$24,600	
Revenue from interest	1,110	
Revenue and expenditure summary	90	
Required taxation		$24,600
Required earnings		1,200
To close the actual and budgetary account into the revenue and expenditure account		

In the case of debt service funds, revenue comparisons between required and actual revenue during the accounting period or studies of the income productivity of investments tend to provide a basis whereby the board of education can make investments of cash in the debt service funds for the best advantage of the school district. The greater the earnings on investments in debt service funds, the lesser the amount of taxes that will have to be assessed, levied and collected in order to retire the long-term debt. Illustration 14.5 shows a balance sheet that can be prepared when the closing entries have been posted to the debt service fund accounts having a balance.

Illustration 14.5
New Douglas School District
Debt Service Fund
Trial Balance
(Date)

Cash	$ 3,740	
Investments	22,000	
Unamortized premium on investments	180	
Unamortized discount on investments		$ 270
Reserve for debt retirement		25,650
Totals	$25,920	$25,920

Having closed the accounts at the end of the accounting period, the debt service fund is ready to begin transactions of the next year. Ultimately, sufficient assets will be accumulated in the debt service fund so that by their conversion into cash at the maturity date of the bond issue, the bonds can be retired (Example 9).

Example 9

Assume that at the maturity of a bond issue for which a debt service fund had been used, the amount of cash on hand is $100,000 and the reserve for debt retirement is $100,000. An entry is made to record matured bonds which have been carried in the general long-term debt group of accounts.

Step 1: The entries to record debt retirement in the debt service fund follow:

Reserve for debt retirement	$100,000	
Appropriation, debt service, principal of debt		$100,000
To record the appropriation of the board of education to retire the principal of matured bonds		

Expenditures, debt service, principal of debt	$100,000	
Matured bonds payable		$100,000
To record the expenditure for retirement of principal of debt		

Step 2: The entry to record the transfer of cash to a fiscal agent for payment of the maturity value of the matured bonds is as follows:

Cash with fiscal agent for debt retirement	$100,000	
Cash		$100,000
To record transfer of cash to fiscal agent for payment of maturity value of long-term bonds		

Step 3: When the report of the fiscal agent is received along with each canceled, paid or redeemed bond, the following entry is made:

Matured bonds payable	$100,000	
Cash with fiscal agent for debt retirement		$100,000
To record payment of matured bonds payable by the fiscal agent and receipt of canceled bonds		

Example 10

Assume that $100,000 of 12 percent serial bonds have been issued, $20,000 maturing at the end of each year for five years, and that the general fund serves as the tax collection agency for the debt service fund. To pay both principal and interest, the following debt service requirements are established prior to issue:

Bonds Outstanding Beginning Year	Interest of Year	Bonds Principal Requirement	Requirement	Outstanding End of Year
1	$100,000	$12,000	$20,000	$80,000

2	80,000	9,600	20,000	60,000
3	60,000	7,200	20,000	40,000
4	40,000	4,800	20,000	20,000
5	20,000	2,400	20,000	0

Step 1: *In the General Fund:*

	Debit	Credit
Cash	$32,000	
Due to debt service fund		$32,000
To record collection of tax that is due to debt service fund		

Step 2: *In the Debt Service Fund:*

	Debit	Credit
Required taxation	$32,000	
Appropriation, principal, bonds		$20,000
Appropriation, interest, bonds		12,000
To record budget for debt service		
Due from general fund	32,000	
Revenue from taxes		32,000
To record assessment and levy of tax by the general fund		
Cash	32,000	
Due from general fund		32,000
To record collection from general fund		
Expenditures, interest, bonds	12,000	
Cash		12,000
To record payment of interest on bonds		
Expenditures, principal, bonds	20,000	
Matured bonds payable		20,000
To record expenditure to assume liability for matured bonds payable		
Matured bonds payable	20,000	
Cash		20,000
To record retirement of serial bonds from debt service fund		

Step 3: Closing Entries

	Debit	Credit
Revenue from taxes	$32,000	
Appropriation, principal, bonds	20,000	
Appropriation, interest, bonds,	12,000	
Required taxation		$32,000

Account	Debit	Credit
Expenditures, interest, bonds		12,000
Expenditures, principal, bonds		20,000
To close budgetary and actual revenue and expenditure accounts		

Example 11

Assume that a tax is authorized to be collected directly by the debt service fund in an amount necessary to retire principal and pay interest. In this case, all accounting for debt service, including assessing, levying and collection of taxes, is accomplished in the debt service fund.

Account	Debit	Credit
Required taxation	$32,000	
Appropriation, principal, bonds		$20,000
Appropriation, interest, bonds		12,000
To record adoption of budget		
Taxes receivable	34,000	
Revenue from taxes		32,000
Estimated uncollectible taxes receivable		2,000
To record assessment and levy of taxes applicable to debt service		
Cash	18,400	
Taxes receivable		18,400
To record collection of taxes receivable		
Cash	14,200	
Taxes receivable		14,200
To record collection of taxes receivable		
Expenditures, interest, bonds	12,000	
Cash		12,000
To record payment of interest on bonds		
Expenditures, principal, bonds	20,000	
Matured bonds payable		20,000
To record expenditure and assume liability for matured bonds payable		
Matured bonds payable	20,000	
Cash		20,000
To record retirement of matured bonds		

At this point, all investments of the debt service fund will have been converted into cash, and the reserve for debt retirement account will have been used for the purpose for which the fund was created. The assets accumulated in the debt service fund will have been used to retire the bonds at maturity.

Therefore, all accounts in the debt service fund will be closed and, for that bond issue, no need exists for the debt service fund to continue in operation.

The advantages that result from the use of accounting principles applicable to debt service funds for each long-term debt issue justify analyzing, recording and reporting through the use of a separate group of self-balancing accounts. This management accounting structure can focus the attention of the board and its administrative officers on the financial requirements of each debt issue throughout its outstanding life and, thus, provide the type of information necessary for the school district to get the maximum amount from every tax dollar for public purposes.

In addition to the accounts illustrated, other accounts may be used such as taxes receivable, allowance for estimated uncollectible taxes, receivable delinquent, allowance for estimated uncollectible taxes delinquent, interest and penalties receivable, allowance for estimated uncollectible interest and penalties, tax liens, and others if the debt service fund assesses, levies and collects its own taxes receivable.

Previous examples have been restricted to long-term bonds, the principal of which matures at one time. Different circumstances surround serial bonds, a portion of which matures during different years. Illustration 14.6 shows a trial balance of the debt service fund after making the above entries.

Illustration 14.6
New Douglas School District
Debt Service Fund
Trial Balance
(Date)

Cash	$ 600	
Taxes receivable	1,400	
Estimated uncollectible taxes receivable		$ 2,000
Required taxation	32,000	
Revenue from taxes		32,000
Appropriation, principal, bonds		20,000
Appropriation, interest, bonds		12,000
Expenditures, principal, bonds	20,000	
Expenditures, interest, bonds	12,000	
Totals	$66,000	$66,000

ADJUSTING ENTRIES

Obviously, an allowance has been made for estimated uncollectible taxes receivable in the amount of $2,000. Observe that taxes receivable amount to $1,400, and there is no need at the present time to have an allowance for more than $1,400. An error was made when the estimated uncollectible taxes receivable was recorded. This error understated the current year's revenue because the error was detected during the year in which it was made. Therefore, the following adjusting entry is made:

Estimated uncollectible taxes receivable	$600	
Revenue from taxes		$600

To reduce the estimated uncollectible taxes receivable to $1,400

If an error is discovered, however, in the balance sheet at the beginning of the period, resulting from transactions of prior fiscal periods, the error is not corrected through current revenue and expenditure accounts but is, instead, corrected through the debt service fund equity account. Corrections of errors of prior years should not affect the current year's revenue and expenditure accounts.

CLOSING ENTRIES

Illustration 14.7 shows the closing entries at this time to the general ledger accounts and to the revenue and expenditure summary accounts.

Illustration 14.7

Revenue from taxes	$32,600	
Appropriation, principal, bonds	20,000	
Appropriation, interest, bonds	12,000	
Required taxation		$32,000
Expenditures, principal, bonds		20,000
Expenditures, interest, bonds		12,000
Revenue and expenditure summary		600
To close revenue and expenditure accounts, both actual and budgeted		
Revenue and expenditure summary	600	
Debt service fund balance		600
To close revenue and expenditure summary account		

Financial statements which are useful to the board of education, administrative officers, investors, financial analysts and taxpayers or each debt service fund are: the balance sheet, the statement comparing required revenue with revenue, the statement comparing expenditures and encumbrances with appropriations, the statement of changes in fund balance, and the statement of changes in financial position. For preparation of the CAFR, refer to ASBOI's website.

Illustration 14.8
New Douglas School District
Debt Service Fund
Trial Balance
(Date)

Assets:	
Cash	$ 600
Taxes receivable	1,400
Less estimated uncollectible	1,400
Total Assets	$600
Fund balance	
Debt service fund balance	$600

In debt service funds, large amounts of financial resources are provided by taxation and interest earned while large amounts of financial resources are applied to pay interest on bonds outstanding and to retire principal of debt. When the statement of changes in financial position is prepared on the total financial resources concept, it will disclose effectively the financial resources provided by tax revenue and interest earned and financial resources applied for debt service, including both interest cost and retirement of bond principal. The problem of combining financial statements for all debt service funds into one set of financial statements to be included in the comprehensive annual financial report is the same as it is for special revenue funds and capital projects funds. Examples of the reporting format for debt service funds follow. Illustration 14.8 shows the balance sheet of the debt service fund after making the closing entries.

Example 12, Part 1

The two following financial statements taken from New Douglas School District, Comprehensive Annual Financial Report for the Fiscal Year Ended June 30, 2009, illustrate the way by which financial statements of each separate debt service fund can be combined. The first (Illustration 14.9) is the combining balance sheet for all debt service funds.

Illustration 14.9
New Douglas School District
Combining Balance Sheet
All Debt Service Funds
June 30, 2009

	Combined Total	Bond Fund	Rent Fund
Assets:			
Cash	$ 158,500	$ 158,500	$ 0
Investments	667,700	667,700	0
Receivables, net of allowance for uncollectible amounts:			
Property taxes	5,195,900	5,026,000	169,900
Corporate personal property tax	217,200	217,200	0
Interest	39,600	39,600	0
Due from other funds	80,200	41,100	39,100
Total Assets	$6,359,100	$6,150,100	$209,000
Liabilities and Fund Balance:			
Liabilities:			
Interest payable	$8,300	$8,300	$ 0
Deferred property tax revenue	2,738,200	2,639,000	99,200
Total Liabilities	$2,746,500	$2,647,300	$99,200
Fund Balance:	$3,612,600	$3,502,800	$109,800
Total Liabilities and Fund Balance	$6,359,100	$6,151,100	$209,000

Example 12, Part 2

The second (Illustration 14.10) is the combining statement of fund operations which presents revenue, expenditures and the changes in fund balance for all debt service funds.

Illustration 14.10
New Douglas School District
Combining Statement of Fund Operations
All Debt Service Funds
June 30, 2009

	Combined Total	Bond Fund	Rent Fund
Revenue:			
Local property tax	$2,697,200	$2,600,100	$97,100
Corporate personal property tax	885,000	885,000	0
Earning on investments	45,500	45,500	0
Total Revenues	$3,627,700	$3,530,600	$97,100
Expenditures, debt service:			
Principal repayment	$1,920,000	$1,920,000	$ 0
Interest payment on bonds	1,107,900	1,107,900	0
Payment on lease/purch contract	102,000	0	102,000
Service charges	3,500	3,500	0
Interest on tax warrants	48,300	48,300	0
Total Expenditures	$3,181,700	$3,079,700	$102,000
Excess Revenue over Expenditures	$446,000	$450,900	($4,900)
Fund Balance—July 1, 2008	$3,166,600	$3,003,600	$163,000
Fund Balance—June 30, 2009	$3,612,600	$3,454,500	$158,100

Example 13, Part 1

The following two financial statements are taken from the Kimberly Hills School District Comprehensive Annual Financial Report, Fiscal Year Ended August 31, 2009. The first financial statement (Illustration 14.11) illustrates how one combined balance sheet can be presented for all debt service funds in the comprehensive annual financial report.

Example 13, Part 2

The second financial statement (Illustration 14.12) illustrates how one combined statement of revenues, expenditures and changes in fund balances can be presented in the comprehensive annual financial report for all debt service funds.

Illustration 14.11
Kimberly Hills School District
Debt Service Fund
Balance Sheet
August 31, 2009

Assets			
Cash in bank		$ 64,863	
Cash with tax collector in escrow		4,962	
Cash with paying agent		363,594	$443,419
Temporary investment—Certificate of deposit		275,000	
Receivables:			
Property taxes—Delinquent:			
2009 tax roll	$17,264		
2008 tax roll	8,117		
2007 tax roll	10,070		
2006 tax roll	31,672		
2005 tax roll	69,018	136,141	
Property taxes—Penalty and interest		25,325	
		161,466	
Allowance for estimated uncollectible taxes	(58.988)	102,478	
Accrued interest on investments			2,145
Total Assets			$813,042
Liabilities and Fund Balance			
Liabilities:			
Accounts payable			$4,962
Fund balance:			
Reserved for debt service			808,080
Total Liabilities and Fund Balance			$813,042

Illustration 14.12
Kimberly Hills School District
Debt Service Fund
Statement of Revenues, Expenditures and Changes in Fund Balance
Budget (GAAP Basis) and Actual
Year Ended August 31, 2009

	Budget	Actual	Variance-Favorable (Unfavorable)
Revenues:			
Property taxes/penalties/interest	$3,591,988	$3,606,866	14,878
Interest on investments	116,000	115,894	(106)
Interest on sale of bonds	20,321	20,321	0
Total Revenues	$3,728,309	$3,743,081	$14,772
Expenditures:			
Retirement of serial bonds	$1,599,000	$1,599,000	$ 0
Interest on serial bonds	2,035,784	2,035,784	0
Paying agent's fees	28,500	28,382	118
Total Expenditures	$3,663,284	$3,663,166	$118
Excess revenue over expenditures	65,025	79,915	14,890

Fund balance, September 1, 2008	728,165	728,165	0
Fund balance, August 31, 2009	$ 793,190	$ 808,090	$ 14,890

Illustration 14.13 shows how a district may present the statement of general long-term debt.

Illustration 14.13
New Douglas School District
Statement of General Long-Term Debt
June 30, 2009

Amount Provided and to be Provided for the Payment of General Long-Term Debt:	
Amount available in Debt Service Fund	$ 1,084,264
Amount to be provided in Debt Service Funds	16,114,736
Total Available and to be Provided	$17,199,000
General Long-Term Debt:	
General obligation bonds:	
Current	$ 833,000
Long-term	16,366,000
Total General Long-Term Debt Payable	$17,199,000

Illustration 14.14 shows how a district may present important information about the total financial impact of bonded debt principal and interest payments.

Illustration 14.14
New Douglas School District
Statement of Changes in General Long-Term Debt
For the Year Ended June 30, 2009

	Balance July 1, 2008	Additions	Balance June 30, 2009
Amount Available and to be Provided for the Payment of General Long-Term Debt:			
Amount available in debt service fund	$ 852,762	$231,502	$1,084,264
Amount to be provided	14,759,238	1,355,498	16,114,736
Total available and to be provided	$15,612,000	$1,587,000	$17,199,000
General Long-Term Debt Payable:			
General obligation bonds			
Current	$ 764,000	$ 69,000	$ 833,000
Long-term	14,848,000	1,518,000	16,366,000
Total general long-term debt payable	$15,612,000	$1,587,000	$17,149,000

Illustration 14.15
Kimberly Hills School District
Schedule of Long-Term Debt
August 31, 2008

Due Fiscal Year Ending 8/31	Principal	Interest	Total
2009	$ 6,109,000	$ 6,102,002	$12,211,002
2010	6,572,000	5,556,479	12,128,479
2011	6,998,000	5,196,155	12,194,155
2012	7,343,000	4,824,235	12,167,235
2013	7,678,000	4,451,157	12,129,157
2014	8,061,000	4,062,593	12,123,593
2015	8,464,000	3,651,511	12,115,511
2016	8,864,000	3,217,783	12,081,783
2017	9,102,000	2,763,020	11,865,020
2018	8,745,000	2,348,077	11,093,077
2019	8,885,000	1,923,553	10,808,553
2020	9,122,000	1,472,264	10,594,264
2021	9,177,000	1,018,649	10,195,649
2022	4,665,000	630,125	5,295,125
2023	2,900,000	380,150	3,280,150
2024	2,975,000	213,000	3,188,000
2025	1,125,000	72,000	1,197,000
	$116,785,000	$ 47,882,753	$164,667,753

SUMMARY

Debt service funds are used to pay principal and interest on bonds payable and to accumulate resources over the outstanding life of a bond issue in an amount equal to the maturity value. The funds are used to provide an orderly and organized accounting for the accumulation and disbursement of money for the payment of interest and the retirement at maturity of long-term bonds.

Serial bonds can be retired and interest on them paid each year from the general fund when revenue of the general fund is adequate. Term bonds are usually retired through use of a debt service fund. When debt service funds are used, interest can be paid either by the debt service fund or by the general fund. While accumulating resources, cash of the debt service fund should be invested.

ACTIVITIES

1. Review the definition of the following terms found in the glossary:

    a. Debt service fund
    b. Long-term debt
    c. Serial bond
    d. Term bond

e. Bonds, maturity value
f. Levy
g. Required taxation
h. Discount
i. Premium
j. Amortization
k. Nominal rate
l. Effective rate
m. Maturity value
n. Self balancing
o. Account
p. Adjusting entry
q. Required earnings
r. Budgeted fund balance
s. Reserve for encumbrances
t. Reserve for debt retirement
u. Appropriation, bond interest expense
v. Appropriation, principal of bond debt
w. Unappropriated debt service fund equity
x. Debt service fund equity account
y. Outstanding bonds
z. Bonded debt
aa. Matured bonds
bb. Fiscal agent
cc. Redeemed bond

2. Distinguish between term bonds and serial bonds.

3. Describe the process for establishing and maintaining a debt service fund.

4. Identify the financial statements commonly prepared from debt service fund accounts.

5. Fort Steven School District uses a debt service fund to retire its long-term bonds. The following transactions took place during the period from January 1, 2008, to December 31, 2008.

January 1 Budgeted for the debt service fund required revenue from taxes of $50,000 and required revenue from earnings of $2,400.

March 15 Taxes collected by the general fund and transferred to the debt service fund amounted to $30,000.

April 1 District purchased 10-year, 10 percent bonds, face value of $30,000, dated January 1, at a premium of $500 with interest payable semi-annually on June 30 and December 31.

June 15 Taxes collected by the general fund and transferred to the debt service fund amounted to $20,000.

July 1 District purchased 20-year, 9 percent bonds, face value of $20,000, at a discount of $600, with interest payable semi-annually on June 30 and December 31.

Instructions:

- Prepare journal entries to record all transactions that occurred in the debt service fund during the year.
- Prepare a trial balance of the debt service fund as of December 31, 2008.
- Prepare closing entries in general journal form.

6. Newbridge School Parish maintains a debt service fund which has accounts with balances as is listed in the following:

Reserve for debt retirement	$300,000
Debt service fund equity	3,090
Cash	60,000
Unamortized premium on investments	100
Earnings on investments	32,900
Investments	260,000
Required taxation	287,000
Unamortized discount on investments	200
Required earnings	16,000
Revenue from taxes	287,000

Instructions:

- Prepare a trial balance for the debt service fund as of December 31, 2008, from the above listed account balances.
- Make the necessary journal entries to close the appropriate accounts as of December 31, 2008.

7. Westbury School Corporation issued $2,000,000 par value of serial bonds on July 1, 2008. The bonds will pay 10 percent per year, to be called in blocks of $200,000 every two years, beginning July 31, 1998. On July 31, 2008, the fund had the following account balances:

Cash	$ 40,000
Taxes receivable	64,000
Estimated uncollectible taxes	32,000
Investments at cost	148,000
Bond interest payable	8,000
Debt service fund equity	12,000
Reserve for debt retirement	200,000

The following transactions occurred on July 31, 2008:

a. Taxes receivable of $30,000 were collected.
b. $138,000 of investments was converted into cash.
c. Interest payable of $8,000 was paid.

d. Following the corporation board's directions, the balance in the reserve for debt retirement was transferred to the debt service fund equity account, and an appropriation for debt service, principal, was made in the amount of $200,000.
e. An expenditure, debt service, principal, was recorded for $200,000, and the debt service fund assumed the liability for matured bonds payable.
f. A check for $200,000 was issued to the fiscal agent to retire bonds presented for payment.

Instructions:

- Prepare a schedule beginning with year 2008 showing the bond principal outstanding during each year and the amount of interest required for each year.
- Record and post the transactions of July 31, 2008.
- Record and post closing entries for the year ended July 31, 2008.

8. Assume a school system issued 9 percent, 20-year bonds having a face value of $1,000,000. What entry would be made to record the school district's bond liability?

9. The Bureau County School System issued 9%, 10-year bonds in the amount of $1,750,000, and serial bonds in the amount of $1,000,000 bearing interest at the rate of 10%, of which $200,000 will become due at the end of the sixth, seventh, eighth, ninth and tenth years.

Instructions:

- Compute the amount of interest payable in future years.
- Record the liability.

10. Notice was given that the general fund had paid $120,000 in interest due on $800,000 of 8%, 10-year bonds and on $500,000 of 9% serial bonds. In addition, the general fund deposited $250,000 in a debt service fund for retirement of general bonded debt.

Instructions:

- Record entries made in the general fund to pay interest and to make annual payments to the debt service fund.
- Record entries made in the debt service fund to show receipt from the general fund.
- Record the effect of interest payment and the principal of debt payment to the debt service fund.

11. At the end of the sixth year, Cuyahoga Schools retired $150,000 of serial bonds from the debt service fund. What entry is made to show retirement of these bonds?

12. Fort Steven School District was authorized to issue bonds of $7,500,000 for providing additional school equipment. The authorization provided for issuance of long-term bonds maturing in ten years with interest at 6% payable semi-annually. The school district was authorized the use of the debt service fund accounting to accumulate resources to retire the bonds at maturity from taxes collected by the general fund. At the end of the year, $960,000 has been provided for retirement of debt in the debt service fund.

Instructions:

- Prepare the necessary journal entry to record the sale of the bonds.
- Record the amount provided in the debt service fund as a result of contributions from the general fund and earnings on investments, totaling $960,000.

13. Mesa City Schools issued bonds to finance new equipment for some classrooms. The issue consisted of serial bonds with face value of $800,000. The amount of $100,000 is to be retired annually from current revenue. Interest of 6% is payable annually.

Instructions:

- Prepare all journal entries necessary to record the issue of the bonds.
- Prepare the general journal entries necessary to record the retirement of the final installment of bonds.

15

General Fixed Assets

INTRODUCTION

A school district makes many investments—in people, in securities, and in tangible items. Over the years, the accumulated dollar value of school district acquisitions of land, buildings and equipment amounts to millions of dollars. Because of this sizable investment, it is important for the school business administrator to accurately account for and report on district possessions. Current practices rely upon computerization of these records. A variety of software is available to users to create individual records for each asset.

OUTCOMES

In this chapter, you will learn how to:

1. Establish an inventory system for land, buildings, and equipment owned by a school district.
2. Produce written records for this inventory.
3. Use double entry accounting to record the dollar value of the land, buildings, and equipment owned by a school district.
4. Produce reports that summarize the dollar value and annual change in dollar value of the land, buildings and equipment owned by a district.

CAPITAL ASSETS

Under GASB 34, school districts are responsible for accounting for, controlling and reporting both current and capital assets. *Financial Accounting for Local and State School Systems, 2003* (Johnson, 2003) states that capital assets have certain properties that distinguish them from other types of assets:

- Tangible or intangible in nature
- Long-lived (have a life longer than one year)
- Of a significant value at the time of purchase or acquisition
- Reasonably identified and controlled through a physical inventory system

DEFINITION OF FIXED ASSETS

Fixed assets are those intended to be used over a period of more than one year. Everett, Lows and Johnson (1996) cited Jensen's definition of fixed assets. Typically fixed assets are categorized as land, buildings or equipment:

1. Land includes all real estate owned by the district, including improvements or upgrades, such as playing fields, driveways and drainage systems.

2. Buildings are district-owned structures, including their electrical, plumbing, HVAC systems and permanent, non-movable, built-in furnishings such as student lockers, closets and cabinets. Also included are renovations, improvements and additions to the original structure.
3. Equipment, which is movable, long-lived furnishings.

Additional items that also are usually classified as fixed assets include: vehicles, machinery, technological assets such as computers and network equipment, works of art and historical treasures, infrastructure and software.

USES OF FIXED ASSET ACCOUNTING

An accurate and current record of fixed assets has many uses (Mutter, Nichols & Honaker, 1985; Office of the State Comptroller, 1990):

1. Inventory records indicate the age and the condition of equipment and buildings. This can aid long-range planning for equipment maintenance and replacement to spread budget expenditures over a period of years while still providing adequate mechanical support for instructional activities;
2. Fixed asset accounting provides records of financing sources which can be used to analyze available revenues for future purchases;
3. Inventory records indicate the location of equipment which can promote equitable distribution of resources among buildings and staff;
4. Comparisons of physical inventories with equipment records can detect theft and unauthorized borrowing of equipment and help discourage such activities in the future;
5. Fixed asset values are necessary for insurance records and claims for replacement of lost, damaged or stolen property.

Current boards of education, communities, state and federal governments are emphasizing school districts account for capital assets for control and accountability. *Financial Accounting for Local and State School Systems, 2003* (Johnson, 2003) states that ". . . a variety of data relating to an entity's capital assets must be maintained to ensure control and accountability over them:

- Quantity and types of assets
- Location of assets
- Life expectancy of assets

BASIS OF CAPITAL ASSETS

According to *Financial Accounting for Local and State School Systems, 2003* (Johnson, 2003), capital assets are included in the financial records at cost. In some situations, the purchase or acquisition documents may not be available for capital assets already on hand. If reliable historical records are not available, an estimate or appraisal of the original cost based on other information, such as price index levels at time of acquisition, may be used. The intent of such valuation is to record a fair value at the date of acquisition and not expend excessive resources in ascertaining exact costs. If capital assets are acquired by gift, then the fair value on the date received is the appropriate amount to include in the capital asset records. Capital assets may be acquired by several methods:

- Purchase
- Lease-purchase
- Construction
- Tax foreclosures
- Gifts and contributions

All capital assets acquired in some manner other than gift are recorded at the cost necessary to place the asset in service. Capital assets arising from gifts or donations are recorded at their estimated fair value at the time of receipt.

CAPITAL ASSET REPORTING

Johnson (2003, 49–50) reported, "GASB Statement 34 establishes reporting requirements for general government capital assets. Previously, financial statement presentation for capital assets of the general government was limited to the general fixed asset account group in the combined balance sheet. No depreciation was recognized on these assets. However, Statement 34 establishes the following new reporting requirements for capital assets:

- Depreciable capital assets should be reported in the Statement of Net Assets (a government wide statement) at historical cost, net of accumulated depreciation.
- The historical cost should include the ancillary charges necessary to place the asset into its intended location and condition for use, including freight and transportation charges, site preparation costs, and professional fees that directly relate to the acquisition of the asset.
- Depreciable capital assets may be reported on the face of the Statement of Net Assets as a single item or by major class. Detailed information will be reported in the notes.
- Significant non-depreciable capital assets that are inexhaustible, such as land, certain non-depreciable site improvements, and infrastructure assets reported using the modified approach should be reported separately from depreciable capital assets on the statement of net assets. GASB has defined an inexhaustible capital asset as one whose economic benefit or service is used up so slowly that its estimated useful life is extraordinarily long. Construction-in-progress should be included with non-depreciable capital assets in the Statement of Net Assets.
- Accumulated depreciation may be reported on the face of the Statement of Net Assets, parenthetically or as a separate line item reducing capital assets. However, regardless of the statement presentation in the Statement of Net Assets, the notes to the financial statements should disclose balances and changes in accumulated depreciation for the period by major asset class, as well as information regarding depreciation methods used."

CAPITALIZATION THRESHOLDS, ESTIMATED USEFUL LIVES AND DEPRECIATION METHODS FOR CAPITAL ASSETS

Since GASB 34, school districts now have to depreciate general capital assets. Boards of education and school administrators are allowed to develop policies and procedures for determining the useful life of a capital asset. Depending upon the state in which the school district is located, there may be rules and regulations regarding capital assets in place.

Capitalization Threshold

The dollar value of purchased assets that will be capitalized rather than an expenditure/expense at the time of purchase is referred to as the capitalization threshold. It is important to remember that many of the school district's assets have value that would affect the district's financial statements. Additionally, the costs of accounting these items may cost more than the value of the assets. Consequently, many local governments determine capitalization thresholds that will allow the business office to report these items as capital assets instead of supplies.

Financial Accounting for Local and State School Systems, 2003 (Johnson, 2003) states that school districts should consider the following factors in determining an appropriate capitalization threshold:

- Total value of all capital assets.
- Impact of the new/revised capitalization threshold on values reported in the statement of net assets.
- Value of any related debt (financial statement presentations may be misleading if significant assets acquired through debt are excluded by the capitalization threshold).
- Costs associated with tracking and reporting assets.
- Applicable state or federal requirements (typically for grant funds).

The Association of School Business Officials International (ASBO International) has published a guide for implementing GASB 34 that includes guidelines for determining capitalization thresholds. Additionally, individual state departments of education may have resources available for school districts to use in making capitalization threshold decisions. These resources are typically available via state websites.

Johnson (2003) reports the federal government uses a dollar threshold of $5,000 for federal grant management purposes. This threshold may have an impact on an entity's policies, particularly as it relates to capital assets that are acquired with federal grant funds.

Estimated Useful Lives

The estimated useful life of an asset is the time that the asset will be used for the purpose for which it was purchased. Depending upon the asset, the useful life may be identified in months or years. *Financial Accounting for Local and State School Systems, 2003* (Johnson, 2003) states the following:

> In determining the estimated useful life of an asset, consideration must be given to the asset's present condition and intended use, maintenance policy, and how long the asset is expected to meet service and technology standards. School districts may use general guidelines obtained from professional or industry organizations, information on comparable assets of other school districts/governments, and internal historical data. The determination of appropriate estimated useful lives is a management decision that is affected by a number of factors:
>
> - Experience with asset management
> - Plans for asset use
> - Property management practices

- Asset maintenance practices
- Applicable federal or state regulations

Many states have issued GASB Statement 34 implementation guides that include sources of information on estimated useful lives and are available to assist in establishing appropriate policies in this area. Many of these websites may be accessed through the GASB website at http://www.gasb.org/. ASBO International's GASB 34 Implementation Guide also provides information on determining useful lives of capital assets.

Determining Costs

There are a number of ways that the dollar value of a fixed asset can be determined. School districts use different cost measures for different purposes.

Historical cost—the original price paid for the item. The physical inventory should include historical costs for all items. Included in this is the price of the item and any additional charges to render the item usable at the site, such as delivery fees and setup charges. Historical costs can be determined by original source documents, such as purchase orders and invoices for equipment and deeds, maps, assessor's records and tax rolls for real property. If the original cost data are not available, estimated costs can be used using one of two methods recommended by the Government Finance Officers Association (additional information is available at their website).

Similar purchase estimation—the school district estimates through written documentation or discussion with knowledgeable individuals the cost of a like item during the time period of its purchase.

Normal costing (or back trending)—the current cost of the item is divided by a price index figure. The index figure, available from appraisal companies, is equal to 1 plus the percentage the item has risen in value from its date of purchase to the present.

Replacement cost—the value of the fixed asset in today's dollars. Replacement costs are found on inventories prepared by commercial appraisal companies and are also used for insurance purposes. Current catalogs and vendors' sales literature can be used to determine replacement costs. Replacement costs for real property include the current market value of the land and the cost of replacing the entire building at its present location, including renovations and improvements. Replacement costs should be updated annually on the inventory records and master inventory file to provide accurate values for adequate insurance coverage.

Actual Cash Value—the replacement cost of an item less accumulated depreciation. Sound insurable value is similar to sound value, except that it does not include uninsurable building structures, such as foundations, excavations, and wiring and plumbing below the surface of the lowest floor of the structure.

Depreciation Methods

Financial Accounting for Local and State School Systems, 2003 (Johnson, 2003) reports that GASB Codification Section 1400.113 states that "depreciation expense should be measured by allocating the net cost of depreciable assets (historical cost less estimated salvage value) over their estimated useful lives in a systematic and rational manner." Although GASB Statement 34 requires governmental entities to depreciate capital assets (other than non-exhaustible assets) it does not prescribe the method. As a result, depreciation methods are a management decision that should be based on the resources necessary to determine the various calculations and the capabilities of asset management systems. In addition to composite or group methods, any established depreciation method may be used (e.g., straight-line, sum-of the-years' digits or double-declining balance).

Johnson (2003) continues, "Depreciation may be calculated for individual assets or it may be determined for a:

- Class of assets
- Network of assets
- Subsystem of a network

The depreciation method can vary for different categories of assets. To simplify the calculations involved, the composite method may be used to calculate depreciation expense. It is applied to a group of similar assets or dissimilar assets in the same class, using the same depreciation rate, but not across classes of assets. The estimated life for the group may be based on the individual weighted average, the simple average of the useful lives of the assets in the group, or the weighted average or assessment of the life of the group as a whole. This method assumes no salvage value for assets; therefore, it simplifies the calculations and the recording of asset dispositions."

Works of Art and Historical Treasures

Financial Accounting for Local and State School Systems, 2003 (Johnson, 2003) states the works of art, historical treasures and similar assets are a special class of capital assets that may require developing a specific capitalization and depreciation policy. These assets are defined as items held singly or in collections that meet all of the following conditions (Statement 34, paragraph 27):

- Held for public exhibition, education, or research in furtherance of public service, rather than financial gain.
- Protected, kept unencumbered, cared for, and preserved.
- Subject to an organization policy that requires the proceeds from sales of collection items to be used to acquire other items for collections.

Technology Assets

Financial Accounting for Local and State School Systems, 2003 (Johnson, 2003) reports that technology-related assets are a class of capital assets that may require special treatment and reporting by school districts based on local or state reporting and accountability requirements or policies. Although technology assets are not dissimilar from other capital assets such as vehicles or furniture and fixtures, the resources dedicated to the installation and on-going support and use of technology by school districts have resulted in an increased level of interest by policymakers and citizens related to the use of resources dedicated to these purposes. Thus, many school districts have instituted special accounting and reporting practices associated with expenditures for technology-related assets. *Financial Accounting for Local and State School Systems, 2003* (Johnson, 2003) states that school districts should account for technology-related expenditures according to the following principles:

- Expenditures related to the technology and media-related activities that support instruction (function code 2230) should be segregated from those associated with administrative technology (function code 2580).

- Expenditures associated with purchased services to support technology should be distinguished from other types of purchased and professional services. Expenditure object codes 351 and 352 have been established for this purpose.
- Expenditures associated with the rental of computer and other technology equipment should be distinguished from other types of rentals. Expenditure object code 443 has been established for this purpose.
- Communications expenditures should include all costs associated with voice, data and video communications charges regardless of the media used (expenditure object code 530).
- Technology supplies should be segregated from other types of supplies. Expenditure object code 650 has been established for this purpose.
- Purchases of technology capital equipment should be specifically tracked for analysis purposes. Expenditure object codes 734 and 735 have been established for this purpose.

The 2003 edition handbook continues, "Using these codes to account for and report on technology-related costs will allow school districts to capture information on both instructional and administrative technology costs and accumulate the total expenditures associated with technology for operating purposes (expenditure object codes 351, 352, 443, 530, and 650) and capital purchases (expenditure object codes 734 and 735)."

CHALLENGES OF FIXED ASSET RECORD KEEPING

Ensuring Complete Inventory Records

A major question with fixed asset accounting is what to include in the physical inventory. To start, the administration and the board of education should determine which fixed assets are of "significant value." This subjective determination is often based on the size of the district, the amount of fixed assets it owns and the abilities of the people making the determination.

Other useful criteria, when trying to determine what to include in—and sometimes more importantly what to exclude from—a fixed asset inventory, are definitions of equipment and supplies. Although large, expensive items, like computers, copying machines and trucks, are easily classified as equipment, smaller items, like pencil sharpeners which resemble equipment in appearance, are actually supplies and therefore should not be included in the inventory. Everett, Lows and Johnson (1996) used Jensen's distinctions between these two kinds of fixed assets. He defines equipment as: a movable or fixed unit of furniture or furnishings, an instrument, a machine, or a set of articles meeting all the following conditions:

1. It retains its original shape and appearance with use.
2. It is nonexpendable; thus, if the article is damaged or some of its parts are lost or worn out, it is usually more feasible to repair it than replace it with an entirely new unit.
3. It represents an investment of money which makes it feasible and advisable to capitalize the item.
4. It does not lose its identity through incorporation into a different or more complex unit or substance.

When inventorying equipment it is common to group like items of smaller value together. For example, a pickup truck worth $30,000 would be listed as a separate item on the inventory; however, all cafeteria tables and chairs of the same make and model, purchased at the same time for the high school, would be listed as two groups: 20 student cafeteria tables in the high school, valued at $150 each or $3,000 total, and 120 student cafeteria chairs in the high school, valued at $25 each or $3,000 total.

Everett, Lows and Johnson (1996) used Jensen's criteria to differentiate supplies as those items meeting any of these qualifications:

1. It is consumed in use.
2. It loses its original shape or appearance with use.
3. It is expendable; thus, if the article is damaged or some of its parts are lost or worn out, it is usually more feasible to replace it with an entirely new unit rather than repair it.
4. It is an inexpensive item, having characteristics of equipment, whose small unit cost makes it inadvisable to capitalize the item.
5. It loses its identity through incorporation into a different or more complex unit or substance.

Ensuring Quality Inventory Records

After the district has decided on its capitalization policy, it should determine whether the inventory will be conducted by in-house staff or contracted with a commercial appraisal company. If done in-house, it is incumbent upon the district to train the inventory workers to perform their tasks in the most complete, accurate and uniform way possible. District-generated forms are useful for this purpose. Most districts use computerized spreadsheet or database software to record this information. The documents discussed below (Everett, Lows and Johnson, 1996) are appropriate for either conducting an initial inventory or updating existing records.

The Initial Inventory Sheet for Equipment is used for the first gross recording of equipment and leads to a list of equipment by building or department. The description, age, condition, building and room location, number of units and original cost should be noted for each piece of equipment (or equipment group as discussed above). The person responsible for the inventory and the date of the count should also be shown for control purposes. An equipment record should be completed for each piece of equipment (or equipment group) listed on an equipment inventory sheet for. The record typically provides information on description, location, quantity (for equipment groups like student desks), acquisition (date of purchase, original cost, and funding source). Changes in the equipment, such as movement to a new location, disposal, or accumulated depreciation (optional) should also be recorded on the record. Combined together, these records form a master equipment inventory list.

A building inventory record, similar in purpose to the equipment item record, provides description, cost and location data as well as an acquisition and disposition history for each district-owned building. A land inventory record documents each parcel of land owned by the district. Information included on the record is similar to that for buildings.

From the inventory records for equipment, buildings and land, a master district inventory file can be compiled. Commercial software packages are also available to handle these records.

Ensuring Current Inventory Records

Most school districts have, at one time or another, undertaken an initial comprehensive inventory of their fixed assets. However, many districts fail to keep their inventories current, resulting in poor accounting and inaccurate insurance records. Inventory records are affected by both acquisitions and disposals of equipment, buildings and land.

Acquisition. Whenever the district acquires new fixed assets, proper purchasing procedures should be used to minimize fraud and to provide an audit trail for accounting in the fund of origin. Expenditure figures in the fund of origin should coincide with historical costs on the inventory records. New fixed assets should be recorded on a master acquisition report; source data for an acquisition list can include purchase orders, original invoices and fund expenditure reports. The information on the master list should then be used to update the inventory records and the master inventory list.

Disposals. Typically, the board of education declares a fixed asset obsolete or of no further use to the district prior to its disposal. Riddance of the fixed asset can then occur in a number ways:

- *Obsolete equipment bid*—Open to the community and other interested buyers, this is a formal procedure which follows state competitive bidding laws. It is often used for higher-priced items, generally over $10,000.
- *Obsolete equipment auction*—This procedure is an opportunity for community members to bid orally for items of their choice. Many school districts turn this into a festive event by combining it with a social activity sponsored by an organization or parent group. The auction is often used for lower-priced items, generally under $10,000.
- *Destruction of equipment*—Equipment is disposed of by burning or trash collection.

TAKING INVENTORY

Counting fixed assets, whether for a comprehensive inventory or to update existing records, should be a planned, organized and thorough project. Everett, Lows and Johnson (1996, 13–15) used Jensen's recommendations for this task:

- *Appointment of property control manager*—This individual, usually recommended by the chief school business official, oversees all aspects of fixed asset accounting.
- *Determining of inventory practices*—To ensure uniformity, decisions must be made regarding level of detail and valuation.
- *Assignment of duties*—Every person involved in the inventory should have a global understanding of the entire inventory process, their role in it, and specific directions for their tasks. The importance of accuracy, completeness, and uniformity in counting fixed assets and recording data should be stressed at this time.
- *Preparation of forms*—Based on the inventory practices previously determined, forms should be prepared to aid inventory workers.
- *Undertaking the inventory*—Each individual involved in the process then counts and values the equipment in their assigned area. Full descriptions should be recorded for each fixed asset, along with their cost value(s).
- *Preparation of master inventory lists*—District-wide inventory records should then be developed. As a minimum, these should include a master list for all fixed assets in the district. Subsidiary lists by location can also be developed; computerization of the master data base can simplify this task.

- *Establishment of change procedures*—Written procedures to record acquisition of new assets, disposal of old assets, and changes in locations and values of existing assets should be established and disseminated to those having responsibility over the assets, such as central office administrators, directors of support services, building principals, and department heads. Inventory records should then be updated annually.

INVENTORY CONTROL SYSTEMS

Although required by GAAP, the main purpose of general fixed asset inventories and accounting is to prevent loss of district property, particularly movable equipment. However, counting fixed assets is only the start; tagging equipment with identification numbers provides further loss control. An ID number displayed in a prominent place on each item not only makes equipment tracking and inventory updates easier but can also make equipment less desirable to steal. Equipment ID numbers should be recorded on the inventory records, the master inventory list and on a master list of inventory numbers.

Sometimes it is impractical to affix an identification tag on each piece of equipment, such as student desks or chairs. In this case, the school district name and/or logo can be painted on each item to discourage theft (Jensen, 1973, 10).

Computer technology is offering new ways of equipment identification and tracking. Tags containing scan bar codes can be affixed to each piece of equipment. The information contained on the individual inventory cards matching each tag code can then be input into a computer, resulting in a data base that makes it easy to obtain accurate and current information on any piece of equipment.

ACCOUNTING FOR FIXED ASSETS

Fixed assets used in the activities of a proprietary fund or internal service fund are accounted for in those funds. Those assets must also be recorded as an expense in those funds. Likewise, fixed assets acquired through trusts and depreciation expenses for assets are accounted for in the non-expendable trust fund. This is in line with the purpose of a trust fund and aids stewardship of trust assets. Also, non-expendable trust funds follow the same accounting practices used in proprietary funds.

All other fixed assets are accounted for in their fund of origin. Illustrations 15.1, 15.2 and 15.3 show typical recording of transactions.

Illustration 15.1
Recording the purchase of a fixed asset

To record the acquisition of a new fixed asset, the appropriate account is debited and the appropriate investment source account is credited. For example, to record the acquisition of a new school bus costing $50,000 purchased from the current year general fund budget:

	Debit	Credit
Expenditures: Equipment, bus	$50,000	
Cash		$50,000
To record the purchase of Bus #107, a 66-passenger GMC bus, model #978534		

To record the acquisition of property ($100,000) and a new facility ($400,000) purchased from the current year general fund budget:

Land	$100,000	
Buildings	400,000	
Bonds and notes		$500,000
To record the purchase, financed through bonds, of a building to be used to house central office administration (lot price: $100,000; structure price: $400,000)		

Illustration 15.2
Recording the sale of a fixed asset without depreciation

To record the sale of an old fixed asset for which depreciation has not been recorded, the appropriate investment account is debited by the original amount of the asset (historical cost), and the appropriate fixed asset account is credited. For example, ten years after Bus #107 was purchased (see example above), it was declared obsolete and sold to the highest bidder for $7,500; to record this transaction:

Cash	$7,500	
Revenues		$7,500
To record the sale of transportation equipment		

Illustration 15.3
Independent School District Statement of Net Assets
June 30, 2008

	Governmental Activities	Business-type Activities	Total
ASSETS			
Cash and cash equivalents	$104,268,980	$5,971,032	$110,240,012
Property taxes receivable (net)	12,182,730	0	12,182,730
Due from other governments	19,968,336	1,268,411	21,236,747
Other receivables	2,252,919	3,783	2,256,702
Internal balances	442,539	(442,539)	0
Inventories and prepaid expenses	1,537,230	1,572,376	3,109,606
Capital assets:			
Land	21,823,682	0	21,823,682
Buildings	262,202,141	0	262,202,141
Furniture and equipment	130,675,133	11,549,456	142,224,589
Less accumulated depreciation	(98,176,725)	(9,016,026)	(107,192,751)
Total capital assets, net of depreciation	316,524,231	2,533,430	319,057,661
Total assets	$457,176,965	$10,906,493	$468,083,458

LIABILITIES			
Accounts payable and other current liabilities	33,305,354	484,151	33,789,505
Deferred revenues	3,117,910	521,035	3,638,945
Long-term liabilities:			
Portion due or payable within one year:			
Bonds, capital leases, and contracts	13,446,974	0	13,446,974
Accrued interest	759,880	0	759,880
Special termination benefits and compensated absences	2,156,000	0	2,156,000
Claims and judgments	5,700,000	0	5,700,000
Portion due or payable after one year:			
Bonds, capital leases, and contracts	70,958,588	0	70,958,588
Accrued interest	16,014,649	0	16,014,649
Special termination benefits and compensated absences	15,460,789	0	15,460,789
Claims and judgments	5,866,721	0	5,866,721
Total liabilities	$166,786,865	$1,005,186	$167,792,051
NET ASSETS			
Invested in capital assets, net of related debt	216,104,020	2,533,430	218,637,450
Restricted for:			
Debt service	5,147,502	0	5,147,502
Campus activities	1,396,569	0	1,396,569
Unrestricted	67,742,009	7,367,877	75,109,886
Total net assets	$290,390,100	$9,901,307	$300,291,407

SUMMARY

Proper stewardship of district assets is the main job of the chief school business official. While these duties usually concern monetary issues, fiduciary responsibility also extends to land, buildings and equipment. Therefore, the proactive school business official will institute a system to maintain accurate, complete and current inventory records and to provide for audit trails and proper accounting procedures in the fund of origin for the acquisition and disposition of fixed assets.

ACTIVITIES

1. Carefully review the definition of the following terms given in the glossary:

    a. Fixed asset
    b. Depreciation
    c. Replacement cost

d. Actual cash value
e. Historical cost

2. The General Fund of the Genesee Central School District had the following opening balances and transactions for the 2008–09 fiscal year. Assume all capital fund expenditures are financed through bonds.

July 1, 2008	Opening balances in these accounts:	
	Land	$1,000,000
	Buildings	$10,000,000
	Equipment	$2,500,000
	Bonds and notes	$10,000,000
	Current Appropriations	$1,000,000
	Gifts	$200,000
	State Aid	$1,800,000
	Federal Aid	$500,000
August 5, 2008	Improvements to land in the form of landscaping (part of a larger capital project paid from the capital projects fund)	$8,500
November 20, 2008	New library facility completed at a cost of (part of a larger capital project paid from the capital projects fund)	$2,250,000
January 21, 2009	Equipment was purchased from the general fund	$35,000
March 10, 2009	State government gave 10 acres of land to the district to build a new sports complex; estimated value of the land	$140,000
May 23, 2009	New heating unit was installed in the high school (part of a larger capital project paid from the capital projects fund)	$55,000

Instructions:

- Record the opening balances and transactions in the General Fund.
- Prepare a Statement of General Fixed Assets (similar to a balance sheet) as of June 30, 2009.

3. For the 2008–09 fiscal year, the Genesee Central School District had the following transactions. Assume account balances for July 1, 2008, are those reported on the Statement of General Fixed Assets as of June 30, 2008 (see #2).

   Assume all capital fund expenditures are financed through bonds.

July 24, 2008	A school bus, number 96, purchased ten years ago by the general fund at a cost of $66,000, was sold for $12,500; proceeds from the sale were directed to be deposited in the general fund.
August 5, 2008	Classroom desks recorded at a cost of $50,000 are considered to be useless, and authorization was received to discard them. The desks were originally purchased by the general fund.
November 2008	Office equipment acquired originally by a capital projects fund was replaced at a cost of $11,000. The old equipment was recorded at an original

	cost of $7,500 and was discarded. The new equipment was purchased from proceeds of a bond issue in a capital projects fund.
February 23, 2009	Special computer equipment for students with disabilities costing $77,500 was purchased with federal special education funds.
May 6, 2009	A local business gave the school district a microwave oven valued at $400 to be used in the Home Economics classes.

Instructions:

- Record the transactions in the appropriate fund.
- Prepare a Statement of General Fixed Assets as of June 30, 2009, and a Statement of Changes in General Fixed Assets as of June 30, 2009, comparing account balances of June 30, 2008, and June 30, 2009.

16

Enterprise Funds

INTRODUCTION

Although school districts are not-for-profit organizations, some of their divisions or departments operate as if they were small businesses concerned with profit and loss. To account for the financial transactions of these special departments, enterprise funds are used.

OUTCOMES

In this chapter, you will learn how to:

1. Understand the history and purpose of enterprise funds.
2. Comply with regulations of various food programs.
3. Account for the financial transactions of enterprise funds.
4. Prepare financial statements for enterprise funds.

DEFINITIONS

Proprietary funds—These funds, also known as income determination funds, non-expendable funds or commercial-type funds, are used for school district operations that provide a product or a service for a fee, similar to a profit-making business in the private sector. There are two kinds of proprietary funds: enterprise and internal service. Enterprise funds account for school district operations that furnish goods or services to the public. The school lunch fund and the school store fund are two examples of enterprise funds used in school districts. Internal service funds account for goods or services rendered to one school district division or department to another. For example, an internal service fund can be established for the district's central computer services department or the central print services department.

School lunch fund—The school lunch fund records the financial transactions resulting from school cafeteria operations that serve meals to students and staff. The fund has three purposes:

1. To avoid commingling cafeteria money with revenues and expenditures used for other purposes.
2. To more easily monitor the profit and loss resulting from cafeteria operations.
3. To more easily record the state and federal support (cash and food commodities) given to school districts participating in various meal/milk programs.

NATIONAL SCHOOL LUNCH, BREAKFAST AND SPECIAL MILK PROGRAMS

The beginning of federal support of school cafeteria operations began in the 1930s when the government aided the nation's farmers by purchasing their surpluses and donating them to schools. This practice continued on an uneven basis until it was formalized in 1946 by the National School Lunch Act, which, by providing nominal funds to school districts to defray the cost of school lunches, became the basis of the modern federal assistance program. The original act had several purposes:

1. To improve nutrition for the nation's children.
2. To bolster the farming economy through the purchase and subsequent redistribution of surplus food to schools.
3. To improve the physical condition of new soldiers. Many World War II recruits were found to be undernourished, and providing an adequate diet during school years was thought to help mitigate this problem.

When the Child Nutrition Act of 1986 became law, the federal government added monetary incentives for free and reduced price meals, promulgated guidelines for menu offerings and started the Breakfast Program. This act improved the nutrition and health of the nation's youth, especially for those from economically disadvantaged areas. The increased federal support also helped schools establish self-supporting lunch programs, which in turn provided more time for actual instruction by virtually eliminating the home lunch option and concentrating student lunches into shorter, well-defined lunch periods (Colucci, 1988 and Goodling, 1990).

The Child Nutrition Program

School districts have a variety of choices of federally subsidized meal programs for children:

1. Subsidized lunch programs are the most common. They allow schools to offer lunches at reduced prices or at no cost to students whose family incomes fall below designated levels and full price lunches to all other students. The districts receive cash and food commodity subsidies from the federal government and cash subsidies from state governments participating in this program.
2. Breakfast programs are not chosen by as many districts as lunch programs. As federal incentives push to institute breakfast programs in schools, there may be more school district participation in the future. Districts receive cash subsidies from the federal government for participation in this program.
3. Special milk programs allow school districts to offer free milk to pre-kindergarten and half-day kindergarten students who meet economic guidelines. Students who are not present during the school's regular lunch periods are eligible for this program. Districts receive cash subsidies from the federal government for participation in this program.
4. Full price and free milk programs offer options for school districts to charge full price for their served meals, as opposed to the free and reduced meal programs cited above. This option allows school districts to sell milk to all students at a cheaper cost due to the federal subsidies received by the district to offset the purchase price of the milk.
5. Full price milk only programs are available to school districts and allow them to offer milk to all students at reduced prices because the district receives federal cash subsidies to offset the purchase price of the milk.

Implementation Procedures

School districts participating in any of the above child nutrition programs must make the program's benefits available to eligible students each year. To help school districts comply with federal guidelines and to ensure smooth implementation of the program's benefits to school children, the state annually distributes to school districts a free and reduced price policy booklet that summarizes federal guidelines and implementation procedures.

MEAL/MILK INCOME VERIFICATION PROCEDURES

The Child Nutrition Program requires that participating school districts verify the eligibility of selected families receiving meal or milk benefits by December 15 of each year. The school district must send a summary of the verification process results to their local or regional office by January 15 of each year. Shearing (1991) identified the steps in the verification process:

1. The school district determines the sample. The most common method used is a random sample of the lesser of 3 percent or 3,000 approved applications for free or reduced price meals and/or milk. Focused samples are also used by some districts.
2. The school district contacts the families in the sample and requests proof of income.
3. The sample families provide proof of income. A family must list the name and social security number of each household member under the age of 21 and provide written documentation of household income. Acceptable documentation includes paycheck stubs, letters from employers, pension award notices, notification from the state employment security office of unemployment compensation or worker's compensation, court decrees or cancelled checks for child support or alimony.
4. The school district then determines the family's eligibility for benefits based upon the income documentation provided by the household.
5. The district then notifies the family in writing of continuation of benefits or ineligibility.

Applications from families who receive food stamps or Aid to Dependent Children (ADC) need not be verified because they are directly certified by the Department of Social Services to receive free meals or milk. Income guidelines for free meals/milk can be obtained from the U.S. Department of Education website that list income levels according to household size and income levels received yearly, monthly or weekly. If an applicant's total household income is the same or less than the amounts on the illustration, the applicant's children may be eligible for free or reduced priced meals or free milk.

The federal and state governments financially assist school districts participating in any of the child nutrition programs by providing cash and commodity support to school districts. Both the state and federal governments pay school districts cash for participation in the programs. Federal cash reimbursement rates per meal can be obtained from the U.S. Department of Education website.

FOOD DISTRIBUTION

The United States Department of Agriculture (USDA) has also indicated the value of entitlement commodities per lunch is $0.1450. The state also provides cash support to school districts in amounts that vary from state to state. Appropriate tables can be obtained from the U.S. Department of Education website or from individual state websites.

ACCOUNTS AND TRANSACTIONS

Budgetary accounts are generally not used in the operation of enterprise funds. Enterprise funds focus on net income as private sector accounting does. An enterprise fund may be created by capital being transferred from the general fund, a special revenue fund, a capital projects fund or from contributions from a local, state or federal unit of government.

The amount of capital originally invested to create the enterprise fund is intended to remain intact. Accounts in the fund equity section of the balance sheet which record the amount of original investment may have titles such as "federal government contribution," "state government contribution" or "contribution from general fund" (see Examples 1 and 2).

Structures, machinery, equipment and other assets such as tools and parts may be acquired through routine purchasing procedures. Sources of revenue may be from sales of finished products, finished jobs, sale of repair parts and supplies or from services provided. Accounting procedures have to be tailored to meet the individual needs of the particular enterprise fund.

Unlike the formal budgetary or governmental type funds, fixed assets used in the operation of an enterprise fund are carried in the fixed assets section of the balance sheet of the enterprise fund. These fixed assets are subject to depreciation. Depreciation is an expense that must be included when setting prices for services rendered or goods produced. By recovering the cost of depreciation in the price for sales or services rendered, it is possible to accumulate an amount equal to the cost of the asset over the useful life of the asset, thereby permitting its replacement without depleting the original fund balance of the enterprise fund.

DEPRECIATION ACCOUNTING

Many different methods may be used to compute the portion of an asset's cost to be properly allocated as an expense during a fiscal period.

Straight-line method—The estimated useful life of each asset is used as the basis for spreading the asset's cost equally to each fiscal period. For example, if an asset cost $50,000 and has an estimated useful life of 10 years, the depreciation is estimated to be $5,000 per year.

Useful hours method—This method estimates depreciation costs using the estimated number of useful hours as the basis for distributing costs to a fiscal period. The total to be depreciated is the difference between the cost of the asset and its estimated scrap value. This total is divided by the estimated useful hours to produce the amount of estimated depreciation per hour. To use this method, records of hours used are required for each fiscal period. The amount is computed by multiplying the number of hours of actual use during the fiscal period by the amount of depreciation per hour.

Example 1

Assume that a school system creates an enterprise fund through which it plans to operate a vocational education project, an automotive repair shop. Capital of $50,000 is to be raised by a contribution from federal sources of $30,000, from state sources of $10,000 and from a long-term advance from the general fund of $10,000.

	Debit	Credit
Due from federal government	$30,000	
Due from state government	10,000	
Due from the general fund	10,000	
Federal government contribution		$30,000
State government contribution		10,000
Advance from general fund		10,000
To record creation of an enterprise fund to operate a vocational education project, an automotive repair shop		

The process of conversion of claims into cash may be lengthy. However, assume that all assets are converted into cash:

	Debit	Credit
Cash	$50,000	
Due from federal government		$30,000
Due from state government		10,000
Due from general fund		10,000
To record receipt of cash from each indicated source		

Example 2

Assume that land of $20,000 is acquired, including all costs of acquisition. A contract is let for construction of a building for servicing the project in an amount not to exceed $25,000. The contract contains a 10 percent retained percentage clause and $22,500 is paid, withholding $2,500 until final inspection is made.

	Debit	Credit
Land	$20,000	
Cash		$20,000
To record purchase of land		
Building	25,000	
Contracts payable		25,000
To record completion of construction of building		
Contracts payable	25,000	
Cash		22,500
Contracts Payable, retained percentage		2,500
To record payment of contract, withholding 10 percent		

Units of output method—When an asset is acquired, the number of units to be produced over the useful life of the asset is estimated. That number is divided into the total amount to be depreciated (difference between the asset's cost and its scrap value) over the useful life. To use this method of depreciation, a record of units produced each period must be kept. The number of units produced each fiscal period multiplied by the rate per unit produces the estimated depreciation.

Other methods—Other methods of estimating depreciation can be used including: useful hours method, units of output method, accelerated depreciation, declining balance, sum of the year's digits, average depreciation rates, composite depreciation rates, blanket rates and reducing charge. Each different method is designed to match the cost of an asset to the accounting period in which the benefits of using that asset are derived. Students may consult additional references for a more in-depth discussion and examples of calculating depreciation.

Enterprise funds keep accounts for fixed assets. The accounts are debited for all costs properly chargeable to the asset account. Such charges are frequently referred to as capital charges. The cost of fixed assets is reported in the balance sheet of the fund. A depreciation expense account is debited at the end of the fiscal period to record the estimated depreciation on each of the fixed assets. The corresponding credit is to a balance sheet account, and the amount contained in the account is subtracted on the balance sheet from the corresponding asset's cost. The difference between the cost of the asset as shown in the fixed asset account and the accumulated depreciation reported in the allowance for depreciation account is referred to as the book value of the asset. The allowance for depreciation account is a balance sheet account and remains on the books as long as the fixed asset does. Fixed assets of an enterprise fund are disposed of by sale, exchange, loss or transfer to the general fixed assets group of accounts, to other enterprise funds or to internal services funds.

An enterprise fund is designed to serve a self-supporting activity or operate to provide services. A credit balance in the retained earnings account indicates that, to date, revenue has exceeded expenses. A debit balance in the retained earnings account indicates that expenses have exceeded revenue.

Cost of goods sold is a major element of cost in the operation of an enterprise fund. Two methods are used to account for cost of goods sold: physical inventory or perpetual inventory. A physical inventory entails physically counting the goods on hand annually or periodically. A perpetual inventory requires an inventory account in which all units purchased are entered at cost, and all units sold or issued are recorded at cost (see Examples 3, 4, 5 and 6).

Example 3

Assume that a physical inventory taken at July 1, 2008, amounted to $2,000. During the year, total purchases amounted to $45,500. Purchases of goods for resale are charged to the purchases account and may be made either by cash or on account. Assume purchased goods in the amount of $400 do not meet the purchaser's specifications because of damage, deterioration or not conforming to the specifications. The goods are returned to the vendor for an allowance:

	Debit	Credit
Purchases	$30,000	
Cash		$30,000
To record purchase of merchandise for cash		
Purchases	15,000	
Accounts payable		15,000
To record purchase of merchandise on account		
Accounts payable	400	
Purchase returns and allowances		400
To record return of purchases found to be unacceptable		

Example 4

Commodities valued at $7,600 are received from the USDA. The commodities should be recorded as having been received and at the fair market value on the date received. Assuming that the cost of transporting those goods was $500, the cost of transportation on all goods purchased for the purpose of resale should be recorded as part of the goods sold.

USDA commodities	$7,600	
Revenue from federal government		$7,600
To record receipt of surplus food from USDA at fair market value on date received		
Freight in	500	
Cash		500
To record payment of freight on goods purchased from USDA		

Example 5

Assume than an inventory on June 30, 2009, the end of the fiscal period, amounted to $2,600. On July 1, 2008, the inventory of goods on hand was valued at $2,300.

Revenue and expense summary	$2,300	
Food inventory		$2,300
To remove the beginning inventory from the accounts and to charge the July 1 inventory to the revenue and expense summary account		
Food inventory	2,800	
Revenue and expense summary		2,600
To record the ending inventory as of June 30, 2009		

Example 6

Assume the New Douglas School District operates a vocational education automotive repair shop and that the accounts of the auto repair shop's enterprise fund as of January 1, 2008, had balances as follows:

Cash	$250	
Accounts receivable	690	
Allowance for uncollectible accounts		$20
Land	3,000	
Building	7,000	
Allowance for depreciation—buildings		700
Equipment	3,500	

Allowance for depreciation—equipment		500
Vouchers payable		680
Advance from the general fund		10,000
Governmental unit's contribution		2,000
Auto repair shop retained earnings		540
	$14,440	$14,440

The following transactions are reported and recorded in summary for the year:

T1	Cash sales for auto services, repairs		$4,700
T2	Repair parts and supplies purchased on account for which a voucher was prepared		2,000
T3	Invoices were received:		
	Electricity	$300	
	Equipment repairs	220	
	Gasoline and oil	750	
	Insurance premiums	830	
	Partially paid $1,780 of the total and vouchered the rest		
T4	Salaries were paid		2,000
T5	Vouchers payable as of January 1 were paid		
T6	Accounts receivable as of January 1 were collected		
T7	Total auto repair services (includes $4,700 from No. 1)		7,000
T8	Interest expense was accrued at 3% on the advance from the general fund		
T9	Estimated depreciation:		
	Buildings	160	
	Equipment	200	
T10	Allowance for uncollectibles was increased	40	

Illustrations 16.1, 16.2, 16.3 and 16.4 show the general journal, balance sheet, income and expenses financial statements and closing entries produced from the above data.

Illustration 16.1
(Example 6)
General Journal

T1	Cash	$4,700	
	Revenue from auto repair services		$4,700
	To record cash sales of services, repairs and/or parts		
T2	Parts and supplies used	2,000	
	Vouchers payable		2,000
	To record repair parts and supplies purchased on account		
T3	Electricity	300	
	Equipment repairs	220	
	Gasoline and oil expense	750	
	Insurance expense	830	

		Debit	Credit
	Cash		1,780
	Vouchers payable		320
	To record invoices paid and vouchered		
T4	Salaries expense	2,000	
	Cash		2,000
	To record payment of salaries		
T5	Vouchers payable	680	
	Cash		680
	To record payment of vouchers payable		
T6	Cash	690	
	Accounts receivable		690
	To record collection of accounts receivable as of January 1		
T7	Accounts receivable	2,300	
	Revenue from auto repair services		2,300
	To record sales on account		
T8	Interest expense	300	
	Interest payable		300
	To record accrued interest for one year at 3 percent on $10,000 advance from the general fund		
T9	Depreciation expense—building	160	
	Depreciation expense—equipment	200	
	Allowance for depreciation—buildings		160
	Allowance for depreciation—equipment		200
	To record depreciation for year		
T10	Loss on uncollectible accounts	40	
	Allowance for uncollectible accounts		40
	To record additional allowance for estimated uncollectible taxes		

Illustration 16.2
New Douglas School District
Auto Repair Shop—An Enterprise Fund
Balance Sheet
December 31, 2008

Assets			
Current assets:			
Cash		$1,180	
Accounts receivable	$2,300		
Less: Allowance for uncollectible accounts	60	2,240	
Total current assets			$3,420
Fixed assets:			
Land		3,000	
Buildings	7,000		
Less: Allowance for depreciation—buildings	860	6,140	
Equipment	3,500		
Less: Allowance for depreciation—equipment	700	2,800	
Total fixed assets			11,940
Total assets			$15,360
Liabilities, Contributions and Fund Balances			
Current liabilities:			
Vouchers payable		$2,320	
Interest payable		300	$2,620
Long-term liabilities: Advance from general fund			10,000
Total liabilities			12,620
Contributions:			
Governmental unit's contribution			2,000
Unappropriated fund balance:			
Retained earnings, January 1, 2008		540	
Add: net income, interest and expense statement		200	
Retained earnings, December 31, 2008			740
Total liabilities, contributions and fund balance			$15,360

SUMMARY

School districts provide many supporting services for educational programs such as school food services, athletic programs, school newspapers, yearbooks and vocational education projects such as farms, automotive repair shops, woodworking shops and homebuilding projects. Services rendered by enterprise funds can be available to the public as well as to students, faculty and staff of the school district. Each activity is intended to be partially, if not fully, self-supporting. The nature of principal revenue source(s) determine whether the activity involved is to be accounted for as a special revenue fund or an enterprise fund. If a substantial portion of the revenue used to finance an activity within a fund is derived from user charges, the fund should be classified as an enterprise fund. In contrast, if only a small portion of the revenue is realized from user charges, the fund should be properly accounted for as a special revenue fund.

Illustration 16.3
New Douglas School District
Auto Repair Shop—An Enterprise Fund
Income and Expense Statement
For the Year Ended December 31, 2008

Revenue:		
Revenue from auto repair sales and services		$ 7,000
Expenses:		
Parts and supplies used	$2,000	
Electricity	300	
Equipment repairs	220	
Gasoline and oil expenses	750	
Insurance expense	830	
Interest expense	300	
Depreciation expense—building	160	
Depreciation expense—equipment	200	
Salaries expense	2,000	
Bad debt expense	40	
Total expenses		6,800
Excess Revenue Over Expenditures		$ 200

Illustration 16.4
Closing Entries

Revenue from auto repair sales and services	$7,000	
Revenue and expense summary		$7,000
To close the revenue account		
Revenue and expense summary	$6,800	
Parts and supplies used		$2,000
Electricity		300
Equipment repairs		220
Gasoline and oil expense		750
Insurance expense		830
Interest expense		300
Depreciation expense—building		160
Depreciation—equipment		200
Salaries expense		2,000
Bad debt expense		40
To close expense accounts		
Revenue and expense summary	200	
Retained earnings		200
To close the revenue and expense summary		

The major objective of an enterprise fund is to determine costs of rendering services. These costs serve as a basis for setting fees to be charged for services or goods consumed.

ACTIVITIES

1. Carefully review the definition of the following terms given in the glossary:

   b. Proprietary funds
   c. Income determination funds
   d. Non-expendable trust funds
   e. Commercial-type funds
   f. Enterprise funds
   g. Internal service funds
   h. Depreciation accounting
   i. Straight-line depreciation
   j. Useful hours depreciation
   k. Units of output depreciation
   l. Book value of an asset
   m. Retained earnings

2. Download the current U.S. Department of Education schedules for income levels, free milk and free meals from their website.

3. Determine the annual, monthly and weekly income eligibility for a single parent family with two school-age children living at home.

3. Assume the remodeling of a cafeteria is begun by a contractor during the current year and that upon completion, 15 percent of total project costs is to be retained until the contractor's work has been inspected and accepted. Prepare the journal entries for the following events:

   a. The contractor submits a bill amounting to the full contract price of $100,000; final inspection and acceptance has not been completed.
   b. Payment is made to the contractor less 15 percent retainage.
   c. Final inspection is satisfactorily completed and the board of education accepts the remodeling project; payment is made.

4. The balance sheet of an enterprise fund for the past year included the following items in the fixed assets section:

Fixed assets:		
Building	$ 80,000	
Less: Allowance for depreciation—building	32,000	$ 48,000
Equipment	70,000	
Less: Allowance for depreciation—equipment	7,000	63,000
Total fixed assets		$111,000

Instructions:

- Assuming a depreciation rate is 5 percent per year, prepare the entries that would be required at the end of the current year.

5. Show the fixed assets section of the balance sheet after recording the entries in #4 above.

6. The Newaygo High School Food Service Fund from Newaygo School District 5 has the following trial balance at the beginning of the school year.

Newaygo School District 5
Newaygo High School Food Service Fund
An Enterprise Fund
Trial Balance
September 1, 2008

	Debit	Credit
Cash	$25,000	
Investments	33,000	
Due from general fund	11,200	
Due from state government	3,500	
Due from federal government	8,900	
Inventories	15,000	
Equipment	75,000	
Accumulated depreciation—equipment		$ 19,000
Accounts payable		27,000
Due to general fund		1,200
Retained earnings		124,400
Total	$171,600	$171,600

The following transactions took place during the fiscal year ended August 31, 2009:

T1	Issued purchased orders for food amounting to $114,500.
T2	Computed the amount due from federal government under the National Child Nutrition Program to be $13,000.
T3	Invoices for the food in T1 amounted to $120,000.
T4	Cash sales to students amounted to $151,000.
T5	Purchase orders for a walk-in cooler and other kitchen equipment were issued in the amount of $7,500.
T6	Cash sales to faculty amounted to $18,000.
T7	Received earnings on investments of $2,000.
T8	Salaries amounting to $28,000 for the year were paid.
T9	Cash contributions from local sources for the breakfast program amounted to $1,500.
T10	Supplies expense for the year of $3,400 was paid in cash.
T11	Received amount due from the state government.
T12	Paid utility bills amounting to $2,800.
T13	Paid $110,000 on account.

T14 Paid the amount due to the general fund.
T15 Received items ordered in T5 above, invoices were for $8,800.
T16 Administrative expenses for the year were paid amounting to $3,000.
T17 Sold equipment costing $4,000 with accumulated depreciation of $3,200 for $900.
T18 Miscellaneous expenses of $3,100 were paid.

Additional information:

a. Ending inventories were determined to be $17,500.
b. Depreciation on equipment for the year was determined to be $4,000.

Instructions:

- Record account balances as of September 1, 2008, in ledger accounts.
- Journalize transaction data, adjusting and closing entries for the year.
- Post to ledger accounts.
- Prepare a post-closing trial balance.
- Prepare a statement of income and expense.
- Prepare a balance sheet
- Prepare a statement of changes in retained earnings.

17

Internal Service Funds

INTRODUCTION

Internal service funds, classified as proprietary funds, are used to "account for the operation of local education agency (LEA), functions that provide goods and services to other LEA functions, other LEAs or to other governmental units, on a cost-reimbursable basis" (Fowler, 1990). Internal service funds are established to centralize operations to promote economic benefits that may result from more efficient and effective operations. For example, a fund may be established to realize economic advantages that may result from centralized purchasing and warehousing. Funds may also be established to obtain economic returns, which may result in the centralization of services such as central data processing, and central printing and duplicating. The objective of an internal service fund is to cover direct and indirect costs of goods and services by assessing appropriate user charges, which produce no significant profit nor result in any significant loss.

OUTCOMES

In this chapter, you will learn how to:

1. Define and identify an internal service fund.
2. Create an internal service fund.
3. Operate an internal service fund.
4. Close the books on an internal service fund.

CREATION OF AN INTERNAL SERVICE FUND

Ordinarily, internal service funds are established in one of three ways:

1. Contributions of cash or other assets from another fund, such as the general fund, an enterprise fund, the capital projects fund or general fixed assets group of accounts.
2. Sale of general obligation bonds.
3. Long-term advances from other funds.

The amount from contributions, sale of bonds or long-term advances becomes the capital of the internal service fund. Since the goal of the fund is to provide goods and services with the LEA on a cost-reimbursable basis without significant profit or loss in the long run, the fund is said to be a non-expendable fund.

The general journal entry should be as follows to record a contribution from the general fund to the internal service fund:

General Journal
Internal Service Fund

Page XXX

Date	Account Title	Debits	Credits
12/01	Cash	$15,000	
	Contributed capital from general fund		$15,000.00
	To record receipt of contribution from the general fund		

OPERATION OF AN INTERNAL SERVICE FUND

Revenue—The internal service fund should record revenue on the full accrual basis of accounting. Interfund transfers from the user department are considered revenues in the internal service fund (and expenditures in the user department). It is necessary to record interfund transfers as revenue in order to obtain proper determination of the fund's operating results. As monies are transferred from the user department to the internal service fund, the general journal entry should be as follows:

General Journal
Internal Service Fund

Date	Account Title	Debits	Credits
12/15	Cash	$2,000	
	Due from other funds		$2,000
	To record collection of accounts receivable from the general fund		

Expenses—In the internal service fund, expenses and not expenditures are recorded. The following transactions represent sample general journal entries for expenses and capitalized items:

1. Gasoline, oil, tires and tubes are requisitioned for maintenance and operating purposes. The cost of materials and supplies issued is recorded as follows:

General Journal
Internal Service Fund

Date	Account Title	Debits	Credits
12/16	Maintenance and operating supplies used	$4,000	
	Inventory of maintenance and operating supplies		$4,000
	To record cost of supplies issued		

2. Assume that a bill was received for a building addition in the amount of $20,000. The journal entry is recorded as follows:

General Journal
Internal Service Fund

Date	Account Title	Debits	Credits
12/11	Buildings and building improvements	$20,000	
	Accounts payable		$20,000
	To record receipt of invoice for building addition		

Fixed assets—The internal service fund is "a fiscal and accounting entity with a self-balancing set of accounts recording cash and other financial resources. Therefore, fixed assets acquired for use by the internal service fund to provide the goods or services for which the fund was created are carried in the accounts of the internal service fund, not in the general fixed assets group of accounts. When materials are purchased or other assets are acquired for use by the internal service fund, asset accounts are created in the internal service fund for them.

TYPES OF OPERATIONS APPLICABLE TO INTERNAL SERVICE FUNDS

Two types of operations are handled through the use of internal service funds. The first is a department-store-type such as would be used by a school district in operating a central supply department. The second may be described as that of a service department. In operating this type of internal service fund, materials, labor and other production costs may be incurred in converting certain materials into goods or commodities that can be used by the school district or that can be used to render a service to a unit of the school system. The operation of a central printing office, a central computer service department and a maintenance department are examples of services that may be provided by an internal service fund.

Costs of goods sold—Two methods are used in accounting for cost of goods sold: physical inventory (or periodic inventory) and perpetual inventory. The physical inventory (or periodic inventory) involves a physical count of goods on hand once each year. The perpetual inventory does not require a physical count of goods on hand, but a record of inventory is maintained to identify the inventory by account. When goods are purchased, the account is debited for the cost of the goods. As goods are consumed, the account is credited for the cost. The balance in the account should reflect the amount on hand.

The two bases most commonly used to determine the value of inventory are cost and lower of cost or market. Tidwell (1985, 462) states:

> In determining cost of inventory on hand, a number of methods have been developed: specific identification; moving-average; weighted average; last-in, first-out; and first-in, first-out. When using perpetual inventory cards, cost can be easily computed, based upon the method of determining cost selected. When using a periodic inventory method, the most economical method of pricing on a cost basis is first-in, first-out. In this case, all units remaining in inventory can be traced to the most recent purchase invoices and to cost identified by item, unit price and quantity.

Job order cost accounting—Tidwell (1985, 462–463) summarizes the essentials of job order cost accounting as follows:

- Asset accounts consist of cash, due from other funds, materials inventory, work-in-process inventory, machinery and equipment, allowance for depreciation of machinery and equipment, and others.
- Liability accounts consist of vouchers payable, salaries payable and others. The fund equity account is the original capital invested in the internal service fund which is to be retained intact and theoretically is not to be increased or depleted. Net income or net loss for each period is closed into the retained earnings account.

- Basically, expense accounts are debited when an expense creates a liability account or when cash is paid. Expense accounts are closed by debiting to a work-in-process account. Work-in-process is an asset account. When a job is completed it is billed to the organization unit ordering and receiving the service and the cost of the job is recorded. Cost of jobs completed is an expense account, which is closed to the revenue and expense summary account at the end of the fiscal period.

CLOSING THE BOOKS OF AN INTERNAL SERVICE FUND

Although the objective of internal service funds is to cover direct and indirect costs of the goods/services by assessing appropriate user charges that produce no significant profit nor result in any significant loss, rarely will revenues match expenses for the year.

The excess of revenues over expenses (or expenses over revenues) may be handled in two ways. One method of handling an excess of revenues over expenses would be to debit revenues and adjust the user departments' accounts. A more practical method of closing the books would be to credit retained earnings for the excess of revenues over expenses and adjust future user charges (Robert Davis Associates, 1981, 367–368).

SUMMARY

Definitions of internal service funds were provided and selected internal service funds were identified. Procedures for creating and operating an internal service fund were discussed. Two methods of closing the books on an internal service fund were given. Robert Davis Associates (1981, 371–372) summarize the essentials of internal service funds as follows:

1. The internal service fund is used to account for services provided by one department exclusively to other departments within the LEA or to other governmental units.
2. A less restrictive budget is needed because the budgets of the user departments act as constraints on the expenses of the fund.
3. The full accrual basis of accounting is recommended for the internal service fund.
4. Transfers to the internal service fund for services provided to user departments are revenue to the fund.
5. Depreciation must be recorded on fixed assets so the full cost of providing services can be billed to user departments.
6. Annual statements required for the internal service fund include:
    a. Balance sheet
    b. Statement of revenues, expenses and changes in retained earnings
    c. Statement of changes in financial position

ACTIVITIES

1. Review the definition for the following terms found in the glossary:

    a. Accrual basis
    b. Capital
    c. Cost of goods sold

d. Cost basis
e. Work-in-process
f. Cost accounting

2. A school bus is purchased for $35,000 and has an estimated useful life of eight years at which time it is estimated that the bus will have a scrap value of $3,000. What is the amount of annual depreciation computed on the straight-line basis?

3. What are two major advantages of operating a central maintenance department of a school system rather than a decentralized department?

4. On July 1, 2009, the board of education of the Kimberly Hills School District created an internal service fund to provide pupil transportation services. To establish this fund, the following were transferred to the school district's Pupil Transportation Service Department:

Cash	$200,000
Transportation vehicles	240,000
Maintenance equipment	60,000
Maintenance and operating supplies	50,000
Prepaid rent, garage (July 1–Dec. 31)	3,000

During the month of July, the following transactions occurred:

July 2	Purchased repair parts on account, $10,000.
July 4	Maintenance and operating supplies requisitioned by mechanics, $1,000.
July 5	Repair parts requisitioned by mechanics, $8,000.
July 10	Purchased additional repair parts on account, $25,000.
July 12	Payment of transportation insurance premium for year beginning July 1, $6,000.
July 12	Payment on account for repair parts purchased.
July 15	Purchased maintenance and operating supplies on account, $10,000.
July 20	Payment on account for repair parts purchased.
July 30	Paid drivers salaries, $5,000.
	Paid maintenance salaries, $2,000.
	Paid heat, light and power bills, $1,500.

(Note: Depreciation on transportation vehicles and maintenance equipment is calculated on a straight-line method. These assets have an estimated life of ten years.)

Instructions:

- Prepare the opening entry on the books of the internal service fund and record the transaction for July in general journal form.
- Prepare a trial balance as of July 31, 2009.

18

Trust Funds

INTRODUCTION

The school district may receive money which is to be used for special purposes. Donors may specify the restrictions on the use of the money in the trust agreement. Due to the nature of trust agreements, accounting principles have been developed to enable a school district to act in the capacity of a trustee or fiduciary. Trust funds entail the management of money or other assets to produce certain results usually specified in the trust agreement. In non-expendable trusts the original amount, or the trust fund principal, is to be retained intact in order to produce an income that may be used to benefit the school system. In expendable trusts, the school district is to use the principal amount and any income produced in accordance with the terms of the trust agreement.

OUTCOMES

In this chapter, you will learn how to:

1. Understand the accounting principles to be applied in non-expendable trust funds.
2. Understand the accounting principles to be applied in expendable trust funds.

TYPES OF TRUST FUNDS

Financial Accounting for Local and State School Systems, 2003 (Johnson, 2003) has developed new trust fund classifications. "These funds are used to account for assets held by a school district in a trustee capacity for others (e.g., members and beneficiaries of pension plans, external investment pools, or private purpose trust arrangements) and therefore cannot be used to support the school district's own programs. Trust funds are generally accounted for on the economic resources measurement focus and the accrual basis of accounting (except for the recognition of certain liabilities of defined benefit pension plans and certain post-employment healthcare plans; refer to GASB 26 and 27 for guidance on the recognition of these liabilities). Trust funds include pension trust funds, investment trust funds, and private-purpose trust funds (as described below).

Pension Trust Funds—used to account for resources that are required to be held in trust for members and beneficiaries of defined benefit pension plans, defined contribution plans, other post-employment benefit plans, or other benefit plans. Typically, these funds are used to account for local pension and other employee benefit funds that are provided by a school district in lieu of or in addition to any state retirement system.

Investment Trust Funds—used to account for the external portion (i.e., the portion that does not belong to the school district) of investment pools operated by the school district.

Private-Purpose Trust Funds—used to account for other trust arrangements under which the principal and income benefit individuals, private organizations or other governments.

NON-EXPENDABLE TRUST FUNDS

Non-expendable trust funds are used to account for trusts in which the principal must remain intact. The accounting principles to be applied in non-expendable trust funds are similar to those that applied to proprietary funds. Therefore, the financial statements applicable to non-expendable trust funds are the balance sheet, the statement of revenue and expense, the statement of changes in fund principal and the statement of change in financial position.

Non-expendable trust funds may be established for a variety of purposes, such as to purchase books for the library, to promote athletic activities or to provide loans to teachers to continue educational pursuits. In the case of loans to teachers to continue educational pursuits, the trust agreement may stipulate that the principal is not to be expended and that the interest charged to teachers on the loan is to be added to the trust fund principal.

Complications may arise in non-expendable trust funds when administrative costs are recovered. If income from the trust fund exceeds the amount of the administrative cost, then no problems exist. If, however, administrative costs exceed the amount of income produced, then payment of the administrative cost would result in a violation of the non-expendable trust agreement transforming the non-expendable trust into an expendable trust. In this event, the financial statements to be prepared would follow those of expendable trusts with a notation that the conditions of a non-expendable trust had been violated.

EXPENDABLE TRUSTS

An expendable trust is created to record transactions that arise from a trust agreement that stipulates the trust fund principal is to be used in accordance with the trust fund agreement. In this case, all assets, principal and any resulting income, may be used to carry out the trust fund agreement and there is no stipulation that the trust fund principal is to be retained intact.

The financial statements applicable to expendable trust funds are the balance sheet, the statement of revenue, expenses and fund equity, and the statement of change in financial position.

SAMPLE TRANSACTIONS

Transactions in the general journal for the above entries would be as shown in Examples 1 and 2.

Example 1—Non-expendable trust fund

1. Assume that Randy Holden donates $10,000 to the Kimberly Hills School District to be used as a non-expendable trust fund principal with income from investments to be used to purchase scientific software.
2. Investments were purchased in the amount of $8,000.
3. Income in the amount of $40 was received from interest on the investment.
4. Software in the amount of $35 was purchased.

General Journal
Randy Holden Software Trust Fund

		Debit	Credit
T1	101 Cash	$10,000	
	721 Contributed capital		$10,000
	To record receipt of donation		
T2	111 Investments	8,000	
	101 Cash		8,000
	To record purchase of investments		
T3	101 Cash in bank	40	
	1500 Earnings on investment		40
	To record earnings on investment		
T4	640 Supplies—software	35	
	101 Cash		35
	To record purchase of software		

Example 2—Expendable trust fund

Assume that Christopher Simpson donates $50,000 to promote swimming activities at Kimberly Hills High School. Any earnings on the principal amount are to accumulate in the fund, however, when the balance (principal and earnings drops below $100 the fund is to be closed and the balance transferred to the General Fund. Investments of $40,000 were purchased. A timing system was purchased for $15,000. Earnings of $75 were realized on the investments:

General Journal
Christopher Simpson Swimming Trust Fund

		Debit	Credit
T1	101 Cash	$50,000	
	770 Unreserved fund balance		$50,000
	To record receipt of $50,000 from Christopher Simpson to be used to promote swimming		
T2	111 Investments	40,000	
	101 Cash		40,000
	To record purchase of investments		
T3	602 Expenditures	15,000	
	101 Cash		15,000
	To record purchase of timing system		
T4	101 Cash	75	
	1500 Earnings on investments		75
	To record earnings on investments		

SUMMARY

The purposes of trust funds were presented and the differences between non-expendable and expendable trust funds were clarified. Accounting principles appropriate to trust funds were noted. Sample transactions affecting non-expendable and expendable trust funds were shown.

ACTIVITIES

1. Why are trust funds created?

2. What happens to the principal in a non-expendable trust fund?

3. What happens to the principal in an expendable trust fund?

4. The Fort Steven School District has a non-expendable trust fund which was established by the donation of $500,000 from John and Freda Hummel. Income, to be deposited in an expendable trust fund, is to be used to promote baseball in the school district. Assume that the principal amount was invested (7/1/2008) to yield an annual rate of 6%. In addition, assume that on 6/30/2009 $2,000 was used to purchase equipment for the baseball team.

Instructions:

- Record the receipt of the principal amount of the non-expendable trust fund.
- Record the collection of interest for the first year in the expendable trust fund.
- Prepare end of the year reports in non-expendable and expendable trust funds at the end of the second year (6/30/2009).

19

Agency Funds

INTRODUCTION

The school district retains custody of and fiduciary responsibility for some money, but exercises no independent control over the use of it. For example, deductions are made biweekly from employees' paychecks for taxes and benefits. Some of these amounts are remitted to the appropriate agency every pay period, but other organizations require monthly, quarterly or annual payments. In other words, the school district, acting in a fiduciary capacity as temporary custodian of these dollars, is not permitted to use the money to finance operations. Therefore, in order to prevent unauthorized use of these assets and to account for their accumulation and disbursement, the school district uses agency funds. In agency funds, assets of the agency should equal the liabilities at all times. Therefore, agency funds have no fund equity.

OUTCOMES

In this chapter, you will learn how to:

1. Understand the purposes of agency funds.
2. Account for transactions in an agency fund.
3. Produce periodic and annual financial statements for an agency fund.

FIDUCIARY FUNDS

Fiduciary funds are used to account for assets held by a school district as trustee or agent. Trust funds were discussed in chapter 18. Agency funds are purely custodial (assets equal liabilities) and do not involve measurements of results of operations.

Agency funds provide a method of accounting for and safekeeping of assets that will be sent to, given to or used by individuals or organizations at some future time. The funds are custodial in nature with assets remaining in the funds for short periods of time. Typically, agency funds are used to account for the financial transactions of a central treasury, tax collection department, payroll department or student clubs (Tidwell, 1985). Separate agency funds are kept for each function. Two types of agency funds will be discussed in this chapter—a central payroll agency fund and the student activity fund.

CENTRAL PAYROLL AGENCY FUND

The central payroll agency fund (sometimes simply called agency fund) is an important part of the payroll process, because it acts as a temporary repository for salaries as the money moves from the fund of origin (e.g., the general fund) to the employees' paychecks or personal bank accounts. The purpose of this agency fund is to hold employee deductions and school district contributions to external agencies for individual retirement accounts, state retirement plans, disability insurance, group health or life insurance, deferred compensation plans, state and federal income taxes, union or professional association dues, social security taxes, wage garnishments and similar purposes from the various funds financing the payroll. A single payment may then be made to each "vendor" for the amount held in custody.

The central payroll agency fund, as do all agency funds, uses the modified accrual system of accounting. This fund contains only asset and liability accounts with no revenue, expenditure, budgetary or fund equity accounts (Fowler, 1990).

SAMPLE TRANSACTIONS IN THE CENTRAL PAYROLL AGENCY FUND

Payroll deductions and withholdings forwarded by other funds to the central payroll agency fund would be recorded in that fund's general journals shown in Illustration 19.1.

Illustration 19.1
General Journal
Agency Fund

Date	Account Title	Acct. No.	Debits	Credits
11/01	Cash	101	$15,000	
	Payroll Deductions and withholdings	471		$15,000
	To record receipt of payroll deductions and withholdings from the general fund			

In the sample transaction in Illustration 19.1, separate liability accounts could have been established for each benefit, i.e., Social Security (471), Retirement (472), Health Insurance (473), etc. (Robert Davis Associates, 1985). Similarly, when the liabilities are paid to the appropriate agencies, the general journal entry would be as shown in Illustration 19.2.

Illustration 19.2
General Journal
Agency Fund

Date	Account Title	Acct. No.	Debits	Credits
11/01	Social Security taxes	471	$5,000	
	Cash	101		$5,000
	To record payment of social security taxes			

FINANCIAL STATEMENTS

An agency fund is used to account for assets held by a school district acting as an agent for individuals, organizations or other governmental units or other funds. As such, the financial statement for the agency fund would be as shown in Illustration 19.3.

Robert Davis Associates (1985) maintains that "agency funds should be used when the volume of transactions, the amount of money involved or the management and accounting capabilities of the school district's personnel make it cumbersome or unwise to account for the money in funds of more general use." Agency funds have been used to handle transactions for student activity funds, central payroll, central treasury and central tax collections. The procedures and detail vary with each agency fund, but basic accounting procedures are similar.

The central payroll agency fund involves greater detail than other agency funds. Procedures need to be established for temporary investment of idle cash, individual earnings records need to be established and maintained and procedures for computing gross earnings, payroll taxes and other deductions need to be in conformity with pertinent guidelines.

Illustration 19.3
Kimberly Hills School District
Statement of Changes in Assets and Liabilities
Agency Fund—Social Security Taxes
June 30, 2009

	Balance July 1, 2008	Additions	Deductions	Balance June 30, 2009
Assets				
Cash	$22,000	$25,000	$28,000	$19,000
Liabilities				
Social Security Tax	$22,000	$25,000	$28,000	$19,000

SUMMARY

The purposes of agency funds were presented and several uses of the agency fund were identified. Procedures were developed for recording financial transactions involving the agency fund and a sample transaction was illustrated. An annual financial statement, statement of changes in assets and liabilities, was shown for an agency fund.

ACTIVITIES

1. Review the definition for the following terms found in the glossary:

   a. Fiduciary fund type
   b. Agency fund
   c. Modified accrual basis

2. Why are agency funds created?

3. How are agency funds different from trust funds?

4. Responsibility for payroll administration of the Kimberly Hills School District rests with the central payroll fund. The following account balances were taken from the central payroll fund's trial balance on September 30, 2008:

Due from general fund	$8,688
Due from cafeteria fund	1,532
FICA taxes payable	1,080
Federal income tax withheld and payable	9,140

During the month of October, the following transactions occurred:

a. On October 1, the employer's FICA tax liability for September was computed. A liability of $918 was applicable to the general fund and $162 was applicable to the cafeteria fund.
b. On October 2, cash was received from the general fund in the amount of $9,606 and from the cafeteria fund in the amount of $1,694.
c. The required monthly deposit of cash for income taxes withheld for both employee and employer's FICA taxes was made on October 2.
d. The semi-monthly payroll voucher was prepared on October 15 as follows: FICA taxes withheld, $540; federal income taxes withheld, $1,250; employee retirement contributions withheld, $1,500; teacher retirement contributions withheld, $1,000; 403b program deductions, $300; net payroll, $29,280. Billings against the general fund were computed to be $32,674 and from the cafeteria fund $5,766.
e. On October 15, cash was received from the general fund in the amount of $24,888 and from the cafeteria fund in the amount of $4,392.
f. Salaries were paid on October 15.
g. The semi-monthly payroll voucher was prepared on October 31 identical in amount to the voucher computed in "d" above.
h. On October 31, the employer's FICA tax liability for October was computed. A liability of $918 was applicable to the general fund and $162 was applicable to the cafeteria fund.
i. Cash was received on October 31 as follows: $41,378 from the general fund and $7,302 from the cafeteria fund.
j. Salaries were paid on October 31.
k. The required monthly deposit of cash for income taxes withheld and for both the employees' and employers' FICA taxes was made on November 5.

Instructions:

- Record the foregoing balances and record the transactions in general journal form on the books of the central payroll fund.

20

Payroll Accounting / Development

INTRODUCTION

Financial accounting and reporting for each fund that employs people can be greatly simplified by using a payroll accounting concept for the entire school district. Accounting principles apply to assets held by the school district for its employees and for local, state or federal governments in the case of withholding and social security/Medicare taxes. The school district deducts federal income tax, social security/Medicare taxes, local and state income taxes from the salaries of employees and remits the amount withheld to the respective governmental entities within a specified time frame. The school district acts as an agent for its employees when it makes other authorized deductions from payrolls for pension, medical/dental insurance, retirement annuities and many other purposes. In these cases, the school district does not determine the purpose for which the assets are to be used, but instead acts as a liaison through which disbursements or distributions are made when the employee grants proper authority, by law or by contract. The school district has the responsibility for establishing adequate internal accounting and management controls needed to safeguard such assets and provide assurance that the assets are being used for the purposes for which they were provided. Increasing demands are being made upon school districts to render services as custodian of assets for others. Therefore, it is necessary that internal controls, accounting procedures and financial responsibility be clearly established by the school district for the efficient and effective use of these assets.

OUTCOMES

In this chapter, you will learn how to:

1. Determine payroll obligations of the school district for its employees.
2. Record transactions used for payroll activities.
3. Determine withholdings and deductions.
4. Identify payroll reports required to be filed with governmental agencies.

EMPLOYMENT AND PAYROLL ACTIVITIES

Administrative decisions needed to make academic, staff, and salary determinations are made by the personnel department. Expenditures are made from the operating funds for the total employment costs. The operating funds generally include:

General fund—certified staff, administrators, educational support staff such as nurse, secretaries, lunch/bus duties, extracurricular duties, cafeteria staff
Building fund—custodial staff, buildings and grounds staff
Transportation fund—transportation staff

The payroll department computes the pay of each employee of the school district. Then the cost distribution applicable to each fund for the total cost of employment that is made up of the employees' gross pay plus the employer's related expenses for taxes and employee fringe benefits is computed. An entry such as below would be made:

Salaries, instruction	XXXX	
Employee benefits, instruction	XXXX	
Salaries, administrative	XXXX	
Employee benefits, administrative	XXXX	
Salaries, support staff	XXXX	
Employee benefits, support staff	XXXX	
Salaries, custodial	XXXX	
Employee benefits, custodial	XXXX	
Salaries, transportation	XXXX	
Employee benefits, transportation	XXXX	
Payroll payables	XXXX	
Cash		YYY
To record issuance of checks for all employment costs for the payroll period		

Based on *Financial Accounting for Local and State School Systems, 2003* (Johnson, 2003), all 100 level object codes are salary accounts. These 100 level object codes should be used for payroll, and only for payroll. The reasoning behind this is that quarterly payroll taxes are based on the 100 level object codes. Appropriate codes from the revised edition are:

100* Personal Services—Salaries. Amounts paid to both permanent and temporary school district employees, including personnel substituting for those in permanent positions. This includes gross salary for personal services rendered while on the payroll of the school district. The third position in this group of objects has been left unused so that a job classification code can be inserted by the school district if desired. (Used with all functions except 5000, Debt Service)

- 101 Salaries Paid to Teachers
- 102 Salaries Paid to Instructional Aides or Assistants
- 103 Salaries Paid to Substitute Teachers

110 Salaries of Regular Employees. Full-time, part-time and prorated portions of the costs for work performed by permanent employees of the school district.

- 111 Salaries of Regular Employees Paid to Teachers
- 112 Salaries of Regular Employees Paid to Instructional Aides and Assistants
- 113 Salaries of Regular Employees Paid to Substitute Teachers

120 Salaries of Temporary Employees. Full-time, part-time and prorated portions of the costs for work performed by employees of the school district who are hired on a temporary or substitute basis.

- 121 Salaries of Temporary Employees Paid to Teachers
- 122 Salaries of Temporary Employees Paid to Instructional Aides and Assistants
- 123 Salaries of Temporary Employees Paid to Substitute Teachers

130 Salaries for Overtime. Amounts paid to employees of the school district in either temporary or permanent positions for work performed in addition to the normal work period for which

the employee is compensated under regular salaries and temporary salaries above. The terms of such payment for overtime are a matter of state and local regulation and interpretation.
- 131 Salaries for Overtime Employees Paid to Teachers
- 132 Salaries for Overtime Employees Paid to Instructional Aides and Assistants
- 133 Salaries for Overtime Employees Paid to Substitute Teachers

140 Salaries for Sabbatical Leave. Amounts paid by the school district to employees on sabbatical leave.
- 141 Salaries for Sabbatical Leave Paid to Teachers
- 142 Salaries for Sabbatical Leave Paid to Instructional Aides and Assistants
- 143 Salaries for Sabbatical Leave Paid to Substitute Teachers

150 Additional Compensation such as Bonuses, or Incentives.
- 151 Additional Compensation Paid to Teachers
- 152 Additional Compensation Paid to Instructional Aides and Assistants
- 153 Additional Compensation Paid to Substitute Teachers

*Account codes that are necessary for the NCES reporting are noted with an asterisk (*).

Using codes other than 100 level (and 200 level only when grossing up salary for board payment), in salary, or using 100 level codes in vendor payments for goods would cause havoc at fiscal year end, when an auditor is trying to verify the quarterly reports. If the 100 level object codes are used inappropriately, the auditor would need to reclassify accounts, and therefore change the amount of quarterly taxes that actually should have been paid to the appropriate governmental level.

It is good practice to have the school district's software provider set up a default-only allowing 100 level accounting codes. This default can be overridden in the few instances where a benefit needs to be included, such as school district paid retirement amounts.

BENEFITS CODING

Financial Accounting for Local and State School Systems, 2003 (Johnson, 2003) provides the following codes to be used for employee benefit accounting:

200* Personal Services—Employee Benefits. Amounts paid by the school district on behalf of employees (amounts not included in gross salary but in addition to that amount). Such payments are fringe benefit payments and, although not paid directly to employees, nevertheless are part of the cost of personal services. The third position in this group of objects has been left unused (i.e., 0) so that a job classification code can be inserted by the school district if desired (used with all functions except 5000, Debt Service).
- 201 Employee Benefits for Teachers
- 202 Employee Benefits for Instructional Aides or Assistants
- 203 Employee Benefits for Substitute Teachers

210 Group Insurance. Employer's share of any insurance plan.
- 211 Group Insurance for Teacher
- 212 Group Insurance for Instructional Aides or Assistants
- 213 Group Insurance for Substitute Teachers

220 Social Security Contributions. Employer's share of social security paid by the school district.
- 221 Social Security Payments for Teachers
- 222 Social Security Payments for Instructional Aides or Assistants

223 Social Security Payments for Substitute Teachers

230 Retirement Contributions. Employer's share of any state or local employee retirement system paid by the school district, including the amount paid for employees assigned to federal programs.

231 Retirement Contributions for Teachers

232 Retirement Contributions for Instructional Aides or Assistants

233 Retirement Contributions for Substitute Teachers

240* On-Behalf Payments. Payments made by the state or other governments on behalf of the school district that benefit active employees of the school district. These payments typically include state matching of the retirement contributions of school district personnel. An equal revenue amount should be recorded in account 2900, 3900 or 4900 depending on the source of the payment.

241 On-Behalf Payments for Teachers

242 On-Behalf Payments for Instructional Aides or Assistants

243 On-Behalf Payments for Substitute Teachers

250 Tuition Reimbursement. Amounts reimbursed by the school district to any employee qualifying for tuition reimbursement on the basis of school district policy.

251 Tuition Reimbursement for Teachers

252 Tuition Reimbursement for Instructional Aides or Assistants

253 Tuition Reimbursement for Substitute Teachers

260 Unemployment Compensation. Amounts paid by the school district to provide unemployment compensation for its employees. These charges should be distributed to the appropriate functions in accordance with the salary expenditures.

261 Unemployment Compensation Paid for Teachers

262 Unemployment Compensation Paid for Instructional Aides or Assistants

263 Unemployment Compensation Paid for Substitute Teachers

270 Workers' Compensation. Amounts paid by the school district to provide workers' compensation insurance for its employees. These charges should be distributed to the appropriate functions in accordance with the salary budget or may be charged to function 2310.

271 Workers' Compensation Paid for Teachers

272 Workers' Compensation Paid for Instructional Aides or Assistants

273 Workers' Compensation for Substitute Teachers

280 Health Benefits. Amounts paid by the school district to provide health benefits for its current employees or employees now retired for whom benefits are paid. These charges should be distributed to the appropriate functions in accordance with the related salary expenditures.

281 Health Benefits Paid for Teachers

282 Health Benefits Paid for Instructional Aides or Assistants

283 Health Benefits Paid for Substitute Teachers

290 Other Employee Benefits. Employee benefits other than those classified above, including fringe benefits such as automobile allowances, housing or related supplements, moving expenses and paid parking. These charges should be distributed to the appropriate functions in accordance with the related salary expenditures.

291 Other Employee Benefits Paid for Teachers

292 Other Employee Benefits Paid for Instructional Aides or Assistants

293 Other Employee Benefits for Substitute Teachers

*Account codes that are necessary for the NCES reporting are noted with an asterisk (*).

RETIREMENT SYSTEM PAYMENTS

School district paid retirement system payments is becoming common for teaching and administrative staff. In most cases, this is simply done by inflating the salary with a separate account code (200 object code) by the amount of the retirement system payments.

Example 1

Salary ($90,000)
District-paid retirement system payment (9%)

Calculate: (90,000/.91)	$98,901.10
Original salary	$90,000.00
Retirement system payment	$8,901.10
Verify: Grossed-up salary amount	$98,901.10
Mulitply by 9%	.09
Total	$8,901.10

This calculation verifies that the salary was grossed-up exactly by the amount of the district-paid retirement system contribution.

Depending upon the state where the school district is located, certificated (licensed) staff members having state retirement contributions withheld for work performed may not have Social Security (FICA) withheld for that same work. Further, any staff hired into the school district prior to March 31, 1986, may not need to have a Medicare deduction withheld. Any staff hired into the district after March 31, 1986, may need to have Medicare withheld.

Retirement system deductions generally are exempt from federal and state income taxes. A typical deduction screen for a retirement system eligible staff member hired after March 31, 1986, would likely include:

Medicare
Medicare Match
Health Insurance Security Fund
School District Match
Retirement System (pension)
Union dues (if the staff is unionized)

Amounts voluntarily withheld by employees as deductions for such things as 403b plans, credit union, medical/dental insurance needs to be remitted to the appropriate agencies in a timely manner. Careful consideration must be given to each of these voluntary deductions for any tax-sheltered effect.

PAYROLL

Many of the school district employees will be placed on a contract, based on a set number of pays. When payroll is opened for processing, these contracts are automatically input. Other employees will be hourly, in which case the number of hours will have to be manually entered for each pay cycle.

After data entry is complete, payroll reports should be run. These reports need to be checked to insure that they balance with entries before the actual checks are printed. This check prevents trying to locate errors discovered at the end of a quarter.

QUARTERLY REPORTING

Electronic funds transfer (EFT) is used by most districts to pay their quarterly payroll taxes. Either via the telephone or the Internet, the school district can key in the type, amount and date of withdrawal for Form 941 taxes. There are state Form 941 and federal Form 941 tax liabilities. The school district is given a verification number when finished entering the information for any future discrepancies. Funds are then electronically deducted from the school district's checking account on the date specified.

Beginning January 2001, if the school district accumulated less than a $2,500 tax liability during the quarter, the district may make only one payment with Form 941 at the end of the quarter.

The two most common types of depositors are monthly and semi-weekly.

> **Monthly depositor**—The school district is a monthly depositor if total taxes on Form 941 were $50,000 or less for the prior fiscal year (July–June). In this case, deposit Form 941 taxes by the 15th day of the following month.
>
> **Semi-weekly depositor**—The school district is a semi-weekly depositor if total taxes on Form 941 were over $50,000 for the prior fiscal year (July–June). The school district should deposit Form 941 taxes on payments made on Wednesday, Thursday or Friday, by the following Wednesday. Form 941 taxes on payments made on Saturday, Sunday, Monday or Tuesday should be deposited by the following Friday.

If the school district accumulates a Form 941 tax liability of $100,000 or more on any given payday, the school district must deposit taxes by the next banking day. The actual Federal 941, State 941, and State Unemployment quarterly forms must be completed and mailed by the end of the month following the end of the quarter. For example: the first quarter reports (January–March) are due on April 30.

ACCOUNTS AND TRANSACTIONS

Individual Earnings Records

For each individual employee, a record of earnings should be kept. This record is generally part of the computerized payroll database. Information about each pay period is recorded into a payroll history database. These records are important because questions may arise in later periods about earnings, social security/Medicare taxes withheld, income taxes withheld, or eligibility for retirement. The record also serves the school system by providing a basis for informational returns covering state and federal income tax and for federal social security purposes.

Payroll Check Register

The payroll check register generally lists the names of each employee, gross earnings, taxes withheld, pension and other benefits, miscellaneous other deductions, net pay, check number and check date.

Employees of the school district are usually employed under the provisions of a salary schedule adopted by the board of education for each classification of employee. Salary schedules are adopted based upon consideration of an employee's qualifications, years of service and other relative data. Once adopted by the board, salary schedules, sick leave policies, benefit programs, provisions for employment of substitutes and methods of computing salaries become the basis for payroll computation.

As a matter of clerical efficiency, the personnel office secures many documents necessary for processing payroll at the time of employment. These documents include a statement from the personnel office that an employee has been added to the staff or faculty. The personnel office gives authority to the payroll department to enter the new employee into the system and to create a payroll check.

Any payroll deduction other than mandatory pension and/or social security/Medicare tax should be authorized in writing by the employee at the time of employment, and furnished to the payroll department. Personnel should have each employee file Internal Revenue Service Form W-4, Employee's Withholding Exemption Certificate, upon which the employee states the employee's social security number, name and address, number of exemptions claimed and filing status (i.e., married or single). In all cases, the social security number is a prerequisite to entering the name of the employee on the payroll.

Notice of any subsequent authorized changes in pay status or deductions, should be furnished in a timely manner to the payroll department. Changes in pay status include contract adjustments, rate adjustments, deductions for leaves without pay and reductions for any time not worked.

Once an employee has been entered into the payroll system, procedures should be developed to furnish the payroll department with documentation indicating the continued employment of the individual. Timesheets/timecards, weekly attendance reports or other written directives should be furnished to the payroll department. Written notice of separation is required for the name of an employee to be deleted from the active payroll roster.

It is important under any set of circumstances that responsibility for initiating all documents that serve as a basis for pay authorization be placed with an administrative officer, rather than with an employee.

The number of recognized days constituting a pay period is important in computing salary. If it is a policy of the board to deduct an amount from salary for absences in excess of authorized leave or sick leave, a daily wage rate is necessary for computing the appropriate salary adjustments. Gross earnings for each employee are calculated for the pay period according to the terms of the individual employee's contract of employment. Under the provisions of the Federal Fair Labor Standards Act (FLSA), commonly known as the Wage and Hour Law, employers are required to pay 150 percent (time and one-half) of the regular rate for all hours worked in excess of 40 hours per week. Executives, administrators and certain supervisory personnel are not covered by the provisions of this law.

Example 2

Assume that John Jones is employed at the rate of $10.00 per hour for the first 40 hours per week and $15.00 for all hours worked in excess of 40 per week. He works as follows: Monday, 8 hours; Tuesday, 8 hours; Wednesday, 9 hours; Thursday, 9 hours; Friday, 8 hours; and Saturday, 8 hours.

Monday	8	8	0
Tuesday	8	8	0
Wednesday	9	8	1
Thursday	9	8	1
Friday	8	8	0
Saturday	8	0	8
Total	50	40	10

Regular time:	40 hours @ $10.00	=	$400.00
Overtime hours:	10 hours @ $15.00	=	$150.00
Gross earnings		=	$550.00

Payroll Taxes (federal, state and local)

The school district is required to report and pay federal, state and local income taxes withheld from salaries and wages of employees. The district is also required to report and pay FICA and Medicare taxes withheld from salaries and wages of employees and also the employer's portion of FICA and Medicare taxes (employee and the district each pay equal shares). The district must also withhold and pay various other kinds of deductions requested by the employee.

Withholding Taxes

In determining whether or not an individual is an employee of the school district, and therefore subject to withholding tax procedures, a distinction must be made between an employee and an independent contractor. The general rule is that if a person is an employee, the school district has a right to direct and control his/her activities and the manner of accomplishing his/her job.

The school district is required by law to withhold federal income tax from salary and wage payments. Generally all wages and salaries paid are subject to withholding taxes. The amount to be withheld is computed by reference to government wage-bracket withholding tables or by the use of a percentage method. Each year the Internal Revenue Service, U.S. Department of the Treasury, publishes Circular E, Employer's Tax Guide. This is available from a local office of the IRS or on the Internet. When the government wage-bracket withholding tables are used, the amount of federal income tax withheld is found by referring to the appropriate table, the wage-bracket in which gross earnings fall, and the column indicating the number of withholding exemptions claimed. Since most payroll systems are now computerized, this Circular E table is loaded into the payroll deduction screens and the appropriate amount of federal and state income tax is withheld. The table must be updated each January 1st.

Tax-Sheltered Annuities

The term *tax-sheltered* describes any program eligible for tax-deferred treatment and in the United States, a special type of plan is available to employees of school districts. Under Section 501(c)(3) of the Internal Revenue Code, a school employee may arrange with the school district to divert a portion of salary before taxes to purchase retirement annuity benefits in accordance with tax-deferral provisions in Sections 403(b), 415 and 457 of the Code and related Treasury Regulations. The principal tax benefit of a tax-sheltered annuity is that the employee is allowed to exclude from gross income the employer's contributions toward the annuity and to postpone the payment of income tax on those contributions until after retirement or a specified age, usually 59 ½. To invest in a tax-sheltered or tax-deferred annuity, the employee and employer enter into a written agreement under which the employee authorizes a reduction in salary in order to release money for the employer to pay as premiums on an annuity contract that is fully vested in the employee.

The Internal Revenue Service ruled that amounts paid into Section 403(b) Tax Sheltered Annuity plans through salary reduction agreements were "wages" for the purposes of social security and Medicare, even though such amounts were not taxable as wages for income tax purposes. Congress passed legislation requiring this change to be effective only for amounts paid after December 31, 1983.

PAYROLL REPORTING

Quarterly

All employers subject to income tax withholding, social security and/or Medicare taxes, must file Form 941 quarterly. At the close of the calendar quarter, the school district must remit amounts withheld from salaries for federal and state income taxes and for social security and Medicare taxes, plus the employer's portion of social security/Medicare, to the Internal Revenue Service Center for the region in which the school is located. Districts that qualify as monthly or semi-monthly depositors will have made timely contributions either by check or EFT relative to each payroll period. In the case of monthly or semi-monthly depositors, only the Form 941, complete with a Schedule B reconciliation would be filed, with no remaining tax due for the quarter.

Annual

Each year the school district is required to notify each employee of total wages paid during the preceding calendar year, what amounts were subject to social security and Medicare taxes and the amounts withheld for federal and state income taxes. This information is provided on Form W-2. Other information contained on Form W-2 includes the name, address and identification number of the school district as well as the name, address and identification number of the employee. Form W-2 is prepared in quadruplicate: two copies are sent to the employee, one copy is submitted to the Internal Revenue Service and one copy is retained by the school district. The school district must submit Form W-3 Transmittal of Wages and Tax Statements along with the W-2s that are sent to the IRS. Electronic or magnetic media filers will submit a Form 6559 with the transmittal of W-2s in a non-paper format.

Compensated Absences

General Accounting Standards Board (GASB), Statement 4, "Accounting and Financial Reporting Principles for Claims and Judgments and Compensated Absences" was issued to provide guidance in application of the requirements of GASB Statement 1 and Statements of Financial Accounting Standards (SFAS) Nos. 5 and 43 issued by the Financial Accounting Standards Board. GASB Statement

4 adopted the criteria of SFAS 43 for recognizing a liability for compensated absences. SFAS 43 requires employers to accrue a liability for employees' compensation for future absences if all of the following conditions are met:

- The employer's obligation relating to employees' rights to receive compensation for future absences is attributable to employees' services already rendered.
- The obligation relates to rights that accumulate or vest, i.e., those for which the employer has an obligation to make payment even if an employee terminates; thus they are not contingent on the employee's future service.
- Payment of the compensation is probable.
- The amount can be reasonably estimated.

Because the central payroll department is in the best position to compute the amount that accrues each year to employees for vested interests for compensated absences and thus the liability of the school district for compensated absences as each payroll period occurs, the responsibility for computation should be placed in the payroll department. Upon computation of the amount that is required to meet vested interest claims for compensated absences, the long-term debt account group would record the amount by which the account, amount to be provided for compensated absences, and the liability account, long-term compensated absences payable is increased or decreased. This assessment should be made at least once each year and the accounts of the general long-term debt account group adjusted accordingly.

Also, the central payroll department is in the best position to inform each fund of the school district using personnel services of employees of the amount that should be included in each fund's budget to pay currently maturing liabilities for compensated absences. In each of these funds using personnel services, expenditure or expense accounts are debited and the current liability is credited to record current costs for compensated absences.

If, in the future, money is provided by each fund using personnel services on a pay-as-you-go basis to a trust fund, that trust fund, in addition to the general long-term debt account group, should record the effect of administering the accumulating compensated absences program upon the financial position and the results of operation of the school district.

LONG-TERM LIABILITY FOR COMPENSATED ABSENCES

The long-term liability for compensated absences should be inventoried and the accounts should be adjusted to increase the amount to be provided for long-term compensated absences and to increase the long-term liability for that purpose. An adjusting entry is made in the accounts:

Amount to be provided for long-term compensated absences	XXX	
Long-term compensated absences payable		XXX
To adjust the accounts to show the estimated long-term liability for compensated absences		

If the annual inventory shows a reduction in the amount of the long-term liability for compensated absences, the following adjusting entry would be made:

Long-term compensated absences payable	XXX	
Amount to be provided for long-term compensated absences		XXX
To reduce the long-term liability for compensated absences		

Direct Deposits

Direct deposit or automated payroll deposit is a method of payment of wages that can reduce the number of payroll checks issued by the payroll department. The school district electronically submits all payroll deductions for direct deposit to a central office bank. That bank, in turn, distributes each individual direct deposit to the individual's bank of choice. In lieu of a paycheck, a direct deposit voucher is issued to each employee, similar to a check stub, which lists gross pay, all deductions and net pay for the period.

Changes frequently occur in payroll taxes to be withheld by the school district. In the case of school employees electing to spread a ten-month salary over a twelve-month period, the payroll usually is prepared in June for the months of July and August ending the contract. Wages are considered to be paid when the employee constructively receives them, when they are credited to the account of the employee or when they are available to the employee to be drawn upon by him/her at any time. The employer must withhold employment taxes on wages when the wages are paid. Therefore, it is appropriate to use the June tax tables to compute the amount to be withheld for federal income tax purposes.

BANK RECONCILIATIONS

Either the treasurer's office will be appointed to issue checks, or the school district may appoint someone within the district, typically the business manager, to act as the treasurer. In either case, procedures must be followed prior to the issuance of checks. Usually, there will be some type of requisition or request for payment submitted for approval. If the school district follows a requisition or purchasing process, a form is completed with all information relevant to the purchase. This form will move through an approval chain from the requestor to a principal, purchasing officer, business manager, or possibly all three, depending on the dollar amount of the requisition.

When the requisitioning process is complete, a purchase order is issued, followed by an invoice for payment. The invoice is matched to the purchase order and an order for payment is sent to the accounts payable department. The accounts payable clerk will verify that invoiced items have been received and create a check for payment to the respective vendor. There are instances where manual checks can be issued for reimbursements or pre-approved expenses, or for immediate payments, such as utilities or telephone charges. Otherwise, no checks can be released unless the board of education has formally approved the bill list.

As each of the payments is processed, most software systems hold the temporary checks in a liability account until they have been reviewed for release. At this time, the checks may be considered as temporary checks or as vouchers payable. In either case, the entry to the general ledger would be a debit to each expense account and a credit to vendor payables. Once the checks have been approved, they are processed through the system and issued permanent check numbers. The entry to record the issuance of checks is a debit to vendor payables and a credit to vendor cash.

As temporary checks (vouchers) are created:

	Debit	Credit
Expense Account	XXXX	
Vendor Payables		XXXX

Once checks have been approved and issued:

	Debit	Credit
Vendor Payables	XXXX	
Cash		XXXX

After checks have been created and a credit has been recorded to cash, the accounts payable clerk will print a check register. The check register lists all of the checks by check number, vendor and dollar amount. The register may be further notated to provide total expenditures by fund.

This information is then forwarded to the treasurer, who keeps records independent of the business office. The treasurer will use the check register to post expenses to the treasurer's ledger. Investments for the school district are held by the treasurer's office. Typically investments will be scheduled to mature when vendor checks are released or when payroll checks are issued. The treasurer then transfers funds from the financial institution holding the matured investments to the bank upon which the district's checks are drawn.

The entries to the treasurer's ledger for this transaction are:

	Debit	Credit
Cash	XXXX	
Investments		XXXX
Distributed to SD#	XXXX	
Cash		XXXX

The entry to the school district's ledger for this transaction is:

	Debit	Credit
Cash	XXXX	
Investments		XXXX

Illustration 20.1
Kimberly Hills School District
Central Treasury—An Agency Fund
Balance Sheet
(Date)

Assets		
Cash on Hand	$ 400	
Deposits:		
Central Bank	$10,650	
1st National Bank	3,620	
National Bank of Commerce	10,330	
Total cash on hand and deposited	$25,000	
Liabilities		
Due to the General Fund		$ 2,200

Due to Special Revenue Fund	1,000
Due to Internal Service Fund	500
Due to Capital Projects Fund	21,300
Total liabilities	$25,000

At the end of the month, a bank reconciliation should be prepared to reconcile cash in the bank with cash recorded on the books. Any interest earnings/fees should be recorded through journal entries. Most districts carry separate checking accounts for each type of check that is issued. The most common checking accounts are payroll, vendor, imprest and student activity accounts. Investments flow through general savings accounts and all maturities with interest, should be recorded into this cash account.

After cash has been reconciled, a balance sheet and statement of position can be prepared for board of education review. Timely and accurate bank reconciliations are necessary to ensure that control over cash is being maintained. Up-to-date cash balances in the ledger are also needed to keep cash flow estimates as current as possible. Illustration 20.1 shows a balance prepared for an agency fund.

SUMMARY

Payroll accounting provides the method to account for assets which are to be held for others by the school district with the board of education acting as agent.

ACTIVITIES

1. Obtain a current copy of Circular Series E from the U.S. Treasury Department website.

2. Given: Payroll is prepared biweekly
   An hourly custodial employee completes a timesheet
   Hourly rate $10.00/hour
   In a two-week period hours worked total 86 (48 hours in week 1 and 38 hours in week 2)
   Contract states that any hours over 40 hours per week is overtime (1.5X)
   The employee is eligible for retirement system (employee rate 4.5%)
   Federal tax rate is 12%
   State tax rate is 3%
   Social security tax rate is 7.65%
   Union dues is $16.09/pay

   Determine:

   - Gross pay
   - Deductions for IMRF; federal tax; state tax; social security tax; union dues
   - Net pay

3. Given: Teacher contract is based on 180 days
   Base contract $55,000

2% stipend for being yearbook sponsor (% of base salary)
Biweekly payroll (assume 26 pays per year)
Stipend also paid over 26 pays
Federal tax rate is 15%
State tax rate is 3%
Medicare rate is 1.45%
Union dues per pay is $26.10

Determine:

- Gross payroll per pay
- Total retirement system reported for entire year
- Total federal tax for year
- Total state tax for year
- Total Medicare for year
- Total union dues for year
- Total net pay for year

4. The following account balances were taken from the Fort Steven School District central payroll fund on September 30, 2008:

Due from general fund	$88,000
Due from cafeteria fund	15,000
Social security taxes payable	10,000
Federal income taxes withheld and payable	93,000

During the month of October, the following transactions occurred:

Oct. 1 Employee's social security tax liability from September was computed. For the general fund, $9,500 was applicable and $2,000 was applicable to the cafeteria fund.

Oct. 2 Cash was received from the general fund in the amount of $96,000 and from the cafeteria fund in the amount of $16,500.

Oct. 2 Required monthly cash deposit for income taxes withheld and for both the employee and employer social security taxes was made.

Oct. 15 Semi-monthly payroll voucher was prepared as follows:

Social security taxes withheld	$ 5,400
Federal income taxes withheld	45,700
Group insurance premiums withheld	12,500
Retirement contributions withheld	15,000
Credit union deductions	3,000
Net payroll	205,800

Billings against the general fund were computed to be $326,700 and against the cafeteria fund to be $57,600.

Oct. 15 Cash was received from the general fund in the amount of $248,900 and from the cafeteria fund in the amount of $43,900.

Oct. 15 Salaries were paid.

Oct. 31 Semi-monthly payroll voucher was prepared as on 10/15.

Oct. 31 Employer tax liability for October was computed; $91,800 was applicable to the general fund and $16,200 to the cafeteria fund.

Oct. 31 Cash was received in the amount of $413,700 from the general fund and $73,000 from the cafeteria fund.

Oct. 31 Salaries were paid.

Nov. 5 Required monthly deposit of cash for income taxes withheld and for both the employee and employer social security taxes was made.

Instructions:

- Record the above balances and transactions in general journal form on the books of the central payroll fund.
- Post to the central payroll fund general ledger accounts.
- Prepare a trial balance as of November 5, 2008.
- Record the general journal entries to the general fund.

5. The annual United Way campaign is taking place in the Michago School System. Students at the system's schools are collecting for the drive, and weekly collections are turned over to the business office. The money is remitted to the United Way, and remitted amounts for the first three weeks follow:

	Friday September 7	Friday September 14	Friday September 21
Westridge High School	$2,000	$2,000	$2,200
Eastside High School	1,800	1,900	1,900
Bayshore Middle School	900	950	950
Woods Middle School	750	750	750
Area 2 Elementary School	1,250	1,200	1,200
South Main Elementary School	1,400	1,400	1,500
Center Elementary School	800	800	800
Total	$8,900	$9,000	$9,300

Instructions:

- Record the receipt of cash by the United Way in general journal form.
- Prepare a trial balance as of January 21, 2009.
- Record the entry by the business office to remit the proceeds of the campaign to the United Way.

21

Internal Cash Control

INTRODUCTION

Internal accounting controls provide a school district with procedures that produce accurate and reliable financial statements that safeguard assets, financial resources and the integrity of every employee charged with the responsibility of handling money or property. This latter part of the accounting function is known as internal accounting control. By products of effective internal accounting control are operational efficiency, adherence to established policies and confidence in the financial administration. Responsibility for its operation extends to every level of authority.

OUTCOMES

In this chapter, you will learn how to:

1. Identify sources of cash receipts.
2. Determine internal controls for cash receipts accounting.
3. Account for cash disbursements.
4. Use vouchers.
5. Use imprest and petty cash accounts.
6. Prepare reports needed to account for cash.

INTERNAL ACCOUNTING CONTROLS

To provide adequate internal accounting control, it is necessary for certain procedures to be developed at the operating level to prevent errors from occurring. A most important internal accounting control procedure is double-entry bookkeeping, the generally accepted procedure that provides the basis for analyzing, recording and summarizing financial transactions. The double-entry bookkeeping concept makes it possible to analyze and record the effect of all financial transactions on each element of each fund used in the operation of the school district.

In an ideal situation, the work of one employee is verified by the work of another, each working separately and independently. One employee should not have control of a complete financial transaction that includes authorizing the transaction, receiving, disbursing, recording and/or posting the transaction to the accounts. Instead, different employees should participate at various stages in the transaction so that each would arrive at the same results independently, and, without unnecessary duplication of work, verify the accuracy of the other. Such a division of duties provides a procedure whereby errors of omission or commission, whether intentional or unintentional, can be minimized.

There are numerous ways of establishing effective and efficient internal accounting controls for a school district. The chart of accounts for each of the funds indicates the nature of the assets, liabilities and fund equity accounts, the sources of revenues and reasons for expenditures. This in itself is a control. Combining financial statements, which requires presentation of the financial position of each of the funds as well as presentation of the results of each fund's operation, provides a form of internal control. Comparisons that take into consideration changes that have occurred between one year's financial statements and those of prior years indicate trends. In this way, some control is provided. In the formal budgetary funds, the use of budgetary accounts that provide for comparisons between estimated revenue and actual revenue and comparisons between appropriations and expenditures plus encumbrances serves as an effective and efficient tool of management control.

The use of an internal auditing department reduces the occurrence of costly, material and time-consuming errors. When an invoice's prices, extensions and footings can be verified and compared with the transaction's authorization, purchase order, receiving reports and voucher prior to recording the transaction, significant losses can be avoided. Such a phase of work frequently is referred to as a pre-audit to contrast this internal control procedure with the post-audit conducted by the outside independent accountants.

The extent to which internal control procedures are to be developed depends upon the circumstances surrounding the individual school district. However, use of those procedures (which provide a school district of checks and balances to safeguard the interests of the taxpayer and the financial integrity of the board, its administrative officers and employees of the school district) is important to the effective operation of the school district and to the accomplishment of its educational goals and objectives.

INTERNAL CONTROL STRUCTURE

Financial Accounting for Local and State School Systems, 2003 (Johnson, 2003, 32) states that internal control is a process—affected by an entity's board of trustees, management and other personnel—designed to provide reasonable assurance regarding the achievement of objectives in the following categories:

- Reliability of financial reporting
- Effectiveness and efficiency of operations
- Compliance with applicable laws and regulations

The 2003 edition (Johnson, 2003, 32–35) further states, "As a result, internal control consists of five interrelated components," which include:

- Control Environment
- Risk Assessment
- Control Activities
- Information and Communication
- Monitoring

Control Environment

The control environment is established on the basis of the attitude of management toward internal control. It is the basis for all other elements of the system of internal control. AICPA Statement on Auditing Standards No. 78 states that the control environment "sets the tone of an organization, influencing the control consciousness of its people. It is the foundation for all other components of internal control, providing discipline and structure." As such, a management philosophy that is dedicated to establishing a sound business process and operating controls would tend to create a stronger internal control environment than a philosophy that is unaware of or unconcerned with internal controls.

The collective effort of various factors affects the control environment, including the following:

- Integrity and ethical values
- Commitment to competence
- Governing board or audit committee participation
- Management's philosophy and operating style
- Organizational structure
- Assignment of authority and responsibility
- Human resource policies and practices

The substance of internal controls is more important than the form because of the risk that controls may not be effectively implemented or maintained.

Risk Assessment

Risk assessment is the entity's identification and analysis of risks relevant to the achievement of its objectives and forms a basis for determining how the risks should be managed. Risks can arise or change as a result of the following factors:

- Changes in operating environment
- New personnel
- New or revamped information systems
- Rapid growth
- New technology
- New grant programs, building projects or other activities
- Organizational restructuring
- Accounting pronouncements
- Federal regulations
- Finance-related statutes

Given the dynamic nature of governmental operating environments, the ability to anticipate and mitigate risks from these changes is a key factor in measuring the strength of internal controls. To the extent that the design of controls for new operations is an important aspect of planning efforts, an entity's level of internal control may be enhanced.

Control Activities

Control activities are the policies and procedures that help ensure that management directives are carried out. Control activities can be divided into four categories:

- Performance reviews
- Information processing

- Physical controls
- Segregation of duties

The application of controls, such as the segregation of duties, is affected to some degree by the size of the organization. In small entities, procedures will be less formal than in large entities. Additionally, certain types of control activities may not be relevant in small entities.

Information and Communication

Information and communication represent the identification, capture and exchange of information in a form and time frame that enable people to carry out their responsibilities. Information systems encompass procedures and documents that do the following:

- Identify and record all valid transactions
- Describe, on a timely basis, transactions in sufficient detail to permit proper classification for financial reporting
- Measure the value of transactions in a manner that permits their proper recording in the financial statements
- Permit the recording of transactions in the proper accounting period
- Present properly the transactions and related disclosures in the financial statements

Senior management should deliver a clear message to employees about their responsibilities and role in the internal control system. Employees should also have a means for communicating the effectiveness and efficiency of these systems to upper levels of management.

Monitoring

Monitoring is a process that assesses the quality of internal control performance over time. On-going monitoring activities include regular management and supervisory activities and other actions taken during the normal performance of management's responsibilities. Further, periodic reviews of internal controls and related activities, performed with internal personnel or external resources, may be undertaken. The nature and timing of these evaluations depend on the effectiveness of on-going activities and the risk that internal controls are not performing as intended by management. Deficiencies in the system of internal controls should be reported to the appropriate level of management.

Management should clearly assign responsibility and delegate authority with sufficient care to ensure that persons who perform control procedures are held accountable for their performance by those who monitor these activities, and persons who monitor the performance of control procedures are held accountable by senior management, the governing board or the audit committee.

If accounting information is routinely used in making operating decisions, management is likely to establish effective controls and hold lower-level managers and employees accountable for performance. In addition, if management routinely uses accounting information in measuring progress and operating results, significant variances between planned and actual results are likely to be investigated. This review may detect the causes of the variances and affect the steps necessary to correct procedures that failed to prevent misstatements."

SOURCES OF CASH RECEIPTS

There is no financial need greater than that of adequate internal control for cash receipts and disbursements. Cash receipts include all money coming into the possession of each organizational unit of the school district. It is within the function of accounting to establish internal control procedures to safeguard, to record and to report all cash collected by all organizational units. Methods of verification should be provided whereby it is possible to reconcile the amount of cash that should have been collected with the amount actually collected. Once money is collected, eventual materials should be provided to show that it was deposited intact in an authorized depository.

Cash receipts should be deposited intact daily. Regardless of the method of verifying cash receipts, if cash collected is used temporarily or permanently without first being deposited, the purpose of the internal control and the effectiveness of its operation are destroyed.

All disbursements, whatever the urgency or nature, should be made only when authorized through the official processes that have been established by the board. Proper authorization may be given by preparation of a pre-numbered voucher. To each voucher is attached supporting documentation with authorized signatures that indicate the need, itemize the goods or services and that specify the amount involved in the request for payment. A system of internal control, which produces a way by which cash receipts can be verified and traced to the depository in addition to requiring properly executed business documents to support each disbursement, provides the basis for safeguarding the integrity of all persons associated with financial transactions of the school district.

To speed the processes related to disbursements of small amounts, a petty cash system may be used. A small amount of money may be entrusted to a custodian of petty cash who is authorized by the board and is given the responsibility to pay small bills upon receipt of a properly authorized petty cash voucher. When a petty cash account operates on an imprest system, internal control continues to be effective. A separation of duties between the person who is authorized to approve payments from the petty cash and the person who is custodian of the money provides a basis for adequate internal control.

Some of the sources of cash receipts of a school district are from:

Collection of taxes receivable—Taxes receivable was debited and a revenue account was credited at the time of the tax levy. It is important to know what taxes have been assessed and levied if the school district is to know how much cash it should receive. Cash collected from taxes receivable is an example of converting an asset into cash.

Collection of revenue directly without being first recorded in an asset account—For example, when a tuition fee is collected, the revenue is realized at the time the cash is collected. If however, collection is postponed until a later date, a receivable should be set up on the books at the time of the enrollment so that a record is made of the amount that should be collected. In the latter case, the collection of a receivable would be another example of converting an asset into cash.

Collection of cash from sources other than revenues—Cash may be received from any of the following sources, which do not provide revenue from:

- *Sale of a fund's assets*—Any asset carried in a fund may be sold. Therefore it is important that the accounting structure include and record all of its assets as an integral part of the accounting structure, particularly if all assets and resources are to be safeguarded. Any change in the balance of an asset account may indicate that cash should have been received and, if that is the case, it is important to determine that the cash was actually received by the school district.

- *Expenditure refunds or rebates*—This source of cash receipts arises after a cash payment has been made and a portion of the payment is returned to the school district. It is a difficult source of cash to trace because it arises after all documents indicating a completed transaction have been processed. However, it may arise as a result of a purchase return or allowance. Close coordination of inventory items with receiving reports and shipping orders provides a basis whereby claims can be established for goods damaged or goods returned. If expenditure refunds or rebates (frequently referred to as an abatement of expenditure) occur, the nature of the transaction should be recorded by adjusting the original expenditure charge or by creating accounts that will indicate that an adjustment has been made as a result of a purchase return or allowance.
- *Creation of liabilities*—Cash may be received from any source that creates liability of the school district. For example, one fund may borrow money from another fund, the school district may borrow money from another organizational unit, or promissory notes, tax anticipation notes or bonds may be issued. In order to provide adequate debt control, each should be authorized and recorded in the minutes of the board meetings. This does not include those purchases authorized by the purchasing agent.
- *Collection of accounts or sales of assets previously written off the books*—This can occur in the case of a school district's having written off taxes receivable or when an asset has been retired but is kept in storage. These sources of cash receipts are difficult to trace, and the way by which the board can best safeguard the assets of the school district is by requiring all tax account write-offs or asset disposal or retirement transactions to be authorized and recorded in the board meeting minutes.
- *Transfers between funds*—A transfer from one fund to another implies that no liability to return the amount is involved on the part of the fund receiving the money. A transfer from one fund to another does not give rise to revenue of the school district, but instead, is a transfer of fund equity.
- *Trust or agency fund receipts*—Examples include the collection of cash for purposes such as United Way, Community Chest or other similar purposes.

In order that the system of internal control for cash receipts operates effectively, the following records or their equivalent should be used:

- *Bill forms*—When a bill is prepared, it should be prepared in sufficient copies so that the department charged with cash collection and the accounting department will have knowledge of and a control over the amount of cash that is to be collected.
- *Receipt forms*—A written receipt shows the collection of money and provides information as to the source from which the money was collected. A receipt should be issued for each collection. All receipts should be pre-numbered, transferred from person to person in writing and accounted for by number. The auditors will be concerned over duplicate receipt numbers or missing receipts and will investigate the circumstances surrounding the case. Receipt forms use allows for the amount of cash that should be collected each day to be compared with actual cash collected. If differences occur, the cause should be determined, and action, if required, should be taken to prevent losses.
- *Deposit tickets*—When cash receipts are deposited in the bank, a duplicate deposit ticket should be secured from the bank, and an entry should be made into the depositor's records. Duplicate deposit tickets should be filed for the auditor's use in tracing deposits from the cash receipts

journal to the bank statement. Reconciliations of the cash account with the bank statement should be made regularly, and they should be brought into agreement.

- *Special journals*—Special journals may be designed to record transactions of a similar nature. Commercial software or spreadsheets may be developed by the school district to track these transactions. A cash receipts journal used to record cash transactions debiting cash and crediting the appropriate accounts is one such example.

Fidelity bonds compensate the school district for known fraud resulting in losses that occur through intentional or unintentional errors of omission or commissions of employees in positions of trust. Not only does a fidelity bond on an employee permit recovery in the case of loss, but it also tends to prevent losses. Bonding companies are likely to prosecute when a person is charged with such a loss rather than the school district would be. In executing a fidelity bond, past employment records of persons covered by the bond are reviewed by the insurer, and the employer is notified by the bonding company if the conduct of any of its employees covered has been in question previously. In this way, employment of persons of doubtful integrity is reduced. Four types of fidelity bonds are available to school districts:

- *Blanket bonds*—secured to cover all employees who actually handle money or property and can be extended to cover those who have access to money or property.
- *Position schedule bond*—secured to cover a particular position regardless of who the employee may be who serves the board in that position.
- *Name schedule bond*—secured to cover losses that may occur in the case of any employee whose name is listed on the schedule.
- *Individual bond*—secured to cover losses in the case of a particular or specified person.

VOUCHERS AND WARRANTS

A voucher or warrant is a business paper prepared by an employee of the school district and signed by a person authorized by the board to approve the expenditure of money for the purpose stated in the voucher. When a voucher or warrant is properly prepared and issued, an accounting entry is made in the fund affected. Depending upon the nature of the transactions, an asset, liability, fund equity, revenue or expenditure account is debited and an accounts payable, vouchers payable or warrants payable account is credited. The voucher is submitted to the school district's treasurer. When a check is drawn in payment of the voucher, a notation is made on the voucher or record of the voucher indicating the date paid and the check number used to make the payment.

The difference between a voucher and warrant is that a warrant is the fund's order drawn upon the treasurer of the governmental unit under which the school district operates, and a voucher is an order drawn within the school district upon the school district's treasurer. In either case, the voucher or warrant gives the treasurer authority to draw a check on a bank account.

CASH FORECASTING

A summary schedule is frequently used that shows each fund's cash balance and the total cash of the school district at a certain date. Such a schedule shows what the cash balance of each fund was at the beginning of the period, what cash has been received by the fund during the period, what cash disbursements have been made by the fund during the period, and the balance of each fund's cash account at the end of the period. Transfers of cash from one fund to another can also be shown on the schedule. Such a schedule is referred to as a schedule of cash position and is attached to the interim financial statements of the school district. Illustration 21.1 shows a summary schedule of cash position.

Illustration 21.1
Schedule of Cash Position
(Date)

	General Fund	Special Revenue Fund	Internal Service Fund	Debt Service Fund	Capital Projects Fund	Total
Beginning Balance	$160,000	$ 30,000	$ 40,000	$ 25,000	$ 0	$ 255,000
Add:						
Cash receipts, Per schedule	40,000	40,000	20,000	25,000	500,000	625,000
Total Cash Available For Use	$200,000	$ 70,000	$ 60,000	$ 50,000	$500,000	$880,000
Less:						
Cash disbursements, Per schedule	75,000	50,000	30,000	0	100,000	255,000
Ending Balance	$125,000	$ 20,000	$ 30,000	$ 50,000	$400,000	$625,000

The schedule of cash position can be used to meet the need of the school district for a systematic, predictable cash forecasting strategy. The forecast may use historical data that is adjusted by variable factors such as estimates for inflation, anticipated salary increases and decreases, changing economic conditions affecting the local, state and federal governments, anticipated major changes in programs, facilities, personnel, equipment, materials and supplies.

IMPREST AND PETTY CASH FUNDS

By resolution of the board, a petty cash account can be established. The resolution should state the amount of the petty cash account. A person is designated as custodian of the petty cash, and based upon the resolution of the board, a check in the amount authorized can be drawn and made payable to the petty cash custodian. An entry in the general fund to establish a $500 petty cash account would be:

	Debit	Credit
Petty cash	$500	
Vouchers payable		$500
To record creation of a petty cash account		

When the voucher is paid and a copy of the voucher indicating the check number used to make the payment and the date on which the check was issued is received by the accounting department, the following entry is made:

Vouchers payable	$500	
Cash		$500
To record payment of the voucher		

At all times, the custodian of the petty cash should have either $500 in cash or $500 composed partly of cash and partly of properly prepared and receipted petty cash vouchers.

When the larger part of cash on hand has been disbursed, the custodian may take the petty cash vouchers to the person authorized to prepare and issue warrants or vouchers. At that time, a warrant or voucher will be issued in the amount equal to the total of all properly authorized, paid and receipted petty cash vouchers presented. If the warrant would amount to $378, the following entry would be made:

Expenditures	$378	
Vouchers payable		$378
To record expenditure to reimburse petty cash		

When notice is received by the accounting department that the voucher has been paid, a general journal entry to record the payment by the general fund would be:

Vouchers payable	$378	
Cash		$378
To record payment of voucher		

In order to avoid the possibility of over-expending an appropriation, an entry should be made in the general fund to appropriate part of the general fund equity in an amount equal to the total of the petty cash account. Note that the petty cash account has changed to being an account that will remain the same until it is increased, decreased or eliminated by action of the board.

OTHER INTERNAL CONTROL ISSUES AFFECTING SCHOOL DISTRICTS

Johnson (2003, 38) also discussed other issues affecting school districts. Regardless of whether districts are component units of another financial reporting entity, are joint ventures of several reporting entities (such as consolidated educational agencies), or meet the definition in GASB Codification, Section 2100, as separate reporting entities, many school districts prepare separate financial statements to accomplish one or more of the following:

- Support state or federal aid applications
- Report financial activities to parent, taxpayer and citizen groups
- Prepare a financial report for use in an official statement for bond issuance purposes

Although school districts are a common type of government, they face a number of unique issues that make them distinct from states, cities, counties or other local governmental entities. These issues often result in internal control and operational challenges that district management must address. This list is not exhaustive:

- **Attendance reporting**—Most school districts receive state aid on the basis of average daily membership (ADM), average daily attendance (ADA) or a similar pupil count method. ADM and ADA data typically are determined at individual school sites and then reported to a central attendance unit. That unit prepares reports for state aid and, in many cases, for federal aid, such as impact aid.
- **Student activity funds**—Most school districts have cash funds or bank accounts at individual schools under the control of school principals or club advisors. These funds may be excluded from the district's normal accounting controls. These funds present a unique control challenge to school districts given their decentralized nature and the production of financial records and reports by non-accounting personnel.
- **U.S. Department of Education requirements**—Federal reporting requirements and others mandated by state-level education agencies are typically more detailed than the account code structures of cities and other local governments. Thus, district accounting systems must have the ability to account for transactions at a level of detail beyond that required by other governments. This issue is particularly complex for school district payroll systems, given the plurality of funding sources for district personnel and reporting requirements for personnel costs.
- **School lunch programs**—Most school districts participate in the U.S. Department of Agriculture (USDA) free or reduced-price food programs. These programs require school districts to segregate food service programs from other programs. School districts that receive federal commodities during the year should recognize the fair value as revenue in the period when all eligibility requirements are met (typically, when the commodities are received). (Guide to Implementation of GASB Statement 34 and Related Pronouncements Q&A, Q152) Because the federal agricultural commodity program involves purpose restrictions in the use of the resources, the value of inventory remaining on hand at fiscal year-end should be reflected as a reservation of fund balance/restriction of net assets. (Statement 33, paragraph 14) USDA-donated commodities may also pose accounting and reporting problems because of restrictive federal rules regulating the use of these commodities.
- **Site-based management initiatives**—Over the past decade, many states and school districts have implemented site-based management initiatives. These initiatives have been designed to delegate to individual schools greater levels of authority to determine the use of financial resources. As a result, local administrators may control and report on the use of financial resources, even though they may lack financial management skills. This issue creates a challenge to district management in controlling financial resources and ensuring that reported results are correct.
- **Educational accountability**—Educational accountability has become a key policy issue at both state and national levels and has resulted in a number of recent reforms. Several educational accountability reforms have required school districts to collect and present school-level financial information. In addition, school-level financial information is often related to non-financial information (e.g., student achievement) in published reports and is used for comparison purposes. As a result, school districts must increasingly focus on ensuring that financial information reported by schools is accurate and consistent across the district. (Johnson, 2003, 38–40)

SUMMARY

This chapter has pointed out the necessity for:

- Providing a proof of the amount of cash that should have been received.
- Determining the amount of cash actually received.
- Accounting for any differences and taking appropriate action under the circumstances of the case in order to safeguard the resources of the school district.
- Depositing all cash receipts as soon as practical and intact.
- Disbursing by cash only by check drawn upon a properly prepared voucher or warrant.

ACTIVITIES

1. Review the definition of the following terms found in the glossary:

    a. Separation of duties
    b. Imprest system
    c. Fidelity bond
    d. Voucher
    e. Warrant

2. Describe internal accounting control.

3. Describe the difference between a voucher and a warrant

4. If a school district central treasury operates as a separate unit, give the journal entries to record:

    a. Receipt of cash by the treasurer from the general fund.
    b. Deposit of cash in the bank by the treasurer.
    c. The receipt of a voucher.
    d. The payment of a voucher.

4. Fort Steven School District's general fund bank statement for March, 2009, indicates a $22,300 balance. The check stub balances and the account balance shows $19,800. A comparison of cancelled checks and memoranda accompanying the bank statement with check stubs reveals the following:

    a. Outstanding checks:

# 2121 for	$1,760
# 2122 for	$1,240
# 2123 for	$ 630
# 2124 for	$1,190

    b. The March 31 deposit of $4,400 is recorded on the books but not on the bank statement.
    c. A $300 bank service charge.
    d. The bank statement shows a credit on the district's account for collection of a $3,500 note receivable left at the bank for collection. No entry is made on the school district's books.
    e. A $1,400 deposit has been erroneously recorded a second time on the check stubs and in the account.

Instructions:

- Prepare a bank reconciliation as of March 31, 2009.

5. A November 1 internal audit of the Lebanon School Corporation accounts at the close of business on October 31 produced the following information:

   a. Cash balance in bank account $52,000.
   b. Bank statement account balance 37,000.
   c. Outstanding checks:

# 401	$170
# 410	50
# 413	210
# 421	675
# 438	300
# 450	1,050
# 456	1,205

   d. October 31 cash receipts of $11,870 were deposited November 1.
   e. The following charges appeared on the bank statement:

Service charge	$ 50
Check payable to district was returned for non-sufficient funds	$120

      (Check was originally received on October 12 and deposited on October 13. It was charged to the district's account by the bank on October 14.)
   f. Check no. 412 for $650 was improperly recorded as $250 on both check stub and cash payments journal. The check was issued to pay for teaching supplies.
   g. An October 28 credit memorandum for $1,100, representing proceeds of a note receivable left at the bank for collection, had not been recorded in the checkbook or cash receipts journal.

Instructions:

- Prepare a bank reconciliation for the Lebanon School Corporation as of the end of October.
- Record the journal entries necessary to bring the general fund accounts into agreement with the correct bank balance.

22

Student Accounting

INTRODUCTION

There are many items that school districts need to count and record, such as dollars, equipment, supplies, staff and students. Although this book concentrates on financial record keeping, counting pupils is just as important. Not only are students the reason for a school's existence, but the numbers and kinds of students determine the district's programs and finances.

OUTCOMES

In this chapter, you will learn how to:

1. Project future student enrollments.
2. Determine the uses of a student census.
3. Identify applications of student attendance.
4. Use present and future data on student counts to aid school district planning.

PLANNING AND STUDENT COUNTS

If it weren't for students, the school district would not exist. The numbers, types and locations of students provide basic planning data for the school business administrator. If student numbers are growing or declining, the school business administrator is faced with a variety of challenges to meet the students' needs. Even if enrollments are stable, the school business administrator needs to be concerned with the types of students in the school district and whether student demographics are changing and the subsequent impact on the school district's programs and finances.

It is imperative that the district be able to accurately determine the number of students presently in the district, and depending upon the funding systems, the attendance and types of students in the district. Certainly technology has aided the school business administrator in these tasks. Commercial student accounting packages that run on mainframe, desktop, or laptop computers are available for any size school district. Larger school districts that have appropriate staff are able to write their own student accounting programs or customize vendor software to their needs. As school administrators become more computer literate, individual applications are shared through networks, professional journals and magazines. Many state systems now accept electronic transmission of data, and that mode of delivery will continue to increase.

ENROLLMENT PROJECTIONS

The school business administrator needs to assess the impact of changing student demographics on the school district operations. The most common measure used is enrollment. Forecasting enrollment involves predicting future numbers and grades of students, and in some cases locations of students.

Enrollment forecasts can also be used to determine future class sizes and building populations, future staff numbers and types of personnel, future building renovation, construction, closing and future financial requirements.

One of the most common methods used to predict enrollments is the cohort-survival method. This uses historical trend data to predict future enrollments at various grade levels. Everett, Lows and Johnson (1996) used Lewis's steps to compute a projection using the cohort-survival method:

Step 1	Determine the number of live births in the school district for each year for the past ten years.
Step 2	Using that birth information, indicate actual first grade enrollment for the first five years.
Step 3	Using the post-enrollment figures for the first five years, calculate the cohort-survival ratio by dividing actual enrollments by resident live births.
Step 4	Complete the table of projected enrollment for all grades.

Lewis cites the following advantages of using the cohort-survival method:

- The method is easy to calculate.
- It can be easily accommodated by the computer.
- Information is easily accessible.

He also cites the following disadvantages:

- Because kindergarten enrollment fluctuates in most school districts, the first grade enrollment should be used as a base to calculate future enrollment.
- Forecasts may be more accurate if first grade estimates are based on the number of four-year-olds counted in the school district census.
- A "pure" situation hardly ever exists; therefore, many variables may influence future enrollments.
- The method tends to be subjective (see Example 1).

In like fashion, the school business administrator can use each grade's prior ten years' data to determine a cohort-survival ratio for that grade to project future enrollments for that grade. Multiplying that grade's cohort-survival ratio by each year's enrollment will produce a projected enrollment for the next five years. The school business administrator should realize that the data projections for the first five years will be relatively accurate since the projections are based on actual live births. Since the second five years combine the survival ratio with trend analysis, the school business administrator should use reasonable care in determining the accuracy of those projections. Ideally, as each new year occurs, actual live birth data can be input to the spreadsheet bringing more reliability to the projections.

In addition to determining actual student enrollment projections, the school business administrator needs to consider additional factors that may affect the enrollment projections including:

- Comparisons with prior enrollment projections noting discrepancies.
- Amount of time lapse between the projection and the present time.
- Economic conditions.

- Special needs of low or high incidence of disadvantaged or gifted students.
- Building, development and housing trends including impact of major new highways, roads or other transportation.
- Impact of non-public schools in the area or home schooling efforts.
- Ethnic background.
- Fertility rates.
- Mortality rates.

Example 1

The New Douglas School District determined that the number of live births in the district for the past ten years and the fall first grade enrollments for the first five years of that period were:

Births		First Grade Enrollment	
Calendar Year	Number of Resident Live Births	School Year	Fall Enrollment
(1)	(2)	(3)	(4)
1995	205	2001–02	180
1996	210	2002–03	182
1997	226	2003–04	191
1998	208	2004–05	179
1999	205	2005–06	175
2000	210	2006–07	?
2001	218	2007–08	?
2002	205	2008–09	?
2003	234	2009–10	?
2004	240	2010–11	?

Illustrations 22.1 and 22.2 show the results of determining the projected enrollments for the next five years.

Illustration 22.1
Example 1, Part 1

Dividing the fall enrollment (Column 4 above) by the number of resident live births (Column 2 below) produces the survival ratio (Column 4 below).

Births		First Grade Enrollment	
Calendar Year	Number of Resident Live Births	School Year	Survival Ratio
(1)	(2)	(3)	(4)
1995	205	2001–02	0.878
1996	210	2002–03	0.867
1997	226	2003–04	0.845
1998	208	2004–05	0.861

1999	205	2005–06	0.854
2000	210	2006–07	?
2001	218	2007–08	?
2002	205	2008–09	?
2003	234	2009–10	?
2004	240	2010–11	?

Illustration 22.2
Example 1, Part 2

Calculate the average survival ratio for those five years, by dividing the sum of the ratios for five years by five ((.878+7.867+.845+7.861+7.854)/5 = .861). Multiplying the average survival ratio for the five years by the number of resident live births (Column 1) produces the projected fall enrollment (Column 5) for the next five years.

Births		First Grade Enrollment		
Calendar Year	Number of Resident Live Births	School Year	Survival Ratio	Projected Enrollment
(1)	(2)	(3)	(4)	
1995	205	2001–02	0.878	
1996	210	2002–03	0.867	
1997	226	2003–04	0.845	
1998	208	2004–05	0.861	
1999	205	2005–06	0.854	
2000	210	2006–07	0.861	181
2001	218	2007–08	0.861	188
2002	205	2008–09	0.861	177
2003	234	2009–10	0.861	201
2004	240	2010–11	0.861	207

DISTRICT CENSUS

School districts may conduct a census to determine the actual number of children residing in the district. Much like the federal government, school boards may decide to conduct a census once every decade, or establish some periodic pattern that would provide the needed information for their school district. Generally, school districts in older, stable communities without changing demographics would not need a census since very little changes from year to year. However, in growing communities or communities undergoing changing demographics, a census could be conducted to provide reliable and accurate data that can be used to:

- Update enrollment projections.
- Determine district demographics to help achieve racial balance in each school.
- Help ensure a staff profile that reflects the ethnic composition of the community.
- Determine the need for special programs.

- Help develop strategies for budget building and support.
- Determine class size.
- Determine staffing needs.
- Determine future building needs including renovation, construction, closing or equity.
- Determine state aid projections when the funding system is pupil-based.
- Complete local, state and federal reports.
- Survey community attitudes and needs to: develop special programs; develop strategies for budget building and support.

STUDENT ATTENDANCE

School districts need to monitor student attendance to provide the district with valuable information or to comply with state requirements. Some common uses of student data include:

- Alerting school administrators to: problem grade levels or buildings; and/or problem seasons, weeks or days of the week.
- Prompting school administrators to take district-wide pro-action.
- Demonstrating school and/or district improvement.
- Determining state aid allocations when the funding is pupil-based.

As previously noted, school districts are increasingly using computer programs to assist them in determining student attendance. Even though smaller districts may be able to determine student attendance manually, reporting requirements from the intermediate, state and federal agencies are necessitating the use of computers to assimilate and report the data.

SUMMARY

This chapter has discussed:

- Planning and student counts.
- Procedures for using the cohort-survival method for enrollment projections.
- Information and benefits that could be obtained by enrollment projections and a school district census.
- Uses of student attendance data.

ACTIVITIES

1. Interview a school business official to identify measures used to determine student census, enrollments and attendance.

2. Obtain at least two commercially prepared student accounting programs and compare them for ease of understanding, input of data, reports produced and costs associated with using each program.

3. Develop a spreadsheet that employs the cohort-survival method of enrollment projection for a school district having grades kindergarten through twelve.

4. Research at least one additional method of forecasting enrollment and compare it to the cohort-survival method citing advantages and disadvantages.

5. Identify the planning process and procedures to be followed for a school district to conduct a district-wide census. Identify potential problems and pitfalls.

6. Fort Steven School District's live births for the last ten years and actual student enrollments for the first five years are:

Births		Kindergarten Enrollment	
Calendar Year	Number of Resident Live Births	School Year	Fall Enrollment
(1)	(2)	(3)	(4)
1995	3,568	2001–02	2,766
1996	3,487	2002–03	2,632
1997	3,502	2003–04	2,687
1998	3,622	2004–05	2,714
1999	3,653	2005–06	2,729
2000	3,598	2006–07	?
2001	3,614	2007–08	?
2002	3,597	2008–09	?
2003	3,612	2009–10	?
2004	3,651	2010–11	?

Instructions:

- Determine the average cohort-survival ratio for the first five years of enrollment data.
- Project the kindergarten grade student enrollments for the next five years.

7. Using the information from problem 4, and knowing the average cohort-survival ratios for the following grades and 2001–02 school year enrollments are:

Grade Level	Enrollment	Percent Change
1	2,841	97.2
2	2,754	102.7
3	2,633	99.5
4	2,644	104.5
5	2,685	100.0
6	2,712	99.3
7	2,683	98.8
8	2,598	98.5
9	3,118	97.2
10	3,425	92.9
11	3,567	94.6
12	3,601	95.0

Instructions:

- Prepare a spreadsheet for Fort Steven School District which projects the district's student enrollment for the next five years.
- Identify major factors that could influence the accuracy of your enrollment projections.

23

Advanced Financial Statements

INTRODUCTION

One of the many primary objectives of financial and managerial accounting for school districts is the preparation of financial statements and reports which present reliable and timely information completely and clearly. Regardless of how clearly information may be presented, if it is not presented in time to serve those who need it, accounting serves only a historical purpose.

A highly desirable goal of accounting for elementary and secondary school districts is the design of financial reports that may be readily understood by reasonably intelligent people to facilitate better communication between schools and the public. Accounting is essentially a communication process. Three types or levels of accounting reports are used:

- The accounting forms required by governmental units.
- The accounting reports prepared by the school district business office personnel for school administrators who must learn what the statements contain and how to use them.
- The accounting reports presented to the school board and public.

OUTCOMES

In this chapter, you will learn how to:

1. Review responsibility for preparation of interim financial statements.
2. Identify requirements for the Comprehensive Annual Financial Report.
3. Review the differences in financial reporting as a result of GASB 34.

FINANCIAL STATEMENTS

Both interim and annual financial statements of the school district are part of the financial statements of the school district. The audited annual financial statements also are the responsibility and formal representations of the school district and its management. The outside, independent auditor, after completing an examination of the financial statements only expresses an opinion on them. The opinion can be an unqualified opinion, a qualified opinion, an adverse opinion, or it can be a disclaimer of opinion. The type of opinion that a school district should try to obtain is an unqualified opinion indicating that the financial statements present fairly the financial position of each fund on the balance sheet date and the results of operation, the changes in fund equity, and the changes in financial position.

The business office staff should prepare interim financial statements throughout the fiscal year for use by operating personnel, administrators, and the board of education. These statements assist the board in making policy decisions and assist administrators in carrying out the financial responsibilities of the board.

The level of reporting in this book has been to provide the managerial accounting structure needed throughout the fiscal period to produce meaningful and timely interim financial statements for all funds used by a school district. The level of reporting that ASBO International is primarily concerned with in its Certificate of Excellence in Financial Reporting by School Systems is the comprehensive annual financial report because it is the one which has award potential. ASBO International has the strong opinion, however, that interim financial statements, properly and timely presented, are an integral part of the management-stewardship function. Accordingly copies of interim financial statements are required to be submitted to ASBO International by participants in its Certificate of Excellence in Financial Reporting program.

Interim financial statements for each fund should be submitted to every member of the board of education and to administrators designated by the board prior to the board's regularly scheduled meetings. To provide a basis for comparability, the format of statements should be consistent with the format of the financial statements of each fund in the comprehensive annual financial statements of the school district. In this way, board members can have an opportunity to compare financial statements and study the financial position and results of operation of each fund at the end of the preceding period. The board and administrators can be in a position to make more reasonable decisions during meetings of the board than if complete financial data were not available.

For management purposes, it is the financial statements of the individual funds that are essential for financial control. Illustrations of interim financial statements have been presented in the preceding chapters to show how financial statements can be prepared for each fund each month during the fiscal year. Based upon these financial statements prepared in accordance with generally accepted accounting principles, the content of interim financial reports should be:

1. A cover letter naming the entity, its address, the period covered by the report and the date of the report.
2. A table of contents.
3. Combining financial statements of fund types or individual funds including:
   - Government funds: General fund, Special Revenue funds, Capital Projects funds, Debt Service funds, Permanent funds.
   - Proprietary funds: Enterprise funds, Internal Service funds.
   - Fiduciary funds: Trust funds, Agency funds.
4. Schedules necessary to demonstrate compliance with legal or other contractual obligations and/or other schedules deemed necessary to lend cohesion and clarity to data presented in the body of the financial statements.
5. Statistics and other pertinent information useful to management.

CONSOLIDATED ANNUAL FINANCIAL REPORT (CAFR)

Financial Accounting for Local and State School Systems, 2003 (Johnson, 2003) presents the revised contents of the Consolidated Annual Financial Report (CAFR). For a comparison of new reporting requirements to the former reporting requirements under Fowler (1990), see pages 74–78 of Johnson (2003).

INTRODUCTORY CHAPTER

Table of Contents
Letter of Transmittal

GFOA Certificate of Achievement
Organization Chart
Principal Officials
Other Material Deemed Appropriate by Management (if applicable)

FINANCIAL CHAPTER

Auditor's Report
Management's Discussion & Analysis
Basic Financial Statements
Government-wide Financial Statements
Statement of Net Assets
Statement of Activities
Fund Financial Statements
Governmental Funds
Balance Sheet
Statement of Revenues, Expenditures and Changes in Fund Balances
Reconciliation to Government-wide Statements
Proprietary Funds
Statement of Net Assets
Statement of Revenues, Expenses and Changes in Net Assets
Reconciliation to Government-wide Statements (if applicable)
Statement of Cash Flows (using the direct method)
Fiduciary Funds (and similar Component Units)
Statement of Fiduciary Net Assets
Statement of Changes in Fiduciary Net Assets
Discretely Presented Component Units
Fund Financial Statements as RSI if component unit does not issue separate financial statements

Notes to Financial Statements

General Disclosure Requirements (Similar to Notes to Financial Statements per the old reporting model as applicable)
Additional Disclosures in Summary of Significant Accounting Policies (Paragraph 115 of GASB Statement 34)
Definition of operating and non-operating revenues
Description of government-wide financial statements including measurement focus & basis of accounting used
Government's policy for applying restricted and unrestricted resources
Description of types of transactions included in program revenues, policies for allocating indirect expenses to functions and elimination of internal activity in the statement of activities
Description of modified approach, if applicable
Policy for asset capitalization and estimation of useful lives GASB 20 policy for proprietary funds and government-wide activities
Additional Disclosures in Summary of Significant Accounting Policies required by GASB Statement 38
Activities accounted for in major funds, internal service, and fiduciary fund types columns
Length of time used to define "available" for revenue recognition

Required Disclosures about Capital Assets (Paragraphs 116–120 of the Statement)
Separately disclosed for governmental and business-type activities: Beginning and ending balances and acquisitions and dispositions for the year for each major class of capital asset and the related accumulated depreciation reported
Required Disclosures on Non-Capitalized Assets (Paragraph 118)
Historical collections that are not capitalized should be described and reasons for not capitalizing should be provided
Required Disclosures on Long-term Liabilities (Paragraphs 116–120 of the Statement)
Beginning and ending balances and increases and decreases for the year for each major long-term liability
Additional disclosure is required for portion of items due within one year
Information on governmental funds that have liquidated the long-term operating liabilities in the past
Any excess of expenditures over appropriation in individual funds
Deficit fund balance or retained earnings of individual funds
Interfund receivable and payables
Disclosures for Donor-Restricted Endowments (Paragraph 121 of the Statement)
Amounts of net appreciation on investment available for authorization for expenditure
How the amounts are reported in net assets
State Law relating to ability to spend net appreciation
Policy for authorizing and spending investment income
Segment Reporting (Paragraph 122 of the Statement)
Provision of Condensed Financial Statements in the Notes:
- Types of goods or services provided by the segment
- Condensed statement of net assets
- Condensed statement of revenues, expenses and changes in net assets
- Condensed statement of cash flows

GASB Statement 38—Violations and actions taken regarding finance-related legal or contractual provisions
Variable-rate debt service on debt and lease obligations
Short-term debt activity
Disaggregation of receivable/payable balances
Interfund Balances and transfers

Required Supplementary Information (RSI) Other Than MD&A

BUDGETARY COMPARISON SCHEDULES

(Paragraphs 130 and 131 of Statement 34; see comment below)

Original and final appropriated budget

Actual amounts (Budgetary basis)
Column to report the variance between the final budget and actual amounts is encouraged, a column to report the variance between the original and final budgets is allowed

COMBINING AND INDIVIDUAL FUND STATEMENTS

Combining statements are limited to non-major funds and are not required under GASB Statement 34

STATISTICAL CHAPTER

The following statistical tables should be included in the CAFR unless clearly inapplicable in the circumstances:

Government-Wide Revenues and Expenses
General Governmental Expenditures by Function
General Revenues by Source
Property Tax Levies and Collections
Assessed and Estimated Actual Value of Taxable Property
Property Tax Rates—All Overlapping Governments
Special Assessment Billings and Collections
Ratio of Net General Bonded Debt to Assessed Value & Net Bonded Debt per Capita
Computation of Legal Debt Margin
Computation of Overlapping Debt
Ratio of Annual Debt Service for General Bonded Debt to Total General Expenditures
Revenue Bond Coverage
Demographic Statistics
Property Value, Construction and Bank Deposits
Principal Taxpayers
Miscellaneous Statistics

New reporting requirements are presented in *Financial Accounting for Local and State School Systems, 2003* (Johnson, 2003). Included are:

- Basic Financial Statements
- Management's Discussion and Analyses (MD&A) and Other RSI
- Component Units

Basic Financial Statements

Under the new financial reporting model, the basic financial statements are:

- Government-wide financial statements
- Fund financial statements
- Note disclosures

The basic financial statements replace the combined general-purpose financial statements (GPFS) required by the former reporting model.

Government-Wide Financial Statements—The purpose of government-wide financial statements is to present the financial position and the operating results of the governmental entity as a whole. The statements are expected to provide users with operational accountability information and to enable them to do the following:

- Understand the true financial position of the governmental entity, including capital and financial assets and long-term as well as short-term liabilities.
- Determine whether the entity is able to continue to provide current service levels and meet its obligations as they become due.
- Determine the operating results of the entity, including the economic cost and the net cost of services, and assess the economy, efficiency, and effectiveness of operations.

GASB Statement 34 allows governments to elect to present budgetary comparison information as part of the basic financial statements, rather than as required supplemental information (RSI) (Statement 34, paragraphs 130 and 131).

The government-wide financial statements are

- Statement of Net Assets
- Statement of Activities

Statement of Net Assets—The Statement of Net Assets presents the financial position of the governmental entity and its discretely presented component units. This statement is required to present all financial and capital resources on the accrual basis of accounting. It encourages the use of a net assets format, which subtracts liabilities from assets to reflect the net assets, rather than the standard balance sheet format, which presents a total for assets equal to a total of liabilities and net assets. However, either presentation is acceptable.

The Statement of Net Assets presents a columnar presentation of the assets, liabilities and net assets of the reporting entity in two categories: governmental activities and business-type activities. Discretely presented component units are reflected in a separate column or columns on the face of the statement. Statement 34 does not alter the requirements for presenting component units as established by Statement 14, *The Financial Reporting Entity* (issued in June 1991) (Johnson, 2003, 78–80).

SUMMARY

Accounting information serves only an historical purpose if it is not presented in a timely basis. It must also be presented in clear form so that it may be readily understood by reasonably intelligent people to facilitate communication and the management of the school district.

ACTIVITIES

1. Identify the primary objectives of financial and managerial accounting for school districts.

2. Interview a school business official to learn what changes/adaptations the district had to make under GASB Statement 34.

3. Interview a school board member to determine:

    a. The financial reports used by the school district.
    b. The procedures for preparation of those reports.
    c. A comparison of the district's reports with the consolidated annual financial report.

4. Discuss the items frequently included in the financial and statistical sections of the consolidated annual financial report and the rationale for including those items.

5. Obtain a copy or download from the NCES website a copy of *Financial Accounting for Local and State School Systems, 2003 edition*. Identify the differences between the new required Statement of Net Assets with the former Balance Sheet.

24

Auditing

INTRODUCTION

School district audits report independently and objectively on the financial position and the results of operation of each fund used in the financial administration of the district. The major purpose of such an examination is to investigate and determine if the financial statements submitted for audit have been prepared in accordance with generally accepted accounting principles and is accomplished by an outside, independent auditor through use of generally accepted auditing standards. Emphasis is placed upon the school district's system of internal control, which should be designed to serve several functions. These functions are to establish and maintain safeguards for conserving and preserving the school district's financial resources and property, to detect intentional or unintentional errors of omission or commission and to detect fraud.

OUTCOMES

In this chapter, you will learn how to:

1. Fairly report the financial condition of the school district.
2. Identify advantages of using independent audits.
3. Prepare specifications, recommendations and presentations of the audit report.

AUDIT REPORTS

Financial accounting for elementary and secondary school districts is technical. Limited sources of revenue and restrictions placed upon the purposes for which money may be used make it as complicated as any area of financial and managerial accounting. The accountants for the school district, the internal auditors and independent auditor have to be well trained. Financial accounting, reporting and auditing for elementary and secondary school districts are fields of specialization. Time and study are required in order to acquire the knowledge and the ability to apply principles, procedures and standards effectively in practice.

The independent audit's objective is an attestation of the auditor regarding the fairness and reliability of the financial statements. In the form of a written audit report, which accompanies the financial statements, the opinion of the auditor is addressed to the board of education. Under GASB 34 preparation requirements, the written audit report is known as the management's discussion and analysis (MD&A). *Financial Accounting for Local and State School Systems, 2003* (Johnson, 2003) identifies the following regarding MD&A:

The management's discussion and analysis (MD&A) is part of the required supplementary information (RSI); however, it precedes the financial statements.

It should be based on currently known facts as of the date of the audit report and should

- Provide a concise, unbiased and easily readable description of the government's financial activities.
- Help users understand the relationship of the results reported in the governmental activities in the government-wide financial statements and the results reported in the governmental funds financial statements (usually focused on the major funds).

The focus of the MD&A should be on the primary government. However, information on any discretely presented component units may be presented as well. GASB has stated that both the positive and negative aspects of the government's operations should be presented to inform the reader about whether the government is in better or worse financial condition than in the prior year. The focus should be on only significant or material items.

MD&A is restricted to the following topics, although there is no limit to the information that may be presented about these topics.

- *Information and discussion on the basic financial statements presented, their relationship to one another and the significant differences in the information they provide*—The discussion should include the different methods of accounting used in the governmentwide and fund financial statements.
- *Condensed financial information comparing the current year and the prior year*—The analysis should include specific economic factors that contributed to the change. Charts and graphs may be used to supplement information in the condensed statements but should not be used in place of it.
- *Objective analysis of the governmental entity's financial condition as a whole*—Analysis of the government's overall financial position and results of operations should address both governmental and business-type activities separately.
- *An analysis of balances and transactions on a fund basis, addressing the reasons for significant changes in fund balances or fund net assets*—The analysis should also include information on whether restrictions, commitments or other limitations significantly affect the availability of fund resources for future use.
- *A discussion on significant variances among the entity's original budget, final budget and actual expenditures for the General Fund or its equivalent and the impact of these variances on the entity's future liquidity.*
- *A description of activity relating to the government's capital assets and long-term debt activity during the year*—This discussion should include commitments made for capital expenditures, changes in credit ratings and debt limitations affecting the financing of planned facilities or services.
- *A discussion of information about the modified approach used to report some or all of the infrastructure assets, if applicable.*
- *A description of currently known facts, decisions or conditions expected to have an impact on financial position and results of operation*—The term *currently known* is limited to events or decisions that have occurred, been enacted, adopted, agreed on or contracted as of the date of the auditor's report. The discussion should address expected effects on both governmental and business-type activities.

Information that does not address the requirements above should not be included in the MD&A but instead may be reported as supplementary information or included in the letter of transmittal.

The entity should ensure that information contained in MD&A is not duplicated in the letter of transmittal. Differences between MD&A and the letter of transmittal are outlined in Table 24.1 (Johnson, 2003, 87).

Table 24.1
Important Distinctions between MD&A and Letter of Transmittal

MD&A

- Presented as part of the Financial Chapter in the Comprehensive Annual Financial Report (CAFR)
- Must present only topics required by GASB Statement 34
- Provides a summary and analysis of the government's overall financial position and operations
- Highly structured and requires information only on currently known facts, conditions or decisions

Letter of Transmittal

- Presented as part of the Introductory Chapter in the Consolidated Annual Financial Report (CAFR)
- Not limited to topics described in GASB standards
- Provides an opportunity to discuss future plans

If the reporting entity provides comparative financial statements by presenting basic financial statements and RSI for two years, a separate MD&A for each year is not required, but it must address both years presented in the comparative financial statements. MD&A should include comparative condensed financial information and related analysis for both years.

Component Units

According to Johnson (2003, 87), it is essential that governmental financial statements provide an overview of the reporting entity that is based on financial accountability, yet allow users to distinguish between the primary government and its component units. GASB Statement 14, *The Financial Reporting Entity*, issued in June 1991, established criteria for evaluating potential component units and provided guidance in the statement presentation of those entities that met the criteria. Component units are defined as legally separate organizations for which the primary government is financially accountable or for which the nature and significance of the relationship with the primary government are such that exclusion would cause the reporting entity's financial statements to be misleading or incomplete (Statement 14, paragraph 20).

Financial accountability for a potential component unit is determined by either of the following:

- Appointment of the voting majority of the potential component unit governing board by the primary government *and either*
  —the ability to impose its will on the potential component unit *or*
  —a relationship of financial benefit or burden with the potential component unit.

- The potential component unit is fiscally dependent upon the primary government.

If a potential component unit does not meet either of the two tests above for financial accountability, an organization may still be included in the financial statements of the primary government based on the criterion that exclusion would result in a misleading or incomplete presentation of the financial reporting entity.

In May 2002, GASB issued Statement 39, *Determining Whether Certain Organizations Are Component Units*, which amended Statement 14 to establish the criteria for the inclusion of organizations on this basis. A legally separate, tax-exempt organization should be reported as a component unit if all of the following criteria are met:

- The economic resources of the separate organization are received or held for the benefit of the primary government, its component units, or its constituents.
- The primary government, or its component units, may access or is entitled to a majority of the economic resources of the separate organization.
- The economic resources of an individual organization that the primary government, or its component units, is entitled to or may access are significant to the primary government. (Statement 39, paragraph 5 in Johnson 2003, 86–88).

This standard continues the requirement for inclusion of organizations based on the GASB Statement 14, paragraph 20 "misleading or incomplete" criterion but emphasizes that "financial integration" may also be a component of all of the aforementioned criteria. Additional guidance on evidence of financial integration is also provided in Statement 39.

Component units may be:

- *Blended*—legally separate from the reporting entity, but intertwined with the reporting entity.
- *Discretely presented*—presentation of financial data separate from the financial data of the primary government.

GASB Statement 34 does not amend the definition of component units or the general reporting requirements.

Some advantages of audits are:

- An outside, independent audit adds credibility to the financial statements.
- The audit tends to discourage fraud and embezzlement on the part of the school district's financial managers and employees.
- Audited financial statements are required by outside creditors, potential bond holders and governmental agencies at the state and federal levels. They provide creditors a more confident basis for decisions about extending credit. They play an important part in state and federal securities laws.
- Independent audits frequently include recommendations for improving internal accounting and management controls and tend to minimize errors and irregularities in the accounting records.
- Audited financial statements provide insurance companies a more confident basis for settling claims for insured losses.
- Audited financial statements provide unions and the board of education an objective basis for contractual agreements.

Through the use of audited financial statements by outside and independent accountants, the board can make complete and timely financial information about the financial affairs of the school district available to the public. In this way, the board can create and maintain confidence in the financial administration of the school district. Examinations made only once every two, three or four years do not provide the value of timeliness of financial information.

REQUEST FOR PROPOSALS

While there is no specific legal requirement to change auditors annually, many boards of education review auditors annually, even if they choose not to change firms. The task of selecting the independent auditors and defining the scope of the engagement should be reserved for the board or for the audit committee composed of board members. Some boards will find, upon examination, that many shortcomings exist in present accounting and reporting practices and procedures, and that adequate financial statements and reports are not being submitted to the board or to the public.

Therefore, the question of how to go about getting improved accounting and reporting practices and procedures arises. The board should ask itself whether professional advice and assistance has been sought for the school district. If so, have recommendations for improving accounting and reporting practices and procedures been secured, adopted and put into operation? It is an obligation of the board either to:

- Staff the business office with people qualified by education, training and experience in accounting.
- Provide in-service training programs for staff members.
- Provide adequate technical and professional advice and assistance to the school district's business officials and administrators to establish effective and meaningful standards of financial accounting and reporting.

After the board has provided either adequately trained personnel or adequate training opportunities for present personnel, annual examinations should be made to determine that generally accepted accounting principles, practices and procedures are being applied.

In those cases where an adequate system of accounting is in operation and the system of internal control is working effectively, the annual cost of audits by outside accountants can be agreed upon by using one of three common methods:

- Per diem basis
- Flat fee basis
- Maximum fee basis

In either the flat fee basis or maximum fee basis, a provision is generally included whereby an adjustment can be made in the contract in the event the scope of the engagement has to be extended to cover unforeseen circumstances which might develop.

In those cases where special services have to be rendered in establishing an adequate accounting system, or where work that should have been done by business office personnel has to be done by the auditing firm, the cost will be greater. Once an accounting system is in operation and an effective system of internal control is established, the work required to be performed by business office personnel can be reduced, and costs should also go down accordingly.

Neither an audit nor ASBO International's Certificate of Excellence program establishes that a school district is fiscally strong. An unqualified audit opinion on each fund used by the school district states that the financial statements present fairly the financial position, the results of operation, the changes in fund balances and the changes in financial position. ASBO International's Certificate of Excellence program recognizes that the consolidated annual financial report is prepared in keeping with generally accepted accounting principles and generally accepted auditing standards. Whether or not a school district is financially strong is an interpretation that must be made by the reader of the financial statements.

The Illinois State Board of Education's publication, *Preparing for Your Local Education Agency Audits*, provides the following general contents of a request for proposal (RFP) and the auditor selection process. The RFP process usually entails the following steps:

- Determination of need by the board of education.
- Preparation of a request for proposal including: an introduction to and description of the school district, scope of the examination, required reports, timing requirements and proposal content.
- Evaluation of proposals/selection of the auditing firm.
- Contract for audit services.

Determination of need—Depending upon the state or province, there may be a legal requirement for the school district to have an annual or some other periodic audit. Barring a legal requirement, the board of education should have a policy stating the need and timing of an independent audit.

Request for Proposal—The school district should provide certain information to prospective auditing firms to enable the firms to have a clear understanding of the school district's needs. By using a standardized format, the RFP provides the school district a better understanding and comparison of services that proposed auditing firms will provide. Illustration 24.1 shows the usual contents of a RFP.

Evaluation of Proposals/Selection of the Auditor—Prior to reviewing the responses from the RFPs, the board should designate a committee to review the proposals received and submit to the board:

- A summary of proposals received.
- A recommendation of the audit firm to be awarded the contract.

The committee selected may include board members as well as business office personnel who will have direct contact with the selected audit firm. This recommendation should include a summary of the basis for their decision as compared to other responding firms.

The designated committee should establish their priorities for selection prior to commencing a review of the proposals. After these priorities are established, each committee member should review the proposals received, summarize the main points and provide any additional comments regarding the proposals. The individual comments and recommendations should be compared to those of the other committee members. Based upon these comments and the established priorities, the committee should be able to submit to the board of education an appropriate recommendation. If there appears to be more than one qualified firm, the committee should consider interviewing the firms in order to make the appropriate recommendation and obtain any necessary clarifications.

Illustration 24.1
Contents of a Request for Proposal

Introduction
The RFP should identify the following:

- Name of the school district requesting the proposal.
- School district contact person, including the title and address, to whom the accounting firm should address the proposal, and to whom inquiries should be made regarding the RFP.
- Fiscal year(s) to be audited.
- Date and time for all proposals to be submitted.
- Number of copies of proposal needed.
- Any special instructions as to how the proposal should be delivered or addressed to indicate the contents.

Description of the School District
The school district information disclosed in the RFP should include:

- Number of students currently enrolled.
- Number of school buildings and facilities currently being occupied by the district.
- Current year budgeted revenues and expenditures.
- Current year budgeted revenues and expenditures from federally assisted programs listed by individual federal program.
- Brief description of the accounting system, including computer/software capabilities used by the school district.
- Number of personnel: certificated staff, support staff and number of people employed in the business office.
- Any other characteristic unique to the school district that the evaluator feels is important for the auditing firm to know in order to gain a basic understanding of the school district.
- Relationship between the school district and school district treasurer.

Scope of the Examination
This section of the RFP should identify the type of audit required and any special audit requirements including type of funds maintained by the school district, so that the auditing firm will know what is to be expected if awarded the contract. This section should specify that the audit should be conducted by the auditing firm under:

- Generally accepted auditing standards promulgated by the American Institute of Certified Public Accountants.
- Requirements under the Single Audit Act or other state and federal regulations.

The school district should also disclose whether the audit and reports are to be based upon a cash, modified accrual, or accrual basis, whether the auditor should express an opinion on the combining and individual fund financial statements, and whether any additional services beyond the normal audit scope are required.

Reports Required
This section should specifically identify the type and number of reports that are to be prepared in connection with the audit examination, such as:

- Financial statements and supplementary information to be included in the annual report of the school district.
- Preparation of any annual financial report needed to be filed with the appropriate state and/or federal office.
- Management's discussion and analysis.
- Any other reports requested by the board of education.

Timing Requirements
The following information should be included to inform the auditor of expected dates so that the audit firm may be able to determine the timing of their audit work:

- The date the accounting records for the year-end audit will be available and when the accounting firm can begin work.
- The date a final audit report should be submitted to the board of education and whether the school district desires to have a representative of the audit firm available for presentation to the board of education.

Proposal Content
In order to alleviate any confusion as to what the audit examination encompasses and who will be performing the audit work, the following requests should be considered for inclusion:

- A statement from the firm regarding the understanding of the work as explained above and a brief description of the audit approach to be used to achieve this objective.
- Qualifications of the public accounting firm, including but not limited to: experience in school district accounting, training programs designed to keep their staff current in the industry, involvement in governmental organizations, the size and location of the firm.
- The approximate timing of completion of the audit to meet the required deadlines stated above.
- Fee information as to the general audit, as well as any additional costs related to state or federal programs. This section should also indicate the extent to which the firm expects assistance from school district personnel.
- Resumes of the individuals that will be assigned to the engagement including school district experience.
- Names, titles, addresses and telephone numbers/email addresses of at least three school district clients who may be contacted for references.
- An example school district audit report.
- Indication of whether any individuals will be available for oral interviews.

When reviewing the proposals, special attention should be devoted to the following items:

- References indicated in the proposal should be checked. Inquiries should be made regarding the following: quality of the audits received, service during the audit as well as throughout the year, timeliness of the audit reports, and integrity and experience of the assigned audit staff.

- Reference checks should include not only the firm, but the individuals.
- Qualifications of the firms should be reviewed to determine: the technical competence of the individuals, experience in the school district industry, adequate manpower to complete the audit in a timely fashion, involvement of the firm with school district organizations, resumes of the individuals should be reviewed to determine if the assigned individuals will have the necessary expertise, the indicated audit approaches should be reviewed as the basis for determining the quality of the audit expected to be conducted, and the costs should be reviewed for reasonableness in conjunction with the services that the district will obtain from the firm awarded the audit.

While costs should be a factor, the decision should not be based solely on fees. Proposals that indicate a greater level of service, including meetings with the board of education and continuing contact throughout the year, may be justification for higher fees. However, the above items should be ranked from each proposal received. After discussion among committee members, the appropriate recommendation should be reached.

Contract for Audit Services—The U.S. Department of Education regulation 34 CFR Part 74, Subpart P (Audit Requirements for State and Local Governments) requires certain standards be followed when arranging for audit services:

- LEAs maintain a code of standards of conduct governing persons awarding and administering contracts using federal funds.
- Officers, employees or agents of the LEA be prohibited from solicitation or acceptance of anything of monetary value, including gratuities and favors from current or potential CPAs.
- The competition for the CPA services be open and free.
- Contracts be made only with responsible CPAs who possess the potential ability to perform the required audit successfully.
- Consideration should be given to such matters as the CPAs integrity, compliance with public policy, record of past performances and financial and technical resources.

Subpart P also requires that small audit firms and audit firms owned and controlled by socially and economically disadvantaged individuals (target firms) shall be given the maximum practicable opportunity to participate in contracts awarded to fulfill the Single Audit Act requirements. The following steps should be taken:

- Assure that target firms are used to the fullest extent possible.
- Make information on forthcoming opportunities available and arrange time frames for the audit so as to encourage and facilitate participation by target firms.
- Encourage contracting with target firms which have traditionally audited LEAs and, in such cases where this is not possible, assure that these firms are given consideration for audit subcontracting opportunities.
- Encourage contracting with a consortium of target firms when a contract is too large for an individual target firm.
- Use the services and assistance, as appropriate, of such organizations as the Small Business Administration in the solicitation and utilization of target firms.

ENGAGEMENT LETTER

An engagement letter is a formal contract between the school district and its certified public accounting firm. The engagement letter confirms the acceptance of the appointment and documents the agreed upon terms. The engagement letter should establish a mutual understanding between the school district and audit firm of the terms, nature and limitations of the engagement. The audit firm should clearly communicate their understanding of the school district's audit and reporting objectives and requirements. This often includes the scope of the audit, the form of reports and any additional responsibilities assumed and can usually be accomplished by referring to appropriate audit guides, standards, laws or regulations.

Likewise, the engagement letter should stipulate the responsibilities accepted by the school district. Generally, government audit agreements are formal written contracts that are legally enforceable and difficult to change once executed. Thus, the exact contents of the engagement letter should be carefully determined by the parties involved. Informal understandings or arrangements are not desirable and should be avoided if possible. Any future modifications to the original agreement should also be in writing.

FINANCIAL STATEMENTS

The objective of financial accounting and reporting is to analyze and record financial transactions in a meaningful way. So many limitations are placed upon the way by which money for school districts can be raised and so many strings are attached to the way it can be used for school purposes, that simplicity and meaningfulness are difficult to achieve.

It is true that all of the assets and financial resources of a school district could be combined into one fund if all sources of revenue are to be used for general operation and if no strings are attached to any of the money. When these circumstances do not exist, however, the separation of financial transactions into self-balancing groups of accounts, which compose various funds, has been found to be the best way of providing meaningful financial statements and effective financial management.

SUMMARY

In preparing financial statements for the school district, the accountant must keep in mind that not only are the technical objectives of analyzing and recording financial transactions to be achieved, but most important is that meaningful statements and reports are to be prepared for use by the administrators, the board and the public. When statements are presented to the public that convey a full disclosure of financial facts, it is possible to secure the support of the public for achieving desirable educational goals and objectives within limits of financial resources available.

ACTIVITIES

1. Discuss some advantages to having outside and independent examinations of the school district's financial records.

2. Discuss advantages and disadvantages of maintaining continuing contractual relationships with outside auditor firms for more than one year.

3. Identify the purpose of the opinion section of the audit report.

4. Interview a school business official to determine for that district:

   a. Procedures used to secure an outside, independent audit.
   b. District procedure for duration of agreement and changing independent auditors.
   c. Process used to compare costs when selecting an independent auditor.
   d. Explanation of any notes to the last fiscal year audit.
   e. Satisfaction of the school board with information provided by the audit.
   f. Community opinion or reaction to the independent audit.
   g. Copies of an engagement letter for auditing services.

5. Prepare a draft request for proposal (RFP) for an independent audit and identify a process that could be used to select an auditor.

25

ASBO International's Certificate of Excellence: Financial Statements and Reports

INTRODUCTION

The school business administrator and his/her staff will spend hundreds of hours every year collecting and preparing information that will go on to a myriad of forms and reports. Some of these forms and reports are mandated by federal, state and local governments, while many others are requested by the board of education, administrators, teachers and other groups. Many of these requests are internal to the school district, while others are from and for those outside of the school district. At times the number of forms and reports seem infinite. Regardless of whether the reports and forms are for financial or managerial purposes, there are several basic goals that should govern their preparation. These basic goals are that reports and financial statements must be accurate, timely and clearly present the information they are intended to communicate.

OUTCOMES

In this chapter, you will learn:

1. What the Certificate of Excellence (COE) is.
2. What the Meritorious Budget Award Program (MBA) is.
3. What benefits can accrue to school districts which earn the Certificate of Excellence and/or the Meritorious Budget Award.
4. What steps are involved in making application for the Certificate of Excellence recognition.

WHAT IS ASBO INTERNATIONAL?

In 1972, the Association of School Business Officials in the United States and Canada (now ASBO International), unveiled a voluntary program that was designed to encourage and recognize school districts whose administrators prepared outstanding financial reports. This was called the Certificate of Excellence in Financial Reporting by School Systems Program, more commonly referred to as simply the Certificate of Excellence (COE). The COE focused on excellence in the preparation, presentation and issuance of a school district's consolidated annual financial report (CAFR).

ASBO International inaugurated the Meritorious Budget Awards Program (MBA) in July 1995 and the program has grown steadily, both in participation and stature in the education arena. The Association created *Standards of Excellence in Budget Presentations* as a hands-on practical guide to the MBA Program in particular and effective school budgeting in general. The current edition provides examples of outstanding budget presentations that meet the MBA Program criteria. In addition, it reflects the minor changes made in the criteria for the current program year.

At the turn of the twentieth century, the United States Office of Education recognized a federal, state and local need to create a means for developing and delivering continuing professional educational programs to those interested and/or involved in the business services side of school districts. An organization was created in 1910 with this goal in mind but it soon expanded its purposes to include other professional school business management related activities. The organization that developed became known as the Association of School Business Officials in the United States and Canada, ASBO International for short. In the mid 1980s, the name of the association was officially changed to more accurately reflect the changing makeup of its nearly 6,000 members. Thus it became known as the Association of School Business Officials International or ASBO International. Throughout its 85-year history, ASBO International members and staff have been actively involved in providing a wide variety of professional development opportunities for school business administrators that would help develop their knowledge and improve their skills relating to their ever-growing responsibilities and complex roles.

The COE was one of the programs that ASBO International developed for its members. It is not a contest, but rather a recognition program wherein every school district that applies *and* meets the requirements can receive the certificate.

ASBO International is involved in not only providing professional development opportunities and the COE but in developing other national standards such as its Meritorious Budget Award (MBA) recognition program. Another is a model preparation program for the initial training of school business administrators that has become the national program standard used by the National Council for the Accreditation of Teacher Education (NCATE) to accredit master's degree-level programs in school business administration in the United States.

THE CURRENT STATUS OF THE CERTIFICATE OF EXCELLENCE

In the March 2004 issue of ASBO International's monthly journal, *School Business Affairs,* COE, a status report for the program can be found. The program continues to grow. Program submissions for the most recent period exceeded 500 and were reviewed by approximately 200 professionals that were organized into COE reviewer panels. ASBO International reports that these reviewers provided well in excess of 10,000 review hours. These reviewers are outstanding governmental accounting and auditing professionals. For the 2003–04 COE year, 26 school districts received this recognition for the first time while 495 school districts were repeat recipients.

BENEFITS OF COE TO SCHOOL DISTRICTS

Surveys have been conducted involving school business administrators who worked in a school district that held the COE. The purpose of these surveys was to identify why a school business administrator would subject their school district to the expense and their staffs and auditors to the extra work the COE process requires. These open-ended surveys simply ask what the school business administrator perceived as being the benefits of receiving the certificate and what local efforts they made to maximize those benefits. The following list reflects a summary of the various statements that school business administrators who responded to the survey provided.

- Enhances the bond rating of the school district, thereby potentially reducing interest costs when borrowing.
- Provides a means to maintain or improve public confidence in the school district/public relations.
- Provides an assurance that the finance department/business office is providing high-quality service.

- Adds credibility to other reports/budget/business office performance.
- Earns the recognition of their professional colleagues.
- Helps to improve managing and accounting processes.
- Validates data/reports.
- Provides an evaluation tool/self-evaluation against national standards.
- Indicates a level of staff professionalism.
- Provides assurance that taxes are needed/being used wisely.
- Creates an expectation to improve/repeat.
- Creates a report that boards can use that is better than the audit.
- Helps pass a referendum.
- Creates pride in the school district.
- Creates a goal for the business office.
- Enhances the resume of the SBA.
- Helps to obtain a line of credit with a financial institution.
- Can be used to establish a common starting point for collective bargaining parties.
- Provides comparability with other COE awardees.

PROGRAM BENEFITS

The COE Program also offers the school business administrator and school district a number of benefits.

Prestigious National Award—Since its inception, the program has gained the distinction of being a prestigious national award recognized by:

- Accounting professionals.
- Underwriters.
- Securities analysts.
- Bond rating agencies.
- Educational, teacher and citizen groups.
- Federal and state agencies.

Fiscal Credibility Validation—Receipt of a Certificate of Excellence validates a school system's fiscal and financial management credibility with its various reporting constituencies, including:

- School board members.
- School system management.
- State and local government offices.
- Federal and state granting agencies.
- Educational, taxpayer and teacher organizations.

Report Presentations Enhancement—Inclusion of a Certificate of Excellence enhances a school district's financial presentations in:

- Annual reports.

- Bond issuance official statements.
- Presentations to the media.
- Budget presentations and hearing.

Uniformity Measure—Adherence to the formatting and terminology as promulgated by the appropriate standard setting bodies (GASB, AICPA, etc.) allows for comparisons between:

- Comparable school systems.
- School system reports from year to year.
- Trend analyses.

Individual Recognition and Development—Receipt of a Certificate of Excellence provides a school system's board and superintendent with a measure of the integrity and technical competence of the system's fiscal administration. The program stimulates personal technical development through:

- Use of technical materials and attendance at professional seminars.
- Completion of ASBO International's self-evaluation worksheet.
- Networking between peers, consultants and CPAs.
- Implementing constructive comments from the Panel of Review.

The program promotes personnel development by documenting technical proficiency. The recognition afforded by receipt of the certificate is personally stimulating and satisfying.

CERTIFICATE OF EXCELLENCE REQUIREMENTS

In order to begin the submission process, a school district must publish a Consolidated Annual Financial Report (CAFR) or in some cases a Component Unit Financial Report (CUFR). Without one of these reports, the school district cannot qualify for the recognition afforded by this program. Whichever report is submitted, it must contain the opinion of the independent CPA that the scope of the audit has not been limited and the opinion is unqualified.

The second component of the survey, How did the SBA use the receipt of the COE to maximize benefits? revealed only three activities/methods were common. First, a special ceremony and/or presentation was arranged at a school board meeting. Second, a press release was prepared and appeared in the local newspaper(s); and third, if the school district was involved in long-term or short-term borrowing the official financial statement prepared in connection with each borrowing included the fact that the school district had received the COE. It seems clear that the recipients of the COE could do much more to enhance and realize greater benefits of this recognition. It appears that the award has more intrinsic than extrinsic value. This seems to be changing.

CERTIFICATE OF EXCELLENCE APPLICATION/SUBMISSION PROCESS

Either the CAFR or CUFR must be completed in a timely manner and submitted to ASBO International no later than six months after the end of the school district's fiscal year. A second "program requirement" is the completion of a "Self-Evaluation Worksheet" that can be obtained from ASBO International. The worksheet is a comprehensive technical document in a question and answer format that requires a specific response to each question with either a "yes" or "no" or "not applicable." A comments section is provided to explain "no" and "not applicable" answers. For example, a question might ask: Are columns captioned with fund type titles? If the answer is "no" or "not applicable," an explanation is required. The worksheet provides a school system with a valuable tool in the preparation of the financial report and acts as a checklist in the review process.

MERITORIOUS BUDGET AWARD

The Meritorious Budget Awards Program (MBA) was established in 1995 to encourage and recognize excellence in school system budgeting. It is an international awards program created by ASBO International to help school business administrators achieve a very high standard of excellence in budget presentation. The program evaluates budget documents against specific criteria or minimum standards. Budgets that meet or exceed these criteria receive the prestigious Meritorious Budget Award.

Any school entity, including local school districts, educational services agencies, private schools, intermediated units and colleges and universities, is eligible to participate in the MBA program. The school entity does not have to be a member of ASBO International to participate.

School entities participating in this program cite the following benefits from their participation in the program:

- Provides clear budget presentation guidelines.
- Defines state-of-the-art budget practices.
- Encourages both short- and long-range budget goals.
- Promotes sound fiscal management practices.
- Promotes effective use of educational resources.
- Facilitates professional growth and development for the budget staff.
- Helps build solid skills in developing, analyzing and presenting school entity budgets.

Those who receive the Meritorious Budget Award are recognized with:

- A handsome plaque and certificate.
- Recognition of their achievement published in *ASBO International Accents*, *School Business Affairs* and their state or provincial ASBO International affiliate's newsletter.
- News releases sent to their local media.
- Letters of accomplishment sent to their superintendent and school board.
- Comprehensive feedback about their budget from peers trained in up-to-date school budgeting techniques.
- Continuing education credits in ASBO International's Professional Registration Program.

Until the development of the MBA criteria, practitioners had no guidelines to follow when attempting to explain the financial plan of the school entity to the public. The MBA format encourages budget developers to present a single document organized in a user-friendly way that translates plans for providing educational services into an easy-to-understand financial story.

In 1993, the ASBO International Board of Directors made a decision to develop a school entity budget awards program and directed the ASBO International president to appoint a task force. The task force was charged with developing a budget recognition program which would promote state-of-the-art practices for the development and presentation of school budgets. The task force was appointed and spent many hours researching what constituted state-of-the-art budget practices. The task force also developed and sent out a membership survey to assess member interest in such a program. The results of the survey confirmed that ASBO International members would enthusiastically support the program. The following year, the task force finished their research and developed the program standards currently used as the MBA criteria.

School entities from representative states and provinces were asked to field-test the criteria by preparing budgets according to the requirements for a test review. Reviewer training workshops were developed, where school business officials were trained to serve as reviewers. A reviewer accreditation workshop was held in conjunction with ASBO International's 1994 Annual Meeting in Seattle and also a Super Session at this meeting further acquainted ASBO International members with the program's standards and benefits.

In 1995, the field-test budget reviews were completed, the criteria were refined, and the program began its first year July 1. Applicants were invited to submit their 1995–96 budgets for review and consideration for the Meritorious Budget Award. During 1995, the MBA Task Force became one of the standing committees of ASBO International officially known as the MBA Committee. The committee is comprised of school business officials who are experts in the field of budgeting. The committee oversees all aspects of the program, provides technical expertise, continuously reviews and updates the program criteria and presents MBA-related workshops.

GROWTH AND SUCCESS OF THE MBA PROGRAM

During the first year of the program, 28 school entities submitted their budgets for review and 16 received the award. In the second program year, 33 school entities submitted their budgets and 21 received the award. Program year 1997–98, which was the third year of operation, was far more successful than the first two years with 51 school entities from 25 states submitting budgets for review and 33 school entities receiving the award. By 2003–04 the numbers had increased to 66. It is expected that the program will continue to grow for many years into the future.

Since 1995, more than 100 dedicated school business officials and accounting professionals have been trained and certified as MBA Program reviewers. Becoming a reviewer is a professional development opportunity that gives an individual a chance to "give back" to the profession. Reviewers lend their expertise to the program by providing feedback to submitting school entities that enables them to create better and more effective budgets in the future.

In 1996, MetLife Resources joined forces with ASBO International to promote the MBA Program. Their sponsorship of the MBA Program supports ASBOI's efforts to educate school business officials about the MBA criteria and to make and expand the programs.

APPLICATION PROCESS

Budgets are submitted in the same form in which they are prepared. Participants are encouraged to pay close attention to the MBA criteria as they develop their budgets. As applicant school systems develop their budgets, they check their budgets against the criteria using the Criteria Location Checklist before final printing. If minor adjustments are needed, participants can incorporate changes into the final document. The guidebook explains the criteria and offers examples of presentations that satisfy the MBA requirements. The document must be submitted to ASBO International within 90 days after the budget's legal adoption by the school entity's governing body.

The submission should include:

- A completed MBA application form.
- A letter explaining criteria that are not relevant to the school entity (see General Requirements for more information).
- A response to any previous review team comments and recommendations.
- Four copies of the school system's budget.
- Four copies of a completed Criteria Location Checklist.
- Payment of the application fee.

The application form requests information on:

- The school entity applying for the award.
- The school official responsible for the application.
- Beginning and ending dates of the budget year.
- The date the budget was legally adopted.
- The size of the budget.
- The names and addresses of officials who should be notified of the review results.

REVIEW AND NOTIFICATION PROCESS

Once ASBO International receives a complete application packet and processes the paperwork, a copy of the budget document and application materials are forwarded to each member of a three-member review team.

To qualify as a member of a MBA review team, a reviewer must work in the school business field, be a member of ASBO International and adhere to certain program requirements, including participation in a reviewer accreditation-training program.

Independently the reviewers evaluate the assigned budget document. The reviewer rates the document against each of the MBA criteria using the following rating categories:

- Exceeds criteria.
- Meets criteria.
- Does not meet criteria.

Applicants are expected to satisfy all of the criteria. The reviewers determine whether the failure to meet any one criterion has a substantial effect on the budget document taken as a whole and is sufficient reason to deny the award.

The reviewer also prepares written comments on criteria that may not be properly implemented in the budget document, how well the budget satisfies the criteria as well as suggestions on how to improve the document. Based upon an overall assessment of whether or not the document meets or exceeds all of the criteria, each reviewer recommends the budget for approval or denial of the Meritorious Budget Award. When the chair of the review team receives the rating sheets and comments from the other members of the review team, the results are compiled and a final decision to award or deny the Meritorious Budget Award is made.

Notification of results is sent to the school entity within 12 to 16 weeks of receipt of the budget submission. The time required to complete an evaluation will vary depending upon the availability of reviewers. During peak submission times, turnaround of reviews may take longer if sufficient reviewers are not available.

When the Meritorious Budget Award is awarded, the school system receives several important forms of recognition. The school administrator who submitted the document receives notification of the award and confidential comments prepared by the reviewers. In addition, the administrator earns continuing education units for ASBOI's Professional Registration Program.

Notification of the award is also sent to the school superintendent/director and school board. The school system receives a personalized plaque and official recognition in ASBO International's membership directory, *ASBO International Accents*, and the affiliate's newsletter. ASBO International also provides a news release that the school system can distribute to its local news media.

If the MBA is denied, a letter of notification is sent only to the school administrator who submitted the budget. In addition, the school administrator receives confidential comments from the review team on how to improve the document.

THE APPEALS PROCESS

A school system can choose to appeal a denial. Within 30 days of receipt of a denial letter, the school system should resubmit three copies of its budget and the original Criteria Location Checklist as well as a letter requesting an appeal and explaining why it believes the denial was inappropriate.

ASBO International will send the resubmitted budget and letter to a separate appeal review team. The appeal team will review the budget and decide to award or deny the Meritorious Budget Award within 90 days. The decision of the appeal review team is final.

CONTINUED PARTICIPATION

Receipt of the Meritorious Budget Award is a special distinction received by few school entities. Because the award is granted for only one year, ASBO International encourages school systems to apply for the award every year. Neither budget documents nor the MBA criteria are static. A school system can demonstrate how well its budget document adapts to changing conditions and standards through perennial participation in the MBA Program.

BUDGET REVIEWER

Another way to participate in the MBA Program is as a budget reviewer. Reviewers not only perform a valuable service for the program but also receive valuable information in return. Through the MBA Program, reviewers gain insight into effective budget presentation through the budget documents they evaluate each year. It is not unusual for reviewers to acquire new techniques and formats they can apply to their own documents.

GENERAL REQUIREMENTS

The MBA criteria are divided into five areas: General Requirements, Introductory Section, Organizational Section, Financial Section and Informational Section. All but the General Requirements criteria apply to specific sections of the budget document. For example, the criteria under the Introductory Section are ones that should be satisfied within the Introductory Section of a school entity's budget.

The General Requirements relate to the overall budget document but do not necessarily apply to a specific section of a document. They set criteria concerning the document cover page, the sectional division and table of contents, page numbering, information not included in the budget document, response to previous review team comments, use of graphs and charts, and the technical preparation of the document.

COVER PAGE (Criterion A-1)

The budget cover page should contain the title "Budget," and include the full name of the school entity, the city/county and state/province in which the entity is located and the budget year covered. Often the school entity's boundaries will include an area in more than one city or county.

MAJOR SECTIONS (Criterion A-2)

This criterion specifies that the budget document should be divided by major sections with consecutive page numbers. Unless a school system chooses to add other sections to its document, the major sections should include those sections delineated by MBA criteria: Introductory, Organizational, Financial and Informational Sections. These and other sections could be divided within the document by divider pages or tabs. Whatever method of division is used, page numbering should run consecutively rather than starting over with each major section.

This criterion also requires that the document include a table of contents. The table should, at a minimum, identify all major sections and precede the Introductory Section. Because the table of contents helps readers to locate specific sections of the document, school entities may also want to list subsections within the table. School systems are given wide latitude regarding the makeup and design of this element of the document.

INFORMATION NOT RELEVANT TO THE SCHOOL ENTITY AND OTHER INFORMATION REQUIRED (Criterion A-3)

If there is any information required by MBA criteria that is not relevant to the school entity and, therefore, is not presented in its budget document, it should be identified and explained by the school entity official submitting the budget document in a cover letter accompanying the application form. For example, information on assessed and market value of taxable property and tax rates required by the Informational Section criteria may not be relevant to school systems which are dependent on a unit of general government for financial support or to an intermediate school unit. If the school system explains what information is not included and why it is not relevant to the school entity, then it will not be counted by reviewers as an omission of required criteria.

Relevance is the only factor, however, that can exempt a school system from meeting specific criteria. Applicants are expected to satisfy all of the MBA criteria. It is expected that a school system can include all the information required by the criteria in its budget document and still conform to legal requirements. The school entity may want to include additional information not required by the MBA criteria in order to meet legal requirements or to provide information required by their governing body, administration or citizens.

In some states, school entities report budget information to state education departments or other governmental agencies, which have oversight responsibilities for the school entity. These state education departments or other agencies have their own form for submitting this information. It is expected in these circumstances that the budget will be prepared according to the MBA criteria and used to communicate to citizens, bond rating agencies and others with an interest in the budget story, and the budget information will also be reported to these oversight agencies according to their required form and format.

The MBA review team alone decides whether a school system has met all of the criteria and whether its failure to meet any one criterion is reason to deny the award.

RESPONSE TO PREVIOUS REVIEW TEAMS (Criterion A-4)

If the school entity has applied for the Meritorious Budget Award previously, a response to the previous MBA review team comments and recommendations by the school official responsible for the school entity submission is required.

USE OF GRAPHS AND CHARTS (Criterion A-5)

Graphs and charts should be an integral part of every budget. The MBA criterion encourages their use in all sections of the document. They are particularly helpful in stimulating readers' interest and aiding their understanding of budget information. The charts and graphs most frequently used in budgets are bar charts, line graphs and pie charts.

Those preparing budgets can use a wide array of charts and graphs to clarify and reinforce budget data and narratives. Graphics and spreadsheet computer software make it particularly easy to prepare effective and attractive budget graphs and charts. Other visuals, such as photographs and maps, can serve the same purpose. Whatever visual device is chosen, it should be used properly. Graphs and charts are best used throughout the document rather than grouped together within a single section.

TECHNICALLY WELL PREPARED (Criterion A-6)

The budget document should be technically well prepared, be easy to read and flow in logical sequence. The narration should be clear and understandable and free from spelling and grammar errors.

SUMMARY

The COE and MBA programs are voluntary programs that encourage and recognize school districts and their administrators that prepare outstanding financial reports and budgets. The programs focus on the comprehensive annual financial report in terms of preparation, presentation and distribution of the annual budget. In addition to the positive recognition the COE/MBA awards bring to the school district, there are many other potential benefits that can accrue.

ACTIVITIES

1. What is the Certificate of Excellence (COE) Program?

2. What is the Meritorious Budget Award Program (MBA)?

3. List the benefits that can accrue to school districts that receive the COE and MBA recognition.

4. Contact ASBO International and arrange to receive the Self-Evaluation Worksheet used in preparing the COE submission.

5. Visit ASBOintl.org and review the COE/MBA information posted.

6. Review the CAFR or CUFR of a school district and compare it against the items listed in the Self-Evaluation Worksheet.

26

Moving Beyond Traditional Measures of Financial Health: What School Districts Have Learned from the Private Sector

INTRODUCTION

For many years, business leaders and owners have attempted to manage current business activities, understand their business better and have a positive impact on their bottom line. Securities analysts have attempted to predict the future performance of marketable securities. Fundamental analysts, likewise, have focused on the analysis of individual companies and their industry groups. Their analysis tends to be long-term in nature. The business owner, the securities analyst and fundamental analyst depend heavily on ratios and other measures to complete their work.

The history and application of fiscal analysis, benchmarking and other fiscal measures in the public sector and specifically school districts, is relatively short compared to the history of their use in the private sector. In the school setting, ratios are not as well understood, developed and used as in business, but it is becoming an important area of school business management research. Developments since the beginning of the new century have shown a growing interest more in measuring than in counting, i.e., placing meaning on the information reported rather than just examining the numbers.

This chapter will explore what ratio analysis is, uses in the private sector, the tie of ratio analysis to accounting and benchmarking and some other measuring techniques. The following chapter (chapter 27) will focus on using similar ideas in the public sector—more specifically the schools and school districts.

OUTCOMES

In this chapter, you will learn how to:

1. Define a ratio and know how it is created.
2. Use ratios in the private sector.
3. Use ratio analysis and know how it can benefit an organization.
4. Define and use other measures of fiscal conditions of an organization.

This chapter begins with a discussion of balance sheets and income statements for private sector companies and then proceeds to discuss ratios and other measures that can be calculated from the balance sheet or income statements that have been developed to guide corporate decision makers. Samples of benchmarks are given for some ratios that are discussed.

PRIVATE SECTOR FINANCIAL STATEMENTS

In the private sector, items important to a fundamental analyst include a company's financial statements (such as the balance sheet and income statement), details regarding the company's product line, the experience and expertise of the company's management and the outlook for the company's industry. While the bottom line approach in the private sector drives the decision making process, especially the decision of whether a company will stay in business, ratio analysis for public schools, while having some similarities, does not carry the same bottom line mentality, i.e., public school districts do not (yet) go bankrupt and close the doors. Creating a knowledge base from which the reader may come to understand ratio analysis and other means of measuring fiscal health and its potential for school districts is useful.

FUNDAMENTAL ANALYSIS IN THE PRIVATE SECTOR: A BRIEF LOOK

One of the most widely used, misused and abused forms of financial analysis is the use of ratios. When used properly, ratios can provide a wide variety of information, used separately or in combination with other ratios that can be used in all aspects of an organization's management and operation. Ratios can help internal managers gain an awareness of their organization's strengths and weaknesses. Because ratios help find weaknesses, ratios can also suggest the move or moves needed to adjust the ratio before irreparable damage is done to the organization thereby removing the weakness.

If a ratio describes a strength, then understanding the components that make up and cause the strength can be useful to managers in keeping an organization strong.

For a starting point, a ratio in its simplest form is nothing more than a comparison of any two numbers. The number on top, called a numerator, can be a single number or a number that is the result of using several other numbers that relate to one another after some computations. The denominator, or bottom number, can also be the result of a series of computations using a variety of other numbers that have relevance to one another. If we compare one number (numerator) to another (denominator) a ratio has been created. However, for a ratio to have some degree of utility, a relationship between the two numbers must be established. Once a ratio is created, a standard or benchmark may also be established so the user of the ratio information can answer some basic questions:

- Does the ratio describe a favorable condition?
- Does the ratio describe an unfavorable condition?
- If managers can act to change the ratio, should the ratio be adjusted by trying to control the denominator or the numerator or both?
- Does the manager want to get from point A to point B with one set of adjustments or many adjustments spread over time?

Administrators and other consumers of ratio information can only assess the appropriateness of the ratios on the basis of some benchmark or standard for comparison.

According to Finkler (1992), there are three principal benchmarks. The first benchmark is the organization's history. This is the result of reviewing the same comparisons or ratios from one time period to the next or even over several time periods. Making these comparisons over time enables one to discover favorable or unfavorable trends that are developing gradually over time, as well as pointing out which numbers have changed dramatically in the long term or short term.

The second benchmark is used to compare the appropriate ratios of one organization with similar ratios of competing organizations. This is accomplished by obtaining the corresponding annual reports and creating and comparing similar ratios. This approach to ratio analysis is valuable in helping to pinpoint why an organization that should be very similar to your own is doing better or worse than your own. By knowing where the ratios differ, one finds what one is doing better or worse than the competition (if a corporation) or neighbor (if a school district).

A third benchmark is industry-wide (or statewide/province-wide in the case of school districts) comparison. Collecting financial data and computing industry-wide ratios allows the determination of relatively how far away from the norms an organization is (Finkler, 1992).

Benchmarks can be established vertically or horizontally, from data in a single report, or by using data from a combination of reports. For example, comparing one category within a section of the balance sheet against the total in that category or the grand total. This comparison will be demonstrated in the next chapter.

Ratios do have their limitations. They don't give a precise picture of the organization. Ratios are meant to serve as *general* conveyors of information from a broader base. It is inappropriate to attempt to interpret minor changes using ratios. The major interest in the ratio develops if a number is particularly out of line with the benchmark selected (i.e., too low or too high). Clearly, ratios should not be interpreted in isolation. Ratios *help* develop a total fiscal profile for an organization. They merely point out what needs to be examined more closely. The ratios do not provide answers in and of themselves. In the near future, a wider variety of new ratios will be developed, tested and interpreted. Benchmarks will be established that will help managers do a better job of managing, both in the private and public sector. Accounting is and will be the basis of these new ratios not only because accounting produces the numbers but the numbers are the result of clearer standardized definitions and better procedures.

The remainder of this chapter illustrates in a cursory or introductory way how ratios and some other measures have been developed and used in the private sector and summarizes a more detailed and comprehensive discussion and treatment of these concepts. For a more detailed look at this subject, examine materials prepared by the *Securities Training Corporation* and others who provide learning materials for people preparing for jobs that require knowledge of balance sheets and other financial reports.

RATIOS IN THE CORPORATE WORLD

One of the key sources of information used by corporations is the balance sheet. The balance sheet represents the financial picture of a company on a specific date. It is divided into three major sections: assets, liabilities and stockholders' equity.

It is called a balance sheet because the total assets will always equal (balance) the sum of the total liabilities and stockholders' equity (Securities Training Corporation, 1985).

Assets represent everything that is owned by the corporation. The liabilities section indicates all items owed by the corporation. The difference between the total assets and total liabilities is the stockholders' equity (also callcd thc company's nct worth).

Assets		Liabilities	Stockholders' Equity
______________		______________	______________
______________		______________	______________
=============		=============	=============
Total Assets	=	Total Liabilities	+ Total Stockholders' Equity

Assets represent everything that is owned by the corporation. The liabilities section indicates all items owed by the corporation. The difference between the total assets and total liabilities is the stockholders' equity (also called the company's net worth).

COMPONENTS OF THE BALANCE SHEET

The assets section of the balance sheet indicates the items owned by the corporation. There are three basic subsections to this category: current assets, fixed assets and intangible assets.

Current assets consist of those items that could be converted into cash within a short period of time (usually within one year). These include:

- *Cash*—Currency, checking accounts and other bank deposits.
- *Marketable Securities*—Securities owned (such as Treasury bills, stocks and bonds) that are readily convertible into cash. They are normally carried on the balance sheet at the lower of cost or market value.
- *Accounts Receivable*—Money owed to the company by customers who purchased goods and have not yet paid. The company would expect to receive these funds within one to three months.
- *Inventories*—The value of raw material, work in progress and the company's finished products that are ready for sale to customers (as applicable).

Fixed assets are items needed by the company in its day-to-day operations to create its products or services. These assets are not intended to be sold or converted into cash. This section of the balance sheet will list the company's physical property such as land, buildings, equipment and furniture. Fixed assets, with the exception of land, lose some of their value each year due to normal use. A company can claim this wear and tear on assets as a deduction against income. Known as depreciation, this deduction may be calculated by either the straight-line or accelerated method. On the balance sheet, fixed assets are shown at a value of their original cost less accumulated depreciation (the amount of depreciation claimed on the asset to date).

Intangible assets do not have any physical value but may add substantial value to a company. Some intangible assets differentiate the company from competitors and are proprietary such as patents, trademarks, franchises and copyrights.

Another intangible asset—goodwill—represents the amount that would be paid above the value of the assets to acquire the company. Factors contributing to goodwill would be a company's potential earning power due to its reputation in the marketplace, customer relations, skilled staff and existing customers.

The liabilities section of the balance sheet indicates the company's debts. Some of these debts must be paid in a short period of time (current liabilities) while other loans do not have to be repaid for many years (long-term liabilities).

Current liabilities are those debts that will become due in less than one year. They are easily identified by the word *payable*. Included in this section are:

- *Accounts Payable*—The amount a company owes for goods and services purchased on credit.
- *Notes Payable*—Short-term loans from banks and other financial institutions.
- *Dividends Payable*—Cash dividends that have been declared but have not been paid.
- *Taxes Payable*—The amount of tax that is owed to the government.
- *Interest Payable*—The amount of interest the company owes on its long-term debt.

Long-term liabilities are debts that a corporation has incurred that become payable in one year or more. Examples include bonds and long-term bank loans.

The stockholders' equity section represents the company's net worth. It indicates the shareholders' ownership interest in terms of the different classes of stock, retained earnings and capital surplus.

- *Preferred stock* is listed in the balance sheet based upon the par value of the outstanding shares.
- *Common stock* is listed in the balance sheet based upon the par value of the company's outstanding common stock. The par value of a stock is only used for bookkeeping purposes.
- *Capital Surplus* is the amount of premium paid by shareholders above par value for shares sold to the public by the corporation. It is also referred to as paid-in capital or paid-in surplus. This does not include funds the company derives from business profits.
- *Retained Earnings* (also called earned surplus) represents net profits that have been retained for future use by the corporation. Dividends are normally paid from retained earnings.

Illustration 26.1 demonstrates how these elements are put together to build a balance sheet.

Illustration 26.1
Corporation
Balance Sheet
December 31, 200X

Assets		Liabilities	
Current Assets		Current Liabilities	
Cash	$ 43,000	Accounts Payable	$ 188,000
Marketable Securities	62,000	Interest Payable	27,000
Accounts Receivable	270,000	Notes Payable	40,000
Inventories	330,000	Taxes Payable	72,000
Total Current Assets	$705,000	Total Current Liabilities	$ 327,000
Fixed Assets		Long-Term Liabilities	
Land	$ 54,000	9% Debentures due 2015	300,000
Plant and Equipment	630,000		
Furniture and Fixtures	280,000	Total Liabilities	$ 627,000
Less: Accumulated Depreciation	(220,000)		
Total Fixed Assets	$754,000		
Intangible Assets		Stockholders' Equity	
Goodwill	40,000	6% Preferred Stock	
		par value $100; 500	$ 50,000
		Common Stock par value $3.00	300,000
		Outstanding shares	600,000
		Capital Surplus	52,000
		Retained Earnings	160,000
		Total Stockholders' Equity	$ 862,000
Total Assets	$1,489,000	Total Liabilities and Stockholders' Equity	$1,489,000

Securities Training Corporation, 1988.

INCOME STATEMENT

An income statement (often referred to as a profit and loss statement) will indicate a corporation's performance during a specified period of time. The purpose of this statement is to detail the company's net income (or net loss). This is accomplished by offsetting the revenues by expenses. A sample income statement is shown in Illustration 26.2. An explanation of each component immediately follows the illustration.

Illustration 26.2
Corporation Income Statement
For period ending December 31, 200X

Sales	$660,000
Less:	
Operating Expenses:	
Cost of goods sold	240,000
Selling and administrative expenses	120,000
Depreciation expense	80,000
Operating Income	220,000
Plus:	
Other income	30,000
Earnings Before Interest and Taxes	250,000
Less:	
Bond Interest Expense	27,000
Earnings Before Tax	223,000
Less:	
Taxes (34% Rate)	75,820
Net Income (or loss)	$147,180

Securities Training Corporation, 1988.

Sales are reduced by day-to-day operating expenses to arrive at operating income. Sales represent the total money received from the company's primary source of business. Operating expenses reflect the daily costs of doing business. Included here is the amount claimed for the depreciation of fixed assets. Operating income is adjusted for other income (or expense) not generated by normal operations leaving earnings before interest and taxes. Other income usually represents income generated by investments (dividends and interest), however, this may also reflect extraordinary items such as earnings from the sale of assets or losses incurred by discontinuing a part of the business. Earnings before interest and taxes are reduced by bond interest and taxes to arrive at net income (or net loss). Bond interest must be paid regardless of the company's profitability. If it cannot be paid, the company is in default. The amount of interest paid is found by multiplying the total par value of the bonds by the coupon rate. Interest is paid prior to taxes.

ANALYZING FINANCIAL STATEMENTS

To this point, the preparation of the balance sheet and income statement has simply been the gathering and organizing of financial data.

A fundamental analyst uses the information from a company's financial statements, the balance sheet and income statement, to determine the financial strengths and weaknesses of a corporation. These statements are the product of the accounting process. This analysis seeks to compare the company's performance to other companies within the same industry.

To conduct fundamental analysis, the analyst will use various calculations and ratios. The accounting produced numbers will be processed through formulas and reveal information regarding the company's liquidity, capitalization, ability to meet fixed costs, profitability and much more.

The following sections provide only a very few samples of what some of the basic ratios, other measures and calculations are and what they help the analyst to do. The discussion is not all inclusive. No in-depth explanation is given since these are shown to illustrate similar ratios and their uses could and should be developed for public institutions. While the final purpose of their use will differ from that in the private sector, there still is a use. Only a few of the many possible ratios are shown. Once again, the reader is reminded that the accounting process and product creates the numbers that are used to create both the ratios and the benchmarks. The ratios are only as good (or useful) as the accounting system that created the numbers being compared. Garbage in/garbage out applies. The ratios and some of the definitions presented in the next section of this chapter come from Securities Training Corporation, *Investment Company Products/Variable Contracts Representative* (Series 6) (1988).

LIQUIDITY RATIOS

In the private sector, liquidity ratios are used to indicate a company's ability to meet its short-term debts as well as convert current assets into cash. Liquidity is normally analyzed by calculating the company's net working capital, current ratio, quick asset ratio, cash asset ratio and cash flow.

A company needs working capital to finance its daily operations. This money bridges the gap between production and sales. Maintaining a comfortable yet appropriate level of working capital is important. Doing so will enhance the company's ability to meet its current obligations, expand its production and take advantage of opportunities.

- Net Working Capital = Total Current Assets (CA) / Total Current Liabilities (CL)

Net working capital is the difference between the current assets and current liabilities. The current ratio indicates the company's ability to pay its current liabilities by using current assets. A low current ratio may indicate a working capital problem.

- Current Ratio = Total Current Assets / Total Current Liabilities

This calculation compares current assets to current liabilities.

- Quick Asset Ratio = Total Current Assets – Inventory / Total Current Liabilities

Quick assets are total current assets reduced by inventories. Total current assets are then divided by current liabilities to find the quick asset ratio.

- Cash Asset Ratio = (Cash + Marketable Securities) / Total Current Liabilities

The most stringent test of a company's ability to meet its current obligations is the cash asset ratio. Cash and marketable securities are divided by current liabilities to assess the company's emergency cash position.

- Cash Flow = Net Income (or Loss) + Annual Depreciation

Cash flow reflects the amount of money generated by a company's operations. Fundamental analysts tend to look at this figure to assess the company's ability to meet current expenses as well as to pay dividends. To find cash flow, the annual depreciation expense is added back to net income (or net loss). These figures are taken from the income statement.

Each business will establish ratio standards, targets or benchmarks for each of the five liquidity ratios and periodically compare current interim ratio calculations against these benchmarks. The results from these comparisons will result in a judgment being rendered concerning the current financial health of the business. As a result, decisions will be made that will change the way the company does business and thereby change the ratios in the desired direction and/or amount over the next reporting period.

CAPITALIZATION RATIOS

In addition to liquidity ratios, many analysts use capitalization ratios to assess the company's risk of bankruptcy. Formulas included in this category are the common stock ratio, preferred stock ratio, bond ratio and debt-to-equity ratio. All of the capitalization ratios analyze the components of a company's long-term capital. Long-term capital is found on the balance sheet. It consists of the entire stockholders' equity section plus long-term liabilities.

- Common Stock Ratio = (Common Stock at Par + Capital Surplus + Retained Earnings) / Total Long-Term Capital

The *common stock ratio* shows the percentage of long-term capital attributable to the common stock.

- Preferred Stock Ratio = Par Value of Preferred Stock / Total Long-Term Capital

The *preferred stock ratio* shows the portion of long-term capital that comes from preferred stock.

- Bond Ratio = Par Value of Bonds / Total Long-Term Capital

The *bond ratio* indicates the percentage of long-term capital that is attributable to bonds. A company with a high percentage of bonds (debt) outstanding is considered to be highly leveraged. This type of company's earnings or profitability is greatly affected by changes in interest rates.

- Debt-to-Equity Ratio = (Bonds + Preferred Stock) / (Common Stock at Par + Retained Earnings)

The *debt-to-equity ratio* compares securities with fixed charges (bonds and preferred stock) to those securities without fixed charges (common stock). It is used to evaluate the credit strength of the corporation.

As with liquidity ratios, a business will create benchmarks for capitalization ratios that will in turn be used to measure certain aspects of the company's fiscal health.

COVERAGE RATIOS

In addition to liquidity and capitalization, coverage ratios may also be calculated. Coverage ratios measure a company's ability to meet interest payments to its bondholders and dividend payments to preferred stockholders. Failing to meet interest payments to bondholders would place a company in default on its debt. By comparing the money available to make interest payments to the amount of interest payments, an analyst can assess a bondholder's degree of safety.

- Bond Interest Coverage = Earnings before Interest & Taxes /Annual Bond Interest Expense

Bond interest coverage is found by dividing earnings before interest and taxes by the annual bond interest expense.

- Preferred Dividend Coverage = Net Income Preferred Dividends / Profitability and Use of Assets

While omitting a preferred dividend payment will not place a company in default, it may affect the market value of the preferred stock. Thus, analysts look to determine the safety of the dividend payment.

- Operating Profit Margin = Operating Income / Net Sales

Profitability calculations show the amount of profit that a company earns from each sales dollar. Analysts often look at both operating profits and net profits to assess profitability. To determine operating profit margin, operating income is divided by net sales. The complement of the operating profit margin is known as the operating expense ratio. If the operating profit margin is 33 percent, then the operating expense ratio is 100 percent minus 33 percent or 67 percent. This would mean that the company is spending 67 cents to produce one dollar of net sales.

- Net Profit Margin = Net Income / Net Sales

To calculate the amount of net profit earned from each sales dollar, net income is divided by net sales.

- Return on Common Equity = (Net Income – Preferred Dividends) / (Common Stock at Par + Capital Surplus + Retained Earnings)

Return on common equity is one of the most important measurements of a company's profitability on a year-to-year basis. This formula compares the amount of income available to the common shareholders each year to the value of the company's common stock.

- Inventory Turnover Rate = Cost of Goods Sold / Inventory

  The inventory turnover rate is calculated by dividing the cost of goods sold by the year-end inventory. The inventory turnover rate indicates the company's efficiency in managing its inventory level. A low turnover may indicate that the company's inventory is too large, representing an inefficient use of the company's assets. A high turnover normally shows that products sell quickly and cost of storing the inventory is low.

- Book Value Per Common Share = (Total Assets – Intangibles – Total Liabilities Preferred Stock) / Number of Outstanding Common Shares

An analyst would look to the balance sheet to determine the amount of assets that back the securities issued by a company. This figure is called the book value per common share, or is also called net tangible asset value.

EVALUATION OF EARNINGS

A major factor that contributes to the market price of a stock is the company's earnings per share (EPS).

- Earnings Per Share = (Net Income – Preferred Dividends) / Number of Outstanding Shares

This calculation indicates the amount of earnings available to the common stockholder. First, any preferred dividends are subtracted from net income. This shows the earnings available to the common stockholders. To find EPS, the income available to the common shareholders is divided by the number of outstanding common shares.

SUMMARY

This chapter is a very brief presentation and discussion of the calculations and uses of ratios and other fiscal health measures used in the private sector. The information provided builds a beginning knowledge base and demonstrates that a wide variety of ratios, measures and uses are well established in the private sector. Much has been written about private sector ratios and their application that go far beyond what is presented here. The next chapter will focus more on ratios, their uses and benchmarking in school settings.

ACTIVITIES

1. Review the definition of the following terms found in the glossary:

   a. Ratio
   b. Ratio analysis
   c. Benchmarking
   d. Corporate income statement

e. Corporate balance sheet

2. What are the three principal benchmarks Finkler describes?

3. Using the corporate balance sheet in Illustration 26.1 and income statement in Illustration 26.2 calculate the following ratios:

   a. Current ratio
   b. Cash asset ratio
   c. Net profit ratio
   d. Quick asset ratio

27

Using Accounting Information to Measure Fiscal Health and Manage a School District

INTRODUCTION

The previous chapter illustrated that the private sector has a highly developed set of ratios that are the product of an accounting system that produces balance sheets and income statements. While the accounting system in the public sector produces audits, annual financial reports and other types of reports, a comparable set of ratios and meaningful benchmarks are not as highly developed presently, but the future trend seems to indicate a change is coming. This chapter will explore common ratios that are used by school administrators, newly developed ratios that are being discussed and benchmarking strategies that are unique to education.

OUTCOMES

In this chapter, you will learn how to:

1. Compute horizontal and vertical ratios using a school district budget, audit or other financial reports.
2. Create and interpret benchmark data that is meaningful and unique to your school district.
3. Use fiscal measures to better manage a district.

RATIOS AND MEASURES OF FISCAL CONDITION

In today's school business administration climate the proper fiscal management of a school district cannot really take place without the creation and use of meaningful ratios and new measures of fiscal condition, and better measures of resource consumption and student outcomes. The growth of the interest in and use of ratios in school business administration is founded in applications that have been successfully used in the business and private sectors for many years. The business ratios and other measures discussed in the previous chapter do not generally cross directly over to school business administration and provide an exact application, but they do suggest that ratios specific to school districts can and will be developed that will facilitate the creation of sophisticated financial management models. In the future these models will have the potential to improve the efficiency and effectiveness of all aspects of school district management. Indicators of financial health and strength of school districts are very important. Indications of fiscal stress and weakness are at least of equal importance if not more important. The importance of ratios is that they can generate the internal information needed by policy makers and administrators of a school district to gain awareness of the school district's strengths and weaknesses. The implication is to do more than just generate interesting data, but to find strengths in order to become stronger and to find weaknesses so that appropriate action can be taken to correct them before long-term damage occurs.

The following illustrate some of the questions that can be partially resolved using ratios or other fiscal measures:

- Can you describe your school district's relative financial condition in terms of comparing it to itself, a neighboring school district, "look alike" school districts and districts statewide of the same type?
- Is your description based on intuition, a hunch, a feeling or can you quantify your description?
- Do you really know how well (or poorly) your school district is performing financially?
- Do you know the cost effectiveness of the school district's educational programs?

INDICATORS OF FINANCIAL DIFFICULTY

Monitoring a school district's financial history and comparing that history to the school district's current condition and performance remains the source of the most relevant comparative information for a school district because every school district is truly unique. Other comparisons can be helpful in planning, evaluating and in the decision making process, but no comparisons are as useful as looking at whether a school district's own performance is changing in the correct direction and in increments that are satisfactory based on existing conditions. In a National School Board Association (NSBA) publication titled *Budgeting School Dollars*, a list of "indicators of financial difficulty" was generated. The authors, Wagner and Sniderman, share the following 30 questions, many of which require ratios being calculated (Wagner and Sniderman, 1987).

As a board reviews fiscal reports it will be apparent that school officials must be alert to indicators of financial difficulty. Obviously, the degree of difficulty may vary. Whenever financial difficulty looms, however, the board's role is to ask administrators to submit plans for alleviating the difficulty, and for preventing similar problems in the future. "Yes" answers to the following questions may be indicative of financial difficulty:

1. Has your system continually engaged in short-term borrowing?
2. Will "second year" tax anticipation warrants be issued?
3. Has your system recently issued working cash bonds?
4. Does your system close out the working cash fund each year?
5. Have the banks notified your system of a limit on its borrowing?*
6. Have loans from restricted funds been made for other purposes?
7. Have all tax referenda attempts in the last five years been defeated?
8. Are present tax rates at non-referendum limits?
9. Has there been a general decrease in the year-end fund balances over the past three years?*
10. Have budgeted expenditures exceeded budgeted revenues for two consecutive years?*
11. Has the system been delinquent in paying on/for any debt instruments, tuition to other school systems or other obligations based on joint agreements, employee's salaries, or payroll tax/pension liabilities?
12. Is the system involved in pending litigation that could adversely affect the system's financial position?
13. Has enrollment declined more than 15 percent since its peak year?*
14. Has the number of attendance centers remained the same although enrollment has declined?
15. Have cash balances decreased each year for the past three years?*
16. Has the student/staff ratio decreased as enrollment declined?*

17. Have interest monies been dedicated for long-term projects or commitments?
18. Has facility utilization dropped below 70 percent at any school site?*
19. Has state ranking of cost-per-student increased?*
20. Did the rate of inflation outpace the school system's prior year's actual revenue increase?
21. Is the property tax collection rate 95 percent or less?*
22. Have payments to vendors been delayed to solve cash flow shortages and minimize borrowing?
23. Has the percent of budget dedicated for maintenance and repair steadily increased at any one school site?*
24. Has the number of building permits issued within your system's boundaries declined?
25. Has there been an increase in the number of accumulated vacation and sick leave days per employee?*
26. Has there been an increase in the number of unpaid invoices at year end?
27. Has there been an increase in the ratio of bonded indebtedness to total assessed value of property?*
28. Has there been a decrease in the rate of growth in revenues from local sources?*
29. Has there been an increase in mandated expenditures as a percentage of total expenditures?*
30. Has there been an increase in fringe benefits as a percentage of total salary costs?*

(* involve ratios)

Over the past decade, several states have developed or have modified their systems for monitoring the fiscal health of public school systems. Each of these systems reflect in their own way what state policy makers consider "indicators of financial difficulty" but also fiscal strength. Even in private sectors companies like Standard and Poor, on a national level, and small school consulting companies, that specialize at the state level, are creating fiscal profile models that districts can use to better make resource utilization decisions.

All of these public and private models require many sources of data that the school district produces from the accounting process that contain information that can be compared. A few of these sources are:

- District budget.
- Audit financial statements.
- Comprehensive annual financial report.
- Monthly treasurer's report.
- Cash flow analysis.
- General state aid claim forms.
- Transportation reimbursement claim forms.

Each state/province will have its own set of reports and working papers that the school district uses to report and manage the school district. Each document will also contain its unique name and format. These forms generally are very consistent, over time only changing slightly. The forms permit vertical comparisons and horizontal comparisons at a single point in time, comparisons over one time period—the short run, or comparisons over the long run—usually multiple years.

Texas, for example, has its Schools FIRST: Financial Integrity Rating System of Texas. Below are listed a few of the questions a school district must address from its financial records.

- Was total Fund Balance less Reserved Fund Balance greater than zero in the General Fund?
- Was the percent of total tax collections (including delinquent) greater than 96 percent?
- Did the comparison of PEIMS data to like information in the Annual Financial Report result in an aggregate variance of less than 4 percent of expenditures per fund type (Data Quality Measure)? (NOTE: PEIMS is a statewide data management system for public education in the State of Texas.)
- Were Debt-Related Expenditures (net of IFA and/or EDA allotment) less than $770 per student? (If the district's five-year percent change in students was a 2 percent increase or more, or if property taxes collected per penny of tax effort were more than $100,000, then answer this indicator YES.)
- Was the percentage of Operating Expenditures expended for Instruction more than 54 percent?
- Was the aggregate of Budgeted Expenditures and Other Uses LESS THAN the aggregate of Total Revenues, Other Resources and Fund Balance in General Fund?
- If the district's Aggregate Fund Balance in the General Fund and Capital Projects Fund was LESS THAN zero, were construction projects adequately financed or adjusted by change orders or other legal means to avoid creating or adding to the fund balance deficit situation?)
- Was the ratio of Cash and Investments to Deferred Revenues (excluding amount equal to net Delinquent Taxes Receivable) in the General Fund greater than or equal to 1:1? (If Deferred Revenues are less than Delinquent Taxes Receivable, then answer this indicator YES.)
- Was the Administrative Cost Ratio less than the standard in state law?
- Was the Ratio of Students to Teachers within the ranges shown below according to district size?
- Was the Ratio of Students to Total Staff within the ranges shown below according to district size?
- Was the Total Fund Balance in the General Fund more than 50 percent and less than 150 percent of Optimum according to the Fund Balance and Cash Flow Calculation Worksheet in the Annual Financial Report?
- Was the decrease in Undesignated Fund Balance less than 20 percent over two Fiscal Years? (If 1.5 times Optimum Fund balance in General Fund or if Total Revenues exceeded Operating Expenditures in the General Fund, then answer this indicator YES.)
- Was the Aggregate Total of Cash and Investments in the General Fund more than $0?
- Were Investment Earnings in all funds more than $15 per student?

Illinois is yet another example of a recent creation of a new system for assessing a school district's financial health. In the spring of 2003, the Illinois State Board of Education (ISBE) started using a new system called the School District Financial Profile, which replaced the Financial Watch List and Financial Assurance and Accountability System developed and used over the past 20 years. While the old system utilized only one financial indicator, the Fund Balance to Revenue Ratio, the new system utilizes that indicator plus four more to expand the state's capabilities to identify school districts at fiscal risk. The five critical indicators in the Illinois system are:

- **Fund Balance to Revenue Ratio**—This indicator has been utilized in the past as well as in this new financial assessment. It indicates the overall financial strength of the district for the prior year. It is the result of dividing the ending fund balances by the revenues for the four operating funds (e.g., Educational, Operations and Maintenance, Transportation and Working Cash funds).

- **Expenditures to Revenue Ratio**—This indicator identifies how much a district expended for each dollar received. It is computed by dividing total expenditures for the Educational, Operations and Maintenance and Transportation funds by the revenues for those same funds.
- **Days Cash on Hand**—This indicator provides a projected estimate of the number of days a district could meet operating expenditure provided no additional revenues were received. It is computed by dividing the total expenditures of the Educational, Operations and Maintenance and Transportation funds by 360 days to obtain an average expenditure per day. Then the total cash on hand and investments for the same funds are divided by the average expenditures per day.
- **Percent of Short-Term Borrowing Ability Remaining**—Districts often incur short-term debt due to several factors (i.e., delays in receipt of local revenues, etc.). For this indicator, the sum of unpaid Tax Anticipated is divided by 85% of the Equalized Assessed Valuation (EAV) multiplied by the sum of the tax rates for the Educational, Operations and Maintenance and Transportation funds.
- **Percent of Long-Term Debt Margin Remaining**—A district often incurs long-term debt for major expenditures such as buildings and equipment. This total is derived by the product of the district's EAV times its maximum general obligation debt limitation less any outstanding long-term debt.

Each indicator is calculated and the results are slotted into a category of a four, three, two or one with four being the highest and best category possible. Each indicator is weighted and the weighted indicators' scores are summed to obtain a district's overall "financial profile score." The sum of the five weighted scores currently ranges from the highest possible score of 4.00 to the lowest 1.00.

The composite score will identify the district as being in one of four designations:

Financial Recognition	3.54–4.00	—best category of financial strength
Financial Review	3.08–3.53	—limited state monitoring
Financial Watch	2.62–3.07	—close monitoring by the state
Financial Warning	1.00–2.61	—districts with the highest financial risk

The examples of Texas and Illinois, given above, set forth a need for school business administrators to understand ratios, how to create them, how they may be used and what actions can be taken to favorably impact specific ratios.

The remainder of this chapter will illustrate how to apply knowledge about ratios to local budgets and other accounting information.

As mentioned in the previous chapter, a simple definition of ratios is a comparison of any two numbers. Any time one compares two numbers, a ratio has been created. Some ratios are useful, and some ratios have absolutely no value or use (Finkler, 1992).

In the financial analysis of a school district, many numbers can be taken from a variety of school district documents and reports and compared, some of which were noted above. The creation of meaningful financial ratios and their appropriate use and interpretations relative to school districts is just beginning to expand and be perfected. While several ratios currently used in education will be presented, the presentation in this chapter is not intended to be all inclusive. Education must generate ratios that are specifically meaningful to education, just as the private sector developed meaningful ratios.

Once again, any two numbers can be compared thereby creating a new ratio, but that comparison is useless if no relationship between the two numbers can be established. The role of research and best practice in establishing meaningful relationships of a wide variety of educational finance variables available is just dawning.

FINANCIAL RATIO ANALYSIS: RESEARCH AND APPLICATIONS

Understanding the financial condition of public educational organizations is an important part of deciding how to respond to internal and external pressures and changes.

To start to develop knowledge of how this works, examine a part of an Illinois school district's budget that is in the appendix. Other state's budget forms will have a different look, but the concepts demonstrated can be applied to any budget. (Note that the appendix is not a complete budget—only selected pages have been used for demonstration purpose.)

The Illinois budget form is divided into four (4) parts:

Part I Estimated Receipts/Revenue
Part II Estimated Disbursements/Expenditures
Part III Budget Summary
Part IV Summary of Cash Transactions

Part I is information about the revenue projections for the year of interest. The budget is organized into lines and columns. Each of the nine columns (Funds) can be thought of as nine separate "mini-budgets" that when thought of in total is commonly called the district budget. One of the columns contains "revenue account numbers" that would correspond to a state's chart of accounts. For the example given in the appendix, revenue account numbers 1110 to 1999 represent Local Revenue. Examine this information (appendix) in terms of the Education Fund only (column 1). Illustration 27.1 shows a correct examination.

Illustration 27.1

Total Local Revenue (line 83)	$17,837,146
Total Flow-Through Receipts (line 87)	$0
General Levy (line 1)	$14,930,032
Special Ed. Levy (line 4)	$ 202,822
Interest or Investment (line 50)	$ 311,686
Grand Total (line 8 of Budget Summary)	$20,971,525

Each of these totals can be compared to the Grand Total:

A. Total Local Revenue / Grand Total = $17,837,146 / $20,971,525 = .8505 = 85.05%

B. Total Flow-Through Revenue / Grand Total = $0 / $20,971,525 = .0000= 0.0%

C. Special Ed. Levy / Grand Total = $202,822 / $20,971,525 = .0097 = .97%

D. Special Ed. Levy / Total Local Revenue = $202,822 / $17,837,146 = .0114 = 1.14%

E. Interest on Investments / Grand Total = $311,686 / $20,971,525 = .0149 = 1.49%

If the entire budget was shown, State Revenue sources, Federal Revenue Sources and Other Financing Sources would be available.

These five ratios give a view of the school district in terms of its local revenue plan. Since all of the numbers used to calculate the ratios come from the same column these ratios are all vertical ratios. These same ratios should be calculated for the prior year, the year before that, and so on and so on. Now that the ratios are calculated and some histories created, one can look for trends of consistency and significant changes.

Once ratios have been created (using either projected information like the budget or real information from the annual audit or annual financial reports) from one year's documents, one may created the same ratios from prior years, organize and display the multi-year results and then attempt to use the information to draw conclusion about the current state of affairs or use it to drive decisions and manage the district.

Illustration 27.2 is an example of creating several revenue ratios over a six-year period. The last column is based on data computed from the appendix using Part III Budget Summary numbers.

Illustration 27.2
Six-Year History of Projected Major Revenue Sources
Reported as a Percentage of Total Revenue
General Fund

	1999–00	2000–01	2001–02	2002–03	2003–04	2004–05
Total Local Revenue Revenue	85.10	83.20	82.25	79.15	78.65	75.20
Flow Through	0.00	1.15	0.80	1.05	0.90	1.00
Total State Sources	13.30	15.00	15.50	18.55	19.05	22.30
Total Federal Sources	1.65	0.80	1.30	1.20	1.30	1.40

(Note: Total percentages in a given year may not equal 100.0% due to rounding.)

What observations can be made? Over the past six years, the revenue mix has significantly shifted in two categories. Total local revenue has become a larger part of the total revenue picture, while total state revenue has declined. Making the observation is one thing, interpreting the observation is another thing. The interpretation is assisted by responding to a set of questions similar to the following:

- What is causing the shift?
- Does the school district control any of the variables?
- What are the variables of the ratio that cause the shift?
- Which variables are controllable?
- Of the variables that the district controls, which values are in the denominator and which values are in the numerator?

- Should all controllable variables be adjusted, only one or a few?
- How much adjustment should be made and in which direction?
- Is the shift a threat to the educational programs of the district?
- If nothing is done, what might be the consequences?

These ratios and the brief discussion concerning comparing financial data in one fund or budget over time can be thought of as vertical ratio analysis—the numbers compared are in the same column.

For a second example, consider another set of revenue ratios that can be calculated. This set compares some of the major separate Local Revenue pieces to the Total Local Revenue. Using the Education Fund in the appendix, the ratios shown in Illustration 27.3 can be calculated.

Illustration 27.3
Major Local Revenue Sources as a Percentage of Total Local Revenue

General Levy / Total Local Revenue = $14,930,032 / $17,837,146 = .8370 = 83.70%

Special Ed. Levy / Total Local Revenue = $202,822 / $17,837,146 = .0113= 1.13%

Corporate Personal Property Replacement / Total Local Revenue =
$677,106 / $17,837,146 = .0379 = 3.79%

Earnings on Investments / Total Local Revenue = $311,686 = .1747 = 17.47%

Food Service / Total Local Revenue = $793,694 / $17,837,146 = .0444 = 4.44%

Pupil Activities / Total Local Revenue = $76,972 = .0043 = .43%

Textbooks / Total Local Revenue = $226,845 = .0127 = 1.27%

Although histories of each of these ratios could be built and an examination undertaken to discover any trends or consistencies, no history will be shown here. Such an exercise is similar to the analysis demonstrated earlier in this chapter and should be completed by the reader. Both of the ratio analyses just illustrated above involve a vertical companion at one point in time.

Horizontal comparisons can also be created and used. Returning to the appendix and looking at line 12 (Account No. 1230) whose revenue description is Corporate Personal Property Replacement Taxes (CPPRT), it should be observed that this one revenue source has been spread across two funds: 1) Education; and 2) Municipal Retirement/Social Security. CPPRT are "unrestricted" dollars, which means that the administrator/board of education has the discretion to put the dollars in any amount into any fund that needs the revenue. (Although these dollars are called "unrestricted," they may still have some conditions as to how the money must be budgeted/used). The ratios of interest dealing with CPPRT compare the amount budgeted in each fund with the total CPPRT projected to be received. From data in the appendix, it can be determined what the total CPPRT revenue is projected to be. This means that the two ratios would be as shown in Illustration 27.4. (Total percentage will not equal 100.00% due to rounding.)

Illustration 27.4
Horizontal Revenue Ratios

Ed. CPPRT / Total CPPRT = $677,106 / $685,106* = .9883 = 98.83%

IMRF-SS / Total CPPRT = $8,000 / $685,106 = .0116 = 1.10%

* Total dollars on line 12 of the appendix.

These ratios are for one point in time. Have these ratios changed over time? To answer this question, the same ratios would need to be calculated from past years. The amount and direction of any significant changes would need to be assessed. Since the revenue sources in this example are discretionary, they are usually allocated last in the budgeting process to make up revenue short falls/declining revenues in other funds or to cover extraordinary expenditures. In any case, a fund that over time requires more and more discretionary funds to balance its revenue plan against its expenditure plan is headed toward difficulty. Efforts should be made to bring program expenditures into line with revenues. Appropriate early actions on the part of administrators and boards of education can help provide program integrity and can help avoid education program stress or distress. Calculating these ratios can help manage this.

When examining a school district budget or other financial reports, one of the first observations that even the novice will make is that the numbers are displayed in rows and columns. As has just been demonstrated and discussed, when one makes relevant comparison of two figures in the same column the ratio is vertical. However, it may be useful to compare two numbers in the same row thereby establishing a horizontal relationship or horizontal ratio. Once again, the compared numbers need to be relevant.

To demonstrate horizontal relationships and then vertical relationships examine the appendix, Part II Estimated Disbursements/Expenditures. Note that the rows represent specific programs of interest, i.e., regular, special education, adult education, gifted, summer school, etc. The columns define the categories of expenditure for each program or for at least accounting purposes, what the expenditure components are, i.e., salaries, employee benefits, purchased services, supplies and materials, capital outlay and the like.

Suppose that the board of education (or anyone else for that matter) is examining salary expenditures. There are many ways to look at this. To demonstrate the use of both types of ratios, examine the salary information for Regular Programs in the appendix. The salary information $10,611,401 is in a row AND a column. If one wants to know what percentage of total instructional salaries is expended in the regular programs then the following calculation is made:

Regular Program Salaries / Total Salaries = $10,611,401 / $15,997,113 = .6633 = 66.33%

If the information of interest is what percent of the money spent on the regular programs goes toward salaries, then the calculation is:

Regular Program Salaries / Total Regular Program Salaries =
$10,611,401 / $12,547,590 = .8457 = 84.57%

The same two calculations can be made for every program listed in the Education Fund. This information will help identify which programs, if any, have a higher or lower percentage of resources going into salaries. If these ratios have also been calculated in prior years, we can see if our resources dedicated to salaries are going up or down in total, or by program. If total costs are going up BUT some programs costs are going down, we can quickly see which programs are causing the increases. The board (and the teacher's unions) may have negotiated a target for salary distribution in a specific program. The ratio calculation helps document that the target (benchmark) is being met or what progress (or lack of same) is being made to realize the target.

In this example, the regular program salary to total salary ratio is a vertical ratio. The regular programs salaries to total regular program expenditure ratio is a horizontal ratio. Note that in both ratios the numerator is the same—it is the denominator that changed.

OTHER INTERNAL RATIOS

In this context, "other internal ratios" means internal to the school district, simply comparing the school district to itself. In some cases this will involve comparing the information within one report. In other cases it may involve comparing data from one report or document with numbers from another report or document.

From a management perspective, the rationale for using other internal financial ratios is that by expressing several figures as ratios, information will be revealed that is missed when the individual numbers are observed. The theory is that managers can then use this information to improve the efficiency and profitability of their operation. By calculating a wide variety of ratios, a profile can be built for the school district or a single program. If a positive profile can be built then a certain measure of success is indicated. This can be done by identifying the presence of factors that measure success or determining that the factors that would signify failure are absent, or some combination of both.

While extensive research has been completed in the private sector on predictors of business failure, similar developments in the public sector are just beginning and becoming more sophisticated. The key ratios currently used in Ohio, Texas, Illinois and other states to identify fiscal conditions validate this being true. The following is a simple list (without standards, benchmarks or discussion) of a few of the ratios currently used by educators. As the reader examines them, it should be noted that some of the numbers to construct the ratio come from different reports and documents.

In some instances, a series of calculations is required to produce the numbers that will be compared:

Total expenditures per pupil
Operating expenditures per pupil
Pupils per teacher
Pupils per administrator
Total revenue per pupil
Operating revenues per pupil
Equalized assessed value per pupil
Instructional expenditures per total expenditure

Administrative expenditures per total expenditure
Local revenue per total revenue
Local revenue per pupil
State revenue per total revenue
State revenue per pupil
General state aid per total revenue
General state aid per pupil
Outstanding debt per equalized assessed value
Total fringe benefit expenditures per total personnel salary
Expenditures
Transportation operating expenditures per total transportation
Personnel expenditure
Total expenditures per total revenues
Building square footage per custodian
Number of lunches served per lunch worker

In *ASAE Operating Ratio Report* (Lang and Edans, 1994), 26 ratios were listed. Each ratio is supported by a brief statement that explains how the ratio is calculated and the potential uses of the ratio information. In some cases, a benchmark is suggested or given. These ratios, referred to as "Key Ratios," are for not-for-profit associations. Although some of these ratios do not apply to not-for-profit school districts they are shown in Illustration 27.5 (on the following pages) to expose the reader further to possible applications.

Illustration 27.5
Key Ratios Based on Balance Sheet Items

(Most ratios are essentially self-explanatory, involving the expression of either income or expense items as a percentage of total income or total expenses. Below are ratios from the "Key Ratios" selections in the report that may require additional explanation. Numbers in the calculation specification refer to the number given to each line on the survey form.)

RATIO	CALCULATION	USES
Operating Efficiency Ratio (Total Income ÷ Total Assets)	Total Revenue (67) expressed as a percent of Total Assets (222)	Indicates how well an organization is using its total assets to generate income. Generally, the higher the number, the more efficient the company.
Total Liabilities ÷ Fund Balance	Total Liabilities (229) expressed as a percent of Total Fund Balances (248)	Indicates how many times over an organization can meet its obligations with net assets. A ratio of greater than 1:1 (such as 2:1) means that an organization cannot meet its obligations with net assets.

Ratio of Expendable Assets to Total Liabilities	Total Assets (222) – Net Fixed Assets (218 + 219 + 220 + 221) ÷ Total Liabilities (229)	Implies the organization's relative liquidity by showing how many times an organization can meet its obligations from cash and other expendable assets. Any ratio of less than 1:1 indicates that the organization could not meet its debts using cash and other expendable assets.
Net Investment in Fixed Assets to Related Debt	Investment in Land, Buildings & Equipment (218) + Other Investments (219) + Land, Buildings & Equipment (220) + Other Assets (221) ÷ Mortgages and Other Notes Payable	Shows potential for increasing long-term borrowing. Generally, the closer the ratio is to 1:1, the more availability there is to borrow with the fixed assets as collateral.
Expendable Fund Balances to Total Expenses	Total Fund Balances (248) – Net Investment in Fixed Assets (218 + 219 + 220 + 221) ÷ Total Expenses (469)	Indicates whether the association could cover expenses if operating income remained stationary. A ratio of .3:1 means that the organization could cover a third of its expenses with expendable fund balances.
Non-Expendable Fund Balances to Total Expenses	Endowment Fund (243) ÷ Total Expenses (469)	Shows the size of the endowment principal relative to the association's operating size. Can serve as a source of financing, since income and capital gains are often used for operating expenses.
Quick Ratio—Cash + Marketable Securities + Accounts Receivable ÷ Current	Cash (208) + Savings (209) + Accounts Receivable (210) + Pledges Receivable (211) + Grants Receivable (212) + Receivables from Officers and Directors (213) + Other Notes and Loans Receivable (214) + Investments – Securities (217) ÷ Accounts Payable (223) + Grants Payable (224)	Measures liquidity by showing how well an organization can meet its immediate obligations, that is, within days.

Cash + Investments ÷ Deferred Revenues	(208 + 209 + 217) + Investment in Land, Buildings and Equipment (218) + Other Investments (219) ÷ Support and Revenue Designated for Future Periods (225)	Another measure of liquidity, it indicates how many times over the organization's cash covers future earnings (e.g., pledges). A ratio of less than 1:1 (such as 3:1) may indicate a weak financial condition because the organization must depend on money it has not yet earned.
Accounts Receivable Turnover	Annual Fees and Sales on Account (410 minus 403 minus 404 minus 405) ÷ Total Accounts Receivable (210 + 211)	Indicates the proportion of outstanding receivables to total product sales and the effectiveness of collection procedures. Can help in setting collection policies.
Average Collection Period	365 Days ÷ Accounts Receivable Turnover as defined above	Indicates the effectiveness of collection policies by the speed in which receivables are collected.
Salary Costs ÷ Total Association Expenses	Total Personnel Salary Costs (416) expressed as a percentage of Total Association Expense (469)	Indicates the proportion of association expense that is used for salary costs.
Benefits Costs ÷ Salary Costs	Personnel Benefits (417) expressed as a percent of Total Salary Costs (416)	Reflects the proportion of total salary costs used for benefits.
Salary Costs ÷ Total Staff Members (FTEs)	Salary Costs (416) ÷ Total Staff (as defined above) (7 + 8 + 9 + 11 + 12 + 13)	Indicates how much is spent per staff member. There are many mitigating factors for variations from these norms.
Benefits Costs ÷ Total Staff Members (FTEs)	Total Benefits Costs (417) ÷ Total Number of Staff Members as defined above	Reflects how much is spent per staff member on discretionary benefits (excludes mandatory, state and federal taxes).
Total Income ÷ Total Staff Members (FTEs)	Total Income (67) ÷ Total Number of Staff Members as defined above	A type of productivity measure. This ratio shows how much of the organization's income is generated per staff member.
Total Expenses ÷ Total Staff Members (FTEs)	Total Expenses (469) ÷ Total Number of Staff Members as defined above	Average expenditure per full-time employee.

Investment Income ÷ Total Expenses	Total Investment Income (403) expressed as a percentage of Total Expenses (469)	Reflects the extent to which income from this area potentially offsets overall organizational expense.

NOTE: Income in each ratio reflects gross income, not net income.

The above list is an important beginning in creating financial models to help administrators manage a school district. While it is simple to create a ratio, it must be clearly understood that not every possible ratio will have meaning or utility. It must also be clearly understood that quality accounting that reflects consistent application of generally accepted accounting standards is essential in order for ratios to have any value to managers.

RATIO ANALYSIS FOR MAKING EXTERNAL COMPARISONS

The best financial comparisons that can be made (as mentioned earlier) are against oneself, but it is human nature to also compare one's performance with others. To this point in the chapter, the ratios that have been suggested are primarily for comparing a school district's performance against itself. There are other comparisons that can be performed.

In order to provide quality educational programs and services, effective financial management tools that address the important relevant indicators are needed. The legislature, the public and other audiences should know whether or not the major financial management tools of a school district are effective and relevant. If the tools that indicate strength or expose signs of financial distress are effective and relevant, the public needs to know why or what corrective actions are available.

An effective means of improving school district financial management will use ratio analysis of variables commonly associated with measuring internally a school district's financial conditions on a longitudinal basis.

Experience has demonstrated that no two school districts are alike. The school district can compare itself with a variety of external entities. For example, the school district can compare itself with 1) a single neighbor school district, 2) several neighboring school districts, 3) school districts within the region or the state that are "close look-alikes" on relevant school finance or educational program variables, and 4) school districts from throughout the nation. The basis for all of these comparisons are ratios, the same ratios as used earlier in this chapter but calculated over time for all school districts to be used in the comparison grouping or for the selected individual school district. They may be similar in some of the important financial and program variables but significantly different on other variables. This makes direct comparisons range from difficult to meaningless so not only must care be exercised, but sound judgment as well when conclusions, analysis and interpretation of ratio calculations are made.

BENCHMARKING: SETTING STANDARDS OF FISCAL PERFORMANCE

As you were studying the material presented earlier in this chapter it may have crossed your mind that calculating ratios is a simple mathematical process but once the ratio has been determined how does one know what to do with the information. Put more simply—when is a number too high, too low or about right? The answer to these questions is obtained through the process of benchmarking. According to Finkler (1992) there are three principal benchmarks. The first is the organization's history, the second is to compare the organization to specific look-alikes and the third (in a school setting) would be statewide.

Benchmarking is the establishment of a standard, a target, or in some cases, a range of values that a school district could use to measure its performance. In the past, these were referred to as "rules of thumb." In today's more sophisticated school business environment these "rules of thumb" are being replaced by measures that are the result of:

- School district experience/past practice
- Research
- Legislation
- State educational agency rules and regulations
- School board policy

In many cases these standards have been little more than arbitrary and capricious. For example, it is not an uncommon situation during the presentation of the annual audit or during the budget process to get involved in a discussion about "beginning balances" or "unrestricted reserves" or "undistributed reserves." The question often asked is "How big should our reserves be?" It is not uncommon to have someone respond "5 percent of anticipated expenditures or 5 percent of projected revenues." When the 5 percent figure is challenged, the defense or justification of the number is seldom satisfactory. In some cases legislatures and state agencies have fallen into the trap of establishing a random number for a rule or regulation that will be applied to all school districts. The 5 percent number in the above discussion is a benchmark. A number less than 5 percent signifies difficulty, the further below 5 percent the more serious the problem. Anything at or above 5 percent is considered to be an acceptable degree of fiscal health.

Research reported by Everett (1992) and by Vadlicka and Hartman (1994) has started to provide a more rational approach, not only to a more definitive answer to the unreserved balance question, but in a broader sense, point future research in a new direction. That new direction is this: what educational agencies need is not a benchmark for each ratio that can be formed but rather to define a uniform process that will define a standard that is unique to each and every school district. Everett's (1992) and Vadlicka and Hartman's (1994) work are examples of this approach. What their work suggests is that 5 percent might be the "right number" for one school district but a higher or lower number might be more realistic for another district. This is not to say that benchmarks will not be found for a school district or school districts but that a specific approach to finding a meaningful benchmark will be the goal. The results will be a "range" of numbers that provide guidance to school district managers. In some instances this range may be very tight, to suggest an absolute value. In other instances, the range may be fairly broad.

It is important to remember that for a single school district the benchmark for each ratio will be different. When a set of ratios is examined together, they create a model that can help manage the fiscal affairs of the district. For these models to be of any use, the accounting information used to create the ratios must be accurate and consistent over time.

One final comment—ratio analysis is not an exact science. The ratios help point out trends and conditions that would otherwise be missed. Much research and reporting and sharing of information in the future will be needed.

SUMMARY

It is not only useful to look at ratio analysis as a tool to help assess overall financial performance, but also as a way to assess the value that certain income and expense categories add to the organization's financial well-being.

Ratio analysis is an important financial tool at any given point in time, but its real usefulness comes from comparing benchmarks over time to gain a sense of perspective on the trends of various fiscal indicators. For this reason, it is recommended that organizations calculate their ratios for the past two or three fiscal years and compare them to the sample norms, noting any significant fluctuations and deviations that could signal the need for analysis. Each organization will have its own particular set of circumstances which explain such variations, but being aware of their existence is valuable financial information to have.

ACTIVITIES

1. Review the definitions found in the glossary.

   a. Ratio
   b. Benchmark
   c. Horizontal ratio
   d. Vertical ratio

2. This chapter listed 30 questions that, when answered, can be indicators of fiscal distress for a school district. Review this list and indicate which could use ratio analysis to resolve the question(s).

3. Review the Schools FIRST: Financial Integrity Rating System of Texas information provided in this chapter and convert the questions into mathematical statements (i.e., TOTAL FUND BALANCE - RESERVED FUND BALANCE > $0).

4. Convert the five critical indicators in the Illinois School District Financial Profile provided in this chapter into mathematical statements.

5. Using the appendix, calculate the following ratios (report as percent).

   a. General Education Levy (EDUCATION FUND) Total Receipts / Revenue from Local Sources
   b. General Education Levy (EDUCATION FUND) Total Revenue / Receipts All Sources
   c. Total State Revenue / Receipts Sources (EDUCATION FUND) to Total Revenue / Receipts.
   d. Total Local Revenue (EDUCATION FUND) to Total Local Revenue (all Funds)
   e. Total Local Revenue (OPERATIONS AND MAINTENANCE FUND) to Total Local Revenue (all Funds)
   f. Total Local Revenue (TRANSPORTATION) to Total Local Revenue (all Funds)
   g. Total Local Revenue (BOND and INTEREST) to Total Local Revenue (all Funds)
   h. Total Local Revenue (MUNICIPAL RETIRE/SOCIAL SECURITY) to Total Local Revenue (all Funds)
   i. Regular Program Salaries (EDUCATION FUND) to total Salaries (EDUCATION FUND)

j. Special Education Program Salaries (EDUCATION FUND) to Total Salaries (EDUCATION FUND)
k. Interscholastic Program Salaries (EDUCATION FUND) to Total Salaries (EDUCATION FUND)
l. Regular Program Salaries (EDUCATION FUND) to Total Regular Program Expenditures
m. Regular Program Employee Benefits (EDUCATION FUND) to Total Regular Program Expenditures
n. Regular Program Purchased Services (EDUCATION FUND) to Total Regular Program Expenditures
o. Regular Program Supplies and Materials (EDUCATION FUND) to Total Regular Program Expenditures
p. Regular Program Capital Outlay (EDUCATION FUND) to Total Regular Program Expenditures
q. Regular Program Other Objects (EDUCATION FUND) to Total Regular Program Expenditures
r. What is the total of the percentages l through q?
s. Total Expenditures (EDUCATION FUND) to Total Revenue (EDUCATION FUND)

6. Assume that benchmarks for the following ratios have been established as shown below. Use the budget information in the appendix to calculate each ratio and compare your results with the benchmarks. Discuss whether the difference is significant and what actions might be taken to move the calculated ratio(s) closer to the appropriate benchmark.

   a. Education Fund General Levy to Total Receipts/Revenues in the Education Fund from all Sources (30.0%)
   b. Total Receipts/Revenue from State Sources to Total Receipts/Revenues in the Education Fund from all Sources (10.0%)
   c. Total Regular Program Salaries and Fringe Benefits in the Education Fund to Total Regular Program Expenditures in the Education Fund (90.0%)
   d. Estimated Fund Balance July 1, 2004, in the Education Fund to 2004–05 Total Receipts/ Revenue in the Education Fund (10%)

28

Future of Financial and Managerial Accounting in the School Setting

It is appropriate that a few ideas and thoughts about the future of the accounting tasks in a school district setting be made at the conclusion of this work. The history of the school business administrator role in the United States clearly documents that the financial accounting or reporting aspect of accounting has been with the role from the very beginning and the managerial aspects of accounting in the school environment are expanding in terms of options and sophistication. As was demonstrated in the first chapter, accounting is the common thread that crosses all topics, duties and responsibilities, and ties the entire profession together.

The almost universal availability of accounting software and the required hardware to run the software has made the financial and managerial aspects of accounting on a timely basis almost a given in school district operations. Detailed reports that were once impractical to create are now expected and demanded almost instantaneously. The degree of detail that can be obtained will be a simple answer to the question, "How much detail do you want and/or need?"

Financial accounting and reporting that were in the past restricted to the district level will become available at the building level, program level, classroom level and even individual student level and this will be available electronically 24 hours a day, 7 days a week. Some school districts have already made significant strides in this direction. In terms of timing, many annual reports will become monthly, weekly and daily in their production and use. This will allow for electronic transfer of information (some of which is already in place) and eventually make paperless reporting a reality on a universal basis. The technology already exists, but getting school district personnel trained to use the technology and having the school district develop the funding to require the technology at the local level is all that keeps this from happening today. Improved accounting will facilitate the proper implementation of site-based management.

Better accounting will drive school finance reform in the future. Accounting reforms will make the student the unit of school finance, define that student unit in terms of program inputs and performance outputs and determine what the state and local financial partnership mix will be for each student based on new measures of local ability. Only a few years ago these measures were unheard of, partially because the accounting definitions and processes could not produce the required information.

The breadth and scope of educational research that depends on accurate, consistent, valid and reliable financial data will be expanded in the future. This improved and expanded information base will allow questions to be asked and hypotheses to be tested that will not only improve accountability and the daily operation of a school district, but also will suggest new approaches to solve more and more complex educational problems.

Accounting for managerial purposes will expand and be perfected. Models and procedures will be developed so that each school district will be able to create meaningful standards and benchmarks that will describe each district's unique fiscal health/fiscal stress and educational health/educational stress. Accounting-produced models will allow for more than a simple description of what is happening; they will actually suggest a set of solutions and prioritize those solutions. The increase in accounting sophistication will allow the linking together of various managerial models that presently stand alone resulting in total fiscal profiles that will allow administrators to act rather than simply react to the information they are producing.

The accounting preparation of school business administrators and superintendents will improve. District-level administrators will request more and better training in the accounting domain in their preparation, but also require seminars as follow-up, in-service type professional development. This will also be true for the Certified Public Accountants that will serve school districts.

Accounting standards, definitions, principles and procedures will become even more uniform in their application. This will facilitate more consistent internal reporting over time and between school districts. All of this will let ratio analysis evolve as a tool. The data that comprise the ratio will be more clearly related and understood and the benchmarks that are established will improve.

Audit documents will improve in presentation and content. Part of this will depend on the preparation and experience of the auditors but also the improved accounting skills and accounting knowledge base of school business administrators and external accountants. School business administrators will become better consumers of accounting information. This will put pressure on those who produce the accounting information, whether internally or externally, to step up a notch in their performance.

Internal auditing will improve. The basic "bookkeeping" of the past will soon be unacceptable even in very small school districts. This idea carries some major implications for those employed to develop professionally. They will need to improve their personal computing skills and their knowledge of accounting.

The Governmental Accounting Standards Board will continue to define new accounting standards, techniques and procedures. GASB 33 and GASB 34 are recent examples of this expansion of the rules that will have an impact on public accounting.

Public entities like legislatures and school boards will develop questions of their own that will require better accounting, and private entities like Standard and Poors will create models that theoretically explain to the public what is happening in the schools in terms of inputs and outputs which will mean better accounting. The bottom line—the use of accounting information for 1) advanced budgeting, 2) financial forecasting, 3) benchmarking, 4) child-based funding, and 5) improved reporting customized to the needs of various constituents to name a few will be the future.

One final observation: Any individual who is preparing to be a school district superintendent, school business administrator, school principal or any other central office position must make sure that their pre-service and in-service professional development activities possess significant components of accounting. Because of time constraints and other limitations, the accounting knowledge and skills needed by school administrators and school business administrators will continue to be different from that needed by Certified Public Accountants. However, the pursuit of improved accounting should always be the objective.

Resources/References/Selected Readings

WEBSITES

The following websites and citations provide other information useful to identifying and describing federal reporting requirements and other reference material relevant to financial and managerial accounting in more detail. This publication contains references to websites on the Internet that were current at the time of publication.

Association of School Business Officials International: http://www.asbointl.org/
Department of Education Program Listing: http://www.cfda.gov
Financial Standards Accounting Board: http://www.fasb.org/
Government Financial Officers Association: http://www.gfoa.org/
Governmental Accounting Standards Board: http://www.gasb.org/
Illinois Association of School Business Officials: http://www.iasbo.org/
Illinois State Board of Education: http://www.isbe.net/
NCES: http://nces.ed.gov/
Title I website maintained by the U.S. Department of Education, Office of Elementary and Secondary Education: http://www.ed.gov/offices/OESE/CEP/

REFERENCES/SELECTED READINGS

Association for School Business Officials International. (March 2004). Year in Review, ASBO's Certificate of Excellence in Financial Reporting. *School Business Affairs,* Vol. 70, No. 3. Reston, VA: Author.

Association of School Business Officials International. (2001). *Association of school business officials international's professional standards.* Reston, VA: Author.

Association of School Business Officials International. (1991). *Model preparation program for school business administrators.* Reston, VA: Author.

Association of School Business Officials International. (2000, September). *Statement 34 implementation recommendations for school districts.* Reston, VA: Author.

Bailey, L. P. (1993). *Governmental GAAP guide, 1993.* New York: HBJ Miller Accounting Publications.

Barr, R. H. (1980). *Financial accounting for local and state school systems.* Washington, DC: Government Printing Office.

Candoli, I. C., et al. (1973). *School business administration: A compilation of exemplary management techniques.* Park Ridge, IL: Research Corporation of the Association of School Business Officials.

Carnahan, O. (1965). *A study of the duties, responsibilities and training of school business officials in cities of the United States between 25,000 and 50,000 population.* Doctoral Dissertation, University of Idaho, Moscow, ID.

Colluci, M. A. (1988, November). Program considerations for school lunch services. *School Business Affairs*, 55 (11). Reston, VA: Association for School Business Officials International.

Everett, R. E. (1992, July). Using cash flow analysis as part of a process to define an adequate beginning fund balance. *The Journal of School Business Management*, 4 (2). DeKalb, IL: Illinois Association of School Business Officials.

Everett, R. E., & Glass, T. E. (1986, May). Survey defines school business officials' responsibilities. *School Business Affairs*, 52 (8), pp. 14–28. Reston, VA: Association for School Business Officials International.

Everett, R. E., & Glass, T. E. (1992). School business administrators in the 1990s. *The Journal of Business Management*, 4 (1), pp. 5–18. DeKalb, IL: Illinois Association of School Business Officials.

Everett, R. E., & Glass, T. E. (1992, July). School business administrators in the 1990s. *School Business Affairs*, 58 (7), pp. 28–36. Reston, VA: Association for School Business Officials International.

Everett, R. E., & Mastro, L. (1994, September). Certification: Little progress for school business administration. *School Business Affairs*, 60 (9), pp. 6–15. Reston, VA: Association for School Business Officials International.

Everett, R. E., Lows, R. L., and Johnson, D. R. (1996). *Financial and managerial accounting for school administrators*. Reston, VA: Association for School Business Officials International.

Federal Register, Volume 53, No. 148 (August 2, 1988). Washington, DC: Department of Agriculture, Food and Nutrition Service.

Finden, R. (2001, November). Applying statement 34's capital asset requirements. *School Business Affairs*, 67 (11), pp 12–14. Reston, VA: Association for School Business Officials International.

Finkler, S. A. (1992). *Finance and accounting for nonfinancial managers.* Englewood Cliffs, NJ: Prentice Hall.

Fowler, W. J., Jr. (1990). *Financial accounting for local and state school systems.* Washington, DC: Government Printing Office.

Gerald, D. E. and Hussar, W. J. (1995). *Projections of education's statistics to 2005*. Washington, DC: National Center for Education Statistics.

Glick, P. E. (Ed.) (1987). *Government fixed asset inventory systems: Establishing, maintaining and accounting*. Chicago: Government Finance Officers Association.

Goodling, W. F. (1990, November). The future of federal funding for child nutrition programs. *School Business Affairs*, 56 (11). Reston, VA: Association for School Business Officials International.

Government Finance Officers Association (1988). Governmental accounting, auditing and financial reporting. Chicago: Author.

Governmental Accounting Standards Board. (1999, June). *Basic financial statements—and management's discussion and analysis—for state and local governments (Statement No. 34)*. Norwalk, CT: Author.

Governmental Accounting Standards Board. (2000, May). *Guide to implementation of GASB Statement No. 34 on basic financial statements—and management's discussion and analysis—for state and local governments: Questions and answers*. Norwalk, CT: Author.

Governmental Accounting Standards Board (GASB). (1992, June 30). *Codification of governmental accounting and financial reporting standards*. Norwalk, CT: Author.

Green, T., Williamson, M. E., & Endris, W. L., Jr. (2000, November). GASB 34: Capitalization and depreciation. *School Business Affairs*, 66 (11). Reston, VA: Association for School Business Officials International.

Haried, A. A. (1988). *Advanced accounting, 1988*. New York, NY: John Wiley & Sons, Inc.

Hess, J. P. & Van Egnond-Pannell, D. (1977, November). Budgeting for food service operations. *School Business Affairs*, 53 (11). Reston, VA: Association for School Business Officials International.

Hill, F. W. (1982). *The school business administrator.* Park Ridge, IL: Research Corporation of the Association of School Business Officials.

Illinois State Board of Education, Department of School Finance. (1993). *Preparing for local education agency audits*. Springfield, IL: Author.

Ingram, R., Peterson, R. I., & Martin, S. W. (1991). *Accounting and financial reporting for governmental and nonprofit organizations: Basic concepts.* New York: McGraw-Hill.

Jensen, P. E. (1973). *Inventory control of fixed assets by school district personnel*. Albany, NY: The University of the State of New York, the State Education Department, Division of Educational Management Services.

Johnson, F. (2003). *Financial accounting for local and state school systems, 2003 edition*. Washington, DC: U.S. Government Printing Office.

Lang, A. and Edans, P. L. (1994). *ASAF operating ratio report, 9th edition*. Washington, DC: American Society of Association Executives.

Lang, A. and Edans, P. L. (1994, June). Benchmarks, performance measurement: Operating ratios as benchmarks. *Association Management*, 46 (6). Washington, DC: American Society of Association Executives.

Lewis, J. Jr. (1983). *Long-range and short-range planning for educational administrators*. Boston: Allyn & Bacon.

Lynn, E. S. & Thompson, J. W. (1974). *Introduction to fund accounting*. Reston, VA: Reston Publishing.

McGuffey, C. W. (1980). *Competencies needed by chief school business administrators*. Park Ridge, IL: Research Corporation of the Association of School Business Officials.

Miller, J. G. and Swanson, G. A. (1989). *Measurement and interpretation in accounting.* New York: Quorum Books.

Municipal Finance Officers Association (MFOA). (1980). *Governmental accounting, auditing, and financial reporting.* Chicago, IL: Author.

Mutter, D. W., Nichols, W. R., & Honaker, K. W. (1985). To count or not to count: All items are not equal when developing a fixed asset system. *School Business Affairs*, 51(10), pp. 42–43, 64–65, 75. Reston, VA: Association for School Business Officials International.

Office of the State Comptroller. (1985–1990). *Financial management: Guide for local governments*. Albany, NY: Division of Municipal Affairs, Municipal Accounting Systems.

Robert Davis Associates. (1981). *Principles of public school fund accounting.* Washington, DC: National Technical Information Service.

Roberts, C. T. & Lichtenberger, R. (1973). *Financial accounting: Classification and standard terminology for local and state school systems*. Washington, DC: U.S. Government Printing Office.

Securities Training Corporation. (1995). *General securities registered representative, Series 2 Study Program.* New York, NY: Author.

Securities Training Corporation. (1988). *Investment company products/variable contracts representative, Series 6*. New York, NY: Author.

Securities Training Corporation. (1994). *Investment company products/variable contracts representative, Series 6*. New York, NY: Author.

Shearing, F. N. (1991, August). *Memorandum to superintendents of public schools*. Albany, NY: Bureau of School Food Management and Nutrition.

Tidwell, S. B. (1985). *Financial and managerial accounting for elementary and secondary school systems (3rd ed.).* Reston, VA: Research Corporation of the Association of School Business Officials.

Vadlicka, S. R. and Hartman, W. T. (1994, February). How much is enough? Sizing a district's fund balance. *School Business Affairs*, 60 (2). Reston, VA: Association for School Business Officials International.

Wagner, I. D. and Sniderman, S. M. (1987). *Budgeting school dollars: A guide to spending and saving*. Alexandria, VA: National School Board Association.

Wood, R. C., et al. (1986). *Principles of school business management*. Reston, VA: Association of School Business Officials International.

Glossary

This glossary is a collection of accounting terminology that reaches beyond the scope of this book. While the significant words, principles and concepts used in this book are defined here, there are also accounting terms defined herein that are not part of this text. This is intentional so that this book can serve not only as a teaching tool, but that it can also be a reference tool, useful as further study is pursued. The following terms and basic definitions are given to assist the reader and students in their development of not only a basic understanding of accounting principles and concepts but to help develop the vocabulary (jargon) of accounting and accountants. This should help facilitate improved communication between school administrators and those who create (internally or externally) financial and managerial accounting information. While the list of terms defined here is comprehensive, it is not all inclusive of terms used in this work. The sources of the definitions given in this glossary come from the following:

Finkler, Steven A. (1992). *Finance and accounting for nonfinancial managers.* Englewood Cliffs, NJ: Prentice Hall.

Illinois State Board of Education. (1993). *Chart of accounts.* Springfield, IL: Author.

Larson, Kermit D. (1989). *Financial accounting.* Homewood, IL: Irwin.

Securities Training Corporation. (1988). *Terminology of the securities industry.* New York, NY: Author.

Tidwell, S. B. (1985). *Financial and managerial accounting for elementary and secondary school systems, 3rd Ed.* Reston, VA: ASBO International.

A

Abatement: A complete or partial cancellation of a levy imposed by a government unit. Abatement usually applies to tax levies, special assessments and service charges.

Abatement of expenditures: Return or cancellation of a part or all of a charge previously made, usually resulting from goods or materials of a quality other than specified for which allowances or refunds are made or which result in a resale of the materials originally purchased. The term can be applied to a loss or damage to property and applies to both current expenditures and capital outlay expenditures. Abatements result in reduction of expenditure accounts only when they occur during the same fiscal period as the expenditure, thereafter they become sources of revenue to the fund.

Abatement of revenue: Return or cancellation of a part or all of any specific revenue previously recorded, usually resulting from a tax refund.

Account: A record of transactions affecting a specific item. An account must provide a space for its title, a space for recording increases in the amount of the item, a space for recording decreases in the amount of the item, a space for recording the year, month and date of each transaction and a space for a posting reference.

Account number: See Coding.

Accounting: A system for providing financial information. It is generally broken down into two principle divisions: financial accounting and managerial accounting.

Accounting entity: Each school district is perceived and treated as if it is a separate entity that is distinct from other school districts, and as such, the financial records and reports of each school district should not include either the transactions or assets of another school district.

Accounting period: A period of time at the end of which and for which financial statements are prepared. See also Fiscal period.

Accounting procedure: The arrangement of all processes which discover, record and summarize financial information to produce financial statements and reports and to provide internal control.

Accounting system: The total structure of records and procedures which discover, record, classify and report information of the financial position, operations, changes in fund equities and changes in financial position of school district or any of its funds, account groups and organizational components.

Accounts payable: Liabilities or amounts owed on open account to private persons, firms, or corporations for goods and/or services received by a school district (but not including amounts due to other funds of the same school district or to other governmental units).

Accounts receivable: Amounts claimed on open account from a private persons, firms, or corporations for goods and/or services received by a school district (but not including amounts due to other funds of the same school district or to other governmental units).

Accrual basis: The basis of accounting under which revenues are recorded when earned and expenditures are recorded as soon as they result in liabilities for benefits received, notwithstanding the receipt of the revenue or the payment of the expenditure in whole or in part in another accounting period. See also Accrue and Levy.

Accrue: To record revenues when earned and to record expenditures as soon as they result in liabilities for benefits received, notwithstanding that receipt of cash or the payment of the expenditure may take place, in whole or in part, in another accounting period. See also Accrual basis, Accrued assets, Accrued expenses, Accrued liabilities and Accrued revenues.

Accrued asset: An asset arising from revenues earned but not yet collected or due, such as accrued interest receivable.

Accrued expense: An expenses incurred during the current accounting period but which is not payable until a subsequent accounting period. See also Accrual basis and Accrue.

Accrued income: See Accrued revenue.

Accrued interest on investments purchased: Interest accrued on investments between the last interest payment date and the date of purchase. The account is carried as an asset until the first interest date after the purchase. At that time, an entry is made debiting cash and crediting the accrued interest on investment purchased account for the amount of interest purchased and an interest earnings account for the balance.

Accrued interest payable: A liability account which represents the amount of interest accrued at the balance sheet date but which is not due until a later date.

Accrued liability: An amount owed but not yet due.

Accrued revenue: Revenue earned during the current accounting period but which is not collected until the following accounting period.

Accrued taxes payable: A liability for taxes which has accrued since the last payment date but which is not yet due. Normally, this liability will be found in the enterprise fund.

Accrued wages payable: A liability for wages earned by employees between the last payment date and the balance sheet date but which is not yet due.

Accumulated depreciation: See Allowance for depreciation.

Activity: A specific or distinguishable line of work performed by one or more organizational components of a school system for the purpose of accomplishing a function for which the school district is responsible.

Activity classification: A grouping of expenditures on the basis of specific lines of work performed by organizational units.

Actual cash value: The value of an investment or other asset at a particular point in time when it is sold or calculated as if the asset were sold.

Actual revenue: Revenue received during the current accounting period.

Actuarial basis: A basis used in computing the amount to be paid or collected periodically to a fund so that the total plus compounded earnings thereon will equal the required collections or payments of the fund. The factors taken into account in arriving at the amount including the length of time over which each collection or payment is to be made and the rate of return compounded on such amounts over its life. A trust fund for a public employee retirement system is an example of a fund set up on an actuarial basis property.

Adjusting entry: An entry that is prepared to correct the asset or liability account and to correct the related revenue or expenditure account.

Administration: The performance of executive duties, supervision, direction, correlation or coordination of a function.

Advance from the general fund: An account in an enterprise or internal service fund which represents the fund's liability to the general fund, possibly for general obligation bonds which have been issued by a school district but whose proceeds have been used to finance facilities and operations of the enterprise fund or internal service fund.

Advance "from" fund: A liability account used to represent a long-term liability owed by one fund to another fund in the same school district.

Advance "to" fund: An asset account which represents a long-term claim by a fund from another fund of the same school district.

Agency fund: A fund consisting of resources received and held by a school district as an agent for others; for example, taxes collected and held by a school district for another school district. Note: Sometimes resources held by one fund of a school district for other funds of the unit are handled through an agency fund. An example is taxes held by an agency fund for distribution among other funds.

Allocate: To divide a lump-sum appropriation into parts which are designated for expenditure by specific organization units and/or for specific purposes, activities or objectives.

Allocation: A part of a lump-sum appropriation which is designated for expenditure by specific organization units and/or specific purposes, activities or objects.

Allot: To divide an appropriation into amounts which may be encumbered or expended during an allotment period.

Allotment: A part of an appropriation which may be encumbered or expended during the allotment period.

Allotment ledger: A subsidiary ledger which contains an account for the un-allotted appropriation for each purpose and showing the amount allotted periodically throughout the fiscal period, the balance available for additional allotment and other related information.

Allotment period: A period of time less than one fiscal year in length during which the allotment is effective. Bimonthly and quarterly allotment periods are common.

Allowance: A deduction from revenue and assets due to some modifying circumstances, for example, time, usage and damage.

Allowance for depreciation: The account in which is accumulated the periodic cost of the related asset which has been charged as depreciation expense. It is a control-asset account. Frequently referred to as accumulated depreciation.

Allowance for depreciation—building: The accumulation of periodic credits made to record the expiration in the service life of buildings which is attributable to wear and tear through use and lapse of time, obsolescence, inadequacy or other physical or functional cause. The account is shown in the balance sheets of enterprise and internal service funds as a deduction from buildings in order to arrive at a book value of buildings. Buildings carried in the accounts of agency or trust funds may or may not be depreciated depending on the conditions prevailing in each case. Frequently referred to as accumulated depreciation on buildings.

Allowance for depreciation—equipment: This account serves the same purpose for equipment as the allowance for depreciation—building serves for buildings.

Allowance for uncollectible accounts: See Estimated uncollectible accounts receivable.

Allowance for uncollectible taxes: An account in which is recorded the amount of taxes estimated to be uncollectible. The balance of this account is shown as a deduction from taxes receivable account to which it relates in the balance sheet.

Amortization: (1) Gradual reduction, redemption or liquidation of the balance of an account according to a specified schedule of times and amounts. (2) Provision for payment of a debt by use of the Debt Service Fund.

Amount available in debt service funds—serial bonds: An account in the general long-term debt group of accounts which designates the amount of assets available in the debt service fund for the retirement of general obligation serial bonds.

Amount available in debt service funds—term bonds: An account which provides the same information for general obligation term bonds as the amount available in debt service funds—serial bonds does for general obligation serial bonds.

Annual budget: A budget applicable for a single, twelve-month fiscal year.

Annual Financial Report (AFR): See Comprehensive Annual Financial Report (CAFR).

Annuities payable: A liability account which records the amount of annuities due and payable to retired employees in a public employee retirement system.

Annuity: A series of equal money payments at equal intervals during a designated period of time. In school accounting the most frequent annuities are accumulations of debt service funds for term bonds and payments to retired employees under public employee retirement systems.

Annuity, amount of: The total amount of money accumulated or paid during an annuity period from an annuity and compound interest at a designated rate.

Annuity period: The designated length of time during which an amount of annuity is accumulated or paid.

Apportionment: See Allotment.

Appraisal: (1) The act of appraising. See Appraise. (2) The estimated value resulting from such action.

Appraise: To make an estimate of value, particularly of the value of property. Note: If the property is valued for the purposes of taxation, the less inclusive term *assess* is substituted for the above term.

Appropriation: An authorization granted by a legislative body, or the school board, to make expenditures and to incur obligations for special purposes. Note: An appropriation is usually limited in purpose, amount and as to the time when it may be expended.

Appropriation account: A budgetary account set up to record specific authorization to spend. The account is credited with original and any supplemental appropriations and is charged with reductions due to budgetary restrictions.

Appropriation bill, ordinance or resolution: A bill, ordinance or resolution which gives appropriations legal effect. It is a method by which authority is granted by the school board to administrative officers to make expenditures for specific periods of time. It is frequently referred to as enactment of the expenditure side of the budget by the school board.

Appropriation, bond interest expense: An expenditure authorized to account for interest due on a bond during the accounting period.

Appropriation expenditure: An expenditure authorized by the appropriation act. Note: Since all expenditures from a budgetary fund or governmental type fund must be authorized by the appropriation act, the term *expenditures* by itself is widely and properly used.

Appropriation ledger: A subsidiary ledger containing an account for each appropriation. Each account usually shows the amount originally appropriated by the budget, budget increases or decreases during the year. On the same page, expenditure accounts and encumbrance accounts are used for budgetary control to determine the amount of the appropriation free for further commitment, encumbrances or expenditures. If allotments are made and a separate ledger is maintained for them, the appropriations ledger usually shows the amount originally appropriated, budget increases or decreases in the appropriation, the amounts allotted and the un-allotted balance of the appropriation.

Appropriation, principal of bond debt: An expenditure authorized to account for principal repayment on a bond during the accounting period.

Arbitrage: Buying and selling the same stock, bonds, etc., at the same time in different markets to profit from different prices. A technique employed to take advantage of price differences in separate markets. This is accomplished by purchasing in one market for immediate sale in another at a better price. With regard to municipalities, the proceeds from the sale of tax-free bonds may not be invested in taxable securities merely for the interest value which would be generated. However, the IRS generally allows such advantages to accrue to the municipality under several special conditions, including the requirement that 85% of the proceeds of the bond issue be used for the purpose for which they were issued within three years from issue date.

Assess: To value property officially for purposes of taxation. Note: The term is also sometimes used to denote the levy of taxes, but such usage is not correct because it fails to distinguish between the valuation process and the tax levy process.

Assessed valuation: A valuation set upon real estate or other property by a government as a basis for levying taxes.

Assessment: (1) The process of making the official valuation of property for purposes of taxation. (2) The valuation placed upon property as a result of this process.

Assessment roll: In the case of real property, the official list containing the legal description of each parcel of property and its assessed valuation. The name and address of the last known owner is usually also shown. In the case of personal property, the assessment roll is the official list containing the name and address of the owner, a description of the personal property and its assessed valuation.

Asset: Property and property right of a school district which has monetary value. Note: Conventionally, debit balances subject to final disposition, such as deferred charges and prepaid expenses, are classified as assets on the balance sheet.

Asset account: An account that is used to record transactions affecting assets.

Audit: The examination of documents, records, reports, systems of internal control, accounting and financial procedures, and other evidence for one or more of the following purposes: (1) to ascertain whether the statements prepared from accounts present fairly the financial position, the results of operations, the changes in fund equity and the changes in financial position of each of the funds and account groups of the school district in accordance with generally accepted accounting principles applicable to the school district and on a basis consistent with that of the preceding year; (2) to determine the propriety, legality and mathematical accuracy of a school district's financial transactions; (3) to ascertain whether transactions have been properly recorded; and (4) to ascertain the stewardship of public officials who handle and are responsible for the financial resources of a school district.

Audit program: A detailed outline of work to be done and the procedure to be followed during an audit, whether it is an internal audit conducted by members of the school district's internal auditing staff, by outside, independent accountants, or by auditors at the local, state or federal level.

Audit report: The report prepared by an auditor covering the audit or examination. As a rule, the report should include: (1) a statement of the scope of the examination; (2) explanatory comments (if any) concerning exceptions by the auditor as to the application of generally accepted auditing standards; (3) opinion; (4) explanatory comments (if any) concerning verification procedures; (5) financial statements including footnotes which are an integral part of the financial statements, and schedules; and (6) sometimes statistical tables, supplementary comments and recommendations. The auditor's signature follows items (3) or (4).

Audited voucher: A voucher which has been examined verified, and approved for payment.

Auditor's opinion: A letter signed by an auditor which states that the financial statements have been examined in accordance with generally accepted auditing standards (with exceptions, if any) and which expresses an opinion on the fairness of presentation of the financial position, the results of operations, the changes in fund equity and the changes in financial position of all of the funds and account groups of the school district that have been examined.

Authority: A governmental unit or public agency created to perform a single function or a restricted group of related activities. Usually such units are financed from service charges, fees and tolls but in some instances they have taxing powers. An authority may be completely independent of other governmental units or in some cases it may be partially dependent upon other governments for its creation, its financing or the exercise of certain powers.

B

Balance sheet: A statement which discloses the assets, liabilities, and equities of a fund of a school district at a specified date. It is properly classified to exhibit the financial position of the fund or account group at that date. Note: If a single balance sheet is prepared for several funds, it must be in columnar or sectional form to exhibit the accounts of each fund and account group individually.

Balance sheet account: An account that is used to record transactions affecting the assets, liabilities and fund equities of a school district. See Balance sheet.

Basis of accounting: The time at which revenues, expenses, expenditures, transfers and related assets and liabilities are recognized in the accounts and are reported in the financial statements of the fund or account group.

Benchmarking: The process of testing a system against its design and purposes using actual data.

Betterment: An addition made to, or change made in, a fixed asset which is expected to prolong its life or increase its efficiency over and above that arising from maintenance and the cost of which is therefore added to the book value of the asset. Note: The term is sometimes applied to sidewalks, sewers and streets but these should preferably be designated as improvements.

Bond: A written promise to pay a specified sum of money called the face value or principal amount at a specified date or dates in the future, called maturity date(s), together with periodic interest at a specified rate. Note: The difference between a promissory note and a bond is that the latter runs for a longer period of time and requires greater legal formality.

Bond anticipation note: A short-term interest-bearing note issued by a school district in anticipation of bonds to be issued at a later date. These promissory notes are retired from the proceeds of the bond issue to which they are related.

Bond authorized and unissued: A bond which has been legally authorized but not issued and which can be sold without further authorization.

Bond discount: The excess of the face value of a bond over the price for which it was acquired or sold. Note: The price does not include accrued interest at the date of acquisition or sale.

Bond equivalent yield: The annual rate of interest paid or earned on bonds purchased at a premium or discount. Interest paid or earned as stated on the face of the instrument plus or minus the amount of the premium or discount amortized for that period of time.

Bond interest expense: The cost of using borrowed money; a stated percentage of the principal amount of the debt charged for a specified period of time.

Bond issue: The term used to describe the process used to sell (market) a school district's bonds.

Bond issued: A bond that is sold.

Bond, maturity value: The value of the bond when it comes due for repayment. Generally this value is also the face value of the bond.

Bond ordinance or resolution: An ordinance or resolution authorizing a bond issue.

Bond payable: The face value of a bond that is outstanding, issued and unpaid.

Bond premium: The excess of the price at which the bond is sold or acquired over its face value.

Bond proceeds receivable: An account used to designate the amount receivable upon sale of bonds.

Bonded debt: That portion of the indebtedness of a school district represented by outstanding bonds.

Book of original entry: The records in which the various transactions are formally recorded for the first time, such as the cash receipts journal, check register, voucher register or general journal.

Book value: (1) The amount shown on the books of the account. (2) The original cost of an asset less the accumulated depreciation to a date specified, if applicable.

Budget: A plan of financial operation embodying an estimate or proposed expenditures for a given period and the proposed means of financing them. Used without any modifier, the term usually indicates a financial plan for a single fiscal year.

Budgetary account: Frequently referred to as a managerial account, a budgetary account is an account which makes it possible for a budgetary type fund (governmental type fund) to show how estimated revenue and revenue realized to date compare and how expenditures and encumbrances compare with appropriations during the fiscal period. Budgetary accounts are estimated revenues, appropriations, encumbrances, reserve for encumbrances and budgeted fund balance accounts as distinguished from proprietary accounts. See also Proprietary accounts.

Budgetary control: The financial control or financial management of a school district or enterprise in accordance with an approved budget for the purpose of keeping expenditures within the limitations of available appropriations and available revenues.

Budgeted fund balance: A temporary account in which the excess of estimated revenue over appropriations is recorded instead of commingling it with the fund equity or fund balance, unappropriated, account when the budget is recorded in the accounts. Changes in the budget can be recorded during the accounting period in this account as long as it has a credit balance. Once a debit balance appears in this account, fund equity, unappropriated, is being absorbed. It is a management information account used during the fiscal period.

Buildings: A fixed asset account which reflects the acquisition value of permanent structures used to house persons and property owned by the school district. If buildings are purchased or constructed, this account includes the purchase or contract price of all permanent buildings and fixtures attached to and forming a permanent part of such buildings. If buildings are acquired by gift, the account reflects their appraised value at the date received.

C

Callable bond: A type of bond which permits the issuer to pay the obligation before the stated maturity date by giving notice of redemption in a manner specified in the bond contract.

Capital: Residual interest in the assets of a school district that remains after deducting liabilities.

Capital assets: See Fixed assets.

Capital budget: A plan of proposed capital outlays and the means of financing them for the current fiscal period. It is usually a part of the current budget. If a capital program is in operation, it will be the first year thereof. A capital program is sometimes referred to as a capital budget. See also Capital program.

Capital expenditures: See Capital outlays.

Capital improvement program: See Capital program.

Capital outlays: Expenditures which result in the acquisition of or addition to fixed assets such as land, buildings and equipment.

Capital program: A plan for capital expenditures to be incurred each year over a fixed period of years to meet capital needs arising from the long-term work program. It sets forth each project or other contemplated expenditure in which the school system is to have a part and specifies the full resources estimated to be available to finance the projected expenditures.

Capital projects fund: A fund created to account for all resources used for the acquisition of designated fixed assets by a school district except those financed by internal services funds, enterprise funds and certain trust funds.

Capital resources: Resources of a fixed or permanent nature, such as land and buildings, which cannot ordinarily be used to meet current expenditures.

Cash: Currency, coin, checks, postal and express money orders and bankers' drafts on hand or on deposit with an official or agent designated as custodian of cash and bank deposits.

Cash basis: The basis of accounting under which revenues are recorded only when actually received, and only cash disbursements are recorded as expenditures.

Cash discount: An allowance received or given if payment is completed within a stated period of time. Note: This term is not to be confused with trade discount.

Cash receipts journal: Any book of original entry of cash receipt transaction.

Character: A basis for classifying expenditures according to the periods they are presumed to benefit. See also Character classification.

Cash in bank: All funds on deposit with a bank or savings and loan institution normally in non-interest-bearing accounts. Interest-bearing accounts are recorded in investments.

Character classification: A grouping of expenditures on the basis of the time periods they are presumed to benefit. The three groupings are: (1) expenses, presumed to benefit the current fiscal period; (2) provisions for retirement of debt, presumed to benefit prior fiscal periods primarily but also present and future periods; and (3) capital outlays, presumed to benefit the current and future capital periods.

Check: A bill of exchange drawn on a bank and payable on demand; a written order on a bank to pay on demand a specified sum of money to a named person, to his order, or to bearer, out of money on deposit to the credit of the maker. Note: A check differs from a warrant in that the latter is not necessarily payable on demand and may not be negotiable. It differs from a voucher in that the latter is not an order to pay.

Claim: A bill representing a demand for payment properly made out on required form, and filed with the board, itemizing items or services for which the claim is made and showing where, when and by whom performed.

Classification: A systematic arrangement of items into classes or related groups for analytical or control purposes.

Closing account: An account that is used to record a closing entry.

Coding: A system of numbering or otherwise designating accounts, entries, invoices, vouchers, etc., in such a manner that the symbol used reveals quickly certain required information.

Combination bond: A bond issued by a school district which is payable from the revenues of the school district but which is also backed by the full faith and credit of a related governmental unit.

Combined balance sheet: A single balance sheet which displays the individual balance sheets of each class of funds and account groups of a school district in separate, adjacent columns. Note:

There are no inter-fund eliminations or consolidations in a combined balance sheet for a school district.

Combined financial report: A financial report that combines individual fund and account group statements.

Commercial-type funds: See Enterprise fund.

Compound entry: An entry that is composed of more than one debit or more than one credit.

Consolidated Annual Financial Report (CAFR): The CAFR of a school district should contain an introductory section, financial section [including (a) an auditor's report, (b) general purpose financial statements, (c) combining and individual fund and account group statements and schedules] and statistical tables.

Construction contracts payable: Amounts due by a school district on contracts for construction of buildings, structures and other improvements.

Construction work in process: The cost of construction work undertaken but not yet completed.

Contingent liability: An item which may become a liability as a result of conditions undetermined at a given date, such as guarantees pending, lawsuits, judgments under appeal, unsettled disputed claims, unfilled purchase orders and uncompleted contracts. Note: All contingent liabilities should be shown on the face of the balance sheet or in a footnote.

Contract payable—retained percentage: A liability on account of construction contracts which have been completed but on which part of the liability has not been paid pending final inspection or the lapse of a specified period of time, or both. The unpaid amount is usually stated as a percentage of the contract price.

Contracts payable: Amounts due on contracts for assets, goods and services received by a school district.

Contribution from the general fund: An equity amount in an enterprise fund or internal service fund which shows the amount of permanent fund capital contributed to the enterprise or internal service fund by the school district from general school revenues and resources.

Contribution from ____ fund: This account is identical to contribution from the general fund except that the specific fund of origin is specified.

Control account: An account in the general ledger in which are recorded the aggregate of debit and credit postings to a number of identical or related accounts called subsidiary ledger accounts. For example, the taxes receivable account is a control account supported by the aggregate of individual balances in individual property taxpayers' accounts. See also General ledger and subsidiary account.

Corporate balance sheet: A balance sheet for a corporation showing liabilities and owner (or shareholder) equity placed to the right of assets.

Corporate income statement: A statement that shows whether or not the business achieved or failed to achieve one of its primary objectives—earning a "profit" or net income.

Cost: The amount of money exchanged for property or services. Note: Costs may be incurred even before money is paid; that is, as soon as liability is incurred. Again, the cost of some property or service may in turn become a part of the cost of another property or service. For example, the cost of part or all of the materials purchased at a certain time will be reflected in the cost of articles made from such materials or in the cost of those services in the rendering of which the materials were used.

Cost accounting: That method of accounting which provides for assembling and recording of all the elements of cost incurred to accomplish a purpose, to carry out an activity or operation or to complete a unit of work or a specific job.

Cost basis accounting: That method of accounting which provides for the assembling and recording of all the elements of cost incurred to accomplish a purpose, to carry on an activity or operation, or to complete a unit of work or a specific job.

Cost ledger: A subsidiary record where each project, job, production center, process, operation, product or service is given in a separate account to which all items entering into its cost are posted in required detail. Such accounts should be so arranged and kept that the results shown in them may be reconciled with and verified by a control account or accounts in the general ledger.

Cost of goods sold: A determination made at the end of an accounting period reflecting the (1) cost of merchandise on hand at the beginning of the period, (2) the cost of merchandise purchased during the period, and (3) the cost of unsold goods that remain at the end of the period.

Cost records: All ledgers, supporting records, schedules, reports, invoices, vouchers and other documents reflecting the cost of projects, jobs, production centers, processes, operations, products or services, or the cost of any component.

Coupon bond: A bearer bond, or a bond registered as to principal only, carrying coupons is evidence of future interest payments.

Credit (adjective): The right side of a T-account. Credit (noun): An amount entered on the right side of a T-account.

Credit (verb): The act of entering an amount on the right side of a T-account.

Credit account: An account that has a credit balance.

Credit balance: An account where the sum of the credits exceeds the sum of the debits for that account.

Credit entry: An entry that is made on the right side of a T-account.

Current: A term applied to budgeting and accounting which designates the operation of the present fiscal period as opposed to past or future periods.

Current asset: An asset which is available or can be made readily available to meet the cost of operations or to pay current liabilities. Some examples are cash, temporary investments and taxes receivable which will be collected within about a year from the balance sheet date.

Current budget: The annual budget prepared for and effective during the present year; or, in the case of some state governments, the budget for the present biennium.

Current expenses: See Expenses

Current fund: See General fund.

Current funds: Funds, the resources of which are expended for operating purposes during the current fiscal period. In its usual application in plural form, it refers to general, special revenue, debt service, internal service funds and enterprise funds of a school system. In the singular form, the current fund is synonymous with the General fund.

Current liability: Debt or obligation of the school district which is payable within a relatively short period of time, usually restricted to those coming due within a year or within an operating period.

Current revenue: Revenues of a school system which are available to meet expenditures of the current fiscal period. See Revenue.

Current taxes: (1) Taxes levied and becoming due during the current fiscal period, from the time the amount of the tax levy is first established to the date on which a penalty for non-payment is attached. (2) Taxes levied in the preceding fiscal period but becoming due in the current fiscal period, from the time they become due to the date on which a penalty for non-payment is attached.

Current year tax levy: Taxes levied for the current fiscal period.

Customer deposits: The liability of an enterprise fund for deposits made by customers as a prerequisite to receiving goods and/or services provided by the enterprise.

D

Debenture: An unsecured bond that depends upon the general credit of the issuing school district.

Debit (adjective): The left side of a T-account.

Debit (noun): An amount entered on the left side of a T-account.

Debit (verb): The act of entering an amount on the left side of a T-account.

Debit account: An account that has a debit balance.

Debit balance: An account where the sum of the debits exceeds the sum of the credits for that account.

Debit entry: An entry that is made on the left side of a T-account.

Debt: An obligation resulting from borrowing of money or from the purchase of goods or services. Debts of school systems include bonds, time warrants, tax anticipation notes payable, accounts payable, vouchers payable, interest payable and salaries payable.

Debt limit: The maximum amount of gross or net debt which is legally permitted.

Debt service fund: A fund established to finance and account for the accumulation of financial resources over a long period of time which are to be used for the payment of interest and principal on all general obligation debt, serial and term, other than that payable exclusively from revenue debt issued for and serviced by the school system. Formerly called a Sinking fund.

Debt service fund requirements: The amounts of revenue which must be provided for a debt service fund so that all principal and interest payments can be made in full on schedule.

Deferred assets: See Deferred charges and Prepaid expenses.

Deferred charge: An expenditure which is not chargeable to the current fiscal period in which it is made but is carried on the asset side of the balance sheet pending amortization or other disposition. An example is discount on bonds issued.

Deferred credit: Credit balance or item which will be spread over the following accounting periods either as additions to revenues or as reductions to expenses. Examples are taxes collected in advance or premiums paid on bonds issued.

Deferred income: See Deferred credit.

Deferred revenue: See Deferred credit.

Deficit: (1) The excess of liabilities of a fund over its assets (frequently referred to as a fund deficit). (2) The excess of expenditures over revenues during an accounting period (frequently referred to as an operating deficit); or, in the case of enterprise and internal service funds, the excess of expense over income during an accounting period.

Delinquent taxes: Taxes remaining unpaid on and after the date on which a penalty for non-payment is attached. Even though the penalty may be subsequently waived and a portion of the taxes may be abated or cancelled, the unpaid balances continue to be delinquent taxes until abated, cancelled, paid or converted into tax liens.

Deposit: Money or securities placed with a bank or other institution or person, either as a deposit subject to withdrawal by check or as a special deposit made for a particular purpose.

Depreciation: (1) Expiration in the service life of fixed assets, other than wasting assets, attributable to wear and tear, deterioration, action of the physical elements, inadequacy and obsolescence. (2) The portion of the cost of a fixed asset other than a wasting asset which is charged as an expense during a particular fiscal period.

Direct debt: The debt which a school district has incurred in its own name or assumed through the annexation of territory or through consolidation with another school district.

Depreciation accounting: Loss in value or service life of fixed assets because of wear and tear through use, elapsed time, inadequacy or obsolescence.

Disbursements: Payments in cash.

Discount: An amount granted by a creditor reducing the amount invested in accounts receivable.

Double entry: A system of bookkeeping which requires for every entry made to the debit side of an account or accounts and entry must be made for a corresponding amount or amounts to the credit side of another account or accounts.

Due from ___ fund: An asset account used to indicate amounts collectible by a particular fund from another fund in the same school district for goods sold or services rendered. This account includes only short-term obligations on open account and not long-term loans. See Advance from ___ fund.

Due from government: Amounts claimed by the reporting school district from a governmental unit. These amounts may represent grants-in-aid, shared taxes, taxes collected by another unit, loans and charges for services rendered by the reporting unit for another governmental unit.

Due to fiscal agent: Amounts due to fiscal agents, such as commercial banks, for paying a school district's maturing interest and principal payments on indebtedness.

Due to ___ fund: A liability account used to indicate amounts owed by a particular fund to another fund in the same school district for money borrowed temporarily, goods sold or services rendered. These amounts include only short-term obligations on open account and not long-term loans.

Due to ___ government: Amounts owed by a fund of the reporting school district to a named governmental unit. See income and revenue.

E

Effective interest rate: The rate of earning on a bond investment based on the actual price paid for the bond, the coupon rate, the maturity date and the length of time between interest dates, in contrast with the nominal interest rate.

Encumbrance accounts: Purchase orders, contracts, and salary or other commitments which are chargeable to an appropriation and for which a part of the appropriation is reserved. They cease to be encumbrances when paid or when actual liability is set up.

Encumbrances: Obligations or commitments in the form of purchase orders, contracts issued or salary commitments which are chargeable to an appropriation and for which a part of the appropriation is reserved. They cease to be encumbrances when paid or when the title to goods or services is received and the actual liability is created. Frequently referred to as commitments.

Endowment fund: A trust fund whose principal must be maintained inviolate but whose income may be expended. An endowment fund is accounted for as a non-expendable trust fund, the income from which is accounted for as an expendable trust fund.

Enterprise debt: Debt which is to be retired primarily from the earnings of publicly owned and operated enterprises. See also Revenue bonds.

Enterprise fund: A proprietary type fund established to finance and account for the acquisition, operation and maintenance of school district facilities and services which may be predominantly self-supporting by users' charges. Examples of enterprise funds are those for food services, bookstores and athletic programs.

Entry: (1) The record of a financial transaction in its appropriate books of account. (2) The act of recording a financial transaction in the books of account.

Equipment: Physical property of a school district having a long period of usefulness, other than buildings and land.

Equity in general fixed assets: A classification of accounts in the general fixed assets group of accounts which indicate the sources from which general fixed assets were acquired. Carrying a credit balance, it is more descriptive of the nature of the accounts than investment in general fixed assets.

Estimated revenue account: If the account is kept on an accrual basis, this term designates the amount of revenue estimated to accrue during a given period, regardless of whether or not it is all to be collected during the period. If the account is kept on a cash basis, the term designates the amount of revenue estimated to be collected during a given period.

Estimated revenue: For revenue accounts kept on the accrual basis, this term designates the amount of revenue estimated to accrue during a given period regardless of whether or not it is all to be collected during the period.

Estimated uncollected accounts receivable: A contra-asset account. It is estimated to be the amount of accounts receivable that is not expected to be collected. It is subtracted from accounts receivable on the balance sheet to arrive at the book value of accounts receivable.

Estimated uncollectible taxes (current or delinquent): A contra-asset account, it is the amount that is not expected to be collected. It is subtracted from taxes receivable (current or delinquent) to arrive at the book value of these accounts. Note: Generally the longer a tax becomes delinquent, the less likely are its chances for being collected.

Exhibit: (1) A balance sheet or other principal financial statement. (2) Any formal financial statement that accompanies or is a part of a financial or audit report.

Expendable trust fund: A fiduciary fund, a trust fund whose resources, both principal and earnings, may be expended.

Expenditure account: A charge incurred, whether paid or unpaid, which is presumed to benefit the current fiscal year.

Expenditures: The cost of goods delivered or services rendered, whether paid or unpaid, including expenses, provision for debt retirement not reported as a liability of the fund from which retired, and capital outlays. Note: Encumbrances are not expenditures. Expenditure accounts are used only in formal budgetary or governmental type funds.

Expenses: Charges incurred, whether paid or unpaid, for operation, maintenance, interest, and other charges which are presumed to benefit the current fiscal period. In budgetary funds, expenditure accounts are used to record expenses but, in proprietary type funds and certain trust funds, only expense accounts are used.

F

Face value: As applied to securities, this term designates the amount stated on the security document.

Fidelity bond: A written promise to indemnify against losses from theft, defalcation or misappropriation of money or property by school officers and employees. See also Surety bond.

Fiduciary fund type: A fund used to account for all transactions of a school district when the school district acts as an agent or trustee for another entity. Trust funds and agency funds are examples of fiduciary funds.

Financial accounting: The recording and reporting of activities and events affecting the money of an administrative unit and its program. Specifically, it is concerned (1) with determining what accounting records are to be maintained, how they will be maintained and the procedures, methods, and forms to be used; (2) with recording, classifying and summarizing activities or events; (3) with analyzing and interpreting recorded data; and (4) with preparing reports and statements which reflect conditions as of a given date, the results of operations for a specific period and the evaluation of status and results of operation in terms of established objectives.

Financial and compliance audit: An audit that determines whether or not the financial statements of an audited school district present fairly the financial position and the results of financial operations in accordance with generally accepted accounting principles and whether or not the school district has complied with the laws and regulations that may have a material effect upon the financial statements.

Fiscal agent: The person or entity charged with handling the financial transactions or services of a school district.

Fiscal period: Any period of time at the end of which a school district determines the financial position, results of operations, changes in fund equities and changes in financial position of each fund and account group. It may be monthly, quarterly, semiannually or annually.

Fixed assets: Assets of a long-term character which are intended to continue to be held or used, such as land, buildings, machinery, furniture and equipment. Note: The term does not indicate the immobility of an asset, which is a distinctive characteristic of a fixture.

Fixture: An attachment to buildings which are not intended to be removed and which cannot be removed without damage to the latter. Note: Those fixtures with a useful life presumed to be as long as that of the building itself are considered a part of such a building; all others are classed as equipment.

Function: A classification of a group of related activities aimed at accomplishing a major service, purpose or program for which a school district is responsible. For example, instruction is a function. See also Activity classification.

Function dimension: The classification of activities or actions which are performed to accomplish the objectives of the school district.

Functional classification: A grouping of expenditures on the basis of the principal purposes for which they are made. Examples are supporting services and community services. See also Activity classification.

Fund: A fiscal and accounting entity with a self-balancing set of accounts recording cash and other financial resources, together with all related liabilities and residual equities or balances, and changes therein, which are segregated for the purpose of carrying on specific activities or attaining certain objectives in accordance with special regulations, restrictions or limitation. See also General fixed assets and General long-term debt group of accounts.

Fund accounts: All accounts necessary to set forth the financial position, the financial operations, the changes in residual equities or balances and the changes in financial position of a fund.

Fund balance: The excess of the assets of a fund over its liabilities except in the case of funds subject to budgetary accounting where, prior to the end of a fiscal period, it represents the excess of the fund's assets and estimated revenues for the period over its liabilities and appropriations.

Fund balance sheet: A balance sheet for a single fund. See Fund and Balance sheet.

Funded debt: Same as Bonded debt, which is the preferred term.

Funded deficit: A fund deficit eliminated through the sale of bonds issued for that purpose.

Fund equity: The excess of a fund's total assets over total liabilities; synonymous with the term *fund balance*.

Fund equity account: An account used to record the financial transactions determining the excess of a fund's assets less liabilities.

Fund group: A group of funds which are similar in purpose and character. For example, several special revenue funds constitute a fund group.

G

General fixed assets: Those fixed assets of a school district which are not accounted for in an enterprise, internal services fund or trust fund.

General fund: A fund used to account for all transactions of a school district which are not accounted for in another fund. Note: The general fund is used to account for the ordinary operations or the basic educational programs of a school district which are financed from taxes and other general revenues. Identified as one of the formal budgetary funds or as a governmental type fund.

General journal: A book of original entry for all entries of financial transactions that are not recorded in special journals such as a cash receipts journal, a voucher register, a cash payments journal or a check register.

General ledger: A book, file or other device which contains the accounts needed to reflect, in summary and in detail, the financial position, the results of financial operations, the changes in equities of a fund or account group used by a school district. Note: In double entry bookkeeping, the debits and credits in the general ledger are equal, and therefore the debit balances equal the credit balances. See also Control account.

General long-term debt: Long-term debt legally payable from general revenues and backed by the full faith and credit of a school district. See Long-term debt.

General long-term debt group of accounts: The account group in which all un-matured general long-term liabilities of a school district are recorded but does not include long-term liabilities of proprietary funds and trust funds.

General obligation bond: A bond for whose payment the full faith and credit of the issuing body is pledged. More commonly, but not necessarily, general obligation bonds are considered to be those payable from taxes and other general revenues.

General revenue: The revenues of a school district other than those derived from and retained in an enterprise. Note: If a portion of the net income in an enterprise fund is contributed to another non-enterprise fund, such as the general fund, the amounts transferred constitute general revenue of the school district.

Governmental accounting: The composite activity of analyzing, recording, summarizing, reporting and interpreting the financial transactions of governmental units and agencies.

H

Historical cost: The price at which an asset was originally obtained. If the asset was purchased, the cost would be the purchase price; if the asset was donated, the cost would be the value, if any, of the asset at the time of donation.

Horizontal ratio: The ratio or ratios that can be created to compare a revenue or expenditure item in one fund with the same revenue or expenditure item in another or all funds (or some combination of funds). For example, salaries expended in one fund compared to all salaries in all funds.

I

Imprest system: A system for handling minor disbursements whereby a fixed amount of money, designated as petty cash, is set aside for this purpose. See also Petty cash.

Improvements: Buildings, other structures and other attachments or annexations to land which are intended to remain so attached or annexed, such as sidewalks, trees, drives, tunnels, drains and sewers. Note: Sidewalks, curbing, sewers and streets are sometimes referred to as betterments, but the term *improvements* is preferred.

Income: A term used in accounting for an enterprise fund or internal service fund to represent the excess of revenues earned over the expenses incurred in carrying on the fund's operations. It should not be used without an appropriate modifier, such as *operating*, *gross*, or *net*. See also Operating income. Note: The term *income* should not be used in lieu of *revenue* in non-enterprise funds.

Indebtedness: The amount of debt of the school district including principal and interest due on bonds issued.

Interest and penalties receivable on taxes: The uncollected portion of interest and penalties receivable on taxes.

Interest payable: The amount of interest that is due on outstanding obligations during a period of time. The amount may span more than one accounting period.

Interest receivable on investments: The amount of interest receivable on investments.

Inter-fund account: An account in which transactions between funds are recorded.

Inter-fund loan: Authorized loan made by one fund to another.

Inter-fund loan payable: The amount of an inter-fund loan that is due to be repaid during an accounting period.

Intergovernmental revenue: Revenue received from other governments in the form of grants, shared revenues or payments in lieu of taxes.

Interim balance sheet: A balance sheet that is prepared at the end of an accounting period other than the end of a fiscal year.

Interim borrowing: (1) Short-term loan to be repaid from general revenues during the course of a fiscal year. (2) Short-term loan in anticipation of tax collections or bond issuance. See Bond anticipation notes.

Interim statement: A financial statement prepared before the end of the current fiscal year and covering only financial transactions during the current year to date. See also Statement.

Internal audit: An appraisal activity within a school district which: (1) determines the adequacy of the system of internal control; (2) verifies and safeguards assets; (3) determines the reliability of the accounting and reporting system; (4) ascertains compliance with established policies and procedures; and (5) appraises performance of activities and work programs.

Internal control: A plan of organization under which employees' duties are so arranged and records and procedures are so designed as to make it possible to provide effective safeguards and accounting control over assets, liabilities, revenues, income, expenses and expenditures. Under such a system, the work of employees is subdivided so that no single employee performs a complete cycle of operations. Procedures to be followed which require proper authorization by designated officials for all actions to be taken.

Internal services fund: A proprietary type of fund established to finance and account for services and commodities furnished by a designated department or agency of the school district to other departments and agencies within a single school district. Amounts expended by the fund are restored to it either from operating earnings or by transfers from other funds, so that the original fund capital is kept intact. Formerly called a working capital fund.

Inventory: A detailed list showing quantities, descriptions and values of property and frequently also shows units of measure and unit prices.

Investments: Securities and real estate held for the production of income in the form of interest, dividends, rentals or lease income. The term does not include fixed assets used in operation of the school district.

Investments in general fixed assets: A widely used classification of accounts used to show the sources from which general fixed assets were acquired in the general fixed assets group of accounts. It has become an ambiguous title because the word *investment* usually implies that it is an asset account which normally carries a debit balance. As this type of account carries a credit balance, the term *equity* in general fixed assets is more descriptive of its nature.

J

Journal: Any book of original entry of a financial transaction. See also Register.

Journal entry: See Entry.

Journal voucher: A business paper provided for the recording of certain transactions or information in place of or supplementary to the journals or registers. The journal voucher usually contains an entry or entries explanations, references to documentary evidence supporting the entry or entries, and the signature or initials of one or more officials who are designated to authorize the transaction.

Journalize: The act of making an entry in the general journal.

Judgment: An amount to be paid or collected by a school district as the result of a court decision, including a condemnation award in payment for private property taken for public use.

L

Land: A fixed asset account which reflects the cost or other valuation basis of land owned by a school district. If land is purchased, this account shows the purchase price and costs such as legal fees, filling and excavation costs and the like which are incurred to put the land in condition for its intended use. If land is acquired by gift, the account reflects its appraised value at date received.

Ledger: A group of accounts in which are recorded the financial transaction of a fund of a school district.

Levy: To impose taxes, special assessments or service charges for the support of school operations. The total amount of taxes, special assessments or service charges imposed by a governmental unit.

Liability: Debt or other legal obligation arising out of transactions in the past which must be paid, renewed or refunded at some future date. Note: The term does not include encumbrances.

Liability accounts: An account used to designate a liability. Encumbrances are not liabilities; they become liabilities when the services or materials for which the encumbrance was established have been rendered or received.

Loan fund: An agency fund whose principal and/or interest is loaned to individuals in accordance with the legal requirements.

Loans receivable: Amounts which have been loaned to persons or organizations, including notes taken as security for such loans; where permitted by statutory authority. The account is usually carried only in the trust and agency fund's balance sheet.

Long-term budget: A budget prepared for a period longer than a fiscal year, or in the case of some state governments, a budget prepared for a period longer than a biennium. If the long-term budget is restricted to capital expenditures, it is called a capital program or a capital improvement program.

Long-term debt: Debt with a maturity of more than one year after the date of issuance.

Long-term liability: A liability that is the responsibility of the school district and that spans a time period greater than the end of the fiscal year.

Long-term loan: A loan which extends for more than five years from the date the loan was obtained and is not received by serial or term bonds.

Long-term note payable: The amount of outstanding debt obligation that is due to be paid during an accounting period.

M

Maintenance expenditure: Repairs to fixed assets that do not clearly increase the value and/or useful life of the asset.

Managerial accounting: Accounting process that is primarily concerned with internal reporting and relates to planning, controlling and evaluating financial performance of the school district.

Matured bonds: Bonds which have reached or passed their maturity date.

Matured bonds payable: Bonds which have reached or passed their maturity date but which remain unpaid.

Matured interest payable: Interest on bonds which has reached the maturity date but which remains unpaid.

Maturity date: The date at which a bond or other debt instrument is due to be repaid to the lender.

Maturity value: The value of a bond or other debt instrument at the maturity date. Usually this will be the face value of the bond.

Modified accrual basis: The basis of accounting under which revenues are recorded when earned and expenditures are recorded when they result in a liability for the school district, but which also allows for some transactions to be made on a cash basis.

Mortgage bond: A bond secured by a mortgage against specified properties of a school district, usually its enterprises. If primarily payable from enterprise revenues, they are also classed as revenue bonds. See also Revenue bond.

Municipal bond: A bond issued by a state or local governmental unit.

N

Net revenue available for debt service: Gross operating revenues of an enterprise fund less operating and maintenance expenses but exclusive of bond interest. *Net revenue* as thus defined is used to compute "coverage" on revenue bond issues.

Nominal interest rate: The contractual interest rate shown on the face and in the body of a bond and representing the amount of interest to be paid, in contrast to the effective interest rate.

Non-expendable trust fund: A trust fund, the principal and sometimes also the earnings of which may not be expended. See also Endowment fund.

Note: A written, short-term promise of the issues to repay a specified principal amount on a date certain, together with interest at a stated rate, or according to a formula for determining that rate, payable from a defined source of anticipated revenue.

Notes payable: In general, an unconditional written promise signed by the maker to pay a certain sum in money on demand or at a fixed or determinable time either to the bearer or to the order of a person designated therein.

Notes receivable: A note held by the school district which contains an unconditional written promise, signed by the maker, to pay a certain sum in money on demand or at a fixed or determinable future time either to the bearer or to the order of a person designated therein. The note may be held by the reporting school district as designated payee or by endorsement.

O

Object: The commodity or service obtained from a specific expenditure.

Object classification: A category of goods or services purchased.

Object dimension: The classification of services or commodities obtained as a result of a specific expenditure by the school district.

Operating budget: A budget which applies to all revenue and expenditures other than capital outlay expenditures. See Budget.

Operating expenses: (1) As used in the accounts of a school district's enterprise funds and internal services funds, the term means those costs which are necessary to the maintenance of the enterprise, the rendering of services, the sale of products, the production and disposition of commodities produced, and the collection of enterprise revenues. (2) The term is also sometimes used to describe expenses for general fund purposes.

Operating income: Income of an enterprise fund which is derived from the sale of its goods and/or services. For example, income from the sale of lunches or from the sale of books is operating income. See also Operating revenues.

Operating revenue: Revenue derived from the operation of an enterprise fund and/or internal service fund of a business character.

Operating statement: A statement summarizing the financial operations, i.e., the revenue and expenses or expenditures of a school fund for an accounting period as contrasted with a balance sheet which shows the financial position of the fund at a given moment.

Outstanding bond: The amount of outstanding debt obligation of the school district for which a bond was sold.

Overhead expenses: Those elements of cost necessary to the production of an article or the performance of a service which are of such a nature that the amount applicable to the product or service cannot be determined accurately or readily. Usually they relate to those expenses which do not become an integral part of the finished product or service, such as rent, heat, light, supplies, management and supervision.

P

Performance audit: See Program compliance audit.

Performance budget: A budget wherein expenditures are based primarily upon measurable performance of activities and work programs. A performance budget may also incorporate other bases of expenditure classification, such as character and object, but these are given a subordinate status to activity performance.

Perpetual inventory: A system whereby the inventory of units of property at any date may be obtained directly from the records without resorting to an actual physical count. A record is provided for each item or group of items to be inventoried and is so divided as to provide a running record of goods ordered, received and withdrawn, and the balance on hand, in units and in cost.

Petty cash: A sum of money set aside for the purpose of paying small obligations for which the issuance of a formal voucher and check would be too expensive and time-consuming. Sometimes called a petty cash fund, with the term *fund* here being used in the commercial sense of earmarked liquid assets. See also Imprest system.

Post: The act of transferring to an account in a ledger the detailed or summarized data contained in the cash receipts book, check register, journal voucher, or similar books or documents of original entry.

Post closing trial balance: A balance sheet statement that is prepared after closing entries are made to the revenue, expenditure and fund equity accounts.

Post to ledger: The act of making an entry to the general ledger. Usually this act will occur when recording an entry from the general journal to the general ledger.

Posting: The act of transferring to an account in a ledger the data, either detailed or summarized, contained in a book of original entry.

Posting reference: The notation made to the location of the account. Usually, the posting reference is the account code number.

Premium: See Bond premium.

Prepaid expenses: Expenses entered in the accounts for benefits not yet received. Prepaid expenses differ from deferred charges in that they are spread over a shorter period of time than deferred charges and are regularly recurring costs of operations. Examples of prepaid expenses are prepaid rent expense, prepaid interest expense and premiums on unexpired insurance. An example of a deferred charge is unamortized discounts on bonds payable.

Prepaid tax revenue: The deposit of money with a school district or governmental unit on condition that the amount deposited is to be applied against the tax liability of a designated taxpayer after the taxes have been levied and such liability has been established. See also Taxes collected in advance.

Principal of bond debt: The amount printed on the face of the instrument; the amount to be paid at the maturity date of the bond, exclusive of interest, premiums or discounts.

Pro-forma: For form's sake; an indication of form; an example. The term is used in conjunction with a noun to denote merely a sample form, document, statement, certificate or presentation, either wholly or partially hypothetical, actual facts, estimates or proposals.

Program: A plan of activities and procedures designed to accomplish a predetermined objective or set of allied objectives.

Program budget: A budget where expenditures are based primarily on programs of work and secondarily on character and object. A program budget is a transitional type of budget between the traditional character and object budget, on the one hand, and the performance budget on the other. See also Performance budget and Traditional budget.

Program compliance audit: An audit that determines the extent to which the desired results or benefits established by the legislature or other authorizing body are being achieved, the effectiveness of the school district and whether or not the school district has complied with significant laws and regulations applicable to the program.

Program dimension: The classification of transactions relating to a group of interdependent, closely related services and/or activities contributing to a common objective of the school district or program.

Project/reporting dimension: The grouping of transactions relating to a particular project that is used to prepare required reports for the school district or project.

Proprietary account: An account which shows actual financial position and operations, such as actual assets, liabilities, fund balances, including reserves of fund equity, revenues and expenditures, as distinguished from a budgetary account.

Proprietary fund: A group of accounts which show actual financial conditions and operations such as actual assets, liabilities, reserves, surplus, revenues and expenditures, as distinguished from budgetary accounts.

Purchase order: A document which authorizes the delivery of specified merchandise to the school district or the rendering of the making of a charge for them.

R

Rate: The percent at which services, commodities or financial obligations are obtained.

Ratio: An expression of a mathematical relationship between one quantity and another.

Ratio analysis: The process of comparing a ratio to its past performance, current conditions or to other similar ratios.

Redeemed bond: A bond that is called for repayment at a specific price prior to the maturity date of the bond.

Refund (noun): An amount paid back or credit allowed because of an over-collection or return of an object sold.

Refund (verb): To pay back or to allow credit for an amount as a result of an over-collection or because of the return of an object sold. To provide for payment of a loan through cash or credit secured by a new loan.

Refunding bond: Bond issued to retire bonds already outstanding. The refunding bond may be sold for cash and outstanding bonds redeemed in cash, or the refunding bond may be exchanged with holders of outstanding bonds.

Register: A record for the consecutive entry of a certain class of events, documents or transactions with a proper notation of all the required particulars. Note: The form of register for accounting purposes varies from one-column to multi-columnar sheets of special design whereon the entries are distributed, summarized and aggregated for convenient posting to the accounts.

Registered bond: A bond that is issued in the name of the owner and recorded in the owner's name on the records of the issuer.

Reimbursement: Cash or other assets received as a repayment of the cost of work or services performed or of other expenditures made for or on behalf of another school unit or department or for an individual, firm or corporation.

Replacement cost: The current cost of an asset that would need to be replaced, usually via insurance, due to loss.

Requisition: A written demand or request, usually from one department to the purchasing officer or to another department, for specified articles or services.

Required earnings: Synonymous or equivalent in meaning to estimated revenue from earnings such as interest income; a budgetary accounting term which indicates the amount of earnings estimated to be earned by the board of education at the time of adopting or revising the budget.

Required taxation: Synonymous or equivalent in meaning to estimated revenue from tax levies; a budgetary accounting term which indicates the amount of taxes levied by adoption or revising the budget.

Reserve: An account which records a portion of the fund balance which must be segregated for some future use and which is, therefore, not available for further appropriation. A reserve for inventories equal in amount to the inventory of supplies on the balance sheet of a general fund is an example of such a reserve.

Reserve for advance to ___ fund: A reserve which represents the segregation of a portion of a fund balance to indicate that assets equal to the amount of the reserve are tied up in a long-term loan to another fund and are not available for appropriation.

Reserve for debt retirement: An account which indicates the amount of the unappropriated debt service fund equity that has been set aside to be used for retirement of outstanding debt at its maturity date; an appropriation of the debt service fund's equity.

Reserve for employee contributions: A reserve in a trust fund for a public employee retirement system which represents the amount of accumulated contributions made by employee members plus interest earnings credited in accordance with applicable legal provisions.

Reserve for employer contributions: A reserve in a trust fund for a public employee retirement system which represents the amount of accumulated contributions paid by the school district as employer plus interest earnings credited in accordance with applicable legal provisions.

Reserve for encumbrances: A reserve representing the segregation or the appropriation of a portion of a fund balance to provide for unliquidated encumbrances. See also Reserve.

Reserve for undistributed interest earnings: An unallocated reserve in a trust fund for a public employee retirement system which represents interest earnings of the system that have not been distributed to other reserves such as reserve for employees' contributions and the reserve for employer contributions.

Reserved fund balance account: A reserve representing that portion of a fund balance segregated to indicate that assets equal to the amount of the reserve are tied up and are, therefore, not available for appropriation. It is recommended that a separate reserve be established for each special purpose. One example of a special purpose would be restricted federal programs.

Restricted asset: Money or other resources, the use of which is restricted by legal or contractual requirements. The most common example of restricted assets in school accounting is that arising out of revenue bond indentures in enterprise funds. Also called restricted funds, but this terminology is not preferred.

Retained earnings: The accumulated earnings of an enterprise or internal services fund which have been retained in the fund and which are not reserved for any specific purpose.

Retired bond: A bond that has been fully repaid.

Retirement fund: A trust fund out of which retirement annuities and/or other benefits are paid to authorized and designated public employees. A retirement fund is accounted for as a trust fund.

Revenue: This term designates additions to assets which (1) do not increase any liability; (2) do not represent the recovery of an expenditure; (3) do not represent the cancellation of certain liabilities without a corresponding increase in other liabilities or a decrease in assets; and (4) do not represent contributions of fund capital in enterprise and internal services funds.

Revenue account: An amount set aside to account for money received for some specified purpose.

Revenue bond: A bond whose principal and interest are payable exclusively from earnings. In addition to a pledge of revenues, such bonds sometimes contain a mortgage on the enterprise's property and are then known as mortgage revenue bonds.

Revenue bonds payable: A liability account which represents the face value of revenue bonds issued and outstanding.

Revenue source: The identification of the specific source from which revenues were derived or to which they are attributable.

Revenue subsidiary ledger: A general ledger account that is used to reduce the size of the general ledger by summarizing individual revenue accounts and that provides budgetary accounting control over each individual source of revenue.

Revenue type: The identification of transactions that are described and coded as to the specific sources from which they are derived or to which they are attributable.

Revenues collected in advance: A liability account which represents revenues collected before they become due.

S

School business administration: The area of educational administration that deals with the financial and ancillary operations of a school district.

School business manager: The person charged with management of specific areas of school business administration.

School business official: A person involved with or working in a specific area of school business.

School business specialist: A person who works exclusively in and is determined to be an expert in a specific area of school business.

Securities: Bonds, notes, mortgages or other forms of negotiable or non-negotiable instruments. See also Investments.

Self-balancing group of accounts: An independent self-balancing group of accounts which is set up to account for either the fixed assets or the long-term debts of a governmental unit which are not accounted for in its individual funds or account groups. See General long-term debt group of accounts.

Self-supporting or self-liquidating debt: Debt obligations whose principal and interest are payable solely from the earnings of the enterprise fund or internal services fund for the construction or improvement of which they were originally issued. See also Revenue bonds.

Separation of duties: The concept of determining responsibilities for people working in various employee classifications.

Serial bonds: Issues redeemable by installments, each of which is to be paid in full, ordinarily out of revenues of the fiscal year in which it matures or revenues of the preceding year.

Shared revenue: Revenue which is levied by one governmental unit but shared, usually in proportion to the amount collected, with another unit of government or class of governments.

Short-term debt: Debt with a maturity of one year or less after the date of issuance. Short-term debt usually includes bond anticipation notes payable, tax anticipation notes payable and warrants payable.

Sinking fund bond: A bond issued under an agreement which requires the school district to set aside periodically out of its revenues, a sum which, with compound earnings, will be sufficient to redeem the bond at its stated date of maturity. Sinking fund bonds are usually also term bonds. In lieu of establishing a sinking fund, today's terminology refers to the fund as a debt service fund.

Sound value—actual cash value: An appraisal term; sound value or actual cash value is based on the cost of reproduction new, less the accrued depreciation to date.

Special revenue fund: A fund that is created to be used to account for financial transactions for designated educational purposes from special sources of revenue and that are not part of the school district's foundation education program.

Standard cost: The predetermined cost of performing an operation or producing a product when labor, materials and equipment are utilized efficiently under reasonable and normal conditions. Note: Normal conditions exist when there is an absence of special or extraordinary factors affecting the quality or quantity of the work performed, or the time or method of performing it.

Statement of changes in assets and liabilities: A financial statement that is prepared at the close of an accounting period to identify the result of transactions occurring during the period that affected assets and liabilities.

Statement of changes in financial position: A financial statement that identifies the amount of financial resources provided from all sources and how those resources were used during the accounting period.

Statements: (1) Used in a general sense, all of those formal written presentations which set forth financial information. (2) In technical accounting usage, those presentations of financial data which show the financial position and the results of financial operations of a fund, a group of accounts or an entire school district for a particular accounting period. See also Exhibit.

Statute: A written law enacted by a duly organized and constituted legislative body.

Stores: Goods on hand in storerooms subject to requisition and use.

Straight-line depreciation: The cost of an asset, less salvage value, is spread in equal periodic amounts over its estimated useful life.

Sub-activity: A specific line of work performed in carrying out a school activity. For example, cleaning buildings and replacing defective lamps would be sub-activities under the activity of operation and maintenance of plant.

Subvention: That which aids; especially a grant, as of money; subsidy; giving of help or relief in danger, distress or difficulty.

Summarizing and closing accounts: See Closing account.

Surety bond: A written promise to pay damages or to indemnify against losses caused by the party or parties named in the document, through nonperformance or through defalcation. An example is a surety bond given by a contractor or by an official handling cash or securities.

T

T-account: A convenient method of displaying the increases or decreases to an account in the form of a "T" where the left side is the debit side and the right side is the credit side of the account.

Tax anticipation note payable: A note (sometimes called a warrant) issued in anticipation of collection of taxes, usually retirable only from tax collections, and frequently only from the proceeds of the tax levy whose collection it anticipates.

Tax certificate: A certificate issued by a governmental unit as evidence of the conditional transfer of title to tax-delinquent property from the original owner to the holder of the certificate. If the owner does not pay the amount of the tax arrearage and other charges required by the law during the specified period of redemption, the holder can foreclose to obtain title. Also called tax sale certificate and tax lien certificate in some jurisdictions.

Tax rate limit: The maximum rate at which a school district may levy a tax. The limit may apply to taxes raised for a particular purpose, or to taxes imposed for all purposes, and may apply to a single school district, or a class of school districts, or to all school districts operating in a particular area. Overall tax rate limits usually restrict levies for all purposes and of all governments, state and local, having jurisdiction in a given area.

Tax roll: The official list showing the amount of taxes levied against each taxpayer or each parcel of property. Frequently, the tax roll and the assessment roll are combined, but even in these cases the two can be distinguished.

Taxes: Compulsory charges levied by a governmental unit for the purpose of financing services performed for the common benefit. Note: The term does not include specific charges made against particular persons or property for current or permanent benefits such as special assessments. Neither does the term include charges for services rendered only to those paying such charges as, for example, water service charges.

Taxes collected in advance: A liability for taxes collected before the tax levy has been made, before the taxes are payable or before the amount of taxpayer liability has been established.

Taxes levied for other units: Taxes levied by the reporting school districts as an agent for other school districts resulting in the need for a taxes receivable account and liability accounts to indicate the amount due to each of the other school districts. When collected, cash will be paid to these districts.

Taxes receivable—current: The uncollected portion of taxes which a school district has levied and which has become due but on which no penalty for non-payment is attached.

Taxes receivable—delinquent: Taxes remaining uncollected on and after the date on which a penalty for non-payment is attached. Even though the penalty may be subsequently waived and a portion of the taxes may be abated or cancelled, the unpaid balances continue to be delinquent taxes until paid, abated, cancelled by order of the board of education or converted into tax liens.

Term bond: A type of bond where the entire principal comes due or matures on one date.

Time warrant: A negotiable obligation of a school district having a term shorter than bonds and frequently tendered to individuals and firms in exchange for contractual services, capital acquisitions or equipment purchases.

Time warrant payable: The amount of time warrants outstanding and unpaid.

Total accrued depreciation: An appraisal phrase; the total accrued depreciation recognizes observed condition with proper consideration of usage, age, maintenance and care, and with such regard for functional and economic factors as are determined relevant.

Trade discount: An allowance, usually varying in percent with the volume of transactions, made to those engaged in certain businesses and allowable without respect to the time when the account is paid. Note: These discounts are commonly considered as a reduction of the sales or purchase price and not as an earning. The term is not to be confused with cash discount.

Traditional Budget: A term sometimes applied to the budget of a school district wherein expenditures are based entirely or primarily on objects of expenditure. See also Program budget and Performance budget.

Transaction: An event affecting an account.

Trial balance: A list of the balances of the accounts in a ledger kept by double entry, with the debit and credit balances shown in separate columns. If the totals of the debit and credit columns are equal or their net balance agrees with a control account, the ledger from which the figures are taken is said to be in balance.

Trust fund: A fund consisting of resources received and held by a school district as a trustee for another entity. See also Agency fund.

U

Unamortized discount on bonds payable: That portion of the excess of the face value of bonds over the amount received from their sale which remains to be written off periodically over the life of the bonds.

Unamortized discounts on investment: That portion of the excess of the face value of securities over the amount paid for them which has not been written off.

Unamortized premiums on bonds payable: An account in an enterprise fund which represents that portion of the excess of bonds proceeds over face value, and which remains to be amortized over the remaining outstanding life of such bonds.

Unamortized premium on investments: That portion of the excess of the amount paid for securities over their face value which has not yet been amortized.

Unappropriated budget balance: Where the fund balance at the close of the preceding year is not included in the annual budget, this term designates that portion of the current fiscal year's estimated revenues which has not been appropriated. Also referred to as budgeted fund balance.

Unappropriated debt service fund equity: The portion of debt service fund equity that is not designated for a specific purpose.

Unappropriated fund equity account: An account that contains amounts of the fund equity that is not designated for a specific purpose.

Unencumbered appropriation: That portion of an appropriation not yet expended or encumbered.

Unreserved fund balance accounts: The excess of the assets of a fund over its liabilities and reserves.

V

Vertical ratio: The ratio or ratios that can be created to compare a revenue or expenditure item in one fund with other revenue or expenditure items (partial or total) in the same fund.

Voucher: A document which authorizes the payment of money and usually indicates the accounts to be charged.

W

Warrant: An order drawn by the school district to the school district treasurer ordering him/her to pay a specified amount to a payee named on the warrant. Once signed by the treasurer, the warrant becomes a check payable by a bank named on the warrant by the treasurer.

Warrants payable: Warrants issued by the school district but not yet signed by the treasurer.

Appendix

2004–05 Adopted Budget

The following is a sample of a *PORTION* of an adopted budget for a school district in Illinois. The budget form is prescribed by the Illinois State Board of Education. This example is provided for readers who may not have access to such a document and is provided to facilitate instruction in that instructors and students can work off of the same set of numbers. Program and function codes may differ slightly from those found in Handbook II. Each spreadsheet page is also available on the accompanying "Financial and Managerial Accounting for School Administrators: Supplemental CD."

PART I - ESTIMATED RECEIPTS/REVENUES

Description	Acct No	(10) Educational	(20) Operations & Maintenance	(30) Bond & Interest	(40) Transportation	(50) Municipal Retirement/ Social Security	(60) Site & Construction/ Capital Improvement	(70) Working Cash	(80) Rent	(90) Fire Prevention & Safety
RECEIPTS/REVENUE FROM LOCAL SOURCES	1000									
AD VALOREM TAXES LEVIED BY LOCAL EDUCATION AGENCY										
1. General Levy	1110	25,667,078	5,916,735	6,624,610	1,753,107	1,016,802				
2. Tort Immunity Levy	1120	1,735,576								
3. Leasing Levy	1130									
4. Special Education Levy	1140	350,621								
5. Social Security/Medicare-Only Levy	1150									
6. Area Vocational Construction Levy	1160									
7. Summer School Levy	1170									
8. Other Tax Levies	1190									
9. TOTAL AD VALOREM TAXES LEVIED BY LOCAL EDUCATION AGENCY		27,753,275	5,916,735	6,624,610	1,753,107	1,016,802	0	0	0	0
PAYMENTS IN LIEU OF TAXES										
10. Mobile Home Privilege Tax	1210									
11. Payments from Local Housing Authority	1220									
12. Corporate Personal Property Replacement Taxe	1230	441,732				8,000				
13. Other Payments in Lieu of Taxes	1290									
14. TOTAL PAYMENTS IN LIEU OF TAXES		441,732	0	0	0	8,000	0	0	0	0
TUITION										
15. Regular Tuition from Pupils or Parents	1311	12,317								
16. Regular Tuition from Other LEAs	1312									
17. Regular Tuition from Other Sources	1313									

ESTIMATED RECEIPTS/REVENUES

Description	Acct No	(10) Educational	(20) Operations & Maintenance	(30) Bond & Interest	(40) Transportation	(50) Municipal Retirement/ Social Security	(60) Site & Construction/ Capital Improvement	(70) Working Cash	(80) Rent	(90) Fire Prevention & Safety
18. Summer School Tuition from Pupils or Parents	1321	44,975								
19. Summer School Tuition from Other LEAs	1322									
20. Summer School Tuition from Other Sources	1323									
21. Vocational Tuition from Pupils or Parents	1331									
22. Vocational Tuition from Other LEAs	1332									
23. Vocational Tuition from Other Sources	1333									
24. Special Education Tuition from Pupils or Parents	1341									
25. Special Education Tuition from Other LEAs	1342									
26. Special Education Tuition from Other Sources	1343									
27. Adult Tuition from Pupils or Parents	1351									
28. Adult Tuition from Other LEAs	1352									
29. Adult Tuition from Other Sources	1353									
30. TOTAL TUITION		57,292								
TRANSPORTATION FEES										
31. Regular Transportation Fees from Pupils or Parents	1411				21,838					
32. Regular Transportation Fees from Other LEAs	1412									
33. Regular Transportation Fees from Private Sources	1413									
34. Regular Transportation Fees from Co-curricular Activities	1415									
35. Summer School Transportation Fees from Pupils or Parents	1421									
36. Summer School Transportation Fees from Other LEAs	1422									
37. Summer School Transportation Fees from Other Sources	1423									
38. Vocational Transportation Fees from Pupils or Parents	1431									
39. Vocational Transportation Fees from Other LEAs	1432									

ESTIMATED RECEIPTS/REVENUES

Description	Acct No	(10) Educational	(20) Operations & Maintenance	(30) Bond & Interest	(40) Transportation	(50) Municipal Retirement/ Social Security	(60) Site & Construction/ Capital Improvement	(70) Working Cash	(80) Rent	(90) Fire Prevention & Safety
40. Vocational Transportation Fees from Other	1433									
41. Special Ed. Transportation Fees from Pupils or Parents	1441									
42. Special Ed. Transportation Fees from Other LEAs	1442									
43. Special Ed. Transportation Fees from Other Sources	1443									
44. Adult Transportation Fees from Pupils or Parents	1451									
45. Adult Transportation Fees from Other LEAs	1452									
46. Adult Transportation Fees from Other Sources	1453									
47. TOTAL TRANSPORTATION FEES					24,000					
EARNINGS ON INVESTMENTS										
48. Interest on Investments	1510	46,446	18,537	37,323	7,661	7,478	100,000	77,189		5,000
49. Gain or Loss on Sale of Investments	1520									
50. TOTAL EARNINGS ON INVESTMENTS		46,446	18,537	37,323	7,661	7,478	100,000	77,189	0	5,000
FOOD SERVICE										
51. Sales to Pupils - Lunch	1611	260,348								
52. Sales to Pupils - Breakfast	1612									
53. Sales to Pupils - Ala Carte	1613	862,386								
54. Sales to Pupils - Other	1614	87,674								
55. Sales to Adults	1620									
56. Other Food Service	1690	17,474								
57. TOTAL FOOD SERVICE		1,227,882								
PUPIL ACTIVITIES										
58. Admissions - Athletic	1711	22,361								
59. Admissions - Other	1719	[5037]	[5283]							

ESTIMATED RECEIPTS/REVENUES

Description	Acct No	(10) Educational	(20) Operations & Maintenance	(30) Bond & Interest	(40) Transportation	(50) Municipal Retirement/ Social Security	(60) Site & Construction/ Capital Improvement	(70) Working Cash	(80) Rent	(90) Fire Prevention & Safety
60. Fees	1720	702,790								
61. Book Store Sales	1730									
62. Other Pupil Activity Revenue (Attach Itemization)	1790									
63. TOTAL PUPIL ACTIVITIES		725,151	0							
TEXTBOOKS										
64. Rentals - Regular Textbook	1811									
65. Rentals - Summer School Textbook	1812									
66. Rentals - Adult/Continuing Education Textbook	1813									
67. Rentals - Other (Attach Itemization)	1819									
68. Sales - Regular Textbook	1821									
69. Sales - Summer School Textbook	1822									
70. Sales - Adult/Continuing Education Textbook	1823									
71. Sales - Other (Attach Itemization)	1829									
72. Other (Attach Itemization)	1890									
73. TOTAL TEXTBOOKS		0								
OTHER REVENUE FROM LOCAL SOURCES										
74. Rentals	1910		57,685							
75. Contributions and Donations from Private Sources	1920									
76. Services Provided Other LEAs	1940									
77. Refund Prior Years' Expenditures	1950									
78. Payment from Other LEAs	1991	168,306								
79. Sale of Vocational Projects	1992									
80. Local Fees	1993									

ESTIMATED RECEIPTS/REVENUES

Description	Acct No	(10) Educational	(20) Operations & Maintenance	(30) Bond & Interest	(40) Transportation	(50) Municipal Retirement/ Social Security	(60) Site & Construction/ Capital Improvement	(70) Working Cash	(80) Rent	(90) Fire Prevention & Safety
81. Other (Attach Itemization)	1999	20,000	15,010		29,000					
82. TOTAL OTHER REVENUE FROM LOCAL SOURCES		188,306	72,695	0	29,000	0	50,000	0	0	0
83. TOTAL RECEIPTS/REVENUE FROM LOCAL SOURCES		30,440,084	6,007,967	6,661,833	1,811,626	1,970,370	150,000	77,189	0	5,000
FLOW-THROUGH RECEIPTS/REVENUE FROM ONE LEA TO ANOTHER LEA	2000									
84. Flow-Through Revenue from State Sources	2100									
85. Flow-Through Revenue from Federal Sources	2200									
86. Other Flow-Through (Attach Itemization)	2300									
87. TOTAL FLOW-THROUGH RECEIPTS/ REVENUES FROM ONE LEA TO ANOTHER LEA		0	0		0	0				
RECEIPTS/REVENUES FROM STATE SOURCES	3000									
UNRESTRICTED GRANTS-IN-AID										
88. General State Aid - Sec. 18-8.05	3001	1,770,114								
89. General State Aid - Hold Harmless/Supplemental	3002									
90. Reorganization Incentives	3005									
91. Other Unrestricted Grants-In-Aid From State Sources (Attach Itemization)	3099									
92. TOTAL UNRESTRICTED GRANTS-IN-AID		1,770,114	0	0	0	0	0		0	0
RESTRICTED GRANTS-IN-AID										
93. Special Education - Private Facility Tuition	3100	76,808								
94. Special Education - Extraordinary	3105	530,098								
95. Special Education - Personnel	3110	553,869								
96. Special Education - Orphanage - Individual	3120	3,996								

ESTIMATED RECEIPTS/REVENUES

	Description	Acct No	(10) Educational	(20) Operations & Maintenance	(30) Bond & Interest	(40) Transportation	(50) Municipal Retirement/ Social Security	(60) Site & Construction/ Capital Improvement	(70) Working Cash	(80) Rent	(90) Fire Prevention & Safety
97.	Special Education - Orphanage - Summer	3130									
98.	Special Education - Summer School	3145	218								
99.	Special Education - Other (Attach Itemization)	3199									
100.	**TOTAL SPECIAL EDUCATION**		1,164,989	0		0					
101.	Vocational Education - Tech. Prep.	3200									
102.	Vocational Education - Coordination Grants	3210									
103.	Vocational Education - Formula	3215	2,195								
104.	Vocational Education - Jobs for Illinois Graduates	3217									
105.	Vocational Education - Secondary Program Improvement	3220									
106.	Vocational Education - WECEP	3225									
107.	Vocational Education - Elementary Career Development Program	3275	3,860								
108.	Vocational Education - Other (Attach Itemization)	3299									
109.	**TOTAL VOCATIONAL EDUCATION**		6,055	0		0	0				
110.	Bilingual Education - Downstate - TPI	3305	5,515								
111.	Bilingual Education - Downstate - TBE	3310									
112.	**TOTAL BILINGUAL EDUCATION**		5,515				0				
113.	Gifted Education	3350	10,560								
114.	State Free Lunch & Breakfast	3360	1,313								
115.	School Breakfast Initiative	3365									
116.	Driver Education	3370	19,170								
117.	Adult Education from Community College Board	3410									
118.	Adult Education - Other (Attach Itemization)	3499									
119.	Transportation - Regular/Vocational	3500				668,583					
120.	Transportation - Special Education	3510				387,062					

ESTIMATED RECEIPTS/REVENUES

Description	Acct No	(10) Educational	(20) Operations & Maintenance	(30) Bond & Interest	(40) Transportation	(50) Municipal Retirement/ Social Security	(60) Site & Construction/ Capital Improvement	(70) Working Cash	(80) Rent	(90) Fire Prevention & Safety
121. Transportation - Other (Attach Itemization)	3599									
122. **TOTAL TRANSPORTATION**		0	0		1,055,645	0				
123. Learning Improvement - Change Grants	3610									
124. Scientific Literacy	3660									
125. Truant Alternative/Optional Education	3695									
126. Early Childhood - Block Grant	3705									
127. Reading Improvement Block Grant	3715	132,094								
128. Reading Improvement Block Grant-Reading Recovery	3720									
129. Chicago General Education Block Grant	3766									
130. Chicago Educational Services Block Grant	3767									
131. School Safety & Educational Improvement Block Grant	3775	141,873								
132. Technology - Closing the Gaps	3792									
133. State Library Grant	3800									
134. Illinois Arts Council Grants	3801									
135. Illinois Scholars Program	3803									
136. Illinois Occupational Info Coordinating Committee	3806									
137. Project Success	3807									
138. IDOT Safety	3808									
139. IDOT Alcohol Awareness	3809									
140. State Charter Schools	3815									
141. Summer Bridges	3825									
142. Academic Early Warning List	3830									

ESTIMATED RECEIPTS/REVENUES

Description	Acct No	(10) Educational	(20) Operations & Maintenance	(30) Bond & Interest	(40) Transportation	(50) Municipal Retirement/ Social Security	(60) Site & Construction/ Capital Improvement	(70) Working Cash	(80) Rent	(90) Fire Prevention & Safety
143. Infrastructure Improvements - Planning/Construction	3920									
144. School Infrastructure - Maintenance Projects	3925									
145. Other Revenue from State Sources (Attach Itemization)	3999									
146. TOTAL RESTRICTED GRANTS-IN-AID		1,481,569	0	0	1,055,645	0	2,700,000	0	0	0
147. TOTAL RECEIPTS/REVENUE FROM STATE SOURCES		2,788,867	0	0	427,086	0	0	0	0	0
RECEIPTS/REVENUE FROM FEDERAL SOURCES	4000									
UNRESTRICTED GRANTS-IN-AID RECEIVED DIRECTLY FROM FEDERAL GOVT.										
148. Federal Impact Aid	4001									
149. Other Unrestricted Grants-In-Aid Received Directly From Federal Govt.	4009									
150. TOTAL UNRESTRICTED GRANTS-IN-AID RECEIVED DIRECTLY FROM FEDERAL GOVT.		0	0	0	0	0	0	0	0	0
RESTRICTED GRANTS-IN-AID RECEIVED DIRECTLY FROM FEDERAL GOVT.										
151. Emergency School Assistance Act	4025									
152. ESEA - Title VII - Bilingual	4030									
153. ESEA - Title VI - Excellence in Education	4035									
154. Community Action Program - OEO	4040									
155. Head Start	4045									
156. Construction (Impact Aid)	4050									
157. EPA Grant Proceeds (Life Safety Purposes Only)	4055									
158. MAGNET	4060									
159. Other Restricted Grants-In-Aid Received Directly From Federal Govt. (Attach Itemization)	4099									
160. TOTAL RESTRICTED GRANTS-IN-AID RECEIVED DIRECTLY FROM FEDERAL GOVT		0	0		0	0	0			0

ESTIMATED RECEIPTS/REVENUES

Description	Acct No	(10) Educational	(20) Operations & Maintenance	(30) Bond & Interest	(40) Transportation	(50) Municipal Retirement/ Social Security	(60) Site & Construction/ Capital Improvement	(70) Working Cash	(80) Rent	(90) Fire Prevention & Safety
RESTRICTED GRANTS-IN-AID RECEIVED FROM FEDERAL GOVT. THRU THE STATE										
161. Title V-Innovation and Flexibility Formula	4100	23,909								
162. Title V-LEA Projects	4105									
163. Title V-Rural and Low Income Schools	4107									
164. Title V-Class Size Reduction	4110									
165. Title V-State Assessments	4120									
166. Title V-Other	4199									
167. TOTAL TITLE V		23,909	0		0	0				
168. National School Lunch Program	4210									
169. Special Milk Program	4215	48,296								
170. School Breakfast Program	4220									
171. Summer Food Service Admin/Program	4225									
172. Child Care Commodity/SFS 13-Adult Day Care	4226									
173. Food Service - Other (Attach Itemization)	4299									
174. TOTAL FOOD SERVICE		48,296								
175. Title I - Low Income	4300									
176. Title I - Low Income - Neglected, Private	4305									
177. Title I - Capital Expenses	4325									
178. Title I - School Improvement	4331									
179. Title I - Comprehensive School Reform	4332									
180. Title I - Reading First	4334									
181. Title I - Even Start	4335									

ESTIMATED RECEIPTS/REVENUES

	Description	Acct No	(10) Educational	(20) Operations & Maintenance	(30) Bond & Interest	(40) Transportation	(50) Municipal Retirement/ Social Security	(60) Site & Construction/ Capital Improvement	(70) Working Cash	(80) Rent	(90) Fire Prevention & Safety
182.	Title I - Migrant Education	4340									
183.	Title I - Other (Attach Itemization)	4399									
184.	**TOTAL TITLE I**		0	0		0	0				
185.	Title IV - Safe & Drug Free Schools - Formula	4400	14,113								
186.	Title IV - Safe & Drug Free Schools -Violence Prevention	4406									
187.	Title IV - Community Service	4420									
188.	Title IV - 21st Century	4421									
189.	Title IV - Other (Attach Itemization)	4499									
190.	**TOTAL TITLE IV**		14,113	0		0	0				
191.	Fed - Spec Education - Preschool Flow - Through	4600									
192.	Fed - Spec Education - Preschool Discretionary	4605									
193.	Fed - Spec Education - IDEA - Flow Through/Low Incidence	4620									
194.	Fed - Spec Education - IDEA - Room & Board	4625									
195.	Fed - Spec Education - IDEA - Discretionary	4630									
196.	Fed - Spec Education - IDEA - Other (Attach Itemization)	4699									
197.	**TOTAL FED - SPECIAL EDUCATION**		0	0		0	0				
198.	VE - Perkins - Title IIA State Leadership	4720									
199.	VE - Perkins - Title IIC Secondary	4745									
200.	VE - Perkins - Title IIC Postsecondary/Adult	4750									
201.	VE-Perkins-Title IIIE Tech Prep	4770	3,640								
202.	VE-Education to Careers-Implementation (DOL)	4777									
203.	VE-Other (Attach Itemization)	4799									
204.	**TOTAL VOCATIONAL EDUCATION**		3,640	0			0				

ESTIMATED RECEIPTS/REVENUES

Description	Acct No	(10) Educational	(20) Operations & Maintenance	(30) Bond & Interest	(40) Transportation	(50) Municipal Retirement/ Social Security	(60) Site & Construction/ Capital Improvement	(70) Working Cash	(80) Rent	(90) Fire Prevention & Safety
205. Federal - Adult Education	4810									
206. Emergency Immigrant Assistance	4905									
207. Title III-English Language Acquisition	4909									
208. Learn & Serve America	4910									
209. McKinney Education for Homeless Children	4920									
210. Title II - Eisenhower - Professional Development Formula	4930									
211. Title II-Teacher Quality	4932	75,216								
212. Goals 2000	4945									
213. Goals 2000 - Leadership	4946									
214. Department of Rehabilitation Services	4950									
215. Federal Charter Schools	4960									
216. School Renovation	4980									
217. IDEA Part B-Supplemental Activities	4981	584,958								
218. School Renovation-Technology	4982									
219. Federal Emergency Management Aid (FEMA/IEMA)	4990									
220. Medicaid Matching Funds - Administrative Outreach	4991	98,972								
221. Medicaid Matching Funds - Fee-For-Service Program	4992	28,654								
222. Other Restricted Revenue From Federal Sources (Attach Itemization)	4999									
223. TOTAL RESTRICTED GRANTS-IN-AID RECEIVED FROM FEDERAL GOVT. THRU THE STATE		877,758	0		0	0	0			0
224. TOTAL RECEIPTS/REVENUE FROM FEDERAL SOURCES		877,758	0	0	0	0	0	0	0	0
225. TOTAL DIRECT RECEIPTS/REVENUE (Total of Lines 83, 87, 147, 224)		34,569,525	6,007,967	6,661,833	2,867,271	1,970,370	2,850,000	77,189	0	5,000

ESTIMATED RECEIPTS/REVENUES

Description	Acct No	(10) Educational	(20) Operations & Maintenance	(30) Bond & Interest	(40) Transportation	(50) Municipal Retirement/ Social Security	(60) Site & Construction/ Capital Improvement	(70) Working Cash	(80) Rent	(90) Fire Prevention & Safety
OTHER FINANCING SOURCES	7000									
226. Permanent Transfer from Working Cash Fund - Abolishment (Section 20-8)	7110	77,189								
227. Permanent Transfer from Working Cash Fund - Interest (Section 20-5)	7120	26,218								
228. Permanent Transfer (Section 17-2A)	7130	37,223								
229. Permanent Transfer of Interest (Section 10-22.44)	7140									
230. Permanent Transfer from Site and Construction Fund (Section 10-22.14)	7150									
231. Perm. Transfer of Excess Accumulated Fire Prev & Safety Tax Proceeds & Int. Earnings (Sec. 17-2.11)	7160									
232. Perm. Transfer of Excess Accumulated Fire Prev & Safety Bond Proceeds and Int. Earnings (Sec. 10-22.14)	7170									
233. Permanent Transfer from Working Cash Fund - Abatement (Section 20-9)	7180									
SALE OF BONDS	7200									
234. Principal on Bonds Sold (Amount of Original Issues)	7210						35,600,000			2,760,000
235. Premium on Bonds Sold	7220									
236. Accrued Interest on Bonds Sold	7230									
237. Sale or Compensation for Fixed Assets (Section 2-3.12 and 17-2.11)	7300									
238. School Technology Revolving Loan Program (STRLP)	7500									
239. Other Sources (Attach Itemization)	7900									
240. **TOTAL DIRECT RECEIPTS/REVENUES AND OTHER FINANCING SOURCES**		34,710,155	6,007,967	6,661,833	2,867,271	1,970,370	2,850,000	77,189	0	5,000

PART II - ESTIMATED DISBURSEMENTS/EXPENDITURES

Description	Funct No	(1) Salaries	(2) Employee Benefits	(3) Purchased Services	(4) Supplies & Materials	(5) Capital Outlay	(6) Other Objects	(7) Transfers	(8) Tuition	(9) Total
EDUCATIONAL FUND (10)										
INSTRUCTION	1000									
1. Regular Programs	1100	16,030,919	1,771,750	300,858	776,066	171,039	33,130			19,084,662
2. Special Education Programs (Total of Function No 1200-1220)	1200	3,446,064	248,826	29,795	35,082	3,000	1,500		419,226	4,183,493
3. Educationally Deprived/Remedial Programs	1250	288,970	14,453	6,930	30,569	900	405			342,227
4. Adult/Continuing Education Programs	1300									
5. Vocational Programs	1400									
6. Interscholastic Programs	1500	516,277	13,332	71,790	23,500	0	11,256			636,155
7. Summer School Programs	1600	72,568			990					73,558
8. Gifted Programs	1650	387,609	21,646	10,800	9,000	3,500	405			432,960
9. Bilingual Programs	1800	86,889	12,363	900	3,300	450				103,902
10. Truant Alternative & Optional Programs	1900									0
11. **TOTAL INSTRUCTION**		20,829,296	2,082,370	421,073	878,507	178,889	46,696		419,226	24,856,957
SUPPORT SERVICES	2000									
SUPPORT SERVICES - PUPILS	2100									
12. Attendance & Social Work Services	2110	348,785	20,067		2,000					370,852
13. Guidance Services	2120	959,812	100,509	97,853	13,850		3,400			1,175,424
14. Health Services	2130	205,601	12,460	650	10,750					229,461
15. Psychological Services	2140	294,097	26,309	13,210	2,000					335,616

ESTIMATED DISBURSEMENTS/EXPENDITURES

Description	Funct No	(1) Salaries	(2) Employee Benefits	(3) Purchased Services	(4) Supplies & Materials	(5) Capital Outlay	(6) Other Objects	(7) Transfers	(8) Tuition	(9) Total
(Fund 10 Continued)										
16. Speech Pathology & Audiology Services	2150	355,614	28,491		3,821					387,926
17. Other Support Services - Pupils (Attach Itemization)	2190									
18. **TOTAL SUPPORT SERVICES - PUPILS**		2,163,909	187,836	111,723	32,421	0	3,400			2,499,289
SUPPORT SERVICES - INSTRUCTIONAL STAFF	2200									
19. Improvement of Instruction Services	2210	382,448	28,369	155,473	154,000	21,000	2,000			743,290
20. Educational Media Services	2220	575,901	47,246	150	70,650	2,000				695,947
21. Assessment & Testing	2230									0
22. **TOTAL SUPPORT SERVICES - INSTRUCTIONAL STAFF**		958,349	75,615	155,623	224,650	23,000	2,000			1,439,237
SUPPORT SERVICES - GENERAL ADMINISTRATION	2300									
23. Board of Education Services	2310	18,638	583,281	354,814	3,500		37,500			997,733
24. Executive Administration Services	2320	181,553	6,829	34,000	2,500	5,000	20,800			250,682
25. Special Area Administration Services	2330									0
26. **TOTAL SUPPORT SERVICES GENERAL ADMINISTRATION**		200,191	590,110	388,814	6,000	5,000	58,300			1,248,415
SUPPORT SERVICES - SCHOOL ADMINISTRATION	2400									
27. Office of the Principal Services	2410	1,570,023	212,356	42,250	54,615	18,305	6,400			1,903,949
28. Other Support Services - School Administration (Attach Itemization)	2490									0
29. **TOTAL SUPPORT SERVICES - SCHOOL ADMINISTRATION**		1,570,023	212,356	42,250	54,615	18,305	6,400			1,903,949

ESTIMATED DISBURSEMENTS/EXPENDITURES

Description	Funct No	(1) Salaries	(2) Employee Benefits	(3) Purchased Services	(4) Supplies & Materials	(5) Capital Outlay	(6) Other Objects	(7) Transfers	(8) Tuition	(9) Total
(Fund 10 Continued)										
30. Direction of Business Support Services	2510									0
31. Fiscal Services	2520	194,321	40,125	76,052	16,000	1,250	11,000			338,748
32. Operation & Maintenance of Plant Services	2540									0
33. Pupil Transportation Services	2550									0
34. Food Services	2560	54,378	7,130	1,184,282	6,800	10,600				1,263,190
35. Internal Services	2570									0
36. **TOTAL SUPPORT SERVICES - BUSINESS**		248,699	47,255	1,260,334	22,800	11,850	11,000			1,601,938
SUPPORT SERVICES - CENTRAL	2600									
37. Direction of Central Support Services	2610									0
38. Planning, Research, Development & Evaluation Services	2620									0
39. Information Services	2630	645,137	27,298	33,066	68,500	40,440	600			815,041
40. Staff Services	2640	262,368	54,149	16,350	4,500	2,500	9,800			349,667
41. Data Processing Services	2660									0
42. **TOTAL SUPPORT SERVICES CENTRAL**		907,505	81,447	49,416	73,000	42,940	10,400			1,164,708
43. **OTHER SUPPORT SERVICES** (Attach Itemization)	2900									0
44. **TOTAL SUPPORT SERVICES**		6,048,676	1,194,619	2,008,160	413,486	101,095	91,500			9,857,536
45. **COMMUNITY SERVICES**	3000									0
NONPROGRAMMED CHARGES	4000									
PAYMENTS TO OTHER GOVT. UNITS (IN-STATE)	4100									
46. Payments for Regular Programs	4110									0

ESTIMATED DISBURSEMENTS/EXPENDITURES

Description	Funct No	(1) Salaries	(2) Employee Benefits	(3) Purchased Services	(4) Supplies & Materials	(5) Capital Outlay	(6) Other Objects	(7) Transfers	(8) Tuition	(9) Total
(Fund 10 Continued)										
47. Payments for Special Education Programs	4120								1,115,635	1,115,635
48. Payments for Adult/Continuing Education Programs	4130									0
49. Payments for Vocational Education Programs	4140								285,439	285,439
50. Payments for Community College Program	4170									0
51. Other Payments to In-State Govt. Units (Attach Itemization)	4190									0
52. TOTAL PAYMENTS TO OTHER GOVT. UNITS (IN-STATE)				0			0	0	1,401,074	1,401,074
53. PAYMENTS TO OTHER GOVT. UNITS (OUT-OF-STATE)	4200									0
54. TOTAL NONPROGRAMMED CHARGES				0			0	0	1,401,074	1,401,074
DEBT SERVICES	5000									
DEBT SERVICES - INTEREST	5100									
55. Tax Anticipation Warrants	5110						192,192			192,192
56. Tax Anticipation Notes	5120									0
57. Teachers'/Employees' Orders	5130									0
58. Corporate Personal Property Replacement Tax Anticipation Notes	5150									0
59. State Aid Anticipation Certificates	5160									0
60. Other (Attach Itemization)	5190									0
61. TOTAL DEBT SERVICES - INTEREST							192,192			192,192
62. Debt Services - Lease/Purchase Principal Retired	5300									0
63. TOTAL DEBT SERVICES							192,192			192,192
64. PROVISION FOR CONTINGENCIES	6000						31,000			31,000
65. TOTAL DIRECT DISBURSEMENTS/EXPENDITURES		26,877,972	3,276,989	2,429,233	1,291,993	280,884	288,196	0	1,820,300	36,265,567
OTHER FINANCING USES	8000									
66. Permanent Transfer (Section 17-2A)	8130									0
67. Permanent Transfer of Interest (Section 10-22.44)	8140									0
68. Other Uses (Attach Itemization)	8190									[3169] 0
69. TOTAL DIRECT DISBURSEMENTS/EXPENDITURES AND OTHER FINANCING USES	***	26,877,972	3,276,989	2,429,233	1,291,993	280,884	288,196	0	1,820,300	36,265,567

ESTIMATED DISBURSEMENTS/EXPENDITURES

Description	Funct No	(1) Salaries	(2) Employee Benefits	(3) Purchased Services	(4) Supplies & Materials	(5) Capital Outlay	(6) Other Objects	(7) Transfers	(8) Tuition	(9) Total
OPERATIONS AND MAINTENANCE FUND (20)										
SUPPORT SERVICES	2000									
SUPPORT SERVICES - PUPILS	2100									
1. Other Support Services - Pupils (Attach Itemization)	2190									0
SUPPORT SERVICES - BUSINESS	2500									
2. Direction of Business Support Services	2510									0
3. Facilities Acquisition & Construction Services	2530									0
4. Operation & Maintenance of Plant Services	2540	2,652,702	390,573	904,237	1,162,199	1,508,513				6,618,224
5. Pupil Transportation Services	2550									0
6. Food Services	2560									0
7. **TOTAL SUPPORT SERVICES - BUSINESS**		2,652,702	390,573	904,237	1,162,199	1,508,513	0			6,618,224
8. OTHER SUPPORT SERVICES - (Attach Itemization)	2900									0
9. **TOTAL SUPPORT SERVICES**		2,652,702	390,573	904,237	1,162,199	1,508,513	0			6,618,224
10. **COMMUNITY SERVICES**	3000									0
NONPROGRAMMED CHARGES	4000									
PAYMENTS TO OTHER GOVT. UNITS (IN-STATE)	4100									
11. Payments for Special Education Programs	4120									0
12. Payments for Vocational Education Program	4140									0
13. Other Payments to In-State Govt. Units (Attach Itemization)	4190									0
14. **TOTAL PAYMENTS TO OTHER GOVT. UNITS (IN-STATE)**				0			0	0		0
15. **PAYMENTS TO OTHER GOVT. UNITS (OUT OF STATE)**	4200									0
16. **TOTAL NONPROGRAMMED CHARGES**				0			0	0		0

ESTIMATED DISBURSEMENTS/EXPENDITURES

Description	Funct No	(1) Salaries	(2) Employee Benefits	(3) Purchased Services	(4) Supplies & Materials	(5) Capital Outlay	(6) Other Objects	(7) Transfers	(8) Tuition	(9) Total
(Fund 20 Continued)										
DEBT SERVICES - INTEREST	5100									
17. Tax Anticipation Warrants	5110									0
18. Tax Anticipation Notes	5120									0
19. Corporate Personal Property Replacement Tax Anticipation Notes	5150									0
20. State Aid Anticipation Certificates	5160									0
21. Other (Attach Itemization)	5190									0
22. **TOTAL DEBT SERVICES - INTEREST**							0			0
23. Debt Services - Lease/Purchase Principal Retired	5300									0
24. **TOTAL DEBT SERVICES**							0			0
25. **PROVISION FOR CONTINGENCIES**	6000						200,000			200,000
26. **TOTAL DIRECT DISBURSEMENTS/ EXPENDITURES**		2,652,702	390,573	904,237	1,162,199	1,508,513	200,000	0		6,818,224
OTHER FINANCING USES	8000									
27. Permanent Transfer (17-2A)	8130									0
28. Permanent Transfer of Interest (Section 10-22.44)	8140							18,537		18,537
29. Other Uses (Attach Itemization)	8190									0
30. **TOTAL DIRECT DISBURSEMENTS/EXPENDITURES AND OTHER FINANCING USES**		2,652,702	390,573	904,237	1,162,199	1,508,513	200,000	18,537		6,836,761

ESTIMATED DISBURSEMENTS/EXPENDITURES

	Description	Funct No	(1) Salaries	(2) Employee Benefits	(3) Purchased Services	(4) Supplies & Materials	(5) Capital Outlay	(6) Other Objects	(7) Transfers	(8) Tuition	(9) Total
	BOND & INTEREST FUND (30)										
	NONPROGRAMMED CHARGES	4000									
1.	Payments to Other Govt. Units (In-State)	4100									0
2.	**TOTAL NONPROGRAMMED CHARGES**								0		0
	DEBT SERVICES	5000									
	DEBT SERVICES - INTEREST	5100									
3.	Tax Anticipation Warrants	5110									0
4.	Tax Anticipation Notes	5120									0
5.	Bonds	5140						1,573,653			1,573,653
6.	Corporate Personal Property Replacement Tax Anticipation Notes	5150									0
7.	State Aid Anticipation Certificates	5160									0
8.	Other - (Attach Itemization)	5190									0
9.	**TOTAL DEBT SERVICES - INTEREST**							1,573,653			1,573,653
10.	Debt Services - Bond Principal Retired	5200						4,221,217			4,221,217
11.	Debt Services - Other (Attach Itemization)	5900			[1246]			10,000			10,000
12.	**TOTAL DEBT SERVICES** (Total of Lines 9,10,11)				[1247] 0			5,804,870	0		5,804,870
13.	**PROVISION FOR CONTINGENCIES**	6000									0
14.	**TOTAL DIRECT DISBURSEMENTS/EXPENDITURES**				[1248] 0			5,804,870	0		5,804,870
	OTHE FINANCING USES	8000									
15.	Permanent Transfer of Interest (Section 10-22.44)	8140							37,223		37,223
16.	Other Uses (Attach Itemization)	8190									0
17.	**Total Direct Disbursements/Expenditures and Other Financing Uses**				0			5,804,870	37,223		5,842,093

ESTIMATED DISBURSEMENTS/EXPENDITURES

	Description	Funct No	(1) Salaries	(2) Employee Benefits	(3) Purchased Services	(4) Supplies & Materials	(5) Capital Outlay	(6) Other Objects	(7) Transfers	(8) Tuition	(9) Total
	TRANSPORTATION FUND (40)										
	SUPPORT SERVICES	2000									
	SUPPORT SERVICES - PUPIL	2100									
1.	Other Support Services - Pupils (Attach Itemization)	2190									0
	SUPPORT SERVICES - BUSINESS	2500									
2.	Pupil Transportation Services	2550	978,119	34,902	994,269	176,100	843,695				3,027,085
3.	Other Support Services (Attach Itemization)	2900									0
4.	**TOTAL SUPPORT SERVICES**		978,119	34,902	994,269	176,100	843,695	0			3,027,085
5.	**COMMUNITY SERVICES**	3000									0
	NONPROGRAMMED CHARGES	4000									
	PAYMENTS TO OTHER GOVT. UNITS (IN STATE)	4100									
6.	Payments for Regular Program	4110									0
7.	Payments for Special Education Programs	4120									0
8.	Payments for Adult/Continuing Education Programs	4130									0
9.	Payments for Vocational Education Programs	4140									0
10.	Payments for Community College Programs	4170									0
11.	Other Payments to In-State Govt. Units (Attach Itemization)	4190									0
12.	**TOTAL PAYMENTS TO OTHER GOVT. UNITS (IN-STATE)**				0			0	0		0
13.	Payments to Other Govt. Units (Out-of-State)	4200									0
14.	**TOTAL NONROGRAMMED CHARGES**				0			0	0		0

ESTIMATED DISBURSEMENTS/EXPENDITURES

Description	Funct No	(1) Salaries	(2) Employee Benefits	(3) Purchased Services	(4) Supplies & Materials	(5) Capital Outlay	(6) Other Objects	(7) Transfers	(8) Tuition	(9) Total
(Fund 40 Continued)										
DEBT SERVICES - INTEREST	5100									
15. Tax Anticipation Warrants	5110									0
16. Tax Anticipation Notes	5120									0
17. Corporate Personal Property Replacement Tax Anticipation Notes	5150									0
18. State Aid Anticipation Certificates	5160									0
19. Other (Attach Itemization)	5190									0
20. **TOTAL DEBT SERVICES - INTEREST**							0			0
21. Debt Services - Lease/Purchase Principal Retired	5300									0
22. **TOTAL DEBT SERVICES**							0			0
23. PROVISION FOR CONTINGENCIES	6000						30,000			30,000
24. TOTAL DIRECT DISBURSEMENTS/EXPENDITURES		978,119	34,902	994,269	176,100	843,695	30,000	0		3,057,085
OTHER FINANCING USES	8000									
25. Permanent Transfer (Section 17-2A)	8130									0
26. Permanent Transfer of Interest (Section 10-22.44)	8140							7,681		7,681
27. Other Uses (Attach Itemization)	8190									0
28. TOTAL DIRECT DISBURSEMENT/EXPENDITURES AND OTHER FINANCING USES		978,119	34,902	994,269	176,100	843,695	30,000	7,681		3,064,766

ESTIMATED DISBURSEMENTS/EXPENDITURES

Description	Funct No	(1) Salaries	(2) Employee Benefits	(3) Purchased Services	(4) Supplies & Materials	(5) Capital Outlay	(6) Other Objects	(7) Transfers	(8) Tuition	(9) Total
MUNICIPAL RETIREMENT/SOCIAL SECURITY FUND (50)										
INSTRUCTION	1000									
1. Regular Program	1100		244,215							244,215
2. Special Education Programs (Total of Function No. 1200-1220)	1200		179,367							179,367
3. Educationally Deprived/Remedial Programs	1250		23,430							23,430
4. Adult/Continuing Education Programs	1300									0
5. Vocational Programs	1400									0
6. Interscholastic Programs	1500		10,093							10,093
7. Summer School Programs	1600		1,108							1,108
8. Gifted Programs	1650		5,547							5,547
9. Bilingual Programs	1800		598							598
10. Truant Alternative & Optional Programs	1900									0
11. TOTAL INSTRUCTION			464,358							464,358
SUPPORT SERVICES	2000									
SUPPORT SERVICES - PUPILS	2100									
12. Attendance & Social Work Services	2110		5,735							5,735
13. Guidance Services	2120		12,628							12,628
14. Health Services	2130		18,998							18,998
15. Psychological Services	2140		9,538							9,538
16. Speech Pathology & Audiology Services	2150									0
17. Other Support Services - Pupils (Attach Itemization)	2190									0
18. TOTAL SUPPORT SERVICES - PUPILS			46,899							46,899
SUPPORT SERVICES INSTRUCTIONAL STAFF	2200									
19. Improvement of Instruction Services	2210		9,278							9,278

ESTIMATED DISBURSEMENTS/EXPENDITURES

Description	Funct No	(1) Salaries	(2) Employee Benefits	(3) Purchased Services	(4) Supplies & Materials	(5) Capital Outlay	(6) Other Objects	(7) Transfers	(8) Tuition	(9) Total
(Fund 50 Continued)										
20. Educational Media Services	2220		19,434							19,434
21. Assessment & Testing	2230									0
22. TOTAL SUPPORT SERVICES - INSTRUCTIONAL STAFF			28,712							28,712
SUPPORT SERVICES - GENERAL ADMINISTRATION	2300									
23. Board of Education Services	2310		4,457							4,457
24. Executive Administration Services	2320		15,003							15,003
25. Special Area Administrative Services	2330									0
26. TOTAL SUPPORT SERVICES - GENERAL ADMINISTRATION			19,460							19,460
SUPPORT SERVICES - SCHOOL ADMINISTRATION	2400									
27. Office of the Principal Services	2410		123,268							123,268
28. Other Support Services - School Administration (Attach Itemization)	2490									0
29. TOTAL SUPPORT SERVICES - SCHOOL ADMINISTRATION			123,268							123,268
SUPPORT SERVICES - BUSINESS	2500									
30. Direction of Business Support Services	2510									0
31. Fiscal Services	2520		32,111							32,111
32. Facilities Acquisition & Construction Services	2530									0
33. Operation & Maintenance of Plant Service	2540		347,933							347,933
34. Pupil Transportation Services	2550		134,730							134,730
35. Food Services	2560		2,207							2,207
36. Internal Services	2570									0
37. TOTAL SUPPORT SERVICES - BUSINESS			516,981							516,981
SUPPORT SERVICES - CENTRAL	2600									
38. Direction of Central Support Services	2610									0
39. Planning, Research, Development & Evaluation Evaluation	2620		[1377]							[1441] 0

ESTIMATED DISBURSEMENTS/EXPENDITURES

Description	Funct No	(1) Salaries	(2) Employee Benefits	(3) Purchased Services	(4) Supplies & Materials	(5) Capital Outlay	(6) Other Objects	(7) Transfers	(8) Tuition	(9) Total
(Fund 50 Continued)										
40. Information Services	2630		28,194							28,194
41. Staff Services	2640		11,878							11,878
42. Data Processing Services	2660									0
43. TOTAL SUPPORT SERVICES - CENTRAL			40,072							40,072
44. OTHER SUPPORT SERVICES (Attach Itemization)	2900									0
45. TOTAL SUPPORT SERVICES			775,392							775,392
46. COMMUNITY SERVICES	3000									0
NONPROGRAMMED CHARGED	4000									
47. Payments for Special Education Programs	4120									0
48. Payments for Vocational Education Programs	4140									0
49. TOTAL NONPROGRAMMED CHARGES			0							0
DEBT SERVICES	5000									
DEBT SERVICES - INTEREST	5100									
50. Tax Anticipation Warrants	5110									0
51. Tax Anticipation Notes	5120									0
52. Corporate Personal Property Replacement Tax Anticipation Notes	5150									0
53. State Aid Anticipation Certificates	5160									0
54. Other (Attach Itemization)	5190									0
55. TOTAL DEBT SERVICES - INTEREST							0			0
56. PROVISION FOR CONTINGENCIES	6000									0
57. TOTAL DISBURSEMENTS/EXPENDITURES			1,239,750				0			1,239,750
OTHER FINANCING USES	8000									
58. Permanent Transfer of Interest (Section 10-22.44)	8140									0
59. TOTAL DIRECT DISBURSEMENTS/EXPENDITURES AND OTHER FINANCING USES			1,239,750				0	0		1,239,750

ESTIMATED DISBURSEMENTS/EXPENDITURES

	Description	Funct No	(1) Salaries	(2) Employee Benefits	(3) Purchased Services	(4) Supplies & Materials	(5) Capital Outlay	(6) Other Objects	(7) Transfers	(8) Tuition	(9) Total
	SITE & CONSTRUCTION/CAPITAL IMPROVEMENTS (60)										
	SUPPORT SERVICES	2000									
	SUPPORT SERVICES - BUSINESS	2500									
1.	Facilities Acquisition & Construction Services	2530					8,711,179				8,711,179
2.	**TOTAL SUPPORT SERVICES - BUSINESS**		0	0	0	0	8,711,179	0			8,711,179
3.	Other Support Services (Attach Itemization)	2900									0
4.	**TOTAL SUPPORT SERVICES**		0	0	0	0	8,711,179	0			8,711,179
	NONPROGRAMMED CHARGES	4000									
	PAYMENTS TO OTHER GOVERNMENTAL UNITS (IN-STATE)	4100									
5.	Payment for Special Education Programs	4120									0
6.	Payment for Vocational Education Programs	4140									0
7.	Other Payments to In-State Governmental Units (Attach Itemization)	4190									0
8.	**TOTAL PAYMENTS TO OTHER GOVERNMENTAL UNITS (IN-STATE)**								0		0
9.	Payments to Other Governmental Units (Out-of-State)	4200									0
10.	**TOTAL NONPROGRAMMED CHARGES**								0		0
11.	Provision for Contingencies	6000									0
12.	**TOTAL DISBURSEMENTS/EXPENDITURES**		0	0	0	0	8,711,179	0	0		8,711,179
	OTHER FIANCING USES	8000									
13.	Permanent Transfer of Interest (Section 10-22.44)	8140									0
14.	Permanent Transfer from Site and Const. (Section 10-22.14)	8150									0
15.	Other Uses (Attach Itemization)	8190									0
16.	**TOTAL DIRECT DISBURSEMENTS/EXPENDITURES AND OTHER FINANCING USES**		0	0	0	0	8,711,179	0	0		8,711,179

ESTIMATED DISBURSEMENTS/EXPENDITURES

	Description	Funct No	(1) Salaries	(2) Employee Benefits	(3) Purchased Services	(4) Supplies & Materials	(5) Capital Outlay	(6) Other Objects	(7) Transfers	(8) Tuition	(9) Total
	WORKING CASH FUND (70)										
	OTHER FINANCING USES	8000									
1.	Permanent Transfer of Working Cash Fund - Abolishment (Section 20-8)	8110									0
2.	Permanent Transfer of Working Cash Fund - Interest (Section 20-5)	8120							771789		771789
3.	Permanent Transfer of Working Cash Fund - Abatement (Section 20-9)	8180									0
4.	**TOTAL OTHER FINANCING USES**								771789		771,789

	Description	Funct No	(1) Salaries	(2) Employee Benefits	(3) Purchased Services	(4) Supplies & Materials	(5) Capital Outlay	(6) Other Objects	(7) Transfers	(8) Tuition	(9) Total
	RENT FUND (80)										
	DEBT SERVICE	5000									
1.	Corporate Personal Property Replacement Tax Anticipation Notes	5150									0
2.	State Aid Anticipation Certificates	5160									0
3.	Debt Service - Other (Attach Itemization)	5900									0
4.	**TOTAL DEBT SERVICE**				0			0	0		0
5.	**TOTAL DISBURSEMENTS/ EXPENDITURES**				0			0	0		0
	OTHER FINANCING USES	8000									
6.	Permanent Transfer of Interest Section 10-22.44)	8140									0
7.	Other Uses (Attach Itemization)	8190									0
8.	**TOTAL DIRECT DISBURSEMENTS/EXPENDITURES AND OTHER FINANCING USES**				0			0	0		0

ESTIMATED DISBURSEMENTS/EXPENDITURES

Description	Funct No	(1) Salaries	(2) Employee Benefits	(3) Purchased Services	(4) Supplies & Materials	(5) Capital Outlay	(6) Other Objects	(7) Transfers	(8) Tuition	(9) Total
FIRE PREVENTION & SAFETY FUND (90)										
SUPPORT SERVICES	2000									
SUPPORT SERVICES - BUSINESS	2500									
1. Facilities Acquisition & Construction Services	2530									0
2. Operation & Maintenance of Plant Service	2540					180,538				180,538
3. TOTAL SUPPORT SERVICES - BUSINESS		0	0	0	0	180,538	0			180,538
4. Other Support Services (Attach Itemization)	2900									0
5. TOTAL SUPPORT SERVICES		0	0	0	0	180,538	0			180,538
NONPROGRAMMED CHARGES	4000									
6. Other Payments to In-State Governmental Units (Attach Itemization)	4190									0
7. TOTAL NONPROGRAMMED CHARGES								0		0
DEBT SERVICES	5000									
DEBT SERVICES - INTEREST	5100									
8. Tax Anticipation Warrants	5110									0
9. TOTAL DEBT SERVICES - INTEREST							0			0
10. PROVISION FOR CONTINGENCIES	6000									0
11. TOTAL DISBURSEMENTS/EXPENDITURES		0	0	0	0	180,538	0	0		180,538
OTHER FINANCING USES	8000									
12. Permanent Transfer of Excess Accumulated Fire Prev. & Safety Tax Proceeds & Int. Earnings (Sec. 17-2.11)	8160									0
13. Perm. Transfer of Excess Accumulated Fire Prev. & Safety Bond Proceeds and Int. Earnings (Sec. 10-22.14)	8170									0
14. TOTAL DIRECT DISBURSEMENTS/EXPENDITURES AND OTHER FINANCING USES		0	0	0	0	180,538	0	0		180,538

PART III - BUDGET SUMMARY

	Description	Acct No	(10) Educational	(20) Operations & Maintenance	(30) Bond & Interest	(40) Transportation	(50) Municipal Retirement/ Social Security	(60) Site & Construction/ Capital Improvement	(70) Working Cash	(80) Rent	(90) Fire Prevention & Safety
	ESTIMATED FUND BALANCE										
1.	**July 1, 2004** [A]			1,664,519	1,874,200	977,030	915,066	5,861,179	8,447,728		945,241
	RECEIPTS/REVENUES										
2.	Local Receipts	1000	30,440,084	6,007,967	6,661,833	1,811,626	1,970,370	150,000	77,189	0	5,000
3.	Flow-Through Receipts/Revenue from One LEA to Another LEA	2000	0	0		0	0				
4.	State Sources	3000	3,251,683	0	0	1,055,645	0	2,700,000	0	0	0
5.	Federal Sources	4000	877,758	0	0	0	0	0	0	0	0
6.	**TOTAL DIRECT RECEIPTS/REVENUES**		34,569,525	6,007,967	6,661,833	2,867,271	1,970,370	2,850,000	77,189	0	5,000
7.	*Receipts/Revenues for "On Behalf of" Payments* [B]	3998									
8.	**TOTAL RECEIPTS/REVENUES**		34,569,525	6,007,967	6,661,833	2,867,271	1,970,370	2,850,000	77,189	0	5,000
	DISBURSEMENTS/EXPENDITURES										
9.	Instruction	1000	24,856,957				464,358				
10.	Support Services	2000	9,857,536	6,618,224		3,027,085	775,392	8,711,179			180,538
11.	Community Services	3000	0	0		0	0				
12.	Nonprogrammed Charges	4000	1,401,074	0	0	0	0	0			0
13.	Debt Services	5000			5,804,870	0	0			0	0
14.	Provision for Contingencies	6000	150,000	200,000	0	30,000	(53,399)	604,357			0
15.	**TOTAL DIRECT DISBURSEMENTS/EXPENDITURES**		36,265,567	6,818,224	5,804,870	3,057,085	1,239,750	8,711,179		0	180,538
16.	*Disbursements/Expenditures for "On Behalf of" Payments* [B]	4180	0	0	0	0	0	0		0	0
17.	**TOTAL DISBURSEMENTS/EXPENDITURES**		36,265,567	6,818,224	5,804,870	3,057,085	1,239,750	8,711,179		0	180,538
18.	**Excess of Direct Receipts/Revenues Over (Under) Direct Disbursements/Expenditures**		(1,696,042)	(810,257)	856,963	(189,814)	730,620	(5,861,179)	77,189	0	(175,538)

	Description	Acct No	(10) Educational	(20) Operations & Maintenance	(30) Bond & Interest	(40) Transportation	(50) Municipal Retirement/ Social Security	(60) Site & Construction/ Capital Improvement	(70) Working Cash	(80) Rent	(90) Fire Prevention & Safety
	OTHER FINANCING SOURCES (USES)										
	OTHER FINANCING SOURCES	7000									
19.	Transfer from Other Funds	7100	140,630	0	0	0	0	0	0	0	0
20.	Sale of Bonds	7200	0	0	0	0		0	0		0
21.	Sale or Compensation for Loss of Fixed Assets	7300	0	0	0	0	0	0		0	0
22.	School Technology Revolving Loan Program (STRLP)	7500	0	0							
23.	Other Sources	7900	0	0	0	0	0	0	0	0	0
	OTHER FINANCING (USES)	8000									
24.	Transfer to Other Funds	8100	0	18,537	37,223	7,681	0	0	771789	0	0
25.	Other Uses	8190	0	0	0	0		0		0	
26.	**TOTAL OTHER FINANCING SOURCES c AND USES**		140,630	(18,537)	(37,223)	(7,681)	0	0	(771,789)	0	0
27.	**ESTIMATED FUND BALANCE d** **30-Jun-05**		(1,555,412)	835,725	2,693,940	779,535	1,645,686	0	7,753,126	0	769,703

c Total of Lines 19-23 minus Lines 24 and 25

d Total of Lines 1, 18 and 26

	Description	Acct No	(10) Educational	(20) Operations & Maintenance	(30) Bond & Interest	(40) Transportation	(50) Municipal Retirement/ Social Security	(60) Site & Construction/ Capital Improvement	(70) Working Cash	(80) Rent	(90) Fire Prevention & Safety
1.	**EST. BALANCE ON HAND JULY 1, 2004** (Cash plus Investments at Cost) [E]	101-5 180	0	1,664,519	1,874,200	977,030	915,066	5,861,179	8,447,726		945,241
2.	**TOTAL DIRECT RECEIPTS AND OTHER FINANCING SOURCES** [F]		34,710,155	6,007,967	6,661,833	2,867,271	1,970,370	2,850,000	77,189	0	5,000
3.	Add Other Receipts: Loans from Other Funds	430	7,311,425								
4.	Loans Repayments from Other Funds	150							5,756,013		
5.	Corporate Personal Property Tax Replacement Tax Anticipation Notes	406									
6.	Tax Anticipation Warrants Issued	407									

Description	Acct No	(10) Educational	(20) Operations & Maintenance	(30) Bond & Interest	(40) Transportation	(50) Municipal Retirement/ Social Security	(60) Site & Construction/ Capital Improvement	(70) Working Cash	(80) Rent	(90) Fire Prevention & Safety
7. Tax Anticipation Notes Issued	408									
8. Teachers'/Employees' Orders Issued	409									
9. State Aid Anticipation Certificates Issued	410									
10. Other (Attach Itemization)	499									
11. TOTAL OTHER RECEIPTS		7,311,425	0	0	0	0	0	5,756,013	0	0
12. TOTAL DIRECT RECEIPTS, OTHER FINANCING SOURCES, AND OTHER RECEIPTS		42,021,580	6,007,967	6,661,833	2,867,271	1,970,370	2,850,000	5,833,202	0	5,000
13. TOTAL AMOUNT AVAILABLE		42,021,580	7,672,486	8,536,033	3,844,301	2,885,436	8,711,179	14,280,928	0	950,241
14. TOTAL DIRECT DISBURSEMENTS AND OTHER FINANCING USES		36,265,567	6,836,761	5,842,093	3,064,766	1,239,750	8,711,179	771,789	0	180,538
ADD OTHER DISBURSEMENTS:										
15. Loans to Other Funds	150							7,586,883		
16. Loan Repayments to Other Funds	430	5,756,013								
17. Corporate Personal Property Replacement Tax Anticipation Notes Redeemed	406									
18. Tax Anticipation Notes Redeemed	407									
19. Tax Anticipation Notes Redeemed	408									
20. Teachers'/Employees' Orders Redeemed	409									
21. State Aid Anticipation Certificates Redeemed	410									
22. Other (Attach Itemization)	499									
23. TOTAL OTHER DISBURSEMENTS		5,756,013	0	0	0	0	0	7,586,883	0	0
24. TOTAL DIRECT DISBURSEMENTS, OTHER FINANCING USES, AND OTHER DISBURSEMENTS		42,021,580	6,836,761	5,842,093	3,064,766	1,239,750	8,711,179	8,358,672	0	180,538
25. Est. Balance on Hand June 30, 2005 (Cash Plus Investments at Cost) (Total of lines 13 less line 24)		0	835,725	2,693,940	779,535	1,645,686	0	5,922,256	0	769,703

About the Authors

Ronald E. Everett, PhD, has spent 41 years in education as a teacher, central office/superintendent, university professor and executive director of the Illinois Association of School Business Officials. Dr. Everett has delivered conference addresses, workshops and taught graduate-level courses throughout the world. He is recognized as a practitioner/scholar at home and as a distinguished visiting scholar abroad. Over the past 25 years, his professional service, research, teaching and primary interests have focused on school business administration.

Donald R. Johnson, EdD, has served the educational administration field for more than 40 years as a university professor, school superintendent, business manager, computer services director, state department consultant and consultant to school districts. He has spoken at numerous local, state, national and international conferences on topics related to school organization, leadership and business management. His current professional efforts have centered on providing electronic and digital access for school leader's professional development.

Bernard W. Madden, EdD, is the assistant superintendent for Finance and Operations in Glen Ellyn School District 89, Glen Ellyn, Illinois. He teaches in the graduate school at Northern Illinois University and has taught and developed a graduate course for the Keller Graduate School of Management at Northwestern University.